BOOKS ON REAL-TIME SYSTEMS AND DATA TRANSMISSION

by JAMES MARTIN

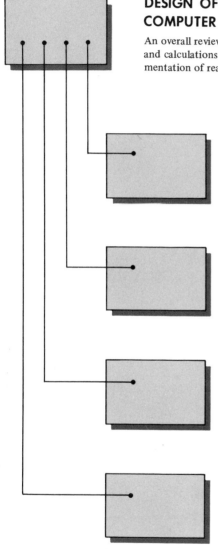

DESIGN OF REAL-TIME COMPUTER SYSTEMS

An overall review of technical considerations and calculations in the design and implementation of real-time systems.

PROGRAMMING REAL-TIME COMPUTER SYSTEMS

Programming mechanisms, program testing tools and techniques, problems encountered, implementation considerations, project management.

TELECOMMUNICATIONS AND THE COMPUTER

A description of the working of the world's telecommunication links and their uses for data transmission.

TELEPROCESSING NETWORK ORGANIZATION

An explanation of the many types of devices and procedures for controlling and organizing the flow of data on today's telecommunication lines.

FUTURE DEVELOPMENTS IN TELECOMMUNICATIONS

An exploration of the foreseeable future in a technology that has reached a period of very rapid change.

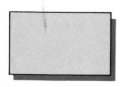

THE COMPUTERIZED SOCIETY

(co-author Adrian R. D. Norman)
Euphoria, Alarm, Protective Action. An appraisal of the impact of computers on society over the next fifteen years.

Prentice-Hall Series in Automatic Computation

George Forsythe, editor

TELECOMMUNICATIONS
AND
THE
COMPUTER

JAMES MARTIN

Staff Member
IBM Systems Research Institute

PRENTICE-HALL, INC.
ENGLEWOOD CLIFFS, N. J.

© 1969 by
PRENTICE-HALL, INC.
Englewood Cliffs, N.J.

Current printing (last digit):

10 9 8 7 6

Library of Congress Catalog Card Number: 78-76038
Printed in the United States of America

PRENTICE-HALL INTERNATIONAL, INC., *London*
PRENTICE-HALL OF AUSTRALIA, PTY. LTD., *Sydney*
PRENTICE-HALL OF CANADA LTD., *Toronto*
PRENTICE-HALL OF INDIA PRIVATE LTD., *New Delhi*
PRENTICE-HALL OF JAPAN, INC., *Tokyo*

PREFACE

This book is based on a course I conduct at the IBM Systems Research Institute in New York City. One purpose of the book is to explain to data processing personnel the workings of the world's telecommunications link. The book may also be used to provide the basis for a one-semester university course in the engineering or computer facilities.

It has been estimated in the telecommunications industry that in the 1970's the revenue from machines talking to machines will be greater than that from people talking to people. This is amazing when one reflects that AT&T has become the world's largest corporation, largely on the revenue from *human* communication. It is also amazing when one considers that data transmission over a voice line can carry at least 20 times as much information as human talking, and much more when digits or characters with logical meaning are sent. But this is only the beginning of a revolution that will far outstrip our educational capacity to handle it.

One cannot doubt that the majority of persons currently employed in data processing will soon be involved in some way with telecommunications.

Unfortunately the majority of computer personnel know little about the technology of telecommunications. In most organizations I have worked with, advising on "teleprocessing" systems, this lack of knowledge has been keenly felt. In many cases, it has impeded the creation of valuable systems approaches.

It is easy to obtain literature on the computer manufacturer's hardware, but surprisingly difficult to acquire the desirable knowledge of the common carriers' technology. To satisfy this need, this book concentrates on common carrier equipment.

The book avoids detailed discussion of the computer manufacturer's hardware (other than modems), and the means for organizing the flow of data in computer networks. This is the subject of another book I have written in conjunction with this one: *Teleprocessing Network Organization,* published by Prentice-Hall, 1969.

The beginning and ending of this text may easily be read by the interested layman, by technical staff in fields other than computing, and by persons involved in telecommunications. It is intended that some of the more detailed sections of the book should be used by computer personnel for repeated reference, and that it will be of value to them in forwarding their careers. It is hoped, therefore, that this book will be owned by such people rather than meeting the sad fate of only being borrowed from a library and read once.

JAMES MARTIN

New York, N, Y.

ACKNOWLEDGMENTS

Any book about the state of the art in a complex technology draws material from a vast number of sources. While many of these are referenced in the text, it is impossible to include all of the pioneering projects that have contributed to the new uses of telecommunications. To the many systems engineers who contributed to this body of knowledge, the author is indebted.

The author is very grateful for the time spent reviewing and criticizing the manuscript by Mr. K. L. Smith in London, Mr. J. W. Greenwood in New York, Mr. "Bill" Accosta and Mr. F. A. Hatfield in the Western Electric plant at Columbus, Ohio, and several unknown members of the Bell Telephone Laboratories. The long-suffering students of IBM's Systems Research Institutes in New York and Geneva also used the manuscript and made many corrections. To all these the author is indebted.

Mr. R. B. Edwards' staff helped enormously in typing and reproducing the manuscript. The author is particularly grateful to Miss Cora Tangney for her help in this. Patient assistance was also given by Miss Kathleen Hill.

Last, and perhaps most important, the author is indebted to Dr. E. S. Kopley, Director of the IBM Systems Research Institute for his constant encouragement. Without the environment that he created, this work would not have been completed.

CONTENTS

8 A. C. TRANSMISSION MEDIA

9 ATTENUATION AND REPEATERS

10 FREQUENCY AND BANDWIDTH

INDEX OF BASIC CONCEPTS

The basic concepts, principles, and terms that are explained in this book are listed here along with the page on which an introductory explantion or definition of them is given. There is a cornplete index at the end of the book.

INTRODUCTION

1 THE FUTURE

This is a book about the technology of the present day. However, rather than begin it, as is often the case with such books, with a survey of the history of the subject, it is probably more interesting to talk about the future.

One of the most exciting technological developments of this exciting century is the marriage of the engineering of telecommunications to that of the computer industry. Both of these fields are developing at a fast and furious rate. Calculated speculation about what either of them is likely to lead to brings awe-inspiring conclusions. Either the computer industry, or the telecommunications industry, alone, is capable of bringing about changes in our society, in the working habits and the government of people, that will change their way of life throughout the world. But the two techniques complement each other. In combination they add power to each other. Telecommunication links will bring the capabilities of the computers and the information in data banks to the millions of locations where they can be used, and computers in return will control the immense switching centers and help divide the enormous capacity of the new linkages into usable channels.

In England, in the eighteenth century, the spinning jenny and a variety of weaving inventions portended a revolution in clothmaking. Around the same time the steam engine was developed. These two inventions also complemented each other. Either, by itself, would have caused changes, but in combination they brought about an upheaval that was to alter drastically the lives of all the people involved. The attractive villages with their cottage industry gave way to the dark satanic mills of the early industrial revolution. The pounding new machines dominated men's lives. Today, as then, the new technologies sweep across our society too fast for the sociologists and politicians to plan the type of world they want to build.

The industrial revolution of the history books depended primarily on man's building machines to harness physical power, such as the steam engine, and applying this to a range of different applications. The computer era we are now embarking upon, often referred to as the second industrial revolution, depends upon harnessing mechanized logic and stored information, and applying it to a wide variety of applications. Man first built an extension of his muscles which gave him power enormously greater than his own frail limbs. He then built an extension of his brain which is giving him mechanized memory of unimaginable magnitude and logic capabilities which can process the data in this memory with absolute accuracy and at speeds millions of times greater than his own head-scratching thought. When this second revolution has run its course it will have wrought a change in mankind's environment even greater than the first.

The sources of physical energy in the first revolution, however, needed means of transportation. Canals were dug and weary horses spent their lives lugging barges of coal from the new mines to the factories. Many factories clustered round the coal fields and whole segments of the population moved there into gloomy, jerry-built rows of houses. It took many years for the means of transportation to become adequate for the needs of the new industry. Later the railways were built, and then electricity was invented so that overhead wires carried the necessary power across hill and dale.

Distribution, likewise, is of great importance in the second revolution. We cannot afford to have a giant set of computer files duplicating data at every location where men need the information. We want one "data base" serving hundreds or thousands of locations. Similarly, we cannot afford to have a powerful computer at every place where men want to use one. Perhaps in the years to come small computers will become as common as adding machines, but there will always be a need to use the *million-dollar* computers and these may be a long way away. Above all, many of the applications that are now envisaged require *fast* access to a machine or to data. A managing director wants a *quick* answer to his question so that he can make a decision. A doctor wants a *quick* analysis of electrocardiac or other data. A factory shop floor is to be controlled in "real-time" as its events are taking place. There is not time to write a letter to the computer center or even to catch a train to it.

Distribution in the computer world will be done largely by telecommunications. We will send data over transmission lines and communicate with the computer, using the same telephone links that we now use to communicate with each other. In the industrial revolution the means for distribution lagged seriously behind the need for it. Today there is such a lag with computing.

In the first decade of widely accepted commercial usage of computers there was hardly any data transmission, except in a handful of pioneering experimental installations. Now, data transmission is fast becoming accepted but there are problems. The telecommunication links were mainly designed for handling voice and television signals, not computer data. With ingenious modification they can be used satisfactorily for data. There are many severe "software" problems. The programs needed for control and supervision of the systems have in many cases become far more complex than was anticipated. When many users can call the computer at random with a variety of requests that all have to be answered quickly, a high degree of organization is needed in the computer system. The programmers are groping toward this but so far many of their control programs have been depressingly inefficient. Large unwieldy teams of programmers have been developed, but there is much yet to be learned about the art of organizing big groups of people, all producing interacting program logic. Slowly, however, the distribution problems are becoming solved and in the next decade or so we can expect to have a vast network for making available computer power and data, as complex as the physical distribution networks of commerce. *network aation*

The telephone lines and probably other newer cables will connect our homes and offices to the computers. One will be able to dial machines using particular programs or data, just as today one can dial a friend, or in England dial a machine that gives the cricket score. It seems possible that this will change our working patterns again just as the first industrial revolution changed them.

There is much work that now can be done from individual homes, using telephone links to computers. Vast quantities of programming are needed. In teaching, for example, computer-assisted instruction can be enormously effective, but only if the programs used for it are very elaborate and are prepared with great care. The amount of programming effort for courses that is needed to make computer-assisted teaching widely accepted runs into thousands, perhaps ten or even hundreds of thousands of man-years. *Enormous* quantities of intelligent human work are needed to carry us forward into this new era—not the work of geniuses, but the ordinary intelligent step-by-step construction and testing of the multitude of programs needed. In general, it is creative, enjoyable work that can be done by married women with children and by the disabled. Some blind people today are happily writing computer programs. Above all it is work that can be done at home, provided that home has a telecommunication link to a computer. And so we may see a return to cottage industry. If we could harness the part-time efforts of the domestic millions, the new era would surge forward. The home spinning wheel would have been replaced by the computer terminal.

The future developments of data transmission are likely to come from two sources. First the telecommunication facilities themselves will improve. Second our ability to use them will develop greatly. Let us look at the former first.

THE INCREASE IN TELECOMMUNICATION CAPACITY

As the need for more transmission capacity grows, many more links will be built. In addition to this, new inventions and engineering developments will greatly increase the capacity of the links. The major telecommunication highways will be able to carry much larger volumes of data than today.

Figure 1.1 plots the capacities of the major telecommunication links against the time when they first became operational. This is done from the date when signals were first sent over transmission wires.

In 1819 Oersted discovered the relation between magnetism and electricity, and Ampere, Faraday, and others continued this work in 1820. Shortly after this the first systems for transmitting information were prepared using suspended magnetized needles. In 1834 Gauss and Weber strung wire over the roofs of Göttingen to make a telegraph system in which information was conveyed by the slow swinging of magnetic needles. A 40-mile telegraph line was set up between Baltimore and Washington by Morse in 1844. The information was coded in dots and dashes, and a steel pen made indentations in a paper strip. In 1849 the first slow telegraph printer link was set up, and by the early 1860's speeds of about 15 bits per second were being achieved. In 1874 Baudot invented a "multiplexor" system (Chapter 6) which enabled up to six signals from telegraph machines to be transmitted together over the same line.

Telephone lines were first constructed in the 1890's. In 1918 the first "carrier" technique (Chapter 10) was used, and 12 voice channels were sent over one wire pair. In the 1940's coaxial cables (page 143) were laid down to carry large numbers of voice channels, and in the 1950's microwave links (page 146) were built. Today in the United States a single long-distance telephone cable or microwave chain commonly carries 11,000 voice channels and already cables with twice this capacity are in use.

The channel capacity achieved by these milestones may be plotted against time. Doing this we find that capacity of the major telecommunication channels has grown exponentially since the earliest days. The points in Fig. 1.1 in fact are so close to a straight line that one is immediately led to speculate that the straight line will continue.

Certainly there is evidence today that channel capacity is going to continue to increase. The Bell Telephone Laboratories has already fully designed what is possibly the next generation of cross-country links. This uses helical waveguides (page 10) and is capable of carrying 100,000 voice channels or more. It seems likely that helical waveguide systems will be laid down in the 1970's. Communication satellites proposed for the late 1970's also have a capacity of about 100,000 voice channels. Beyond this the laser will provide an even greater jump forward. The potential of the laser, if we can learn how to fully utilize it, seems so great that the straight line of Fig. 1.1 may start to swing sharply upward.

The dotted line in Fig. 1.1 extrapolates the straight line growth rate into the future. It is important to note that the vertical axis is drawn logarithmically. If this diagram were drawn with a linear axis representing capacity, and the entire past history occupied the height of one page of this book, then the next seventy years would need a scale about one mile in length! It will be seen that, in terms of what one could transmit over such a channel, the increase in capability would be enormous.

Where might this increase come from in terms of physics? The speed of motor cars will not increase indefinitely because of physical limitations. Could there be physical limitations that will prevent us climbing the dotted line in Fig. 1.1?

In general, the increase in channel capacity of the past has been achieved by increasing the *range of frequencies* with which signals are transmitted. Indeed, as is discussed in Chapter 11, the quantity of information we can send down a channel is approximately proportional to its *bandwidth* or range of frequencies usable. Figure 1.2 shows the electromagnetic spectrum. Just as we may have a rainbow-colored spectrum of light by separating the visible frequencies, so all the frequencies of physics may be laid out in a spectrum; this is drawn in Fig. 1.2. Visible light is only a small part of this wide spread of frequencies which travel through electrical conductors, or through the air. Higher frequencies can be transmitted through space in the form of radio waves. As the frequencies become higher the waves suffer less diffraction and tend to travel in straight lines. Long radio waves are reflected by the iono-sphere. Microwave signals are not, and therefore they must be sent between antennas that are normally within sight of each other. Because microwave signals start at a higher frequency, they can carry a proportionately higher information content. If we increase the frequency the waves become infrared, or heat radiation. If we increase it further it becomes visible light. The increase of the frequency of light beyond the visible spectrum turns it into ultraviolet radiation, then x-rays, and at very high frequencies, indeed, γ-rays.

How much of this spectrum have we used for transmitting information? Only a small portion of it is indicated in Fig. 1.2. How much will we use in the future? No one can be sure but it seems likely that new inventions of which we have no inkling today will utilize many parts of this spectrum higher than at present. Already, for example, laser beams have been used in com-munications from satellites in space (page 158). These are very much higher in the spectrum than anything used for public telecommunications. We

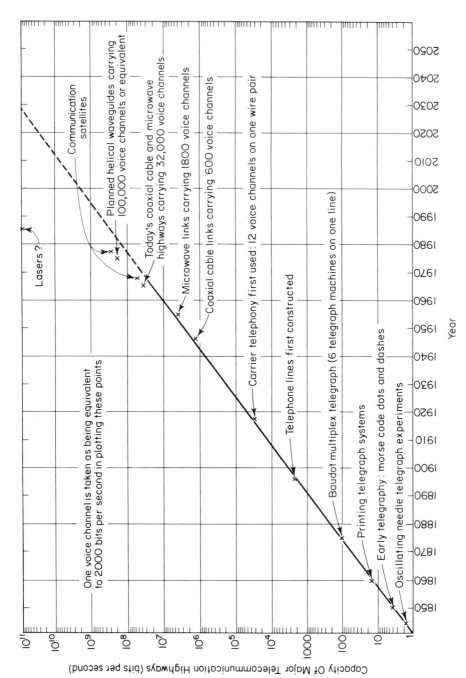

Fig. 1.1. The sequence of inventions in telecommunications.

8

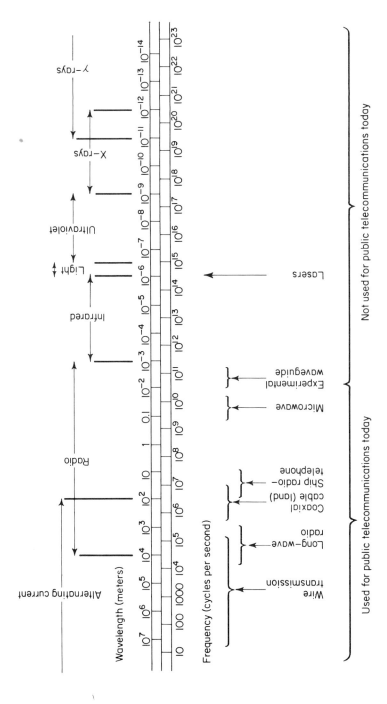

Fig. 1.2. The electromagnetic spectrum.

9

have no idea how we would amplify or modulate (Chapter 10) most of the possible frequencies on this scale. But then some of the systems in our laboratories now were entirely beyond the technologies of scientists 20 years ago.

Again note that the scale of frequencies in Fig. 1.2 is logarithmic. If we drew this diagram with a *linear* scale so that that part of the spectrum used today for commercial communication links occupied the width of this page, then the part of the spectrum as yet unused would require a sheet of paper stretching from Earth to a point twice the distance of the Sun! Theoretically the quantity of information the medium can carry is proportional to the distance on this scale.

The theoretical capacities suggested by examining the electromagnetic spectrum enormously outstrip the requirements of the dotted line in Fig. 1.1. Probably we are only beginning to utilize telecommunications just as we are only beginning to utilize computer potentialities. These are the toddler's first halting steps.

In addition to the channel capacity increasing, the number of channels built can be increased to fulfill any future we can dream of. This would not be true if we were talking about radio links. The radio wavelengths are already becoming notoriously overloaded in parts. Microwave systems are a little better. Here the signal is transmitted in a narrow beam with little scattering so that separate transmissions can coexist fairly near each other without interference; but there is a limit to the number of such channels. There is virtually no limit, however, other than cost, to the number of coaxial cable channels that could be built across a country. Each cable in use today is capable of carrying more than 10,000 voice (telephone) channels, or the equivalent. For tomorrow's technology, there is again virtually no limit to the number of helical waveguide channels that could be built, each equivalent to 100,000 voice channels or more.

Another spectacularly successful development that has arrived quickly, precipitated by the space race, is the communications satellite. The Early Bird satellite and its successor, INTELSAT II (Chapter 20), both working better than their designers' specifications, herald a decade of new satellites, already planned, and each design of higher capacity than the previous ones. The cost of long-distance telecommunications will drop. A novel feature in satellite economics is that it will be no more expensive to phone or send data to the other side of the world than it will be to send it from New York to Chicago. Where necessary, the computer data highways will be global in scale.

There is no foreseeable limitation in telecommunication capacity. We can build all we can pay for. Although today systems analysts can be heard to complain sometimes about the cost and difficulty of obtaining high-speed lines, channels *can* be built fast enough for most purposes we can think of. One system being developed today can transmit at a speed of 220 million bits per second. At this speed the entire text of this book could be transmitted in one fortieth of a second. As the capacities of individual channels increase, the cost of transmitting a given quantity of information will come down. The high-capacity channels will be split into many low-capacity channels (Chapter 15). Also, as the usage of telecommunications goes up, mass-production methods will lower the cost.

The next question is: How will we use this capacity? This question is exciting enough even if we only consider the transmission channels of today. Compared with what will probably be achieved in the next few decades, we have hardly started to use the facilities we have invented. The computers of today have a potential far beyond their present use. In fact, if all hardware development were to cease now, and we spent fifty years learning how to program and how to use today's machines, and building up data banks for them, we could accomplish what now would seem like miracles.

THE INFORMATION EXPLOSION   The new technology of information processing and transmission has turned up just in time for the needs of scientific progress. Looking at the history of technology one observes a number of fundamental inventions which arrived in one field of research just when they were needed to permit progress elsewhere. The thermionic vacuum tube, for example, arrived just in time to allow development in telecommunications. The moon shot depends on a variety of recently developed technologies, and if any one of them had been developed a few decades later the shot would probably have been impossible. We have reached a state now in man's learning when the quantity of information being generated in industry, in governments, and in the academic world is reaching alarming proportions. The press euphemistically calls it the "information explosion," but that is not a good term because explosions quickly end their violent growth. The growth of man's information has no end in prospect, only greater growth.

The sum total of human knowledge changed very slowly prior to the relatively recent beginnings of scientific thought. But it has been estimated that by 1800 it was doubling every 50 years; by 1950, doubling every 10 years; and that by 1970 it will be doubling every 5 years.[1] This is a much greater growth rate than an exponential increase.

Certainly, the number of documents an employee in the computer industry would like to read is going up by leaps and bounds. The first computer programmed by this author had one manual of operation which contained all that had to be known about the machine. . . . Then came the "second

---

[1] Edgar C. Gentle, Jr.: "Data Communication in Business." New York: American Telephone and Telegraph Company, 1965.

generation" of computers, and before long there were ten manuals that described parts of the software for the machine. Now we have the "third generation." This author has not counted all the manuals, but there are well over 100. The rack by a typical test-center computer has six feet of tightly packed manuals, and yet they are not complete. It is happening in other fields too. The weight of the drawings of a jet plane has been stated to be greater than the weight of the plane. In many fields of research, even one as old as medicine, more papers have been published since World War II than in all prior human history.

Clearly, automated means of filing and indexing research papers, engineering drawings, and other types of documents is becoming essential, and must be coupled with means of searching for, and retrieving, the required information. Computer storage coupled with computer-processing ability seems the answer, or part of it. Telecommunication links will enable people needing information to search with computer assistance through what is available. Many information-retrieval systems today are operating without the telecommunication link. Jet engine manufacturers are storing details of their part specifications on computer files. A large number of privately set-up files of technical reports are being used in different organizations. If I want to search the literature on computers for information on a certain topic, I can fill out a "profile" of the subjects in question, making the field as narrow as possible, otherwise I shall be deluged with reports that are not quite relevant. The files are then searched, and computer-printed abstracts sent back to me after a delay of a week or so. Perhaps one in twenty of these abstracts will be relevant, and I can either obtain it from the library or ask for a copy of it to be printed.

Files like this will eventually be available "on-line," so that users can interrogate them, probably using a machine with a screen something like a microfilm reader, and a keyboard like that on a typewriter. With a small unit like this the user will dial a number to connect him to the data file and its computer. In searching for reports on a given topic the user would carry on a two-way conversation with the distant computer. The computer might suggest more precise categorizations of what he was seeking. He might browse through many data indices, titles, and abstracts before he found what he wanted.

The telecommunication link will make the searching much faster and more efficient. The computer helps the user in his search, and he can determine whether a report is, in fact, the one he wants by simply scanning through it. More important, the data file could be made "public" so that a large number of people can use it, and a large variety of people can contribute to the building up of the data in the system.

Banks of data on many subjects will grow in the years and decades to come. After an enormous quantity of coding and classification work has been done, the biochemist will be enabled to check what reports have been written on a particular topic, the lawyer will have the mass of literature he needs electronically available to him, and the patent agent will be enabled to carry out a search in "real-time."

GOVERNMENT INFORMATION
Government and police records are also growing alarmingly fast. If one accepted the civil servants' statements of what records are necessary to run our increasingly complex society, then, without automation, in a few decades we would all be employed governing and policing ourselves, and would have no time to do anything else.

Among the data that are under active consideration for automation in local and state government are the following:[2]

1. *Personal Identity Data.* Social security number, recognizable physical characteristics, address, race, relatives, etc.
2. *Personal Employment Data.* Employer, previous employers, occupation, earning, etc.
3. *Personal Education Data.* Schools, courses, degrees, achievements, etc.
4. *Welfare Data.* Periods of welfare, aid received, basis for aid, etc.
5. *Health Data.* Physical deficiencies, reportable diseases, immunization, x-ray data, etc.
6. *Tax Data.* Details of income tax returns, dependents, investments, life insurance, etc.
7. *Voters' Registration Data.*
8. *Licenses and Permits.* Type, number, date issued, issuing agency, expiration date, etc.
9. *Law Enforcement Data.* Records of offenses, outstanding warrants, exconvict registration, suspects, missing persons, etc.
10. *Court Actions.* Plaintiff and defendant, court, date, type of action, result.
11. *Probation/Parole Data.* Probation number, agency, court, offense, terms, conditions.
12. *Confinement Data.* Type of confinement, period, place, reason, treatment, escapes, etc.
13. *Registered Personal Property.* Cars, motorcycles, boats, firearms, radios (in the U.K.), dogs, ambulances, elevators, etc.
14. *Vehicle Registration Files.* Owner, license number, make, engine, body, axles, wheel base, whether registered in other states, etc.
15. *Land Details.* Zoning, uses, assessed value, taxable value, deeds, water and mineral rights, drainage, productivity data, soil type, details of buildings, owners, sales, etc.

---

[2] Edward F. R. Mason and Raymond J. Mason give more details in *A Data Processing System for State and Local Governments.* Englewood Cliffs, N.J.: Prentice-Hall, 1963.

16. *Owner/Occupant Files.*   Names, address, licenses, occupation group, race, place of work, children in school, income group, vehicles owned, police records, etc.
17. *Street-Section Records.*   Name, class of street, length, limits, intersections, surface, drainage, traffic data, parking data, street lights, curbs, sewers, signals, accidents, etc.

There are many other items that are stored by government bodies in addition to these. Many such records are being or have been put into data-processing systems. Now there is emphasis on obtaining access to them more readily, and minimizing the work of keeping the files up to date. This will be done mainly by centralizing the storage of the data on random-access files, and providing telecommunication links to all its likely users. There will probably be many different locations where data are stored. Data which are used largely within one county will be stored in that county to minimize transmission costs. And so, as in other applications, a network will grow up for transferring data from one place to another as and when they are needed. The locations of the files, and the question of what data are stored where, will be determined largely by the balance of cost between data storage and data transmission.

Today there is much duplication in the records that are kept. There is duplication, indeed, in our filling in of government forms. How many times do we write on these forms our address and physical description. Perhaps in the future a social security number will be all we will need (possibly social security number and name for checking purposes). The computer, with a data link to the relevant file, will provide the rest.

Spectacular use is already being made of data transmission in some American police systems. Police, stopping a suspect, radio his name and other data to an operator at a computer terminal. The computer gives information about whether the suspect is wanted, whether his car is a stolen one, or whether he has failed to pay his parking tickets. In this way a policeman can interrogate a data bank from his patrol car. At the time of writing the data banks contain information for a limited geographical zone. Soon they will become nationwide.

Much of this sounds 1984ish. It is difficult to escape the conclusion that in the era of data transmission much of the preceding personal documentation will be generally accessible to government officials. We can pass laws to stop Big Brother from watching us too closely if we act quickly. We should certainly pass laws to prevent abuse of this system. Our data files should not be accessible to just anybody. Computers, like other inventions that change civilization, are a force for great good or great evil depending on how countries use them. There is no doubt about how the systems we envisage would have been used in Germany in the 1930's. Sometimes great civilizations fall under despotic rule, and when the computer techniques we describe are perfected, the totalitarian state will have a new means of maintaining control.

CHANGING
FILES
Many of the files which it would be most useful to interrogate are those which contain data that are constantly changing. Two processes must then go on simultaneously: (1) the updating of the information in the files, and (2) the answering of the queries based on it.

A variety of telecommunication-based systems in industry provide management or operating personnel with up-to-the-minute information on which decisions can be based. Today, when you book an airline seat, for example, the girl you deal with is quite possibly carrying on a conversation with a distant computer at the same time as she talks to you. She finds out which seats have been booked, and sometimes other information about the flight. On an advanced system she enters details of your booking: your name, telephone number, the time limit by which you are going to collect your ticket, and any other comments that will be relevant. Next time you telephone the airline, perhaps from a different city, perhaps in a different country after having traveled half of the journey, you usually talk to a different girl. She may display in a few seconds, on a screen in front of her, a summary of your booking, and surprise you by knowing such details as your telephone number and the fact that you are taking your pet dalmatian on board. Meanwhile the airline has tighter seat-inventory control and probably fills its planes more fully.

FINANCE
SYSTEMS
The world of finance employs many files of constantly changing information. Among the earliest "real-time" computer systems were those in savings banks where tellers used machines to update customers' passbooks. A central computer kept records of all customers' accounts and these were updated by the machine at each teller's counter (Chapter 2). The teller had the information he needed about the account automatically transmitted to him. The same system often provided information to management on request.

From this small, but successful, beginning a change threatens to sweep through the financial community that might eventually revolutionize our entire monetary system. Many financial transactions will be made without using cash or checks, as are credit-card transactions today. The bank customer must have some way of identifying himself to a telecommunication terminal and details of the transaction will be keyed into the terminal. This data will reach the computers which hold the records of the payee and payer. The latter's record will be debited and the former's credited. In this way, financial transactions will be made by means of data transmission, without paperwork —or at least paperwork will be *external* to the system, not internal as it is today, and will merely have the purpose of informing the users of what transactions have taken place. Payrolls, for example, will be worked out by a firm's computer and transmitted to the appropriate bank computer. When the employee then buys something at a store, the store's computer will find out if the cash is in his account.

In such a system the user might be permitted to overdraw his account by a given amount. Overdrawing has long been normal practice in Britain and certain other European countries, though it is only now being introduced by American banks in certain states, and in a limited form. In Britain the bank manager decides from his personal knowledge of the customer how much an account can be overdrawn. The bank computer has this limit on the customer record, and permits overdrawing to this level. In the future we envisage an individual's credit worthiness will, if he wishes, be stored on a file that is accessible by telecommunications. A store will have automatic access to this when he tries to purchase goods with a credit transfer. In a limited form, credit-checking systems of this type are already in operation in the United States today.

One of the problems in this financial network is the proper identification of each individual. Today a recognized credit card acts as a means of identification for some. This, however, is only given to individuals who are deemed to be a good credit risk. Some banks are offering check-guarantee cards to credit-worthy customers, and these serve a similar purpose. Probably an extension of the card-carrying facilities, combined with the use of data transmission for checking a customer's credit, will enlarge the population who can make automatic credit transfers. The introduction of a national, machine-readable identification card could further extend this and other uses of computers.

Research is now under way on more fundamental methods of recognizing an individual. Pattern-recognition techniques, for example, can enable the computer to recognize certain identifying characteristics of the human voice. It is within reach of our technology to build a machine into which an individual reads his social security number over the telephone. The computer interprets the digits and looks up a record containing details of that individual's voice characteristics. Just as the police use details of a fingerprint to identify a suspect, the computer uses details of the voice sound to verify that the person speaking is the one with that specific social security number. It is not yet sure how uniquely the machine will eventually identify the speaker. A mimic after weeks of practice might fool the machine, just as a forger can falsify a signature. However, it seems likely that voice "forging" would be more difficult than signature forging. Another problem is that the computer might not recognize the digits spoken by everybody. A Scotsman with a broad accent might attempt to buy goods in a store only to find that the machine cannot understand the digits he speaks. He will have to go home and practice speaking more computer-recognizable English, or else pay by check!

Some writers have envisaged a completely checkless, and others a cashless, society. It seems unlikely that we will ever do away with cash entirely. For small transactions, such as buying a drink or tipping a porter, cash is needed. However, the use of large sums of cash and checks will probably decline rapidly as credit transfer gains acceptance and the different systems spread, interlinking, across the nation.

The development of such systems could be easier in a country like England than in the United States, because in England the General Post Office (GPO) owns and operates all telecommunications and the nationwide, computer-run GIRO banking system. The commercial banks are also largely nationwide and some are planning to interconnect over 2000 branches into one giant, on-line computer network. The United States, on the other hand, has a patchwork collection of small banks with all manner of restrictive state regulations. Nevertheless one suspects that, as in other areas, Americans will, in fact, lead the way. If only England could invest courageously in technological innovation, it could make spectacular use of the new computer techniques. The country is geographically small and data highways of massive capacity could interlink it at a fraction of the cost of those in the United States.

DATA TRANSMISSION IN BUSINESS

In industry the uses of data transmission are growing fast. Many links not connected directly to a computer are used for sending data from one point to another, or for collecting information from the factory work areas; and now many systems are growing up in which the transmission links and the computer are inseparable parts of the same system. Most of these systems are tailormade to carry out a specific set of operations in a given company.

Most data-processing installations with earlier generations of machines have exclusively used "batch processing." Several hundred transactions would be grouped into a batch. In a punched-card installation, many trays of cards would be fed through one machine before the setup of that machine was changed for its next function. The "batch" would then have to wait for the next operation to be performed on it, possibly a sorting or merging operation ready for another "run." Similarly, with the use of magnetic tape on computers, large tape files would be processed with one program before the file was sorted ready for the next operation. It is economic to have large batches. A cycle of operations, perhaps a weekly cycle, is adhered to, and so it is normally a long time before any one particular transaction is processed.

Now, instead of operating run by run, printing out results which will be read at a later time, the computer can deal with transactions immediately if necessary, or in an hour or so if that is good enough. It can complete all the processing associated with one transaction at one time. It can provide management with information *when* they ask for it. It can give quick answers to inquiries about the status of a job, the load or a machine tool, or the amount of an item in stock. The answer will not be a week out of date but up to the minute. Instead of filling in documents on the shop floor, the workers enter data into a computer terminal, and the computer then builds in its files records with the current situation. When exceptional conditions arise, as they do frequently in most factories, these can be dealt with immediately, and the appropriate person in the organization notified.

These techniques are needed in order to achieve minute-by-minute *control* of a commercial situation in the same way that control is maintained over, say, a chemical plant. The computer may schedule work through a factory and reschedule it whenever new requirements occur, or the situation on the shop floor changes. It can control the selling of airline seats all over the world. Immediate insurance quotations can be given, and claims and payments handled more quickly. Salesmen's orders from all over the country can be processed in time for the following day's production. The computer can control a steel mill and optimize its efficiency. It can monitor a commercial process in the same way it monitors a manned space flight. Traffic in a turbulent city has been speeded up by computers which maneuver it into groups of vehicles and change traffic lights at the best moment; in a similar way, the events in an industrial process can be regulated in an optimum manner. The benefits of such control are not necessarily the traditional saving of manpower. Often they accrue from increased efficiency, better customer service, or more profitable utilization of facilities.

Many companies are widely dispersed geographically and so data links are being used to connect separate plants, to link warehouses, to connect large numbers of sales offices or service centers to a central information system, and so on. As in other fields, paperwork is being replaced by electronic storage and data transmission. The airline office does away with its filing cabinets of cards for each passenger. Industry branch offices will enter and retrieve data on a device like a television set with a keyboard, and a computer will have centralized control and centralized information on all the new developments.

A board room or *management control room* in industry in the future may be designed with wall-size computer display screens, and individual consoles for communicating with the computer. It may look something like today's computerized military war room.

Already management control rooms are being built in which a group of men assist the computer in controlling the flow of work through the organization. Such rooms have a number of functions. First, they are necessary in many systems to control errors: often errors made in human input to the system, or errors found in the filed data. Second, they handle exceptional conditions that arise and require human intervention. Third, they represent a recognition that it is not necessarily the best policy to make the computer do *all* of the processing that is needed. There are some transactions or situations that need human judgment, and so the computer requests help and transmits details to the man with the relevant experience or judgment ability. Fourth, they enable management to obtain information it needs or to test the effect of possible actions. Many members of management will not have the ability to communicate with the computer fluently, and so they do this via the staff in the control room.

Such systems in industry today appear to be more a tool of middle management than top management. They can handle the logistics of production scheduling and inventory planning, but they aid little in top management policy making. The potentialities, however, are to a large extent unexploited as yet. In the future it can be expected that the display screens, the data banks, and the telecommunication links will be indispensable in computer-assisted decision-making in big companies. As with the other applications, the limitation is no longer in the hardware. It is in the programming and the organization of the vast quantities of information involved.

MAN–MACHINE
INTERACTION
There are certain thought processes which will always remain in the domain of human rather than machine activity. Others, however, are better done by machine. When the two can be efficiently combined, the result is more powerful than either process on its own.

The computer can store vast quantities of data and retrieve individual items quickly. It can carry out well-defined calculations or logic processes at enormous speed. It can keep files up to date and take controlling actions the moment they are required. The repertoire of procedures which can be built in a computer does not become distorted or forgotten as in the human brain. The human brain, on the other hand, can select goals and criteria, select approaches, detect relevance, and formulate questions and hypotheses. It can handle the unforeseen.

With the logic power of the computer and mass-information retrieval available to it, the capability of the human brain for tackling certain types of problems can become immensely greater. The human operator may formulate hypotheses and immediately test them on the data concerned. The computer can help formulate and evaluate the effect of management policies. It can assist in producing engineering drawings or PERT charts or simulation programs. It can help in planning complex schedules. It can help programmers write programs, keying them directly into a terminal and changing them where necessary as they go along. In this way, complex programs can be produced much more quickly than with conventional methods.

Much research is needed, and is being done, on the combined use of man and computers. Using time-sharing techniques, a man may use a part share in a powerful computer and its files, at a fraction of the cost of the whole system. The term *man–machine symbiosis* is used to describe this new type of thinking—part machine, part human.

Among the possibilities that are now becoming reality are the following: *Designers* of various types may use computers to assist them. A circuit designer, for example, may store details of all the components available to him, and quickly make the computer investigate the effect of various arrangements or modifications. *An architect or bridge engineer* can use a display tube to produce plans, fitting elements of the design together and modifying the results as required. A linkage of steel girders in a building or a bridge may be built up on a display screen, and the computer will place figures by each object, indicating the results of stressing calculations. The designer may change his linkages and investigate the stresses caused by different loadings, and thus optimize his design. An *automobile designer* may sketch surfaces of body panels or fender designs on the graphic input device. The computer will fit a mathematical expression to the surface and then "rotate" the surface on the screen so that the designer may observe its shape from all viewpoints. The computer will apply constraints that are forced by mechanical or manufacturing considerations and the designer will then adjust his shapes to achieve a compromise within the constraints that must apply.

If these processes were done by hand or with a batch-processing computer, they would take a long time, so long that the designer would be restricted in the full use of his imagination or inventive ability. Most design processes are 1% inspiration or art, and 99% calculation and the laborious working out of detail. The object of using a real-time computer for design is to take away as much as possible of the tedious work and enable the designer to observe as quickly as possible the effects of his ideas. In a trial-and-error process, if there are three months between the trial and the error, the designer can lose much of his original ideas. Where it is possible to explore the effect of these ideas in real-time, much more fruitful and exciting thinking can sometimes be stimulated.

Similarly, *simulation* or mathematical "models" may be "built" at a display terminal, to investigate the passage of work through a factory, the flow of traffic through a city, or any other situation capable of being simulated. A standard simulation "language" may be used for this, the model being tested as it is built. The effect of different actions may be investigated using such models. A model of the functioning of an organization may be permitted to "grow" until it steadily becomes a more accurate representation of the behavior of the organization. Sales forecasts may form inputs to a model used for planning. The effects of different policies may be investigated, and experiments carried out with the model. As in a design process, the work of building a simulation model today can be long and laborious. If somebody asks, "What would be the effect of changing so-and-so?" the answer may come two weeks later. This is too slow for many purposes, especially in the racing turmoil of the commercial world. To demonstrate to management that quick and effective answers can be obtained from simulation, real-time methods may be needed.

The surprising effectiveness of computers used for *teaching* has already been demonstrated. Many pupils can be handled at once and different subjects taught. The computer gives individual treatment to students, and modifies its behavior according to their progress in a much more adaptable way than simpler machines.

The computer used in this way becomes a type of storehouse for human learning and thinking. An effective teaching program can be used throughout the world in many types of computer, and is likely to be constantly improved as student reactions are observed.

Languages for writing teaching programs are now being developed so that a professional educator with little knowledge of computers can write them. As the potentialities of this become understood and developed, it is likely that many educators throughout the world will set to work writing and improving computerized instruction courses.

MEDIC'NE   *Doctors* will one day make use of a distant computer as a help in diagnosis. A patient's symptoms will be transmitted to the distant machine. The machine will make suggestions to the doctor and perhaps ask for additional information. Already electrocardiograph results have been transmitted from patients' bedsides over the telephone for immediate analysis by a distant computer. The computer would not in any way replace the human qualities of the doctor, but it would add to his limited store of information. The computer is also carrying on a type of information-retrieval work, but probably with more logical or analytical programming than straightforward information retrieval.

Another likelihood is the storing and automatic retrieval of patient case histories. The case history accessible to the computer would contain details of the patient's past diseases and symptoms, diagnostic tests performed, inoculations, drugs given, the effectiveness of treatments attempted, side effects, and so on. This could be retrieved by the doctor to help him in his diagnosis, and might even in the future be processed by the computer so that the accumulated experience of the medical profession might be of help in the case.

The case histories accumulated in this way would provide an excellent base of information from which medical statistics would be gathered. Medical research would use this body of data widely. The effects of new drugs would be monitored. Any undesirable side effects would be detected as quickly as possible and communicated to the doctors who need to know them.

As with other personal information files, laws need to be passed restricting access to this data, otherwise the individual is going to lose much of the privacy he cherishes today. If all of the organizations who want to record things about an individual have their way, much of his past life is going to be accessible to the machines.

PUBLIC USE OF COMPUTERS   We could list many applications of computing-plus-data-transmission. They reach into almost all walks of life, almost all industries and professions.

It now becomes apparent that we are going to need a public use of computers. People everywhere must be able to dial up a computing facility appropriate to their needs. They may have a portion of a file reserved for them personally in a distant machine. The grocer on the street corner will transmit the paper tape from his cash register and have his accounts done. Doctors' assistants will transmit details of charges to patients to their bank's computer, which will bill them and keep accounts. An engineer will do his routine calculations on a teleprinter or on a terminal that looks like a desk calculating machine. Computer programmers will develop programs at a remote input/output device.

There will be "on-line" files of many kinds of data, with automated means for searching them. Commercial and economic data files will be interrogated for business planning. A private investor can check his hypotheses about how to make money on the stock exchange against files of data on past stock movements. One visualizes the clergyman of the future preparing his Sunday sermon at a computer terminal with ability to retrieve appropriate literature and perhaps past sermons. The result will probably be better than some of the sermons we get today. The architects, the electronic designers, the market researchers, and many other professional prople are already having application-oriented programs written for them.

There is a commonality between most of the uses of this vast spectrum of applications. The same types of computer could handle most of them. The files needed vary in size and speed of access but are conventional computer files. None of the preceding applications need a file technology unique to itself. The telecommunication links are the same, though some applications could economically use a faster link than others. There is more variation in the input/output devices envisaged, but although many special-purpose devices will undoubtedly be built, two or three types of machines could handle the majority of the applications. Only the programs will be widely different, and these will be as diverse as the applications themselves. The programs, however, will be stored, along with data, on the computer files, and the user will request the program he needs to use before he begins.

COMPUTERS IN THE HOME   Many of the applications of this technology can be carried out from individuals' homes. Today only a small number of persons have a computer terminal in their home, but sooner or later this is going to become a mass market. Perhaps, in the beginning, they will be paid for by the firms the users work for. Perhaps advertising, catalog scanning, and computer-assisted purchasing will help to pay for them. Perhaps people will buy them because they are the latest and greatest status symbol. They need not be expensive. The addition of two keys to a Touch-Tone® telephone[3] can give a "voice answer-back" input/output device of some versatility.

However it is done, the computer manufacturers are well aware that once they can penetrate the *domestic* market, their revenue is going to soar. The airline industry, the automobile industry, telecommunications, and other complex technical industries, all spent two decades or so of limited growth, but then expanded rapidly when there was general acceptance and usage of their product by the public. Probably data transmission is going to help this happen to the computer industry also.

Certainly when the layman, the dedicated amateur, the experimenting engineer, and the inventive academician can all tinker with terminals, the quantity of computer time that will be *wasted* will be phenomenal. Computing is like a narcotic. Once their programs begin to work, people cannot let it alone. If Colman's made a fortune out of the mustard left on the side of the plate, how much more will the computer manufacturer make out of time wasted at on-line terminals?

Experiments are being done which involve adding keyboards and adaptors to conventional television sets so that they can be used for a man–computer dialog. The signal from the computer in this case is a coded alphabetic signal, and the letters and digits the computer sends appear on the television screen. If the receiving device has an appropriate form of storage, still pictures could be sent also. A conventional dial-up telephone line is used for transmission.

A device like this in the home could be used for many purposes. It could give access to a wide variety of data banks and computers. The user might do calculations, store details for his tax return, learn French, scan the local lending library files, or play chess with a computer. It is likely that "news-

---

[3] "Touch-Tone" is an A.T. & T. trade-mark copyright.

papers" will be presented in this way in the future. The user will quickly flip through pages, or indexes, for what he wants to read. With satellite communications he might read the London "papers" for no more cost than the New York ones.

The television screen of the future is likely to become much bigger than today. Manufacturers are experimenting with techniques for making screens several feet in width. By increasing the television transmission bandwidth (Chapter 10) by a factor of ten, wall-sized screens could be filled with high-quality pictures. The user could relax in his armchair and watch such a screen, using a detached keyboard in his lap.

Whereas a man, perhaps, uses his home terminal for writing programs, his wife might go shopping with it. In the American advertisers' paradise, all manner of highly colored catalogs will become available the moment the new medium exists, and there will be varied enticements for exploring them. Very elaborate presentations of products will become possible. Perhaps critical consumer guides will also become automated to aid the exploration. Having scanned the relevant catalogs and inspected pictures of the goods in detail, the shopper can then use the same terminal to order items. The money will be automatically deducted from her bank record and added to that of the seller. Again with satellite transmission, dialing a shopping catalog in a machine thousands of miles away will be no more expensive than dialing one in the next town, and one visualizes New Yorkers "shopping" in Paris and Tokyo.

If telecommunication capacity goes on increasing, however, as projected in Fig. 1.1, the day is going to arrive when we have a link of much higher capacity than a telephone line coming to our home. The capacity needed for television transmission along a cable is about a thousand times greater than that used for the telephone. Already, however, broadcast television is delivered to some homes by coaxial cable. It seems likely then that a switched cable system will be coupled to homes sometime in the future. The Bell System is planning to actively market their Picturephone® set[4] in the near future (Fig. 1.3). This requires a total line capacity about 500 times that of a conventional telephone. Already broadband switching centers (Chapter 18) are coming into operation.

This opens up great new opportunities. The Sears Roebuck catalog could now have film sequences on it! But still the user would be free to "turn the pages," to use the index, to select and reject. The day's news film footage could be scanned selectively like a newspaper. A historian or documentary film maker could scan through relevant indexed film segments on his screen, duplicating the parts he wishes to use. It would need a massive quantity of storage by today's computer standards to store films electronically in this

---

[4] "Picturephone" is an A.T. & T. trademark copyright.

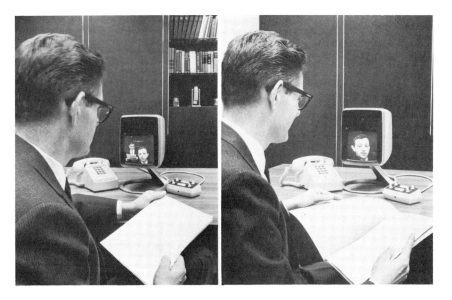

The electronic zoom feature of the Bell System's Model II Picturephone set enables the user to enlarge the field of view of the camera simply by turning a knob on the control unit. A camera iris automatically adjusts the lens aperture to compensate for any change in light intensity between the two scenes.

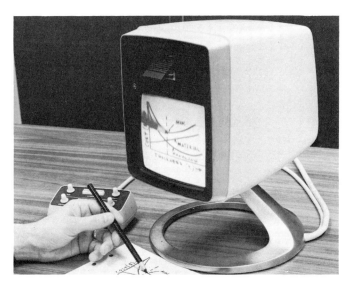

The set being used to transmit drawings or charts by setting the camera focus at one foot. Here the "self-view" option is being used to position the graph while it is being transmitted.

Fig. 1.3. Picturephone: the start of a new era in telecommunications? When these machines are installed in offices or homes, the communication links to those buildings will have a capacity about 500 times that of a conventional telephone line. This capacity will become usable for data transmission also; and such speeds will change much of our current computer systems thinking.

way, but there is no reason why film warehouses should not be constructed so that the films can be automatically selected, loaded, and viewed under computer control. The home user may feel like watching an Antonioni film. He displays on his screen a list of these, selects one that he has not seen before, and requests it. The evening's entertainment is set. There will be no advertisements. He can stop the film for a while if he wants to make coffee. And his bank balance will be automatically depleted.

Dialable video channels will also be used for Picturephone. You may dial a relative's home and he can connect the channel to his television camera, or a video-tape recording he made of the children during the weekend. Video-tape films for use on such systems are already being made, and will soon be distributed like phonograph records. In England, an experiment is under way using them in schools. Business video calls have many possible uses, and probably many office buildings will have their own screen unit. It would be very useful for a systems analyst, for example, to be able to discuss block diagrams or code with distant colleagues in this way. The screen would be also useful in selling. It seems likely that board rooms will have a set of screens for conference calls, and the screens for data in the management control room will also perhaps become video links.

As we will see later in the book, the Picturephone channels planned by the Bell System will carry their picture and sound to individual homes or offices on three wire-pairs, which, surprisingly, need only a minor modification of today's telephone lines.

THE SYMBIOTIC AGE   We are moving into an age when intelligent men in all walks of life will need, and constantly use, their computer terminals—this will be a *symbiotic age* when the limited brain of man is supplemented by the vast data banks and logic power of distant machines. Probably all of the professions will have their own data banks and possibly their own languages. The nonprofessional man will use the terminals for doing calculations, working out his tax returns, computer dating, planning vacations, or just for sheer entertainment. In Britain and some other countries, the possibility of setting up a government-controlled "national grid" of computers is being examined. In private enterprise, telecommunication companies, computer manufacturers, and third parties are setting up schemes in which users lease an input/output device just as a telephone is leased, and are then billed for the computer time they use. The input/output devices include Touch-Tone telephones, teleprinters, and specially manufactured computer terminals.

Although some general-purpose systems have been put into operation which can be programmed to meet most of the needs of most types of users, it seems likely that in the beginning, at least, the majority of systems will be much more specialized than these. Part of the reason for this is machine efficiency. The ratio of productive to nonproductive computer utilization can be considerably higher on the special-purpose, or restricted, system. Second, the massive files that are envisaged for certain applications are more likely to reside on their own special system. Third, special-purpose systems are, in general, easier to implement than the big system which does everything for everybody. And last, we have not mastered the art of building computers of the gigantic size that would become necessary for a general-purpose system with a large number of users.

The user, then, is likely to have a catalog of remote systems which he can dial for different operations. He will, we hope, use his same input/output machine, or possibly a group of machines, for all of the various computers he communicates with.

The language the user employs in "conversing" with the machine is a problem. Some of the systems can only be communicated with by programming. However, if they are to be used by the massive public that is hoped for, or by management, clerks, salesmen, and so on, in industry, it must be possible to communicate with them in a much easier form than a programming language. The computer must speak or display the language of its user, and, much more difficult, it must be able to interpret what the user tells it. Man–machine communication is one of the big difficulties and there is much scope for ingenuity and research in this area (some examples are given in Chapter 24).

Public time-sharing schemes of this type are beginning to work successfully. The next generation of such schemes will improve upon them enormously, and before long it can be expected that this field will reach that critical point in the stages of growth of a technology when it will achieve mass acceptance, and mass-produced machines will be sold. The systems will grow, multiply, and interlink. A countrywide, and probably a worldwide, network of computers that can be dialed on the existing telecommunication facilities will be available to us before many years have passed.

The range of users will extend into many fields. We will find enthusiastic users in these fields adding programs and data to the files that are for public use. Dedicated amateurs will probably begin to write and sell programs to the computer companies. We must achieve mass participation in the enormous quantity of programming work that lies ahead if such schemes are to flower fully. In computer-assisted teaching alone the programming work ahead is of unimaginable magnitude. The technique can only achieve maturity after thousands of talented and dedicated teachers have been harnessed into the work of preparing the programs. This is equally true in other fields.

This technology is bringing the computer to the masses. People everywhere will be able to participate in using and building up an enormous quantity of computerized information and logic.

We are at the beginning of a chain reaction. The ingredients already exist. The fuse has been lit. It is clear that we now have a tool so powerful that it will take many decades for us to use it to its full potential. But its full potential is far beyond our cleverest imagining today.

2 MACHINES THAT USE DATA TRANSMISSION

A vast and ever-growing array of machines can be attached to telecommunication lines for transmitting and receiving data. This chapter gives examples of these devices. The reader who is familiar with computing hardware may skip this chapter.

Transmission may take place directly between computers. One computer may be connected via a telephone line, or a higher speed line, to another computer and will send data to it as though it were writing on its own output units. A computer may be assigned a telephone number and another computer can automatically dial it on the public telephone network (generating with an automatic call unit under program control the requisite dial impulses on the line which is connected to the local town exchange), and transmit or request data.

More commonly, however, transmission takes place between input/output machines which are connected remotely to a computer center to form a "system." A wide variety of such machines exist. They may be permanently connected to the computer on a private line leased from the telephone companies, or be attached to a device with a telephone dial so that the connection must first be established by dialing, as with our telephone at home.

Much data transmission does not involve a computer at all. Machines such as paper tape readers, card readers, teleprinters, and so on, send data to each directly. The Telex and telegraph networks have been doing this for many decades. Today it may be done faster and with a wide variety of data processing machines, but in essence it is similar to conventional telegraphy.

TYPES OF MACHINES FOR DATA TRANSMISSION Computer input/output devices, and also machines which transmit to each other without the intervention of a computer, fall into two categories, those for dealing with a mass of data and those for handling single items or a small number of items.

For massive output, high-speed printers are used. For massive input there are card readers, paper tape readers, optical readers of documents with marks or characters, magnetic-ink character readers, and so on. Fast output punches are also used. Transmission may also take place to and from remote storage media, such as magnetic tapes or disk file units.

All of these devices may be connected to a distant computer by telecommunication links. If the input/output device is attached directly to the computer in this manner, it is said to be *on-line*. Often, however, one of these machines transmits to another machine without a computer being involved. This is referred to as *off-line* transmission.

These devices are slow by comparison with computer speeds. They are sometimes not connected to the main computer, but may be on a separate, less expensive, line-control computer. This may, for example, write transmitted data to magnetic tape or disk for later processing by the main computer, and disseminate output from some storage medium to the remote devices. However, with many modern systems they are attached to the main computer and work in such a way that their operation is fully overlapped with other computing.

The cost of off-line telecommunications facilities is often lower than on-line for a small number of lines. Figure 2.1 shows a means of transmitting paper tape which is inexpensive for small quantities of data. For larger quantities of data and long lines it becomes more economic to use a machine with a modem (Chapters 10 and 13) gives a higher transmission speed. For a large number of lines it becomes cheaper and easier to use on-line rather than off-line communications.

The economics of the communication facilities are tied up with what response time or turn-around time is needed. For a response time in minutes, on-line facilities are demanded. For a response time in hours, off-line facilities are good enough if they are in fact cheaper than on-line. A turn-around time of eight hours or so, depending upon distance, may be attainable using delivery vans. If two days or so is acceptable, the mail services might provide the cheapest answer.

Input and output of single transactions or small groups of transactions are done by a variety of different machines. These can be devices into which data are entered by human operators or which collect data automatically. Data collected automatically may be in analog form, such as temperature or pressure readings; or may be in the form of impulses, as from flow meters or

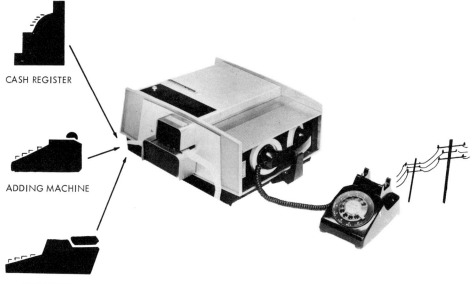

CASH REGISTER

ADDING MACHINE

TYPEWRITER

Fig. 2.1. An inexpensive way to transmit small quantities of data. The Digitronics Audio-verter Model 8050 transmits five- or eight-channel paper tape over a dial-up telephone line. No separate data set (modem) is required because the machine is acoustically coupled to a conventional telephone handset, and the data travels in the form of audible tones. Five-channel tape is transmitted at 43 characters per second; eight-channel tape at 30 characters per second. *Courtesy Digitronics Corporation.*

devices for counting. For efficient handling on a data-transmission system they may be first converted to digital characters. Analog-digital converters are used either remotely, or on the computer site if the computer is close to the instrumentation.

Similarly, the output devices can be either analog, impulse-countrolled, or digital. They can present information for human use, or can control machines, valves or other devices automatically.

Devices for human use may be typewriters or other keyboard machines. They may permit a two-way "conversation" with the computer, or may be a remote equivalent of the computer room input/output devices. Paper tape readers and card readers may provide input over communication lines. Printers may provide the output. An example of a range of low-speed general-purpose input/output units is the Datel equipment provided by the GPO in Britain. Figure 2.2 shows a Datel 300 card reader and keyboard.

Devices which transmit single transactions may be either on-line or off-line, as with those designed for batches of data. If, however, they are intended

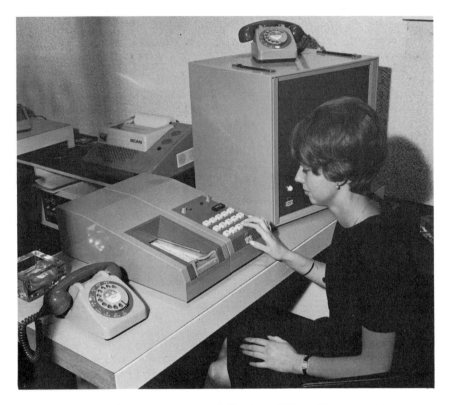

Fig. 2.2. Datel 300 equipment available from GPO in Britain provides card and keyboard transmission over a dial-up voice line at up to 20 characters per second using multifrequency tones. *By courtesy of H.M. Postmaster General.*

to give a fast response to their user, it is necessary for them to be on-line. This is true with the many machines today that are designed to give a conversational interaction with their user.

Machines which give real-time answers to human operators must be designed to give the most efficient man–machine interface. The operators obtain their image of the system from the terminal device they are using. These devices should present information in a form as familiar as possible, and should respond sufficiently adroitly to avoid making the operator impatient. In some environments, especially robust machines are needed, for example, where a terminal is operated by a burly manual worker who is likely to thump the machine if it does not respond to his pressing keys!

The information given to the operator may have to be in *hard copy* form or it may not. If not, a versatile device like a cathode ray tube may form the output facility, or voice answer-back over a telephone might be used. Using a visual display screen, looking something like a television set, a variety of fast and efficient means of man–computer interaction have been devised. One of the most appealing of these, but on early machines one of the most expensive, uses a "light pen." This is a light-sensitive electrical stylus. When brought into contact with the display by the operator, the computer can detect its position, and as the machine scans the screen continuously, so the light pen adds lines or other shapes to the image or it can be used to convey information symbolically to the computer. The light pen is often used in conjunction with a foot pedal or keyboard. Sometimes the keyboard may be covered with a variety of templates so that different input signals may be indicated with the light pen and keyboard, and these may be changed by changing the template and program associated with it. Figures 24.18 and 24.19 show terminals with light pens.

Various means have been devised for making the computer talk with a human voice. At first this was regarded as a cute piece of laboratory showmanship, entertaining but of no practical value. Now, however, it is being installed by many firms because it is the cheapest way to make the computer give information over the telephone network. On some systems an unlimited number of human-voice words may be stored in digital form on the files. A person wanting information from the machine dials it on the telephone. After establishing contact he dials his enquiry in a coded form. The machine assembles appropriate words in reply and speaks them clearly over the telephone.

Table 2.1

Document Transmission Terminals	Human-Input Terminals	Answer-Back Devices and Displays
Paper tape readers/punches	Keyboard-like typewriter	Typewritten
Card readers/punches	Special keyboard	Printer
Magnetic tape units	Matrix keyboard	Teleprinter
Badge readers	Lever set	Passbook printer
	Rotary switches	
	Push buttons	
Optical document readers	Teleprinter	Display tube
Microfilm	Telephone dial	Light panel
	Touch-Tone telephone keyboard	
Plate readers		Graph plotter
Facsimile machines	Light pen with display tube	Strip recorder
	Coupled stylus	
	Facsimile machine	Dials
	Plate reader	Telephone voice answer-back
	Badge reader	Facsimile machine

Table 2.1 lists some of the devices in use for input of data from documents, and for human input and replies. Many machines use combinations of the facilities listed, and a great variety of shapes and sizes exist.

Some systems use big display boards as their output, so they can give information to a large number of people at once. Group displays may be used so that the computer may be interrogated by a member of the group.

The remainder of this chapter gives some specific illustrations of remote input/output devices.

TELEGRAPH
EQUIPMENT

The common carriers and associated manufacturers produce teleprinters, paper tape readers and paper tape punches for use on telegraph and telephone lines. These form one of the least expensive ranges of remote input/output devices, and are generally machines of high reliability. In the United States these are called teletype machines when marketed by the telephone companies. The word teleprinter is common elsewhere.

Seven types of on-line devices can be obtained. In American terminology these are sometimes referred to with abbreviated initials as follows:

1. TD *Transmitter Distributer*
   –Reads and transmits punched paper tape.
2. ROTR *Receive-Only Typing Reperforator*
   –Receives the signal and punches paper tape, printing characters on the edge of the tape, or over the perforations for chadless tape (chadless tape does not have the paper completely removed when a hole is punched, but instead remains attached, like a flap, so that the entire tape can be printed over.
3. RT *Reperforator–Transmitter* (in effect a TD + ROTR)
   –Combination of a transmitter distributer and a typing reperforator. Sometimes used as a store-and-forward device in manual message switching
4. RO *Receive-Only Page Printer*
   –Receives the signal and prints continuous stationery. It has no keyboard but does have page-positioning keys.
5. KSR *Keyboard Sending and Receiving Unit*
   –Receives the signal and prints as with an RO. There is a keyboard on the same device which transmits data.
6. KTR *Keyboard Typing Reperforator*
   –Receives the signal, punches and prints paper tape as with the ROTR. In addition, the keyboard can transmit a signal, punching and printing paper tape at the same time. No tape reader or page printer.
7. ASR *Automatic Sending and Receiving Unit*
   –This combines all of the preceding devices into one machine con-

taining a keyboard, page printer, reperforator, and tape transmitter. Paper tape can be prepared off-line. This can take place while printing is occurring from the transmission line.

Another machine used in conjunction with these is a device for punching paper tape off-line, ready for transmission. This is called a *perforator*. Machines equivalent to these exist in other countries, sometimes with different names. American teleprinters, in common with other telegraphic devices, operate at a variety of speeds up to 150 bits per second; English teleprinters operate at 50 bits per second using the 5-bit Baudot code (Fig. 6.2). Among today's most common telegraphic equipment is Western Union's Model 28 series.

The Teletype Corporation's Model 30 Series operates at 75 to 150 bits per second and transmits 7-bit ASCII code (Fig. 6.3). Figures 6.7 to 6.9 show typical teletype equipment.

MACHINES OPERATING AT TYPEWRITER SPEEDS   The computer manufacturers have produced a wide variety of data transmission machines which operate in the same speed ranges as the faster telegraph devices. These are intended for use on voice or subvoice lines. Their advantages over telegraph machines are that they may be faster, may have better error control features, may be able to handle punched cards or other media, and may have lights and keyboard arrangements better suited to a specific application. They may have buffers and line-control units which give better line utilization. A disadvantage is that they are often more expensive than telegraph machines.

In some of these devices the basic printing unit is an electric typewriter, and all of the components are built to operate at the maximum speed of the typewriter. Figure 2.3 illustrates the IBM 1050 series, for example. This range of equipment operates at 14.8 characters per second. It consists of a typewriter-like printer and keyboard, a paper tape reader and punch, and a card reader and punch. These can be arranged in a wide variety of combinations. It is possible to transmit from keyboard to printer, from tape to printer, from tape to card, and so on. Combinations of these may take place at the same time. All of the transmission has automatic error detection, and retransmission takes place when a transmission error is found. Some computer systems have large numbers of these machines permanently attached on leased lines. In time-sharing systems a user may have one of these machines temporarily connected to a computer via the switched public telephone network. He may use it for only a small portion of the day and when he does so he dials the computer that he wishes to work with.

Fig. 2.3. The IBM 1050 series, a range of general-purpose terminals operating at 14.8 characters per second over a 150-baud or voice line. The series includes a card reader (foreground, left), card punch, (background, left), a paper tape reader, tape punch (background, right), as well as the keyboard and printer at which the girl sits. Here the operator has dialed a computer, or other 1050. Commonly, however, 1050's and similar terminals are installed on private leased lines with many terminals on one line to reduce line costs. In the foreground, right is the data set that connects the 1050 system to the communication line. *Courtesy IBM.*

**MACHINES DESIGNED
FOR A SPECIFIC
APPLICATION**

The 1050 series, like the teletype machines, are general-purpose terminals. They were not built with any particular type of application in mind, but rather so that they could be used in the widest possible variety of applications. Some terminals, on the other hand, are constructed to meet the needs of one application or one type of user only, such as a bank teller or an airline reservation agent. Figure 2.4 shows an NCR terminal specifically designed for use by tellers in savings banks. This terminal updates the customer's pass-book.

The first essential for man to be able to communicate with a computer system is that they should use a common language. This is one of the major problems that stands in the way of a widespread and sophisticated use of man–computer communication. It is a problem that affects both the programming or "software" design, and the design of the unit which the man uses to carry on the conversation.

When a man with programming training communicates with the system, he has great flexibility in what he says through the use of program statements. When an airline reservation agent or an administrative clerk carries on what is a fairly complex conversation with the system, he cannot be expected to be a programmer, and so he needs a system which is carefully planned for his particular type of input. This may mean careful design of the coding that is used, and examples of this are given in the next chapter. On the other hand, the problem may be largely solved in the design of a special-purpose input/output device. Sometimes the best way of designing a system, if it can be afforded, is to use both a "problem-oriented" language and a special input/output unit.

**VISUAL
DISPLAYS**

In many forms of man–machine conversation, the machine does much more talking than the man. The computer can be prolific in producing output whereas the man is slow. On the other hand, it is difficult to program the computer to understand human statements unless they are very simple or else precisely formulated. In some "conversations" designed for fast and accurate input of information, the computer leads its distant user through a series of logical steps obtaining one fact from him at a time, until all of the details about a particular item are recorded. At each step the user's entry is a very simple one. The next chapter gives illustrations of this. On the other hand, the user may be searching for information from the computer. He may scan through quantities of data quickly until he finds what he is searching for, or obtains clues to where he might find it. He may have to work through a logic tree of indexes or other data before he finds what he wants.

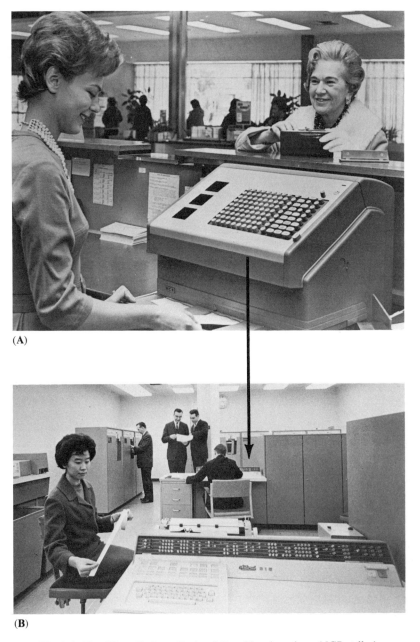

(A)

(B)

Fig. 2.4. The Dime Savings Bank of Brooklyn has these NCR teller's machines in five branch offices. The NCR 315 computer updates customer passbooks and bank records in real time for almost one-half million savings accounts. *Courtesy National Cash Register Co.*

(A)

(B)

Fig. 2.5. The reason for using data transmission is often to obtain access to a centrally updated set of files, rather than to obtain access to a computer alone. The IBM 2314 shown here, has been used for many such remote "data banks." One unit gives direct access to up to 233 million characters (bytes) with an average "seek" time of 75 milliseconds. The disks containing data can be removed and stored like tape. *Courtesy IBM.*

Typewriter speed output is often too slow for fast and efficient man–machine "conversation" of these types. Typewriter-speed devices are sometimes used on voice lines which are capable of ten times that speed. To use a faster printer, say 120 characters per second, would be more expensive, possibly too expensive on a system with a very large number of individual output units. This problem has been solved elegantly by the use of visual displays which have a screen something like a domestic television set. Output can be written on the face of a cathode ray tube at the maximum speed the communication line is capable of. It is noteworthy that the introduction of these devices changed the whole nature of man–machine conversations in commercial and administrative systems, in scientific applications, in computer-aided teaching, and in other fields.

In commercial applications, records which once occupied many filing cabinets are now stored on magnetic disk files in a computer system (Fig. 2.5). Office personnel who need facts from the records obtain them via display screens attached to the computer by telephone line. The display unit has a keyboard, often a typewriter-like keyboard, but sometimes a special keyboard. With this the operator interrogates the system, enters new data, and modifies existing data. Often the system is such that the average input "transaction" from the operator is very short, whereas the reply is a screenfull of data. The cost of these alphabetic "television set" units can be lower than the cost of typewriter-like units if several of them are situated in one location sharing the same control unit and the same voice line. Figure 2.6 shows a room full of typical small display units.

Many visual display units are not designed to display alphanumeric data alone but also analog data so that the screen can show any line drawing. Often a light pen is used with such a system to draw lines or make some coded input. It should be noted that a high-capacity transmission link is needed if a screen of this type is to be filled quickly. To fill a screen that can hold 1200 alphanumeric characters (but no line drawings) could take about 4 seconds over an efficiently organized leased telephone line. To fill a screen designed for line drawings and made up on a matrix of 800 by 800 dots would take $4\frac{1}{2}$ minutes over the same line. This is because each alphanumeric character on the former screen can be coded using six bits, and so the screen can be filled with 9600 bits (or somewhat more than this because of error checking), as opposed to 640,000. The information sent to a graphic screen must, then, be more cleverly coded than this. What is transmitted is likely to be an abbreviated set of operation codes instructing a terminal with a high degree of logic circuitry how to compose the image. Nevertheless some graphic displays require too much transmitted data to be used efficiently on a voice line.

The alphanumeric screen, therefore, is commonly used on telephone lines,

Fig. 2.6. IBM 2260 terminals. All of the terminals in this room can be attached to one voice line. The speed normally used, 1200 or 2400 characters per second, is fast enough to enable the computer to fill the screen with alphanumeric data in less than a second. On average in this application, the response to the screen might consist of about 200 characters. Users interrogate the distant computer less than once per minute and so response time will be fast provided so that an efficient method interleaving the data messages is used. *Courtesy Robert Isear Studio.*

Fig. 2.7. A Bunker-Ramo Telequote 70 terminal, in a stock broker's office, connected to a remote computer by voice line. Two separate screens are employed. The right-hand one displays alphanumeric data. The left-hand one shows charts composed of dots in such a way that they can be transmitted in a sufficient number of bits to give a fast response time over a voice line. *Courtesy Bunker-Ramo.*

whereas the screen for line drawings is sometimes not. The latter is located close to the computer so that a high-speed (wide band) channel can connect it to the computer. Figure 2.7 shows a graphic screen which is designed for use on a voice line. The terminal has two separate images. The left-hand one shows stock charts composed of dots in such a way that they can be transmitted in a sufficiently small number of bits to give a fast response time.

VOICE ANSWERBACK DEVICES

The least expensive way of receiving detailed answers over the telephone from a computer is to receive them in human-voice form so that a conventional telephone receiver is the output device.

There are two basically different ways of making the computer transmit human sounds. One is to record the sounds in an analog form as they are recorded on a domestic tape recorder. Sounds may be recorded in a magnetic form, as with tape, on the surface of a drum. In a typical system, the drum surface is divided into fixed-length slots of time and each of these contains one human word or part of a word. A series of magnetic heads are able to pick up selected words. The sounds selected are amplified and connected to the telephone line. Selecting the requisite words or parts of words is done under control of the computer program. Where a word occupies more than one slot on the drum the computer will transmit the appropriate slots sequentially. The switching between drum heads is sufficiently fast so that there is not a perceptible break between the slots transmitted.

A device of this type is used for giving up-to-the-minute quotations of stock prices on the New York Stock Exchange to brokers. The broker or his client dials a code which represents the stock in question. Details of the latest price of the stock are stored in the stock exchange computer files. This computer has data transmission devices on the floor of the exchange, into which jobbers enter all changes. In response to the enquiry, the computer selects the requisite words and fractions of words from its drum, and, as the drum rotates past the pick-up heads, these words are transmitted down the line to the broker's telephone. He receives a clear audible statement, spoken twice, of the stock price he requires.

The other audio response technique does not use analog recording of this type, but rather digital recording. The analog recording method has two limitations. First, the vocabulary is limited by the size of the voice answerback drum. On a typical system, the maximum number of words that can be used is 128. Second, if the system uses fixed-length time slots the reply must be composed of short fixed-length blocks of sound. This can make it sound disjointed. The New York Stock Exchange system, for example, sounds more staccato than a recorded voice announcing an incorrect telephone dialing.

As will be discussed in Chapter 14, any sounds transmitted over a telephone line can be converted into digital form, converted, for example, into a stream of 1 and 0 bits (*off*-or-*on* pulses). One second of telephone sound can be represented by 56,000 bits and when it is reconverted to sound it has suffered little detectable distortion beyond that already introduced by the telephone. A smaller number of bits could be used, for example, 20,000, but then the distortion would be more noticeable. Strings of bits such as this are the form of data which a computer program can manipulate, and which can be stored readily on computer tape, disk, or other bulk storage. A small computer disk unit capable of storing, say, 100 million bits, could therefore hold a very large human-voice vocabulary in this fashion. The computer program can manipulate the words (and pauses) as wished, assemble sentences, store them on tape, and so on. Words or phrases can be stored which are fully variable in length, and thus the staccato fitting together of fixed-length sounds is avoided.

Another advantage of the latter method is that a device can be built for

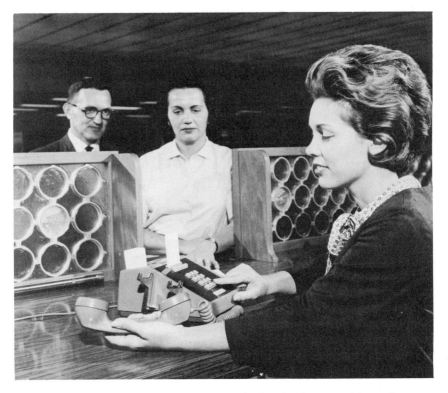

Fig. 2.8. Touch-Tone banking. Here a bank teller inserts a data card into her dialing telephone and is connected directly to the bank's computer. The computer answers the call and gives a tone signal that it is waiting for the transaction.

The teller then inserts the customer's personal account card into her telephone so that the computer knows who the customer is and is prepared to receive further instructions.

Next the teller keys into the computer the amount of deposit or withdrawal. The computer will then give the new balance in the customer's account. *Courtesy AT & T.*

the user to record, or digitize, new words and phrases with ease. This is a much more difficult laboratory job if the words have to fit exactly into short fixed-length time slots.

The user of a voice answer-back system needs an inexpensive way of sending small amounts of data to the computer so that he can phrase enquiries or enter facts. On some systems, such as the New York Stock Exchange system, this is done by using the dial of the telephone itself. Sometimes the ten keys of a Touch-Tone telephone are used (Fig. 2.8). The provision of two keys beyond the basic ten is now standard on the Touch-Tone telephone. The digit keys can all be given a second meaning through the use of the extra keys

Fig. 2.9. The Bell System Touch-Tone telephone keyboard originally had 10 keys. Now 12 keys are standard; the extra two nonnumeric keys are needed for data transmission. With this telephone, plastic keyboard overlays could be used to give the numeric keys a variety of different meanings. The additional keys may be used to condition the meaning of the numeric keys. An example of this is given on page 421.

to indicate when they mean digits and when they have the alternate meaning (Fig. 2.9).

On a typical system using a simple telephone dial, the telephone is first connected through to the computer by dialing its telephone number in the normal way. The user knows when the connection is established because the computer sends a "data tone," usually a high-pitched note of a few seconds' duration. The user then dials a stock number, account number, or other information. This is stored by the computer program and is used to anwer the enquiry.

Sometimes a low-cost punched-card reader or other input device is attached to the telephone for the input of prepunched data. Sometimes a card-dialing telephone is used into which a plastic card is inserted to generate a given sequence of dial pulses.

FACSIMILE TRANSMISSION

Facsimile terminals are devices which can transmit and reproduce documents. At a sending station a document is scanned and converted into signals suitable for transmission. At the receiving station the signals are decoded and a copy of the original document is printed.

As with audio response from computers, the document can be coded in either an analog or a digital fashion. Many facsimile transmission devices use digital coding. With these, the original document may be coded as though it was entirely black and white, or it may be in shades of grey, thus permitting half-tone pictures to be sent. Often the former is used and this permits the document to be transmitted in a shorter time period. As the document is scanned, it is in effect divided up into small squares. In the case of black and white transmission each of these would be sent as either a 1 or 0 bit (on-or-off pulse). In half-tone transmission each point would be sent as a group of bits or character).

A page of print $8\frac{1}{2} \times 11$ inches is likely to take 5 minutes or more to

Fig. 2.10. Sperry Rand Corporation's UNIVAC DCT-2000 Data Communications Terminal, a combination card punch, high-speed printer and card reader, control unit and operator's console. It can send and receive information via voice-grade telephone lines at speeds of 300 characters per second. The printer, at left, can be ordered separately should printed output alone be required.

transmit over a telephone (voice) line. If half-tone reproduction or a high degree of resolution is needed, the time could be considerably longer than this. Higher speed facsimile transmission is performed using high-capacity telecommunication channels.

A much simpler form of machine is used to transmit handwriting. In this, as a ball-point pen moves on paper, varying tones are generated to represent the movement of the pen. They are transmitted, and a pen at the receiving end reproduces the movement of the original. Electronic blackboards have been used in classrooms with the lecturer using a telephone line from far away. The telephone relays his voice while a second line transmits his handwriting. The latter is projected onto a screen, thus providing an "electronic blackboard."

BULK TRANSMISSION

The devices described in the last few pages are used mainly for transmitting single items or small groups of items. Much of the transmission that takes place to and from computers is of large batches or "files" of items. There is a variety of batch transmission machines which operate at a higher speed than most of the devices discussed. Figure 3.2 shows one such machine designed for high-speed transmission from magnetic tape. This requires a wideband circuit, which is expensive and may be difficult to obtain. Many terminals for bulk transmission consequently operate at speeds geared to the capacity of a voice line. Figure 2.10 shows one of these.

3

PRESENT-DAY SYSTEMS
USING DATA TRANSMISSION

Chapter 1 surveyed uses conjectured for data transmission. This chapter and the next examine in a little more detail some of the systems that are already working.

ON-LINE AND OFF-LINE SYSTEMS   In systems using data transmission and computing, the telecommunication lines may be "on-line" or "off-line" to the computer. "On-line" means that they go directly into the computer with the computer controlling the transmission. "Off-line" means that telecommunication data do not go directly into the computer but are written onto magnetic tape or punched into paper tape or cards for later processing.

Figure 3.1 shows a computer with both on-line and off-line transmission links. Transactions arrive on paper tape, perhaps from distant depots or warehouses, and replies are returned in the same manner, possibly with a teleprinter network. Whereas the data transmission links are still off-line, the system permits a number of enquiry or data-entry stations to be used on-line. On many systems these stations are exclusively within the same building or factory and it is referred to as an "in-plant" system. Strictly, "in-plant" means based on an internal private telecommunication system. Units on the other end of public telephone or telegraph lines are referred to as "out plant."

The vehicle in the upper corner carries the printouts of the computer to where they are needed. A delivery van, or mail, is much cheaper than data transmission for bulk data. For bulk data, telecommunications are only justified where a significantly faster turnaround time is needed.

Off-line entry of data into the system is relatively simple in that it avoids software (control program) problems. Therefore it was common on early systems. Today, however, standardized software is becoming much more elaborate and thus it is becoming easier to have the links on-line.

In a system with many more data transmission links than in Fig. 3.1, the handling of paper tape becomes congested. Furthermore, the cost of the paper tape units, with adequate checking and retransmission facilities and their operators, becomes greater than the cost of taking the communication lines directly into the computer. The system therefore becomes on-line, rather than off-line.

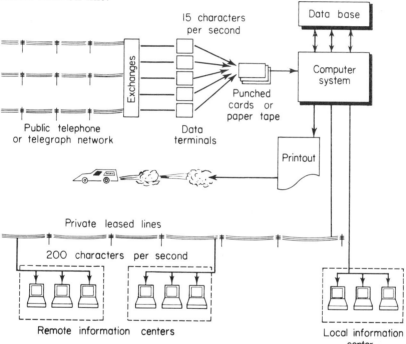

A system in which information is sent to the computer center on off-line dial-up public lines, from many locations, with low cost terminals. A few information centers with higher cost terminals are connected on-line by private leased lines of higher speed. A van is used to deliver computer printouts.

Fig. 3.1. Off-line data transmission links; on-line in-plant enquiry stations.

There are many other reasons for using an on-line system. Validity checks can be made on transactions at the time they are entered, and so mistakes may be picked up immediately while the distant terminal operator is present. The terminal can be used for enquiries, or for communicating with the computer, which can be instructed to take certain types of action. The computer may process the transaction before the operator leaves the terminal, and check for any exceptional conditions that the operator may be able to do something about.

Many firms have a need to move large quantities of data from one location to another, and this is often carried out off-line. Over a voice line or higher-capacity link, data is transmitted from one machine to another—from card reader to card punch, magnetic tape to magnetic tape, or other combinations of data-handing machines. Where the quantity of data that must be transmitted is large enough, wideband links are used. These are normally circuits leased from the common carriers, although some firms have installed privately owned microwave links or other facilities.

Figure 3.2 shows a wideband link used by IBM in the early 1960's to connect its computer center in the Time-Life Building, New York, with computers used for software development in Poughkeepsie, 80 miles away.

Fig. 3.2. Use of a wideband link. Data from IBM magnetic tape transmission units below flowed in both directions at once over a wideband channel transmitting at a rate of 15,000 characters per second.

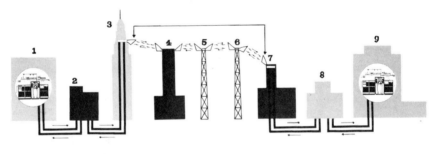

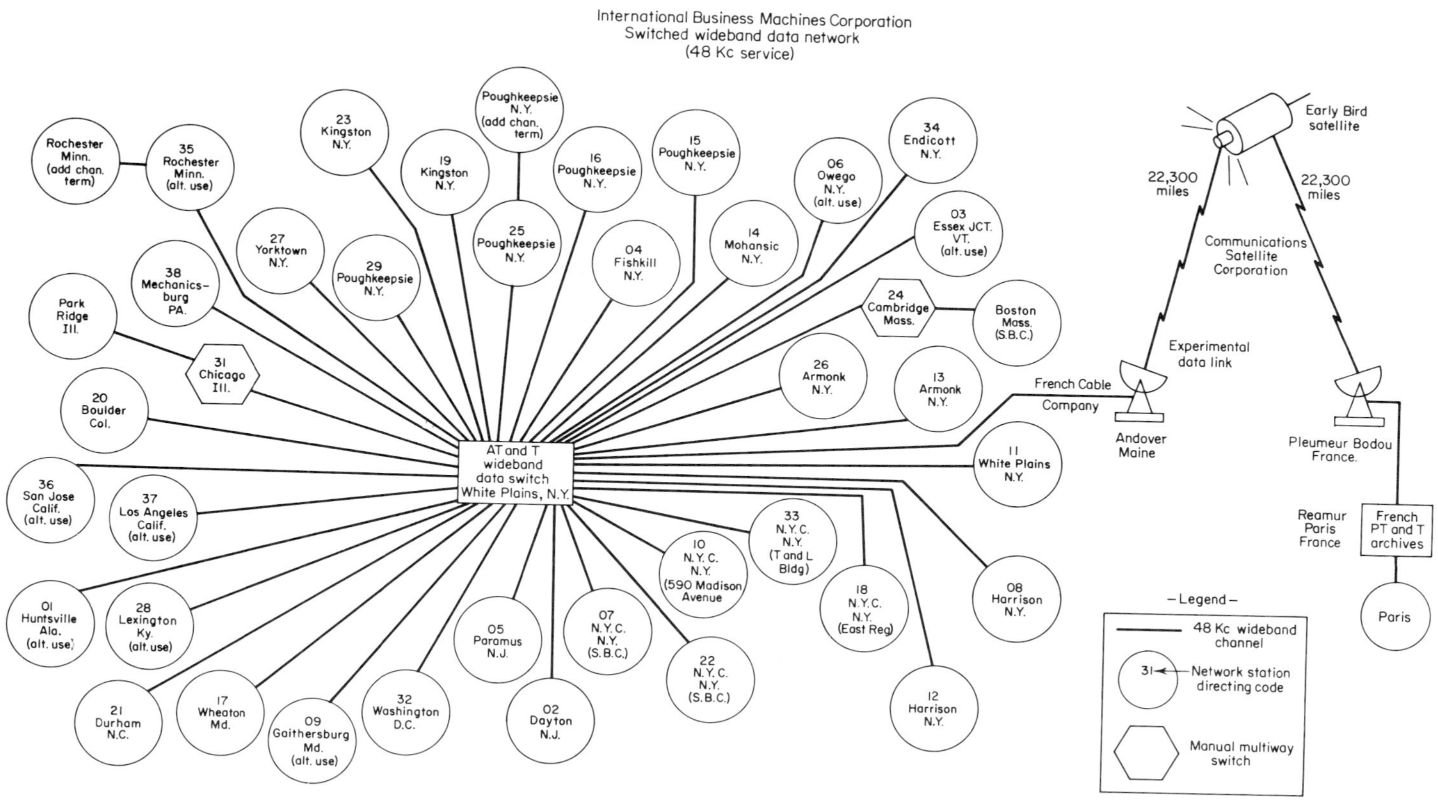

Fig. 3.3. IBM switched wideband data network (48-kHz service).

51

This microwave link gave magnetic tape-to-tape transmission at 15,000 characters per second. This speed was necessary to facilitate the running of programs on the distant computers.

The use of the link was highly successful and within a few years wideband data transmission in IBM developed into the network shown in Fig. 3.3. A private leased wideband exchange enabled dial-up interconnection of IBM locations throughout the United States with a transmission speed of 40,800 bits per second. By 1966 the total wideband circuit distance was 14,000 miles, and an average terminal on the network was in use 80 hours per month, transmitting or receiving at this high speed. The network was soon extended to include satellite channels to England and Paris. Other world-wide locations may be linked up in this way.

In firms with a lower volume of data to transmit, a similar network with voice grade lines is used, with a private exchange. Often such lines are used alternately for voice or data.

REAL-TIME AND NONREAL-TIME SYSTEMS

There is a fundamental distinction between a system which must give an answer within a certain short period, and a system which stacks transactions for processing as soon as it works its way to them. An operator at a terminal carrying on a fairly complex conversation with a computer normally needs a fairly quick reaction from it.

Response time is the time the system takes to react to a given input. If a message is keyed into a terminal by an operator, and the reply from the computer is typed at the same terminal, "response time" may be defined as the *time interval between the operator pressing the last key and the terminal typing the first letter of the reply.* For different kinds of terminal, response time may be defined similarly, as *the interval between an event and the system's response to the event.*

If the computer reacts to its input data quickly, completes its processing, and takes action within a short period of time, the term "real-time" is sometimes used.

A real-time computer system may be defined as one which controls an environment by receiving data, processing them, and taking action or returning results fast enough to affect the functioning of the environment at that time.

"Real-time" is a term that is defined differently by different authorities. The question of response time may enter into the definition. Some authorities use the term "real-time" to imply a response time of a few seconds. Others expand the definition to include any response which controls the minute-by-minute or even hour-by-hour functioning of an environment, but this use of the term "real-time" is disputed.

In using a computer to *control* a set of operations, a low response time is usually necessary. The speed of response differs from one type of system to another according to their needs. In a system for radar scanning, a response time of milliseconds is needed. Airline reservation systems in operation give a response time of about 3 seconds. A warehousing control system may have a response time of 30 seconds. In a system used for controlling a paper mill, a 5-minute response time may be adequate. On some systems the response time is higher than this, perhaps half an hour or more, but above this it is certainly arguable whether the system should still be described as "real-time."

TIME-SHARING SYSTEMS

Most systems with manually operated terminals are time-shared, meaning that more than one user is using them at the same time. When the machine pauses in the processing of one user's item, it switches its attention to another user.

The term "time-sharing," however, is commonly used to refer to a system in which the users are *independent*, each using the terminal as though it were the console of a computer and entering, testing, and executing programs of their own at the terminal. The work on programs of one terminal user is quite unrelated to those of other users.

In many systems the users do not *program* the system at the terminal, and neither are the users entirely independent. They are each *using* the programs in the computer in a related manner. They may, for example, be insurance or railroad clerks possibly using the same programs and possibly the same file areas. In many time-shared systems, however, the computing facility is being divided between separate users who can program *whatever they wish* on it, independently of one another. There are in common use three categories of on-line systems differing by the degree of independence of the users:

1. Systems which carry out a carefully specified and limited function, for example, a banking system, a factory control system, or an information retrieval system.
2. Systems in which programmers can program anything they wish at the terminals, providing they all use the same language, an interpreter or compiler for this being in the machine. Normally each user has the same type of terminal.
3. Systems in which programmers can program anything by using a variety of different languages. Often a wide variety of terminals is permitted also.

The latter two types of system are, in effect, dividing up the computing facility "timewise" and giving the pieces to different programmers to do what they want with the pieces. The files are also divided according to use. It cannot be known beforehand how much space in the files the various users will occupy. This is quite different from category 1, in which the file size and organization is planned in detail.

APPLICATIONS There is a wide variety of different systems in operation. The remainder of this chapter selects certain examples of these for discussion.

1. *Airline Reservations*

Many of the world's major airlines now have real-time systems for seat reservations. These systems, however, differ very widely in scope, functions, complexity, and cost. Some airlines are on their second real-time system, having started with a relatively simple one and later changed to a more complex and comprehensive system, often from a different manufacturer.

Most of the systems make spectacular use of communications. Some have a thousand or more terminals, all obtaining very quick responses from a far distant computer. Some have communication links that circle the world, and in so doing employ most of the different communication facilities discussed in this book. Pan American, for example, has a large room full of agents in London, near Picadilly, who answer telephone calls about bookings from most of England. While they talk to the passengers on the telephone, they are carrying on a "conversation" with a computer in the Pan American Building in New York. Standing in the room watching them, it is difficult to believe that the replies they are receiving, with a response time of a second or so, are coming from the other side of the Atlantic.

Figure 3.4 shows the world-wide data network of Pan American in a simplified form. Figures 3.5 and 3.6 show details of the American and European parts of that network. This was the network before the advent of satellite communications (Chapter 20). The latter will bring about a major change in the economies of long-distance lines, and different channels are likely to be used.

The real-time terminals of Pan American are on private leased voice-grade lines with many terminals connected via concentrators to one line. The voice-grade lines on Fig. 3.4 will be seen to cover America and Europe, and extend from Honolulu to San Juan. To take them further than this would have been uneconomical. The rest of the world is reached, therefore, by private telegraph lines, and Telex. These lower-speed circuits often travel their long distances by radio and where this is so have a much higher proportion of data errors than the voice-grade lines or land telegraph lines. The telegraph circuits are used for administrative messages of all types, as well as for reservations. They go through message switching centers some of which are manually operated or semiautomatic, and this means that there is a delay in some reservation signals reaching the computer. Special procedures therefore have to be programmed for the offices that do not have conversational terminals.

With the hardware available today it would be economic to include functions other than reservations in an airline real-time system. The planning now being done in several airlines is towards an airline *operating* system, of which reservations handling is a subset. The computer complex might handle real-time and nonreal-time functions such as revenue and cost accounting, crew scheduling, scheduling of maintenance services, passenger check-in, load and trim calculations, spares inventory control, cargo handling, and so on. Such a system might include different computers in different parts of the world connected by communications lines.

However, the programming and systems analysis involved are exceedingly complex, and therefore many airlines have installed a system which carries out the reservations functions alone to begin with, other data processing being done on a separate computer.

There are three main objects in designing a reservation system:

1. To improve the service given to passengers and potential passengers.
2. To save staff in sales offices and in control offices where reservations are processed and space on aircraft is controlled.
3. To improve the load factor on flights.

If a system handles cargo reservations, the objectives here will be to save staff and to optimize the loading of cargo.

Some systems have been planned with staff savings being the main or sole justification. However, a major payoff, where it can be achieved, is the potential increase in the loading of flights. Most airliners take off today with a large number of seats empty. Many airlines have an average load factor of only about 50%. When this load factor can be increased, it gives a direct increase in revenue for the airline.

To achieve these objectives, there are several functions which the system may carry out. Many reservation systems do not carry out all of these functions. Although interrelated, they can be thought of separately and in many cases have to be automated separately.

Function 1. Giving flight information to distant sales points, and especially answering requests about what seats are available.

Function 2. Centralized inventory control of seats booked and canceled at distant locations. This has been done without passengers' names being used, but to be done efficiently these are needed to eliminate duplicate bookings and invalid cancellations.

Function 3. Control of space allocation to offices not on-line to the computer, or

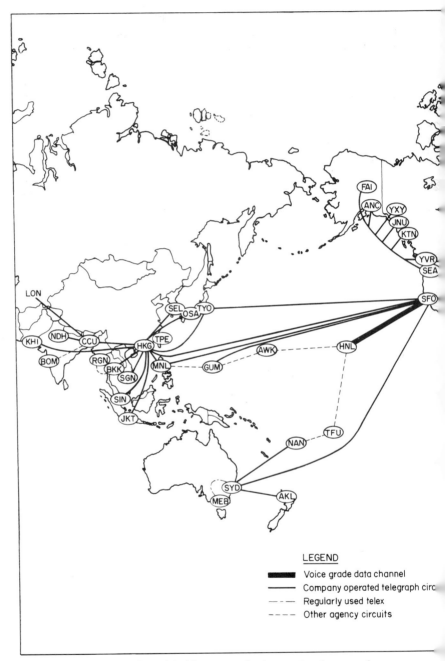

Fig. 3.4. Pan-American's world-wide communications network as used with their Panamac computer system before the advent of satellite communications. *Courtesy Pan-American.*

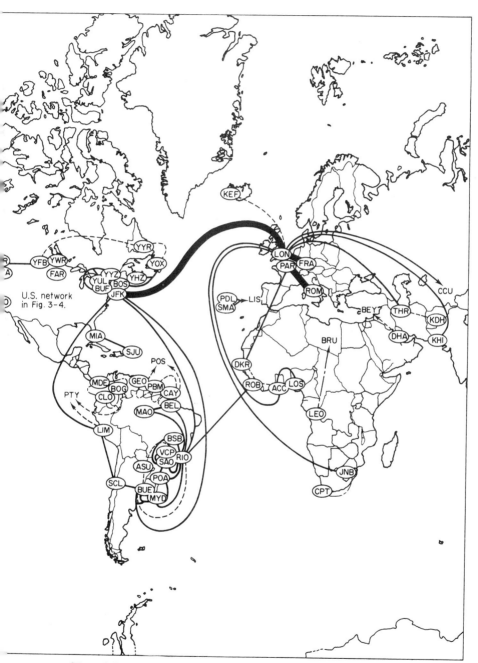

U.S. network in Fig. 3-4.

Figure 3.4. *(cont.)*

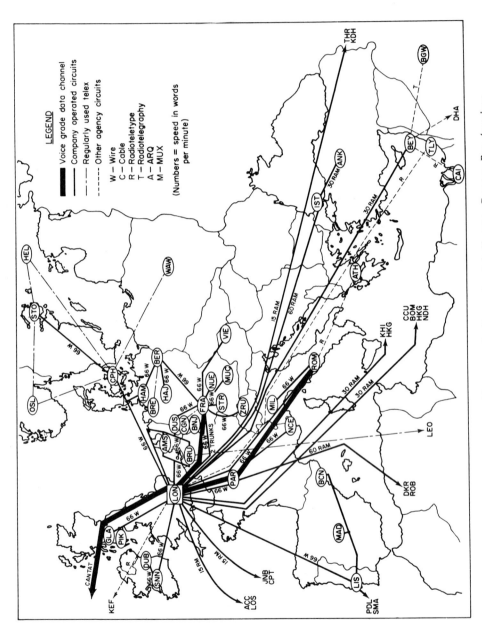

Fig. 3.5. Pan American's world-wide communications network in Europe. *Courtesy Pan American.*

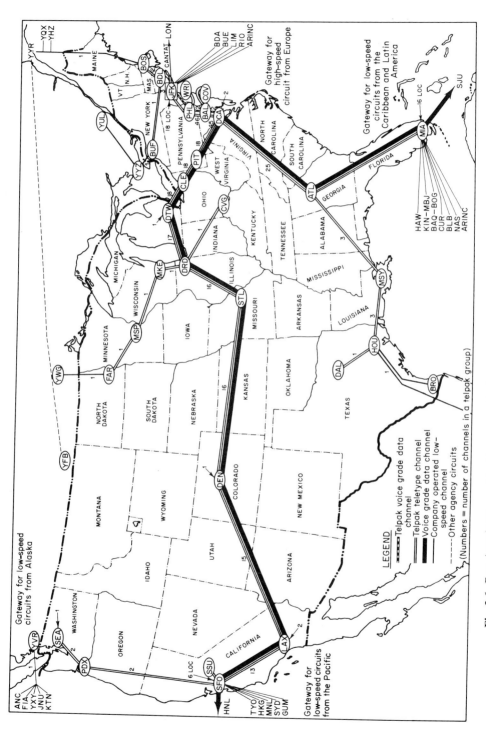

Fig. 3.6. Pan American's world-wide communications network in America. *Courtesy Pan American.*

Fig. 3.7. The American Airlines SABER computer center. The IBM computers shown are on-line to more than 1000 terminals for airline reservations. The terminals operate in real time, giving a response time of less than 3 seconds to the input messages. *Courtesy American Airlines.*

offices of other airlines. Small offices or offices in remote parts of the world, to which leased voice-grade lines are still too expensive, are likely to be off line. They send telegraph signals to the computer and these may take many hours to reach it. From a knowledge of the booking patterns on given routes, allotments of seats to be sold by various offices must be set, and as the bookings build up "status" limits must be set.

Function 4. Mechanization of passenger files. These have previously been maintained manually in the sales offices. To keep them in the files of the distant computer and maintain them in a real-time manner, using the facilities needed for the preceding functions, will give major labor cost savings, and improve the service given to passengers.

Function 5. Waitlisting, reconfirmation, checking ticket time limits, and other operations concerned with manipulation of the passenger files. If, for example, a passenger does not reconfirm or collect his ticket when he should, the computer notifies the appropriate sales office.

Function 6. Provision of special facilities for the passenger such as renting a car or booking hotels in a distant location, providing a baby carrier, wheelchair, facilities for pets, and so on.

Function 7. Message switching. Airlines need large message switching centers for routing off-line teletype bookings and other messages to the control points. Many of the teletype booking messages will be from other airlines. A computer can be used for this as part of the reservation system.

Function 8. Passenger check-in at airports. Manifests giving details of passengers are sent to the airport check-in desks. The check-in clerks have the facility to make enquiries on the distant computer and use this in allocating seats.

Function 9. Load and trim calculations done in a real-time fashion just before the aeroplane takes off can be combined with passenger check-in. Weights of passengers' baggage and estimated weights of passengers are used for the calculations. The results determine last-minute acceptance of cargo and passengers.

Function 10. Cargo reservations may also be controlled by the system, and the weight and approximate volume of cargo used in the load and trim calculations.

Not all of these functions are mechanized on all airline reservation systems. Today, however, it is probably economic to put all of them on the same system in large airlines.

Some airlines only mechanize Function 3; others, Functions 1 and 3; and still others, Functions 1, 2, and 3. Several are now taking the complex step of mechanizing 4, 5 and 6. There is therefore a wide variation in cost and complexity between one airline reservation system and another. Some airlines use separate computers for message switching. Some use a separate system for Functions 8 and 9. However, the more the functions can be combined onto one system the more economic the operation becomes.

Most of the reservation systems now being installed used terminals with keyboards and screens. When a passenger wishing to make a booking telephones the airline, or walks into its office, he talks to an agent operating such a terminal. The agent does not use a timetable but obtains information about possible flights on his screen. The passenger might say, for example, that he wants to travel to Los Angeles on March 25 at about 5 p.m. The agent keys in this fact in a coded form, and on the screen appears the four best flights with seats to fill the requirement. If for some reason none of these is suitable, it can be instructed to scan outwards from this time and produce the next four, and so on. The screen tells the agent fares and all the other details he needs to know.

When it has been agreed on which flight the passenger will travel, the agent then enters details about the booking into the system. The passenger's name, home and business telephone numbers, ticketing arrangements, and other pertinent information are sent to the computer and stored on its disk files.

The computer checks that all the pertinent details have been entered. It makes various checks for validity. It may compare the name with other names booked to ensure that it is not a duplicate booking. When all of the details are entered correctly and checked, the computer stores this information in the relevant files. Some examples of the conversation that takes place between the agent and the distant computer are given in the next chapter.

Passengers may call later to confirm, change, or cancel a booking. This happens with the majority of seats sold. While a passenger is on the telephone, his details will be retrieved from the system, and the agent will make the desired changes. The appropriate seat inventory will be reduced when cancellations or changes are made. The system will check that this is a valid reduction: that the seat being canceled has in fact been booked. Tight checks and controls ensure that most of the errors which occur on a noncomputerized airline reservation system cannot happen here.

The response time of the system to each agent's action must be low enough to permit efficient "conversation" with the computer while talking to a passenger on the telephone. The contract on a typical system says that 90% of all messages must have a response of less than 3 seconds. In fact, on most working systems, the majority of messages receive a reply in a second or so.

2. *Factory Control Systems*

Whereas some airline reservation systems are global in scale, many factory control systems use communication links within one building only. Others, however, extend to distant locations: other factories, warehouses, head offices and in some cases terminals are placed in sales offices. The functions of these systems vary considerably from one system to another. Manufacturing firms differ widely in their methods, their needs, and their attitude toward automation.

The events in the production cycle are never exactly predictable, and in order to maintain control over the various stages in the production process, data about goods received, operations completed, items that transfer location, and so on, are fed back into the computer. The computer constructs and updates records of the status of the events that must be controlled. These may be records giving the levels of stock and details relating to the reordering of stock, records giving the status of each customer order, records giving details of the loading of each machine, and records relating to the work given to each employee. In general, each type of facility that is employed in the production process may have a record giving its current status or loading, and the jobs to be done at each work center may be recorded with indications of priority. These records are kept up to date. They may be used either by the computer or by management and foremen in planning, scheduling, progress chasing, reordering, and so on. The computer will use them for such functions as producing work tickets giving instructions to operators, giving loading instructions, handling new orders, and notification of exceptional conditions or situations that have become critical and need expediting. Management will use them for displaying the facts they need for decision-making.

This type of mechanism may be used in the operation, not only of a manufacturing process, but of any environment in which a large number of discrete events must be controlled in order to achieve certain results.

In a railroad, for example, the movement and use of the cars must be constantly rescheduled to convey the maximum quantity of goods in an acceptable time with the minimum cost. Details of each car, its contents, its actual movements, and its future intended movements would be stored in the computer files, and these records would be used by the computer or by management, or more probably by both, to optimize the operation. In an airline, the scheduling of aircraft operations, crew movements, and maintenance is a severe problem aggravated by circumstances that cannot be planned for in detail, such as the need to ground aircraft for unscheduled maintenance, crew changes due to sickness, fog and other holdups. At the time of writing, this problem has not been tackled by computers, but several airlines are directing their sights on it. They may possibly use the same transmission links as in reservations traffic. It is a problem that in some respects is analogous to manufacturing control. The analogy can also be seen in other types of industry.

The transmission and processing techniques required depend upon the time scale on which events take place. The time for job completion, for example, varies widely from one industry to another. In some firms the main criterion is using the machines fully. In others it is desirable to rush orders through the production shops as quickly as possible.

In many production shops, the events that must be controlled occur in rapid succession even though individual jobs take several hours. The control system that governs these must be at least as dynamic as the events it is controlling. A typical system needs to respond in 3 seconds or so to human inquiries and data input, but need not respond to events taking place on the shop floor in seconds. Rescheduling, new job allocation, or other response to events may be fast enough if it happens in half an hour, or in some factories, half a day.

Therefore we usually need a system with two or three levels of activity going on: an almost immediate response on an interrupt basis to on-line human and sometimes nonhuman input; a queue of jobs that need to be tackled fairly quickly but not immediately on a random basis, some jobs possibly having higher priorities than others; and a background activity of work for which there is no time pressure. In addition, a real-time clock may trigger off other activities at preset intervals.

Basically, the following elements are needed in controlling a factory shop floor:

1. A means of deciding what parts are to be made, and by when. This is obtained by breaking down the orders or forecast, and comparing this with what is in stock.
2. A means of scheduling: building a schedule of work for each machine tool and worker. These schedules will have to be constantly modified as events take place.

Fig. 3.8. A terminal on the RCA Spectra 70/630 data gathering system used to transmit data from a warehouse or factory shop floor. *Courtesy Radio Corp. of America.*

3. A means of issuing the orders to the shop floor.

4. A means of collecting data about the status of events on the shop floor.

5. A set of records giving the current status of orders, schedules, jobs, machines and workers.

6. A means of communicating data to management when they need it for planning purposes.

7. A means of dealing with exceptional conditions and sorting out things that go wrong. This must never be deemphasized. It is folly to imagine that when a computer is in control events will run like clockwork.

One could enlarge this list considerably by extending it into other areas beyond the shop floor operation.

One of the first steps into telecommunications is often to put terminals for data collection near each work station on the shop floor. Using these terminals the worker reports when he starts and completes a job. If he leaves his work he reports the percentage completion of the job. He identifies himself by inserting his man badge into the machine. The job may also carry a small plastic badge, or the machine tool may have a badge which is used for identifying these. He may also enter details such as scrap values, stock shortages, and so on.

Figure 3.9 shows an arrangement which has worked well. Computer files containing a record for each machine tool, each worker, and each job, are kept up to date by the on-line data collection system. In some factories the data-collection system is off-line, though with today's software it can be used on-line without too much difficulty. Many exceptional conditions arise such as material running out, tools breaking, and the workers entering invalid data. These are reported immediately to staff in a control room, which has one or more representatives on the shop floor who can walk over to the work stations to sort out any problems. The control room staff alerts the shop floor representative by radio, and he goes to the relevant work station. From the work station he can talk by telephone to his control room

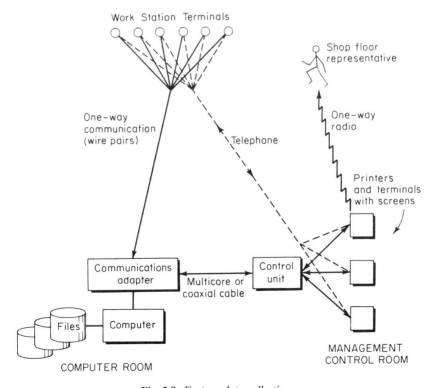

Fig. 3.9. Factory data collection.

partner who sits at a computer terminal and can interrogate the system.

The dispatching of work to the shop floor and the giving of instructions to workers might also take place via on-line terminals, or off-line. When one job is completed the computer issues the next job for that work station, always keeping at least two jobs ahead in order to give the worker or foreman time for preparation. Again the control room is an essential buffer needed to take care of errors and other problems.

The control room staff also carry on functions such as answering management enquiries, maintaining file integrity by correcting errors if they are discovered, modifying schedules, and perhaps in an advanced system testing the effect of possible management decisions using techniques such as simulation. Management might want to know, for example, what the effect on other orders will be if a certain large order is accepted or brought forward.

A typical control room might have a small number of printers, perhaps teleprinters, on which the exception notices are printed, and some terminals with cathode ray tube screens for fast display of records, schedules, and so on. The controllers use these terminals for changing data in the system.

A computer in a main factory may carry out some processing for subsidiary plants too. Often sales offices, warehouses, and depots have terminals on-line to the main computer, and sometimes a firm with computers in different locations has a data link between them.

Figure 3.10 shows an arrangement typical of what a number of medium-sized and large firms are installing today. The main plant in this illustration has a powerful data-processing center, using random-access files and tape. The laboratories have a large scientific computer. Some of the subsidiary plants have small card computers which they use for routine work, such as payroll and invoicing. The small plants use the large computer at the main plant for production scheduling and other jobs needing a machine with a larger core and random-access files. Some of these jobs need a fairly fast response and produce a fair quantity of printing, so the small computer is directly connected to the large computer, and the small computer's printer is used. The smallest plant of those on the diagram does not have a computer. It has a medium-speed card reader and printer attached to the main plant's computer, and this does all the data-processing work of the plant.

A network of enquiry terminals is used in sales offices, depots, and in the subsidiary plants. Some of the messages from the subsidiary plants need a reply which takes a considerable amount of printing, and so this is returned, possibly a little delayed on the printer of their computer.

A high-speed magnetic tape link is used to the laboratory computer. The engineers and market research staff in the main plant can then use this, if they wish.

Engineers at the subsidiary plants can also use it by sending their data to the main plant for retransmission. In the diagram this connection is a fast, tape-to-tape, off-line link. A broadband channel capable of transmit-

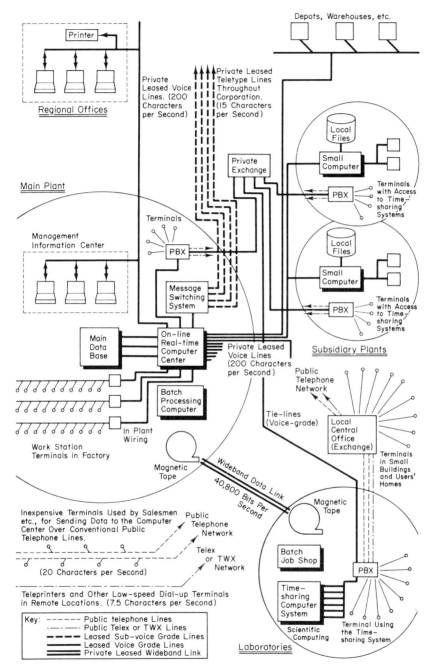

Fig. 3.10. Large computer center in main plant with links to computers in subsidiaries and laboratory. An in-plant data collection system and on-line terminals in sales offices and depots.

ting 5000 characters per second is used because a large bulk of information is to be sent involving many millions of characters per day. Faster lines than this are available though they are rarely needed in today's data processing. Applications envisaged for the near future, however, will need them. The link is off-line for simplicity. Unless a fast response is required, there is no need to put it on-line.

With many real-time and on-line systems two computers are used. This increases the certainty of receiving a reply, as when one computer breaks down, and the other comes on-line. Most airline reservation systems, for example, *duplex* the computers and peripheral machines in this way. It does not necessarily mean that one computer sits idle because the installation can be planned so that machines share the load, or so that the off-line machine has other work to do. Some of the very complex installations, however, have achieved little other productive work on the stand-by machine.

3. *General-Purpose Time-Sharing Systems*

Both of the preceding types of system are tailor-made for one application. A type of system that is spreading rapidly is one which gives a user remote access to a computer and allows him both to program anything he wants in that computer, and to use programs which are made available to him in the computer's files. In this system the user dials the computer on a conventional telephone or telegraph line (a private line could be used also). The responses he receives at the terminal are normally fast. On most systems the user will receive a reply in approximately 3 seconds, unless the computer is doing a lengthy computation, and so he receives the impression at the terminal that he is the only user of the system. In fact, the computer has many such users, and switches its attention from one to another at high speed. By chopping up its work into small slices of time and scanning from one user to another, the computer ensures that nobody is kept waiting unduly long at the terminal. There is a wide variety of different possible scheduling arrangements and hardware configurations to permit the paying of attention to many users at once.

Some authorities reserve the words time-sharing for this type of system, while others include all on-line real-time systems in that category. Still others, especially in Europe, broaden its usage to other types of system doing several tasks at once. The term multiaccess system is also used to refer to a computer system with many on-line users.

There are four main reasons for using a time-shared system:

1. *Cost.* Time-sharing permits users who could not afford their own computer to have a part share in a machine. As communication lines give them fast access to it and fast replies, it can behave much as though they had a machine on their own premises. Bulk input/output, as in high-speed printing, for

example, will be limited on their premises by the speed of the communication lines used. However, economical and accessible computing services can be provided for scientific engineering business groups previously unserved.

2. *Low-Turnaround Time.*   On a batch-processing system or a system with a lengthy job queue, the turnaround time can be long. It is still longer if the computer is remote from its user. To obtain a run on a heavily loaded computer may take half a day. If the data have to be sent and returned by station wagon, this may be a day; by mail, two or more days. Off-line transmission links have been installed to bridge both long and short distances. On-line batch systems are also in use so that the work is entered directly into the computer's job stream on disk or tape. On-line batch systems may reduce the turnaround time to an hour or so, depending upon how heavily loaded the systems are, and how long individual jobs run. However, in time-sharing systems we are generally talking about conversational turnaround times of only a few seconds, and problem–solution times are measured in minutes. The programmer can locate and correct half a dozen bugs in an hour rather than a week. The engineer or scientist can solve problems while sitting at the terminals of the system.

3. *Conversational Mode of Operating.*   The user at the terminal is once again in direct contact with the machine. He can use the power of the machine to supplement his own thinking, as in the old days when he might have had a computer all to himself. He is even better off now because he can use modern languages, and the computer probably has a large random-access store in which elaborate supervisory programs, compilers, and all manner of program routines are kept. He can "experiment" with his programs at the terminal, testing the effect of modifications. For example, he can change parameters or logic elements of a simulation program and observe the effects of this. Man–machine interaction is being shown to expand vastly the creative power of skilled users. In some ways the most exciting results of the early time-sharing systems, especially the university ones such as Project MAC, have been entirely new ways of using computers that have emerged from the real-time combination of a highly skilled man and a powerful machine.

4. *Communication between Users.*   The files holding programs and data are commonly divided into "private" and "public" areas. The private areas hold the programs and work that belong to individuals while the public areas contain those programs and data that are made available to any user. One of the most surprising developments on M.I.T.'s Project MAC and other such systems has been the growth rate of the public files. Many users wrote programs or compiled data that were deemed valuable for other users. These were made available and very rapidly the public files became filled with useful items. When this happens, as it will, on a nationwide or global scale, time-sharing systems will provide a powerful storehouse for human thinking. The work of one programmer will be picked up and developed by interested parties elsewhere. Today we are confronted with a bewildering array of technical literature to read; tomorrow we will have an equally bewildering array of on-line programs to use.

Probably the best known of the world's general-purpose time-sharing systems is Massachusetts Institute of Technology's Project MAC. MAC stands for *M*ultiple *A*ccess *C*omputer, or, alternatively, *M*achine *A*ided *C*ognition. It is an experimental project financed by the Department of Defense to investigate ways of achieving more effective man–machine interaction.

The system at the time of writing has about 300 authorized users in a variety of different departments and laboratories. This number is increasing, and a spectacular variety of differing uses is being accomplished. The input and output are mainly via teleprinters which can dial the MAC installation, but there are also devices in given locations near the computer for graphical output and input using a light pen. Experiments are taking place in collaboration with other universities to gain experience in long distance use of such a system. The system has been used, for example, at Cambridge University in England.

In this and other systems, the user must first "log in." He types an identification, and can only proceed when the computer recognizes it as a registered user number. He then instructs the machine to load a program for him, either from his own private store on the files or one of the computer center's "public" programs. The computer switches its attention to this user at intervals of perhaps once every two seconds. During the time when the computer

Fig. 3.11. Keydata Corporation's on-line computer center for general commercial service. The UNIVAC 491 real-time system processes data transmitted over leased telephone lines from subscribers throughout the Boston area. *Courtesy Sperry Rand.*

is not actually working on a user's program and operational data, it is to be transferred out of the working core to a backing store, and then brought back when it is needed again.

Many of the research workers using the MAC system have reported that it speeded up the work on the system enormously. In some cases the dynamic interaction with the machine enabled the user to change parameters as a calculation proceeded and so direct it to an optimum solution in one machine session of a problem that otherwise would have taken a month of separate machine runs. New methods of solving complex problems are evolving.

A number of time-sharing systems less versatile in scope than Project MAC have been offered for lease by the computer manufacturers. Examples of these are General Electric's BASIC system and IBM's QUIKTRAN. Such systems restrict the user to one or a small number of languages rather than the variety of languages available in Project MAC. Both systems permit a user to dial up the computer on the General Electric system by using a teleprinter, and on the QUIKTRAN system by using an IBM 1050 or 2740 terminal. The user can compose and test a program at the terminal, enter it prepunched on paper tape with General Electric, or on cards with IBM. He can store his programs and data on the files of the system with safeguards to ensure privacy and protection from loss. Examples of QUIKTRAN and BASIC use are given in Chapter 24.

4. *Special-Purpose Public Time-Sharing Systems*

In addition to general-purpose systems in which the user can program anything he wants, other systems for carrying out specific operations are made available for public lease. The user in these systems does not necessarily have to program the machine, but merely uses its services.

Some banks throughout America, for example, are offering professional billing services. Doctors and dentists have a small terminal in their office. Their nurse or secretary dials the bank computer and sends details of the charges to patients. These may be punched into cards or tape, and transmitted as a group later. The bank computer bills the patients, credits payments to the doctor's account, and sends receipts. It compiles complete tax information for the user, and perhaps for this reason the service is not quite as popular as it might have been otherwise.

The Keydata Corporation operates a time-sharing system in the Boston area for offering business services to users. Initially, the system offered such functions as on-line invoicing, order entry, inventory checking and updating, and credit-checking. In addition many off-line services are available. It is intended that the system should expand its scope to include functions for scientists and engineers also. In so doing, it could grow into a general-purpose system which the user could program. Conversely, the general-purpose systems such as QUIKTRAN are making available special-purpose programs so that they can become useful to nonprogrammers.

The author used a time-sharing system to help in the preparation of part of this book. This was IBM's *Datatext* system. This, in effect, provides a typewriter similar to an ordinary office typewriter, linked to a distant computer. A secretary using the typewriter can store sentences, paragraphs, insertions, or whole documents in the computer's storage. She uses these for compiling letters or a report, and uses the computer to help her in editing, correcting, and inserting items into documents.

The average secretary spends a large amount of time correcting, revising, and retyping material that has been typed before. When perfect copy is required, she may have to retype a whole page because of a misplaced comma. To assemble a bulky proposal or legal agreement, she may have to copy and recopy standardized paragraphs, or items from previously prepared documents. In preparing a book like this, the manuscript becomes modified many times before it is fit for the printer.

5. *Military Systems*

To a large extent, the pioneering work for systems combining telecommunications and computers was done in the military. One of the first, and still one of the most spectacular, was SAGE, the United States Air Force *Semi-Automatic Ground Environment*, designed in the early 1950's to protect the United States from surprise air attack.

SAGE became operational with one computer center in 1958, and has grown to many centers in the 1960's. A system to back up SAGE, called BUIC (*Back-Up Interceptor Control*), is also being implemented to provide some of the SAGE functions with much greater dispersion, the intention being that if SAGE is knocked out BUIC still survives to give some protection.

SAGE is designed to maintain a constant watch on the air space over North America, provide early warning of airborne attack, and give its Air Force operators the information needed for conducting an air battle. Its input comes over data transmission links from a variety of radars which unceasingly sweep the skies of the continent. These include the CADIN line (*CAnaDian Integration North*), and many other land-based radars. Input also comes from observation aircraft, ground observer corps stations, and picket ships. The computers digest this constant stream of data and prepare displays for their output screens. In addition, the system contains aircraft flight plans, weapons and base status reports, weather data, and other information. Figure 3.13 gives a highly simplified diagram of one sector of SAGE, and Figure 3.12, the division of the United States into SAGE sectors,

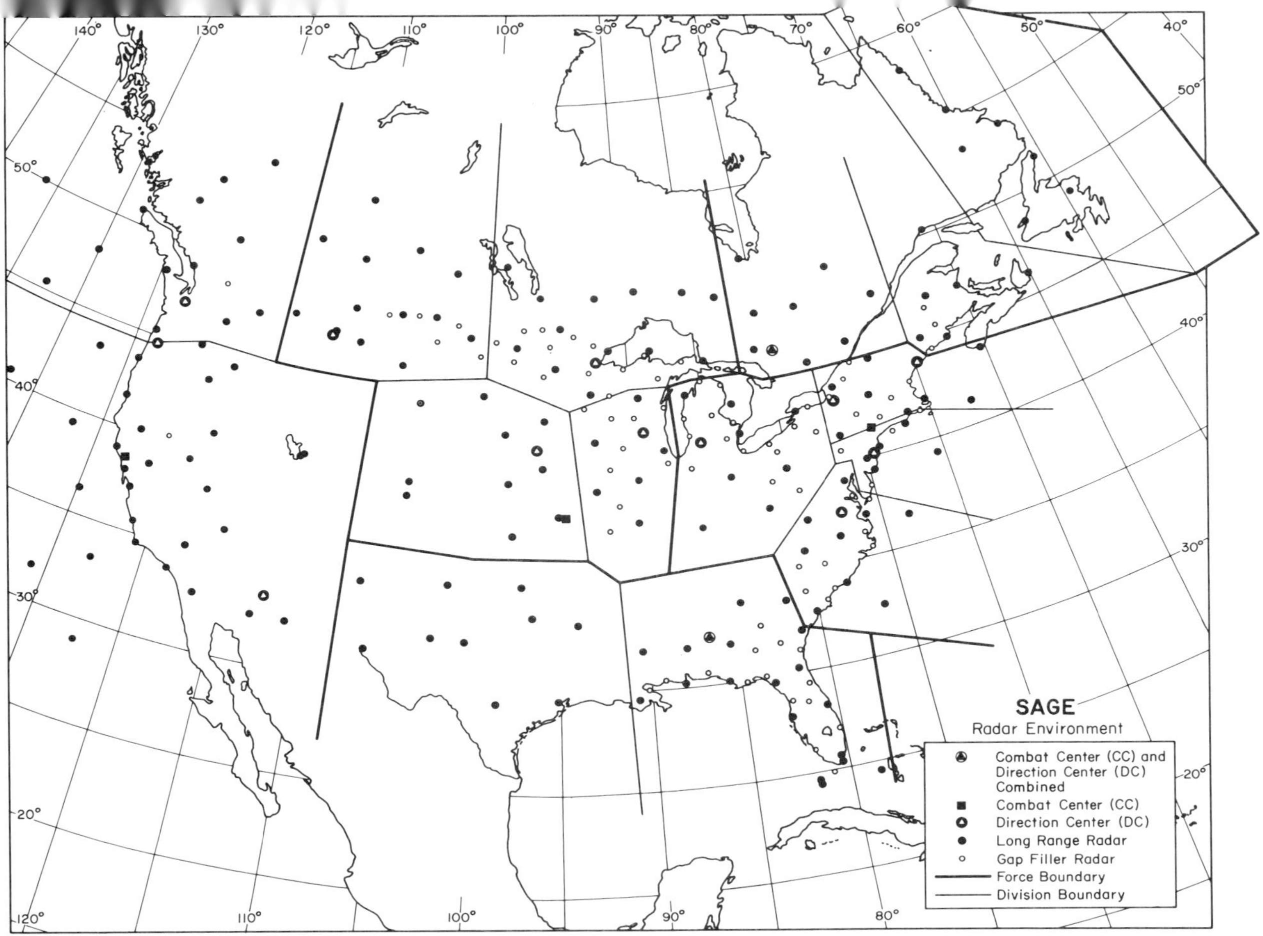

Fig. 3.12. *Courtesy SAGE.*

73

Fig. 3.13. One sector of SAGE. *Redrawn from "Sage—A Data Processing System for Air Defense," by R. R. Everett, C. A. Zroket, and H. B. Benington. Eastern Joint Computer Conferences, 1957.*

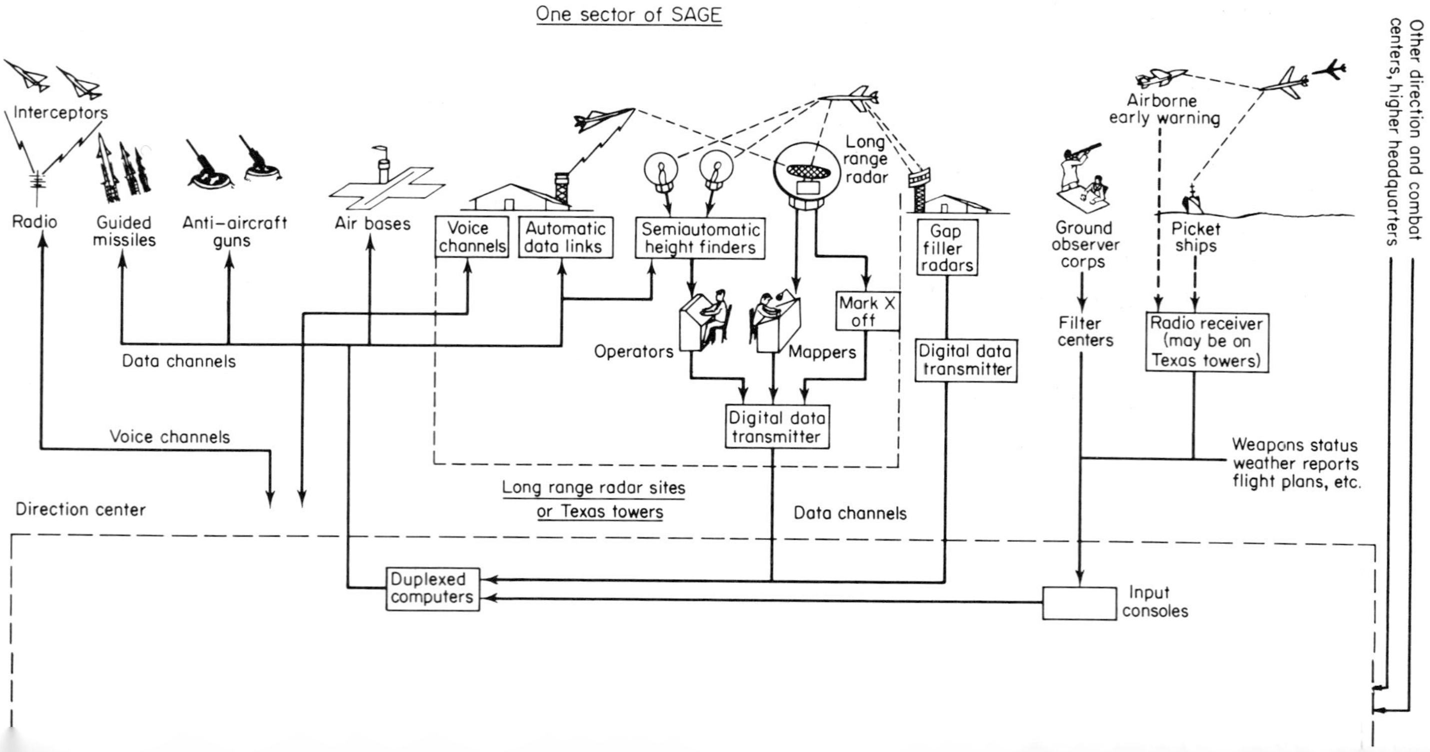

One sector of SAGE

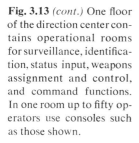

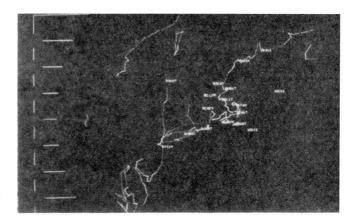

Situation display New England coastline.

Air surveillance room. Operators using consoles attached to the computers.

Fourth floor of direction center.

Fig. 3.13 *(cont.)* One floor of the direction center contains operational rooms for surveillance, identification, status input, weapons assignment and control, and command functions. In one room up to fifty operators use consoles such as those shown.

with the approximate locations of the radar sites and computer centers. These locations are all connected to the computers, and the computers are interlinked by telegraph and telephone lines carrying digital data.

Air Force personnel sit in front of screens on console units designed for their different responsibilities. They communicate with the computer by using a light pen—a forerunner of the light pen on today's commercial systems. They can request displays stored in the computer of particular situations, and can command the machines to compile certain special displays for their use. The computer on its own initiative, will flash on the screen displays of particular urgency. If an unidentified aircraft approaches, the system notifies command personnel who will then use the screen to investigate, and if necessary, dispatch interceptor aircraft or activate weapons.

Since SAGE, many command and control systems have been installed and planned. The United States Marine Corps has the *Marine Tactical Data System* (MTDS), which is in effect a mobile SAGE, transportable to an operational theater by helicopters. The United States Navy has the *Naval Tactical Data System* (NTDS), which has computers and screens on board ships linked together on a worldwide basis to form a vast mobile command and control system. The Pentagon can obtain on its screens positions and status of its ships anywhere, and can display data that ars being used by the Navy on the other side of the world.

The United States Army, meanwhile, is planning a command and control system of immense complexity for operation in the 1970's. This is called CCIS–70 (*Command and Control Information System*), and will be used by every level of command and will handle intelligence and logistics information. Information on tactical operations, fire support, personnel, and other administrative matters will be kept up to date in the system. The output will be available again either on individual consoles or large group displays, and the Pentagon will be placed directly in touch with the theaters of warfare.

The BMEWS system (*Ballistic Missile Early Warning System*) uses giant radar units for the detection of potentially hostile missiles aimed at the West. Its duplexed computers in the United States and England scan the radar signals they receive ceaselessly and notify appropriate military personnel if they conclude that an attack might have been launched. It is these computers that would give us 20 minutes grace prior to nuclear devastation, in which time we could launch our counterattack and do whatever else needed to be done in that interval.

SPADATS (*SPAce Detection And Tracking System*) uses its own computers in different locations with phased array radars to keep up-to-the-minute records of every object orbiting in space—a job which becomes more involved as the quantity of satellites and discarded "space junk" increases. The objects observed have their orbits compared with those recorded for the known satellites. Any deviations are reported.

There are many other American military information systems in addition to these, each system having as integrated components, computers, files, display and input units with highly trained operators, and a variety of tele-communication links. An all-embracing system is now under design, called NMCS (*N*ational *M*ilitary *C*ommand *S*ystem). It is intended that this should tie the global systems of the Army, Air Force, Navy, and other Government agencies into one enormous, integrated complex. The President of the United States or the Chiefs of Staff could then display details of all military affairs. The task of linking the other systems, however, is one of Herculean magnitude because of the incompatibilities between their different record formats and means of display. No doubt the Communist countries are also involved in massive military automation and the prospect of these systems grappling in some future warfare is a systems analyst's nightmare!

In setting up such systems, a massive use is made of telecommunications of all types. The military communication systems are, in general, kept separate from the civilian ones. It is perhaps not surprising to find that by the late 1960's, the American military had at least 24 synchronous telecommunication satellites, whereas the civilian organizations had only three.

The United States Defense Communications Agency has set up two vast telecommunications networks: AUTOVON for voice, and AUTODIN for data. These were first installed internally in the United States, but the domestic network functions as an integral part of a rapidly developing global system. The networks must give precedence to priority traffic. When a General telephones, his call must, if necessary, preempt lower priority calls. The system must be able to handle the unusually high traffic volumes that may occur in times of emergency. It must present no unusually attractive target to potential attack, and so its facilities are as well distributed as pos-sible. Above all, it must have sufficiently widespread alternate routings to survive massive nuclear attack. A configuration of trunk groups, in the form of multiple overlapping hexagons and diagonals, links the many switching centers in the United States with many alternate paths. We may sleep assured in the knowledge that if most of the United States were annihilated, the computers in the parts that remained would still be able to transmit to one another!

SECTION **II**

THE WORLD'S
TELECOMMUNICATION LINKS

4 ORGANIZATIONS INVOLVED IN TELECOMMUNICATIONS

Before describing the technicalities of the telecommunications links, let us discuss briefly some of the organizations involved with this industry. Some of these will be referred to in subsequent chapters.

1. *The United States Common Carriers*

The companies in America which furnish communication services to the public are referred to as "common carriers." Legally, the name applies to all companies who undertake to carry goods for all persons indiscriminately. Reference to the communication companies by this name dates back to days when messages were carried by a stagecoach clattering through the sagebrush.

The telecommunication common carriers offer facilities for the transmission of voice, data, facsimile, television, telemetry, and telephoto pictures. Some of them are now offering on-line computer services also, and it is possible that their business could branch out widely in this direction. Many computer manufacturers and independent companies are also offering on-line computer services to the general public, and so run the risk of being classed as public utilities for this part of their business in the future, and being subject to the various government controls on public utilities.

It is surprising to note that there are more than two thousand telecommunication common carriers in the United States. Many other countries have only one such organization, which is run by the government. Most of these common carriers are very small. Only about 250 of them have more than 5000 subscribers. The largest common carrier is the American Telephone and Telegraph Company whose subsidiaries and associated companies operate more than 80% of the telephones installed in the United States.

When a common carrier provides data transmission facilities he may lease the lines and their termination equipment, and lease or sell the machines such as teleprinters which use the lines. Alternatively, some other manufacturer may supply the data transmission machines. Sometimes another manufacturer provides the line termination equipment—modems or data sets (Chapters 10 and 23)—leaving the common carrier to provide only the lines. At worst, a data transmission link could consist of the products of four suppliers—one providing the line, one the modems, another the computer, and yet another the terminal machine. Liaison between these manufacturers would be needed to ensure compatibility and a working link. There are advantages in not having too many suppliers in one system, as difficulties can arise as to who is responsible when failures occur.

2. *The Bell System (USA)*

"The Bell System" refers to the vast network of telephone and data circuits with many switching offices, and to the television and other links which are operated across the United States by the American Telephone and Telegraph Company (AT&T) and its subsidiaries and associated companies. AT&T owns all or the majority of the stock in most of the 24 Bell operating companies, and its Long Lines Department provides much of the U.S. interstate long distance service. AT&T also owns the Western Electric Company. AT&T and Western own the Bell Telephone Laboratories. Western Electric is the main manufacturing company for the Bell System. It manufactures and installs most of the equipment in use. The Bell Telephone Laboratories, which is claimed to be the world's biggest research organization, has done much of the development work that has made today's telecommunications possible. It was there that the transistor was invented, Shannon's work on information theory was done, the solar battery was invented, and the first communication satellite, Telstar, was designed and built.

Many of the line types made available by the Bell System are summarized in Chapter 5. AT&T leases private lines of a wide range of capacities and provides terminal equipment for data transmission. It also provides a direct dial-up teletypewriter service called Teletypewriter Exchange Service (TWX) using equipment such as page printers, keyboards, paper tape readers, and punches. Any teletypewriter on this service can be dialed from any other. Also the public telephone dial-up networkcan be used for interconnecting data transmission machines. AT&T's DATA-PHONE[1] service makes it possible to send data over normal telephone lines, and provides the modem (Chapter 8) required for the termination of such lines.

---

[1] DATA-PHONE is a trademark and service mark of the Bell System.

3. *General Telephone and Electronics Corporation (USA)*

General Telephone and Electronics' network of telecommunication facilities is known as the General System. This has about 7% of American telephones, the second biggest slice of the telephone business after AT&T. General System equipment is compatible with Bell System equipment in most areas, to allow direct interconnection. The system offers a wide range of data services, as well as telephones. Like the Bell System it provides dial-up TWX facilities.

Two subsidiaries of GT&E manufacture equipment for it, and for the rest of the telephone industry, which includes the Automatic Electric Company, and the Lenkurt Electric Company, Incorporated. Western Electric equipment is also used in the General System where GT&E does not manufacture it.

4. *The United States Independent Telephone Association (USITA)*

The remainder of the two thousand or so telephone companies are mostly very small. Many of these are members of the United States Independent Telephone Association which coordinates their practices. The tariffs are established by committees, and literature is distributed to the member companies.

5. *Western Union (USA)*

The Western Union Telegraph Company has provided America with telegraph links since the days of the Wild West. It operates a national telegraph message service to all parts of the United States and overseas via suboceanic cables. Western Union also leases private communication links, and it operates the American telex system, a direct dial-up teleprinter service. The Western Union leased line facilities now include voice, and data and facsimile services of a wide range of speeds. Many of these are summarized in Chapter 5.

Recently Western Union has done much experimenting with on-line computer systems and now offers a wide range of computer services which might be extended widely in the future.

6. *The Federal Communications Commission*

With so many common carriers, many of which monopolize the services they offer, it is desirable to have some regulating authority. There is at least one such authority for each American state, as well as a national authority for controlling interstate lines and foreign facilities originating in the United States. The latter is the Federal Communications Commission (FCC).

The FCC is an independent federal agency which regulates radio, television, telephone, telegraph, and other transmissions by wire or radio. The powers of the FCC are defined in the Communications Act (1934).

Every subject common carrier must have its plans for facilities offered to the public approved by the FCC before they come into effect. To achieve this, schedules must be filed with the FCC giving details of the intended service, the charges, classifications, regulations, and so on. These documents are called *tariffs*, and they form the basis of the contract between the common carrier and the user. It is intended that the FCC should regulate these for the benefit of the public, and that all common carriers provide service at "reasonable charges on reasonable request." Some of the tariffs become standards which other companies use. There is no requirement for a company to file a new telephone or telegraph tariff if it can use an existing one from another carrier. For this reason some of the more important tariffs are common to many suppliers.

7. The State Public Utility Commissions

What the FCC does for interstate links and foreign links originating in the United States, the State Public Utility Commissions do for links within one state. Different states have different tariffs for the same grade of service, and there can be a wide difference in the prices of facilities from one state to another. Interstate tariffs, however, are uniform across America.

8. The General Post Office (GPO) (Britain)

In many countries the job of delivering mail and providing telecommunications is undertaken by the same organization. This came about because the first use of telecommunications was in telegraph message delivery, which was an extension of the mail. It may make sense again, before long, as it may become cheaper to transmit letters in facsimile form and reproduce them, than to deliver them physically.

Britain's General Post Office handles mail, telecommunications, and broadcasting. It is a government department and a total monopoly, though its status will be changed soon to that of a government-regulated commercial company. It has its own research laboratories, though most of its equipment is manufactured by private industry.

For data transmission, the GPO offers a variety of links under the heading of *Datel Services*. It operates a Telex network of dial-up teleprinters and paper tape machines; it provides facilities for sending data over the dial-up public telephone network; and it offers private leased lines of varying speeds.

It provides private wideband circuits with a capacity 12 to 60 times voice circuits between about 180 selected towns. The delay in obtaining these facilities, however, is sometimes much greater than in the United States. The lines are not always compatible with the American ones, as will be discussed in later chapters, and sometimes equipment that works well in the United States cannot be installed in Britain. British facilities are also summarized in Chapter 5.

9. Telecommunication Departments in Other Countries

Most of the countries of the world have a government-controlled monopoly providing their telecommunications, like Britain's GPO, and offering or planning to offer facilities for data transmission which are broadly similar. In Germany there is the Deutschen Bundespost and in France, the Postes Téléphonique et Télégraphique. In most of these, the finance comes from government, not public, sources. For the Swedish Telecommunications Administration, for example, the State, through the Riksdag (Parliament), decides the amount of investments and makes the necessary grants. Some countries manufacture most of their own telecommunication equipment. Others import it. India, because of her currency problems, tries to manufacture as much as possible internally. The Indian Posts and Telegraphs Department has an active research department which works closely with private firms, such as Indian Telephone Industries Ltd., and Hindustan Cables Ltd., to produce modern equipment at low cost.

There is much duplication between the research of different countries. Certainly in Europe, close technical cooperation seems to be needed between the different countries' telecommunications organizations, as in other fields, if Europe is to compete with America. As will be mentioned in later chapters, there are certain minor incompatibilities between national networks that are causing increasing expense now that international telecommunication is growing so rapidly.

10. The International Telecommunications Union (ITU)

Although incompatibilities exist the degree of *compatibility* is remarkable. This is largely due to the International Telecommunications Union. This organization, centered in Switzerland, has 124 member countries throughout the world. Its consultative committees carry out very detailed studies of world telecommunications, and make recommendations for standardization. The recommendations are put into practice widely throughout the world, with some notable dissensions.

There are three main organizations within the ITU. These are: *The International Frequency Registration Board* which attempts to register and standardize radio frequency assignments and to assist in the elimination of harmful radio-frequency interference on the world's radio communications circuits; *The Consultative Committee on International Radio* (CCIR), which deals with other standards for radio, especially long-distance radio telecommunications; and *The Consultative Committee on International Telegraphy and Telephony* (CCITT).

11. *Comité Consultatif International Télégraphique et Téléphonique (CCITT)*

The Consultative Committee on International Telegraphy and Telephony, based in Geneva, is divided into a number of study groups which make recommendations on various different aspects of telephony and telegraphy. There are study groups, for example, on telegraphy transmission, performance, telegraph switching, alphabetic telegraph apparatus, telephone channels, telephone switching and signaling, noise, and several others. The study group which is perhaps the most concerned with the subject of this book is the special committee on data transmission. This has produced reports of great thoroughness giving recommendations for standards for data transmission. These are widely accepted. Some examples of CCITT standards will be given later in the book.

12. *International Telephone and Telegraph Corporation*

ITT is the world's largest company engaged internationally in operating telecommunication services and manufacturing telecommunication equipment. It has been diversified in the last decade to include electronics and other products and services such as hotels and Avis Rent-a-Car. It embraces more than 150 associated companies and has activities in 57 countries, manufacturing telecommunications equipment in many of them. It operates a worldwide communication network of thousands of cable, radio, and satellite circuits.

ITT connects telegraph users in the United States and other countries by means of radio and cable facilities. It also provides communications between certain foreign countries. The United States has three "gateway" cities for international traffic—New York, Washington, and San Francisco. At these cities the Bell System or Western Union lines, or those of other carriers, connect to the ITT international lines. Subscribers in the gateway cities can connect directly to the ITT lines, otherwise they are routed in on lines of other carriers.

ITT operates an international telex system. An ITT telex subscriber in America can dial-up numbers overseas, in London or Rome, for example, without manual intervention. It also operates a radio-telephone service and leases private international lines, and has over 110 traffic offices in countries outside the United States.

13. RCA Communications

The Radio Corporation of America Communications, a wholly owned subsidiary of RCA, also provides international circuits. It provides worldwide telegraph service, telex service to 105 countries, and radio-photo service to 53 foreign cities. Fully automatic telex dialing is available between several countries and communications also provide private leased international telegraphy lines, radiotelephone circuits in the Pacific area, and ship-to-shore communications.

In demonstrating M.I.T.'s Project MAC in England, an RCA Datatelex link was used to connect teleprinters in England to the time-sharing computer in the United States.

14. The Communication Satellite Corporation, COMSAT (USA)

The COMmunications SATellite Corporation (COMSAT) is a private company responsible for the launching and operation in America of commercial communication satellites with worldwide coverage. It works in conjunction and cooperation with other countries to achieve this, and at the time of writing has agreements with 55 other countries to share in the ownership and operation of a world-wide system of satellites and earth stations. COMSAT files applications with the FCC for the launching of its satellites. The first satellite it launched was the Early Bird satellite in 1965. COMSAT is a company chartered by the American Congress in the Communications Satellite Act of 1962. It is not a government agency, but a shareholder-owned company, with widely distributed stock.

International telecommunications is growing at a phenomenal rate. A spokesman for NASA, the United States Civilian Space Agency, told a Congressional Committee in 1962 that American overseas telephone calls alone would grow from 4 million in 1960 to 20 million in 1970, and to 100 million by 1980. It now appears that the growth might be much greater than this, and that television may swallow a large part of the available capacity. International data transmission, at the time of writing, is not very extensive because of its prohibitive cost, but it is likely to expand enormously as the satellite facilities become used. COMSAT, and its partners in other countries, have a very major role to play in expanding world commerce, and in opening the windows between nations.

COMSAT was set up primarily with the intention of developing international communications. However, the success of satellite technology and the design of the future satellites now makes it seem likely that this form of transmission will become the lowest cost form of long-distance domestic link in the United States. Consequently, in 1966 COMSAT made proposals to the FCC for a system of satellites and earth stations that would serve all types of telecommunication users in the United States. Several American common carriers also filed proposals and comments, and the Ford Foundation proposed an independent system of satellites for noncommercial television. COMSAT, at the time of writing, claims that it alone is authorized to provide satellites for services in the United States (by the 1962 Communications Satellite Act and the 1934 Communications Act). Some other organizations, including the Ford Foundation, dispute this claim.

15. *The International Telecommunications Satellite Consortium, INTELSAT*

The INternational TELecommunications SATellite Consortium (INTELSAT) is, in effect, a partnership of owners in the Early Bird system and its successors. At the time of writing, 56 countries are members, and agreements are open for signing by any of the 124 nations which are members of the International Telecommunication Agency.

The international agreements were formulated in 1964 whereby it became possible for all nations to use, and share in the development of, one satellite system. The participating organization from each country shares in the financing and owning of the satellites with their tracking and control equipment, but not in the earth stations. The latter are owned by the individual countries or corporations who use them. The participating countries receive revenues derived from share in the ownership.

As new countries join, the percentage interest of each member drops, but the 1964 agreements state that COMSAT, the American partner, cannot have its interest drop below 50.6%.

Some countries, for example, Italy and Japan, have set up a company similar to COMSAT to participate in INTELSAT. In most countries, the government telecommunications agencies, such as the General Post Office in Britain or the Deutschen Bundespost in Germany, are the INTELSAT participants.

Countries who are not members of INTELSAT, and who have not signed the agreements, can still use the satellites by paying a lease cost for the circuits.

COMSAT, in addition to being the United States participant in INTELSAT, and a member of its governing body, has the role of manager in the design, development, and operation of the satellites. COMSAT is engaged in research and development work on satellite systems. It submits the satellite programs to be implemented for approval by an INTELSAT committee.

Satellites launched by COMSAT since 1966 have the name INTELSAT. INTELSAT II satellites were developed in 1967 and are a major improvement of Early Bird; INTELSAT III satellites were developed in 1968, and further advanced satellites are planned for the 1970's (Chapter 20).

5   A SUMMARY OF TYPES
OF LINES AND TARIFFS

The facts about the transmission links which most concern a systems analyst are the cost of the link and the rate at which data may be sent over a link of that cost. This can have a major effect on the feasibility of different systems approaches. All the common carriers issue a price list describing their facilities. Let us begin our description of communication links by summarizing what is available. The illustrations in the following summary are taken from the offering of the carriers in the United States and Britain. Those of other countries are broadly similar. Countries with less well-developed data transmission have less to offer in the way of wideband (high-capacity) facilities.

The services which a common carrier offers to the public are described in tariffs. A tariff is a document which, in the United Sates, is required by the regulating bodies who control the carriers. The United States Federal Communications Commission must eventually approve all interstate facilities, and similar state commissions control those within state boundaries. By law, all tariffs must be registered with these bodies. In most other countries, the telecommunication facilities are set up by Government bodies and thus are directly under their control.

In the United States the subject of communication rates has become very complex. The amount and structure of charges differ from one state to another. In other countries, such as England and Germany, the rates for more conventional channels remain relatively straightforward; however, as the carriers are Government organizations, they are not obliged to publish tariffs for all of their facilities. The price for less common channels, such as broadband, may have to be obtained by a special request to the carrier. In general it is desirable, when designing a system, that the carrier in question should be called in to quote a price for the facilities needed.

TELEPHONE
CHANNELS

When from your home telephone you dial a number in the same locality your call goes to a nearby public exchange, referred to as a *central office*. The equipment in this building connects the wires from your telephone to those of the party you called. These wires are permanently connected from your local central office to your telephone and are referred to as a *loop*. No other subscriber uses them, unless you have a party line. Thousands of such wire connections lie under the streets of a city in cables like that in Fig. 8.3.

Loops to a company building normally terminate at a switchboard, which has several extension lines to telephones in the building. The switchboard may be manual with interconnections made by an operator using cords, or may be automatic, in which case the user can dial his own connections. Switchboards at such premises are described as Private Branch Exchanges (PBX), Private Automatic Exchanges (PAX) or sometimes Private Automatic Branch Exchanges (PABX).

A circuit between two switching equipments is referred to as a *trunk*. When you dial a person whose telephone is not connected to the same central office as your own, your call will be routed over an *interoffice trunk*. The switched *public network* consists of a complicated system of switching offices and interconnecting trunks which will be described in a later chapter. Trunks between switching offices are normally designed to carry many telephone conversations, not just one as on the local loop.

A *tie line*, or tie trunk, is a private, leased, communication line between two or more private branch exchanges. Many companies have a leased system of telecommunication lines with switching facilities. To telephone a person in a distant company location, an employee must first obtain the appropriate tie line to that person's private branch exchange. On an automatic system this is done by dialing a tie-line code before the extension number, thus:

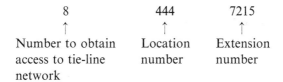

8	444	7215
↑	↑	↑
Number to obtain access to tie-line network	Location number	Extension number

The tie line (or lines) to that location may be busy, in which case a "busy tone" ("engaged signal" in British parlance) can be heard before the extension number is dialed.

All of the lines above can be used for data transmission as well as voice. Where one voice line is used the transmission speed is limited to a few thousand bits per second depending, as will be discussed later, on the equipment used at each end of the line. This is the data capacity of a telephone line. Often, however, the tie-line system has more than one voice line connecting two locations. At the time of writing, the common carrier tariffs in the United States make a broadband channel giving 60 voice lines or equivalent considerably less expensive than leasing 60 individual voice channels. If broadband link is used, a group of voice lines may be taken over together for high-speed data transmission.

One typical large corporation uses its tie-line groups in this manner as a broad-band data network during its second and third shifts. The lines are transferred to data automatically, as a group, and so telephone calls in progress on those lines may possibly be interrupted. The corporation tie-line directory contains the following note:

> "When a transfer is about to occur, callers will hear a special interrupt tone that is introduced during a conversation. Callers hearing this tone should hang up and redial the call after a 30-second interval. Normally, these transfers will only occur after 6: 00 p.m. Eastern Time."

LEASED VERSUS SWITCHED LINES   Voice lines and telegraph lines can be either switched through public exchanges (central offices), or permanently connected. Facilities for switching broadband channels are also coming into operation in some countries, although these channels, today, are normally permanent connections.

When you dial a friend and talk to him on the telephone, you speak over a line connected by means of the public exchanges. This line, referred to as a "public" or "switched" line could be used for the transmission of data. Alternatively, a "private" or "leased" line could be connected permanently or semipermanently between the transmitting machines. The private line may be connected via the local switching office, but it would not be connected to the switch-gear and signaling devices of that office. An interoffice private connection would use the same channelizing equipment as the switched circuits (multiplexing equipment discussed in Chapters 10 and 15). It would not, however, have to carry some of the means of signaling which are needed on a switched line, as we shall see in Chapter 17. This is one reason why it is possible to achieve a higher rate of data transmission over a private line. Another reason is that private lines can be carefully balanced to provide the high quality that makes higher speed data transmission possible.

There are also in operation several large *private* line systems which are also *switched*. It is possible to engineer these to the same quality as private lines, and hence provide a switching system of better quality than the public network.

Some private line systems are wholly owned by their user rather than leased. Typical of such systems are communication links within a factory, private microwave connections and other radio links, lines along railroad tracks, and, today, in some laboratories, private wiring of terminals to a time-sharing computer.

In the same way you can either dial a telephone connection or else have it permanently wired, so with other types of lines. Telegraph lines, for example, which have a much lower speed of transmission than is possible over voice lines, may be permanently connected, or may be dialed like a telephone line using a switched public network. Telex is such a network; it exists throughout most of the world, permitting transmission at 50 bits per second. Telex users can set up international connections to other countries. Some countries have a switched public network, operating at a somewhat higher speed than Telex but at less speed than telephone lines. In the United States, the TWX network gives speeds up to 150 bits per second. TWX lines can be connected to Telex lines for overseas calls. Also certain countries are building up a switched network for very high-speed (wideband) connections. In the United States, Western Union has installed the first sections of a system in which a user will indicate *in his dialing* what capacity link he needs.

ADVANTAGES OF PRIVATE LINES   The private line has certain advantages for data transmission over the switched connections:

1. If it is to be used for more than a given number of hours per day, it is less expensive than the switched line. If it is used for only an hour or so per day, then it is more expensive. The break-even point depends upon the actual charges, which in turn depend upon the mileage of the circuit, but it is likely to be of the order of several hours per day.

2. Private lines can be specially treated or "conditioned" to compensate for the distortion that is encountered on them. In this way the number of data errors is reduced, or alternatively, a higher transmission rate can be made possible. The switched connection cannot be conditioned beforehand in the same way because it is not known what path the circuit will take. Dialing one time is likely to set up a quite different physical path to dialing at another time, and there are a large number of possible paths. Line termination equipment has been designed now which conditions dynamically, and adjusts to whatever connection it is used on. When this comes into more common use, it will enable higher speeds to be obtained over switched circuits. Conditioning is discussed in Chapter 12. Many carriers have separate tariffs for conditioned telephone lines from those for unconditioned lines or charge extra for conditioning.

3. Switched voice lines usually carry signaling within the band that would be used for data (at frequencies such as those shown in Figure 17.2). Data transmission machines must be designed so that the form in which the data are sent cannot interfere with the common carrier's signaling. With some machines this also makes the capacity available for data transmission somewhat less than over a private voice line. A common rate over a switched voice line at the time of writing is 1200 bits per second, whereas 2400 bits per second is common over a specially conditioned, leased voice line. Some machines equipped with suitable modems transmit satisfactorily at 4800 over the leased line. Because of improved modem designs, however (Chapter

13), it is likely that 3600 bits per second over switched voice lines, and 7200 bits per second over conditioned, leased voice lines, will be used before long.

4. The leased line may be less perturbed by noise and distortion than the switched line. The switching gear can cause impulse noise which causes errors in data. This is a third factor which contributes to a lower error rate for a given transmission speed on private lines.

The cost advantage of switched lines will dominate if the terminal has only a low usage. Also the ability to dial a distant machine gives great flexibility. Different machines can be dialed with the same terminal, perhaps offering quite different facilities. A typewriter terminal used at one time by a secretary for computer-assisted text editing, may at another time be connected to a scientific time-sharing system and at another time dial a computer-assisted teaching program. Machine availability is another consideration. If one system is overloaded or under repair, the terminal user might dial an alternative system. Often this dialing is done over the firm's own leased tie lines.

SIMPLEX, DUPLEX, AND HALF-DUPLEX LINES

In designing a data-processing system it is necessary to decide whether the line must transmit in one direction only or in both directions. If the latter, will the machines transmit in both directions at the same time?

Transmission lines are classed as simplex, half duplex, and full duplex. In North America, these terms have the following meanings:

Simplex lines transmit in one direction only.

Half-duplex lines can transmit in either direction, but only in one direction at once.

Full-duplex lines transmit in both directions at the same time. One full-duplex line is thus equivalent to two simplex or half-duplex lines used in opposite directions.

The above are the meanings in current usage throughout most of the world's computer industry. Unfortunately, however, the International Telecommunications Union defines the first two terms differently—as follows:

Simplex (circuit)—A circuit permitting the transmission of signals in either direction but not simultaneously.

Half Duplex (circuit)—A circuit designed for duplex operation but which on account of the nature of the terminal equipment can be operated alternately only.

"Simplex" and "half duplex" are thus used differently by European telecommunications engineers, and computer manufacturers (especially American ones) using the same facilities.

Throughout this book, the words will be used with the former meanings exclusively.

Simplex lines (American meaning) are not generally used in data transmission because, even if the data are only being sent in one direction, control signals are normally sent back to the transmitting machine to tell it that the receiving machine is ready, or is receiving the data correctly. Commonly, error signals (positive or negative acknowledgment) are sent back so that there can be retransmission of messages damaged by communication line errors. Many data transmission links use half-duplex lines. This allows control signals to be sent and two-way "conversational" transmission to occur. On some systems full-duplex lines can give more efficient use of the lines at little extra line costs. A full-duplex line often costs little more than a half-duplex line. Data transmission machines which can take full advantage of full-duplex lines are more expensive, however, than those which use half-duplex lines. Half-duplex transmission is therefore more common at present though this might well change.

The question of whether a line can support transmission in both directions at the same time or not will depend on the speed desired and on whether it is two wire or four wire (discussed in Chapter 9). The circuit from your telephone to the local telephone exchange is usually a two-wire path, that is, only two signal-carrying wires leave your telephone and disappear into the wall plaster. Most intercity lines, on the other hand, are four-wire or four-wire equivalent. A two-wire telephone circuit can generally be used in a half-duplex fashion and a four-wire circuit can always be used in a full-duplex fashion. It is possible to use certain two-wire circuits in a full-duplex manner if they have an appropriate arrangement of amplifiers. To do so needs a special modem, and the maximum speed obtainable would clearly be less than with a four-wire circuit. The specifications of data sets which connect a data-handling machine to the line state whether they operate in a half-duplex or full-duplex manner, and whether they need a two-wire or four-wire circuit.

In order to achieve full-duplex transmission then, it is necessary to have a line suitable for this which could in some cases be a two-wire line, and also to have data sets suitably designed taking into account whether the circuit is two-wire or four-wire.

VOICE AND SUBVOICE LINE TYPES

The main categorization of line types relates to the speed of transmission possible. The line may be specifically adapted by the common carrier for data transmission, in which case a fixed transmission speed may be quoted in the description of the line. On the other hand, it may be a normal voice, or other, line with no special devices for data. In this case the speed obtained over the line will depend upon the data sets or transmission mode which the user employs.

Table 5.1. THE MAIN TYPES OF COMMUNICATIONS LINKS IN USE TODAY*

| | Speed (bits per second) | United States | | | United Kingdom | Half Duplex or Full Duplex |
		AT&T (New Terminology)	AT&T (Old Terminology)	Western Union		
Sub-voice grade:	45	Type 1002	Schedule 1	Class A		FDX/HDX
	50				Telegraph, Tariff H	FDX
	55	Type 1002	Schedule 2	Class B		FDX/HDX
	75	Type 1005	Schedule 3	Class C		FDX/HDX
	100				Datel 100, Tariff J	FDX
	150	Type 1006	Schedule 3A			FDX
	180			Class D		FDX/HDX
	200				Datel 200	FDX
Voice grade:	600			Broadband exchange Schedule 1		FDX
	1200			Broadband exchange Schedule 2		FDX
	1200	Type 3002	Schedule 4	Class G	Datel 600 Tariff S	FDX/HDX
	1400	Type 3002 plus C1 conditioning	Type 3003	Class E	Tariff S with line improvements	FDX/HDX
	2400	Type 3002 plus C2 conditioning	Type 3004	Class F	Ditto	FDX/HDX
	4800	Type 3002 plus C4 conditioning	Type 3005	Class H		FDX/HDX
Wideband:	19,200 fixed	Type 8803				FDX
	40,800 fixed	Type 8801		Wideband channel	Special quotation	FDX
	105,000	Type 5700 or 5800	Telpak C	Telpak C	Special quotation	FDX
	240,000				Special quotation	
	500,000	Type 5800	Telpak D	Telpak D	Special quotation	FDX

*The terminology for these line types has been subject to many changes recently, and may well change again. Also the data speeds, in bits per second, on some line types are likely to improve with better modem design. For up-to-the-minute information, the reader should refer to the Common Carrier or FCC tariffs.

Table 5.1 lists the main types of communication links in order of increasing speed. The speeds have been listed in terms of the number of data bits per second that may be sent over the line. Communication lines fall into one of three categories of speed:

1. *Narrow-Band.* Lines designed for telegraph and similar machines transmitting at speeds ranging, in the United States, from 45 to 150 bits per second. Some countries have lines of higher speed than their telegraph facilities, but still much less than the capacity of voice lines. England, for example, has a Datel 200 service operating at 200 bits per second. All of these lines are today commonly obtained by subdividing telephone channels.

2. *Voice-Band.* Telephone channels normally transmitting today at speeds from 600 to 2400 bits per second. Speeds up to 4800 are in use by some of today's machines, and speeds of 7200 and possibly higher can be expected in the near future. Today leased, conditioned lines are necessary for speeds above 1800. Speeds up to 3200, however, may soon become possible in the public network.

3. *Wideband.* Lines giving speeds much higher than voice channels, using facilities which carry many simultaneous telephone calls. Speeds up to about 500,000 bits per second are in use, and higher bit rates are possible if required.

All of these line types may be channeled over a variety of different physical facilities. This chapter, and indeed the tariffs themselves normally, say nothing about the medium used for transmission. It could equally well be wire, coaxial cable microwave radio, or even satellite. Chapter 8 discusses the various media available.

In the terminology of the United States telephone companies, Schedule 4 used to refer to voice lines. This was replaced by the term Series 3000 lines. A Type 3002 line refers to a voice line used for data transmission. Western Union refers to it as a Class G line. Type 3002 lines with conditioning were referred to by AT&T as Type 3003, 3004 and 3005 lines, however these terms have now been dropped and one refers to a "Type 3002 line with Type C1, C2 or C4 conditioning." Western Union refers to lines with those three levels of conditioning as Class E, Class F, and Class H lines. The speed at which one can transmit over such lines varies with the type of modem that is used.

In AT&T terminology, schedules 1, 2, 3, and 3A used to refer to lines of much lower capacity which were obtained by sending several separate channels over one voice links (see Chapter 15). These are now called series 1000 lines. A type 1002 line refers to 45 and 55 bits-per-second teletypewriter lines which used to be called schedule 1 and 2 lines. A type 1005 line is the old schedule 3 line giving teletypewriter service at 100 bits per second. A type 1006 line permits data transmission at 150 bits per second; this used to be called schedule 3A.

In Western Union tariffs, teletype and other low-speed lines are listed as class A, B, C, and D. Classes A, B, and C are equivalent to AT&T's schedules 1, 2, and 3 (now types 1002 and 1005).

This is all summarized in Table 5.1.

In the United Kingdom, today's teletype circuits can be used to transmit at 50 or 100 bits per second (full duplex). These are referred to as tariff H and tariff J lines, respectively. The 100 bits-per-second links are new and are available only between selected locations. This is referred to as the *Datel 100* service. The United Kingdom voice lines are used, split into separate channels, to give a *Datel 200* service at 200 bits per second, a *Datel 300* service in which multifrequency signaling permits the transmission of up to 20 characters per second (only), and a *Datel 600* service with a speed range of 600 to 1200 bits per second. The latter is referred to as tariff S. A conditioned voice line giving speeds of 2000 bits per second is referred to as *Datel 2000*. The term "Datel" generally means that the GPO is leasing modems to provide data transmission over the circuit, and these are included in the tariff. The voice line can sometimes be leased for part of the day only, and this is referred to as tariff E. If it is leased for two hours per day (the minimum) its cost will be approximately a quarter of tariff S.

**LINE
CONDITIONING**

As has been mentioned, private, leased, voice lines can be *conditioned* so that they have better properties for data transmission. Tariffs specify maximum levels for certain types of distortion. *An additional charge is made by most carriers for lines which are conditioned.*

AT&T, for example, has three types of conditioned voice lines, the conditioning being referred to as types C1, C2 and C4 (formally types 4A, 4B and 4C). Their properties are given in Table 5.2. The types of distortion listed in this table will not be discussed until Chapter 12, but nevertheless it is convenient to place the table here in the summary of line types. The reader can refer back to it when he reads Chapter 12. In addition to the figures listed in the table, the telephone companies often publish objectives for maximum levels for thermal noise, cross talk, and echoes on conditioned lines.

**WIDEBAND AND
TELPAK TARIFFS**

TELPAK is a private line, "bulk" communications service offered in the U.S. by the telephone companies and Western Union. It transmits high-volume point-to-point communications in various forms—voice, telephotograph, teletypewriter, control, signaling, facsimile and data.

The service, introduced in 1961, is designed for businesses and government agencies with large private line communications requirements. TELPAK has a flexible capacity and can be tailored to the customer's needs, providing, if required, wideband communications or subdivided for use with

Table 5.2. Specifications of Conditioned Voice Lines in the U.S.A.

	Type C1 conditioning "Class E" lines Line Type 3003 Type 4A conditioning		Type C2 conditioning "Class F" lines Line Type 3004 Type 4B conditioning		Type C4 conditioning "Class H" lines Line Type 3005 Type 4C conditioning	
Name of conditioning: Telephone companies: Western Union: Former names: Telephone companies:						
Voice lines applicable to:	Two Point or Multipoint Half or Full Duplex Two Wire or Four Wire		Two Point or Multipoint Half or Full Duplex Two Wire Four Wire		Two Point Half or Full Duplex Two Wire or Four Wire	
Specifications for amplitude variation:	Amplitude Variation	Frequency Range	Amplitude Variation	Frequency Range	Amplitude Variation	Frequency Range
	-2 to $+6$ db $+1$ to $+3$ db -2 to $+6$ db	300–999 1000–2400 2401–2700	-2 to $+6$ db -1 to $+3$ db -2 to $+6$ db	300–499 500–2800 2801–3000	-2 to $+6$ db -2 to $+3$ db -2 to $+6$ db	300–499 500–3000 3001–3200
Specifications for envelope delay:	Envelope Delay (Microseconds)	Frequency Range	Envelope Delay (Microseconds)	Frequency Range	Envelope Delay (Microseconds)	Frequency Range
	Less than 1000	1000–2400	Less than 500 Less than 1500 Less than 3000	1000–2600 600–2600 500–2800	Less than 300 Less than 1500 Less than 1500 Less than 3000	1000–2600 800–2800 600–3000 500–3000

teletypewriter equipment. A base capacity channel could be employed for high-speed transmission of such data as magnetic tape, computer memory, and facsimile.

The TELPAK customer pays a monthly charge based on the width of the communications channel he selects, the number of airline miles between locations, and the type and quantity of channel terminals. He has use of this channel on a full-time basis.

There were originally four sizes of TELPAK channels: TELPAK A, B, C, and D. However, in 1964 the Federal Communications Commission ruled that rates for TELPAK A (12 voice circuits) were discriminatory in that a large user could obtain a group of channels at lower cost per channel than a small user who could not take advantage of the bulk rates. In 1967 the TELPAK A and B offerings were eliminated.

TELPAK A had a base capacity of 12 voice channels (full duplex)
TELPAK B had a base capacity of 24 voice channels (full duplex)
TELPAK C has a base capacity of 60 voice channels (full duplex)
TELPAK D has a base capacity of 240 voice channels (full duplex)

Each TELPAK voice channel can itself be subdivided into one of the following:

(a) Twelve teletype channels, half or full duplex (75 bits per second).
(b) Six class D channels, half or full duplex (180 bits per second).
(c) Four AT&T type 1006 channels, half or full duplex (150 bits per second).

There cannot be mixtures of these channel types in a voice channel.

As will be discussed further in Chapter 16, TELPAK C normally transmits data at speeds of 105,000 bits per second but higher rates are possible; TELPAK D has a potential transmission rate of 500,000 bits per second. Line termination equipment is provided with these links and each link has a separate voice channel for coordination purposes.

The TELPAK channels thus serve two purposes. First, they provide a wideband channel over which data can be sent at a much higher rate than over a voice channel. Second they provide a means of offering groups of voice or subvoice lines at reduced rates—a kind of discount for bulk buying.

Suppose that a company requires a 40,800-bit-per-second link between two cities, and also 23 voice channels and 14 teletypewriter channels; or perhaps 30 voice channels and no teletypewriter links. Then it would be likely to use the TELPAK C tariff. In leasing these facilities it would have some unused capacity. If it wishes it can make use of this at no extra charge for mileage, though there would be a terminal charge.

Government agencies and certain firms in the same business whose rates and charges are regulated by the government (e.g., airlines and railroads) may share TELPAK services. Airlines, for example, pool their needs for voice and teletypewriter channels. An intercompany organization purchases the TELPAK services and then apportions the channels to individual airlines. Most of the lines channeling passenger reservations to a distant office where bookings can be made are TELPAK lines, and so also are the lines carrying data between terminals in those offices and a distant reservations computer. There has been some demand to extend these shared TELPAK facilities to other types of organizations who could benefit from them by sharing, but in the late sixties, this was still not permissible.

TELPAK originally was proposed as an interstate service, but since then it has become generally available intrastate as well.

Although not a TELPAK offering, Series 8000 is another "bulk" communications service in the U.S.A. that offers wideband transmission of high-speed data, or facsimile, at rates up to 50,000 bits a second; the customer has the alternative of using the channel for voice communication up to a maximum of 12 circuits. A type 8801 link, part of this series, provides a data link at speeds up to 50,000 bits per second with appropriate terminating data sets and a voice channel for coordination. A Type 8803 link provides a data link with a fixed speed of 19,200 bits per second, and leaves a remaining capacity which can be used either for a second simultaneous 19,200-bits-per-second channel or for up to five voice channels. These links must connect only two cities. The separate channels cannot terminate at intermediate locations.

Most countries outside North America also offer tariffs similar to the Series 8000, and in most locations quotations for higher speeds can be obtained on request. At the time of writing obtaining a wideband link in many such countries can be a slow process. This is particularly so if the termination is required in a small town or rural area rather than a city to which such links already exist. No doubt as the demand for such facilities increases, so the service of the common carriers in providing them will improve.

TARIFFS INCLUDING   Some common carrier tariffs are designed espe-
DATA SETS   cially for data transmission, and the cost of the
                               link must include the common carrier modems
(data sets) needed for efficient transmission. Data sets are discussed in Chapters 10 and 13. A picture of some is shown in Figure 10.7. The tariff will then state the speed or speeds in bits per second at which the link will transmit.

An example of this is the Bell System Dataphone service. A data set (Fig. 10.7) is provided which connects to the data-processing machine. A call may be dialed by an operator with the data set switched to "Voice." When she has established the call she hears a characteristic whistling tone from the data set at the dialed machine and she then switches the data set to "Data." The GPO *Datel* Services are such a tariff in Britain.

MULTIDROP LINES

To lower the cost of the network of communication lines, it is often desirable to attach more than one terminal, or more than one concentrator, to a single leased line. A line such as this with several "drop-off" points is termed a *multidrop* line.

When several devices all share a communication line, only one can transmit at once, though several or all points can *receive* the same information. Each terminal must have an address of one or more characters, and it must have the ability to recognize that a message is being sent to that address. For example, a line may have 26 terminals with addresses A to Z. The computer sends a message down the line which is to be displayed by terminals A, G, and H. The message is preceded by these three addresses and each terminal has circuitry which scans its own address. Terminals A, G, and H recognize their addresses and display the message simultaneously. The other terminals do not recognize their address, and so ignore the message. The network may also have a "broadcast" code which causes all terminals on a line to display those messages preceded by it.

Where there are several locations, then, which will transmit to a computer, a leased line may wander around all of these locations as in Figure 5.1. An additional charge, apart from the charge for the data set, may be made for each "drop."

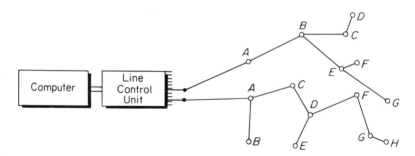

Fig. 5.1. Multidrop lines. The path selected between the locations is that which has the lowest cost without overloading the lines. There may be more than one data terminal at each location.

TELEX   Telex is a world-wide switched public teleprinter system. It operates at 66 words per
minute (50 bits per second), and uses the Baudot code. It is operated in the
United States by Western Union. Any teleprinter on the system can dial
any other teleprinter in that country, and Telex machines can be connected
internationally without speed or code conversion. The United States can dial
Canada and Mexico directly, but to other countries, operator intervention
is needed. Some countries permit the Telex facilities to be used for other
forms of dial-up data transmission. Each Telex call is billed on a time and
distance basis.

Each subscriber has an individual line and his own number, as with the
conventional telephone service. His teleprinter is fitted with a dial, like a
telephone, with which he can dial other subscribers. The teleprinter used may
or may not have paper-tape equipment also. The teleprinter can be unattended. When a message is sent to an unattended teleprinter, it will switch
itself on, print the message, and then switch itself off. Figure 5.2 shows two
typical Telex installations.

TELETYPEWRITER   The Bell System and other telephone com-
EXCHANGE   panies offer a service in the United States and
SERVICE   Canada which is competitive with TELEX.
Again, each subscriber has a dial-up teletype-
writer with his own number listed in a nation-wide directory. This service is
called the Teletypewriter Exchange Service (TWX), and it uses the telephone
circuits combined with several TWX channels so that they can be sent over
one voice channel. The combining or "multiplexing" is done at the local
switching office where the dc signals are changed to equivalent bursts of
appropriate frequencies. The link between the local switching office and the
subscriber is often a conventional telephone line, and in this case the teletypewriter needs a data set to convert the dc signals to appropriate frequencies
in the voice range.

Other manufacturers' data transmission equipment can be connected to
TWX lines, and can transmit at speeds up to 150 bits per second, half or
full duplex. This requires special terminal arrangements at additional cost.
There are three types of access lines to the TWX network, as follows:

(1) TTY-TWX.
    This is an access line with a teletypewriter (e.g., Fig. 6.8) provided
    by the common carrier. The speeds of transmission are either 6
    characters per second in Baudot or 10 characters per second in Data
    Interchange Code. (DIC).

(A)

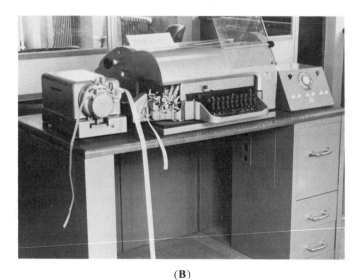

(B)

Fig. 5.2. Typical Telex installations. Many countries have this dial-up telegraph service operating at 50 bits per second (66 words per minute). Such Telex machines have been incorporated in computer systems. *Courtesy General Post Office, London.*

(2) CPT-TWX.

CPT stands for "Customer Provided Terminal"; and to this access line the customer can attach any device operating with one of the above two speeds and codes, and adhering to normal TWX line control. The device could be a computer with an appropriate adapter on its input/output channel.

(3) CE-TWX (formally called "TWX Prime").

CE stands for "Customer Equipment." This can now be any device and is not restricted to a specific code or character speed. Two TWX subsystems are accessible, one which operates at speeds up to 45 bits per second, and the other up to 150. A CE-TWX terminal can communicate only with another CE-TWX terminal.

TWX directories are published listing TTY-TWX and CPT-TWX subscribers.

MODES OF TRANSMISSION

The facilities described can be used by machines in a variety of different transmission modes. Machines may transmit, for example, in a simplex, half-duplex, or full-duplex fashion. Using full duplex, some send data in both directions at once; some overlap control signals traveling in one direction with data traveling in the other. Many machines use a full-duplex link only to eliminate the time taken to reverse the transmission direction, and actually never send data in both directions at once.

Some machines use *parallel* transmission. Eight separate paths between the same locations, for example, may be used to convey eight-bit characters parallel by bit as described in Chapter 23. This can reduce terminal costs, but where the separate paths are *physically* separated, it is only likely to be used over short, and therefore low cost, lines. However, the separate paths may be obtained by splitting up *one* physical path in a manner discussed in Chapter 15. Some very inexpensive data-handling machines transmit a group of frequency-separated signals over a single leased or dial-up voice line.

Machines may use *start–stop transmission*, as in the telegraphy machines described in the next chapter; or they may use synchronous transmission in which equally spaced bits are sent in a continuous stream with timing carefully controlled at each end of the line often by use of a precise oscillator.

A wide variety of techniques exists for controlling the flow of characters on the lines. To make the most efficient use of the expensive links, many terminals may be placed on one line and control techniques of considerable complexity may be used. A variety of different machines exists to connect the transmission facilities to computers and other data-processing machines. In planning a communication-based computer system the systems analyst can be faced with a complex variety of different methods and machines to choose from.

6 TELEGRAPHY

In the nineteenth century, electronics had not been invented. From the 1830's when electrical communication was first used, until the 1910's when electronic vacuum tubes were perfected, there were no electronic amplifiers, repeaters, multiplexors, modulators, or other such devices which make modern communications what it is. The invention of the vacuum tube, and the new technology that grew up around its use, revolutionized the communications industry. From that time on, all manner of developments became possible that were hitherto undreamed of. We have now reached another point in time when a new technology is going to bring equally sweeping changes. The use of logic circuits such as those in computers promises to alter again the whole nature of telecommunications.

Telegraph transmission somewhat similar to that of the era before electronics is still used extensively, and is one of the means of remote data input to computers. Data transmission today used with computers has adopted and modified the methods of telegraphy. All of the techniques discussed in this chapter will recur again later in the book, in a modified form.

Telegraph systems in the past were generally designed to communicate intelligence with the minimum transmission line requirements. The machines sent simple pulses such as those in Fig. 6.1 at a slow speed. Teletype lines in the United States operate at speeds up to 150 bits per second. Telex and many European lines operate at 50 bits per second. On most modern lines, as we will see in later chapters, these pulses are converted so that they can be transmitted in an AC form with voice channels being subdivided into many telegraph channels.

Teletype signals are formed simply by switching an electrical current on and off, or by reversing its direction of flow. The upper part of Fig. 6.1 shows

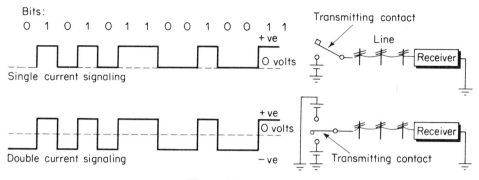

Figure 6.1

a *single-current* telegraph signal in which the information is coded by switching the current on and off at particular times. The lower part shows the same signal on a *double-current* telegraph system in which positive and negative potentials are applied at one end of the line, thus reversing the direction of current flow. The means for producing these current changes are some form of make-and-break contact. The instruments for sending signals such as teleprinters or paper-tape readers make and break the circuit at appropriate times. The on and off pulses form a code which is appropriately interpreted by the receiving device. Single current telegraph signaling is also known as "neutral" or "unipolar" signaling. Double current signaling is called "polar" or "bipolar." In the United States, neutral signaling is used 100% by AT&T, and about 30% by Western Union. In Europe, bipolar (there usually called "double current") signaling is the most common. The adaptors for connecting telegraph equipment to computers may be planned to use either neutral or bipolar signals, whichever is appropriate.

On some telegraph circuits, signals are still sent in the DC form shown in Fig. 6.1. However, with the enormous growth of the telephone network, voice lines, with amplifiers designed for voice, became far more common than DC teletype circuits. In order to use these voice lines efficiently, the DC signal is converted into an AC signal by a modem, in a way which will be described later. It is then transmitted in AC form over the voice line equipment. One voice channel is often subdivided electronically into 12, or sometimes more, AC teletype channels. At the other end of the line the AC signal is converted back to the DC form of Fig. 6.1.

TELEGRAPHY CODES

The ones and zeroes of Fig. 6.1 have long been referred to in telegraphy as "marks" and "spaces." In single current signaling a mark may be represented by the presence of current and a space by the absence of it. A variety of codes has been used for making the marks and spaces represent letters and digits. Codes for operating machinery use fixed length marks and spaces arranged in different combinations. Many telegraphy machines throughout the world today use a code with five "bits" of information. The five bits are preceded by a START bit, which is always a "space," and followed by a STOP bit, which is always a "mark." The STOP is commonly of 1.5 or 1.42 times longer duration than the other bits. On other equipment it is the same length as the data bits or two data bits.

The receiving machine has, in essence, a clocking device which starts when the START bit is detected and operates for as many bits as there are in a character. With this, the receiving machine can distinguish which bit is which. The STOP bit was made 1.5 or so times longer than the data bits in case the receiver clock was not operating at quite the same speed as the transmitter.

To a large extent the five-level code has now been superseded by higher level codes, and in particular by the United States ASCII code, in which a character has seven information bits (many machines are designed to transmit eight, of which one is today unused) plus one START bit and one or two STOP bits.

Figure 6.2 shows the common five-bit telegraphy codes. These were used for almost all telegraphy transmission until the acceptance of higher level codes in recent years. Outside North America they are still the most widely used but are likely to be displaced by the higher level codes.

Figure 6.2 shows the common methods of allocating the 32 permutations to the ιpper- and lower-case characters on a teleprinter. Because there are only 32 possible combinations of the five bits, *figures shift* and *letters shift* characters must be used. These are printed ↑ and ↓, respectively. When a *figures shift* character is sent, the characters that follow it are uppercase characters until a *letters shift* character is sent. Similarly, the characters following a *letters shift* are letters—until a *figures shift* is sent. Like the *carriage return*, *line feed*, and *space* characters, the *letters shift* and *figures shift* are recognized in either upper or lower case.

International standardization of telegraphy codes has come into general acceptance, but there are still some minor differences between codes used in the United States and other countries. CCITT has laid down standards for telegraph codes. These have been adopted by most countries of the world. The United States, however, has not adopted them fully. At the time the standards were laid down Western Union had several thousand teleprinters in service using the Western Union Murray code. In Europe a version of the Baudot code was in general use, and this differed in almost every character from the Murray code. Europe made a major concession to international standardization and abandoned its telegraphy code. The resulting international code, however, differed slightly from the Western Union code in the upper case of the teleprinter keyboard. The United States participated in the conference which agreed upon the international code, but did not sign

● Denotes positive current

Code signals:

Start	1	2	3	4	5	Stop	Lower case	Upper case: CCITT standard international telegraph alphabet No.2	Upper case: U.S.A. teletype commercial keyboard	Upper case: AT & T fractions keyboard	Upper case: Weather keyboard
	●	●				●	A	—	—	—	↑
	●			●	●	●	B	?	?	5/8	⊕
		●	●	●		●	C	:	:	1/8	○
	●			●		●	D	Who are you?	$	$	↗
	●					●	E	3	3	3	3
	●		●	●		●	F	Note 1	!	1/4	→
		●		●	●	●	G	Note 1	&	&	↘
			●		●	●	H	Note 1	#		↓
		●	●			●	I	8	8	8	8
	●	●		●		●	J	Bell	Bell	'	↙
	●	●	●	●		●	K	(	(	1/2	←
		●			●	●	L	)	)	3/4	↖
			●	●	●	●	M	.	.	.	.
			●	●		●	N	,	,	7/8	⦶
				●	●	●	O	9	9	9	9
		●	●		●	●	P	0	0	0	∅
	●	●	●			●	Q	1	1	1	1
		●		●		●	R	4	4	4	4
	●		●			●	S	,	,	Bell	Bell
					●	●	T	5	5	5	5
	●	●	●			●	U	7	7	7	7
		●	●	●	●	●	V	=	;	3/8	⌽
	●	●			●	●	W	2	2	2	2
	●		●	●	●	●	X	/	/	/	/
	●		●		●	●	Y	6	6	6	6
	●				●	●	Z	+	"	"	+
						●	Blank				−
	●	●	●	●	●	●	Letters shift	↓			
	●	●		●	●	●	Figures shift	↑			
			●			●	Space	■			
				●		●	Carriage return	<			
		●				●	Line feed	≡			

Note 1: Not allocated internationally; available to each country for internal use.

Fig. 6.2. Baudot 5-bit telegraphy code.

the agreement. Today the Western Union teleprinter code in normal use differs from that of other countries as follows:

Letter	Upper-Case Character	
	Western Union	CCITT
D	$	Who are you?
F	!	Private Allocation
G	&	Private Allocation
H	#	Private Allocation
V	;	=
Z	"	+

Some telegraph services use sequences of characters for certain functions, for example to indicate the start or end of a message. Table 6.1 lists the sequences in common use. These are standardized sequences, again following a CCITT recommendation.

Table 6.1. THE USE OF SEQUENCES OF TELEGRAPH CHARACTERS FOR SPECIAL PURPOSES

Purpose of Sequence	Sequence	Notes
Start of message	ZCZC	
End of telegram	ZZZZ or ++++	Used in retransmission systems and store-and-forward devices
End of message	NNNN	
Suppression of delay signals	HHHH	Used to prevent the retransmission of delay signals used for error-corrected radio-telegraph channels
Connection of reperforator or equivalent device	CCCC	Switching into the circuit by remote control a reperforator or equivalent device
Disconnection of reperforator or equivalent device	FFFF	Switching out of the circuit by remote control a reperforator or equivalent device
Connection of data equipment	SSSS	Switching into the circuit, by remote control, data transmission equipment

Several codes other than the five-bit codes above have for some time been used for telegraph transmission. Widely used are the Friden *Flexowriter Code* (six bits, plus parity and control, which provides 64 characters) and the United States Military Standard *Fieldata Code* (seven bits, plus parity, providing 128 characters). The computer manufacturers have used a variety of different codes for transmitting data.

BIT 7:			0	0	0	0	1	1	1	1
BIT 6:			0	0	1	1	0	0	1	1
BIT 5:			0	1	0	1	0	1	0	1
BIT 4:	BIT 3:	BIT 2:	BIT 1:							
0	0	0	0	NULL	DC$_0$	ƀ	0	@	P		
0	0	0	1	SOM	DC$_1$	!	1	A	Q		
0	0	1	0	EOA	DC$_2$	"	2	B	R		
0	0	1	1	EOM	DC$_3$	#	3	C	S		
0	1	0	0	EOT	DC$_4$ (STOP)	$	4	D	T		UNASSIGNED
0	1	0	1	WRU	ERR	%	5	E	U		
0	1	1	0	RU	SYNC	&	6	F	V	UNASSIGNED	
0	1	1	1	BELL	LEM	' (APOS)	7	G	W		
1	0	0	0	FE$_0$	S$_0$	(	8	H	X		
1	0	0	1	HT / SK	S$_1$	)	9	I	Y		
1	0	1	0	LF	S$_2$	*	:	J	Z		
1	0	1	1	V$_{TAB}$	S$_3$	+	;	K	[		
1	1	0	0	FF	S$_4$ (COMMA)	<	L	\			ACK
1	1	0	1	CR	S$_5$	−	=	M	]		①
1	1	1	0	SO	S$_6$	·	>	N	↑		ESC
1	1	1	1	SI	S$_7$	/	?	O	←		DEL

EXAMPLE: Character "R" is represented by 0100101

LEGEND:

NULL	Null / Idle	DC$_0$	Device control reserved for data link escape
SOM	Start of message		
EOA	End of address	DC$_1$–DC$_3$	Device control
EOM	End of message	DC$_4$ (Stop)	Device control (stop)
EOT	End of transmission	ERR	Error
WRU	"Who are you ?"	SYNC	Synchronous idle
RU	"Are you...?"	LEM	Logical end of media
BELL	Audible signal	S$_0$–S$_7$	Separator (information)
FE$_0$	Format effector	ƀ	Word separator (space, normally nonprinting)
HT	Horizontal tabulation		
SK	Skip (punched card)	<	Less than
LF	Line feed	>	Greater than
V$_{TAB}$	Vertical tabulation	↑	Up arrow (Exponentiation)
FF	Form feed	←	Left arrow (Implies / Replaced by)
CR	Carriage return		
SO	Shift out	\	Reverse slant
SI	Shift in	ACK	Acknowledge
		①	Unassigned control
		ESC	Escape
		DEL	Delete / Idle

Fig. 6.3. The American Standard Code for Information Interchange (ASCII).

111

The proliferation of different codes is clearly disadvantageous because it may prevent the machine of one manufacturer communicating with that of another. In Britain alone, at least five different codes have been used for five-track tape. In the United States more than 25 different codes have been used for six-bit character representation in computers. To solve this problem, ASCII, the American Standard Code for Information Interchange, was designed as a universal data transmission code which, it was hoped, all manufacturers would use. If a computer using one data coding needed to communicate with computers using different coding, it would do so in ASCII. The various machines would then need the facility to convert ASCII into their own code and back, but not need to be able to convert every other machine's code.

ASCII has been widely accepted and put to use in North America although there is still a major use of other codes. It would be to the benefit of the rest of the world to follow America's lead and give it general acceptance as an international standard.

The ASCII code was described in an American Standards Association document dated June 17, 1963.[1] Subsequent standards have prescribed the means of implementing the code in paper tape, punched cards and other media. Figure 6.3 shows the ASCII code as described in the standard above.

Although the ASCII code uses seven bits, many data transmission machines transmit it as an eight-level code. Those numbers of bits most economically handled by machines are powers of two. The Bell System teletypewriter equipment, for example, transmits and receives eight information bits. In most such teletype machines at the time of writing, the eighth bit is not used for information; it is always a "mark." It could be used, however, either for parity checking the character, or to extend the character set beyond the present 128 possible combinations. In some data transmission schemes the eight-bit character is used for sending two four-bit numeric characters.

START-STOP INSTRUMENTS   Figure 6.4 shows the keyboards of some typical instruments using telegraph lines.

Such devices normally use start-stop transmission. The character generated by one key-depression begins with a START bit and ends with a STOP bit or bits. The "marks" and "spaces" of such characters are shown in Fig. 6.5, a mark representing positive voltage on the line and a space, zero or negative voltage.

In some transmissions, the START and STOP bits are used for starting and stopping the receiving instrument at the beginning and end of each character.

---

[1] American Standard Code for Information Interchange. Published by the American Standards Association Incorporated, 10 East 40th Street, New York, N.Y. 10016, June 17, 1963.

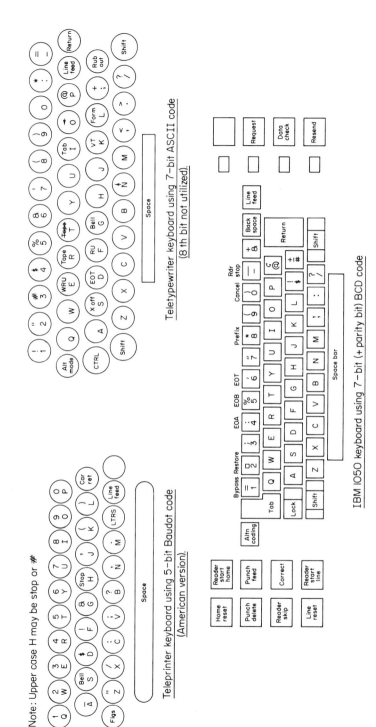

Figure 6.4

113

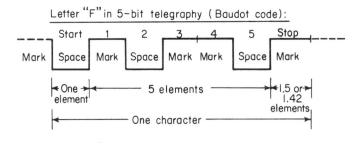

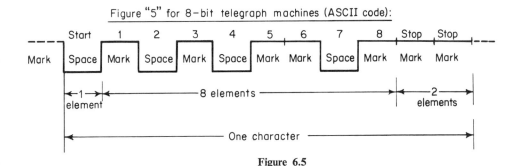

Figure 6.5

In others, the instrument operates without stopping, the STOP bit being used only to give a mark-space transition for the next START bit.

Using this start-stop transmission there can be an indeterminate period between one character and the next. When one character ends, the receiving device will wait idly for the start of the next character. The transmitter and the receiver are then exactly in phase, and will remain in phase while the character is sent. The receiver will thus be able to attach the correct meaning to each bit it receives.

When the STOP bit is represented by positive current flowing as with the codes in Fig. 6.2, this positive current may remain on the line until the start of the next character. In other words, the line's idle condition is a "mark" rather than a "space." As soon as a space is detected the receiving device starts and will then be in synchronization with the transmitting device. The STOP bit thus has a minimum duration which is 1.42 (or 1.5 or 2) times the length of the other bits, but can go on much longer than this. The STOP bit line condition lasts until the next START bit.

When an automatic machine such as a paper-tape reader is sending START/STOP signals the length of the STOP condition will be governed by the sending machine. It will be short, always 1.42 (1.5 or 2) times the other bits, so as to obtain the maximum transmission rate. When a typist uses the keyboard of a start-stop machine, on the other hand, the duration between her keystrokes will vary. The transmission will occur when she presses each key, and so the STOP condition will vary in length considerably. When a scientist uses a teleprinter on a time-sharing system he may be doing work which involves a great amount of thinking. Between one character and another there may occasionally be a very long pause while he thinks or makes notes. The STOP "bit" will last for the duration of this.

Figure 6.6 illustrates the principle of operation of mechanical start-stop instruments. The sending device and the receiving device each have an armature, A, which can rotate at a constant speed when a clutch connects it to an electric motor in these machines. Brush contacts on the armatures connect an outer ring of contacts B, to an inner ring C. In Fig. 6.6, the armature is in its "STOP" position. Consequently, current from the battery in the sender flows via the outer contact labeled "STOP," through the armature and onto the line. This current causes the contact of a receiver relay, D, to be in the position shown, and thus no current from the battery in the receiver flows to any of the operating magnets shown.

Now suppose that a girl operating the sending device presses the **H** key on the keyboard. In accordance with the code in Fig. 6.2 the **3** and **5** data contacts now close. Also the **START** contact closes and the armature of the sender begins to rotate counterclockwise. The armature connects the contacts on the outer ring to the line in sequence: **START, 1, 2, 3, 4, 5, STOP**. The **3, 5** and **STOP** contacts convey current; the others do not. As soon as the armature of the sender travels to its **START** contact, the positive currents on the line ceases. The contact of the relay, D, flips across, and positive current from the battery of the receiver flows through the inner ring C, armature A, and outer ring B, to the start magnet, E. The start magnet causes the armature of the receiver to rotate counterclockwise at the same speed as that of the receiver.

When the receiver armature is over contact **3**, current will again flow on the line. Receiver relay, D, will again move to the position shown in the figure, and so as the armature of the receiver passes over the **3** contact on the outer ring, current will flow to the select magnet **3**. Similarly, select magnet **5** will be operated. These will cause the letter **H** to be selected on the type mechanism of the receiver. When the sender armature reaches its **STOP** contact, the receiver armature will pass over the contact, **F**, and current will flow to the print magnet. The letter **H** will be printed. Both armatures will then come to rest in the position shown in the figure, unless the sender is ready to transmit another character immediately.

There are several variations of this basic operation principle, but the

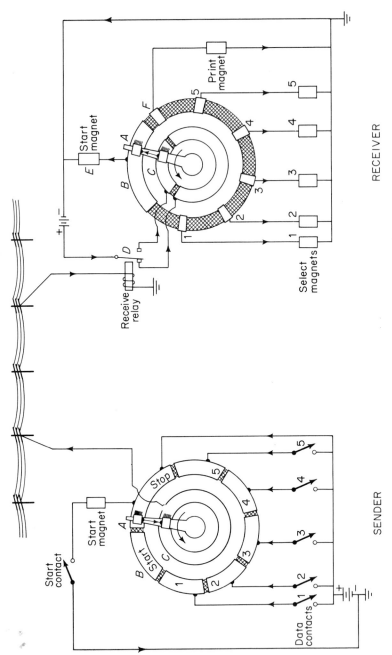

Fig. 6.6. The principle of start-stop telegraph equipment.

116

speeds and timing have become standardized. This means that a variety of different telegraphy machines can communicate with one another. A computer can send data to a telegraph machine by sending pulses with the same timing as the sender in Fig. 6.6.

Teletype speeds in common use are listed below. Such speeds are often quoted in "words per minute." An average teletype word is considered to be five characters long. As there is a space character between words, there are, then, six characters per word, and x words per minute $= 10x$ characters per second.

Speed in Bauds (bits per second)	Number of Bits in Character	STOP Bit Duration (in bits)	Information Bit Duration	Characters per Second	Words per Minute (nominal)
45.5	7.42	1.42	21.97	6.13	60
50	7.42	1.42	20	6.74	66
50	7.50	1.50	20	6.67	66
74.2	7.42	1.42	13.48	10	100
75	7.50	1.50	13.33	10	100
75	10	1.00	13.33	7.5	75
75	11	2.00	13.33	6.82	68
150	10	1.00	6.67	15	150

Figures 6.8 to 6.10 show typical start-stop instruments. Paper tape such as that in Fig. 6.7 is very widely used in telegraphy. Some teleprinters have a paper-tape punch and reader attached to them. In operating a teleprinter for conversing with a distant time-sharing computer, a program may be typed in a language such as BASIC. At the first attempt this will probably contain errors. The program can be debugged at the teleprinter, and then, when correct, the computer can be requested to punch it into tape at the teleprinter. The operator then has a correct version of the program which he can use next time.

A considerable amount of distortion can occur in the length and positioning of the start-stop pulses without the receiver misinterpreting them. As will

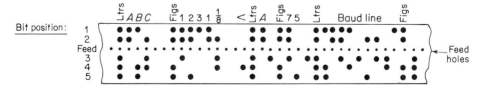

Fig. 6.7. Five-channel paper tape illustrating the use of figures and letters shift in Baudot code.

Fig. 6.8. British General Post Office teleprinter No. 15 for operation over 50-baud telegraph or telex lines (66 words per minute), using Baudot code (Fig. 6.2). *Courtesy of H. M. Postmaster General, England.*

be seen on Fig. 6.6 the contacts **1, 2, 3, 4, 5,** and **F** on the receiver are much narrower than their counterparts on the sender. The sender's pulse can therefore become shortened or lengthened, or it can be late or early, by an amount somewhat less than half the pulse width, and the receiver will still interpret it correctly. Of course, if it is delayed by one pulse width then it will be wrongly interpreted. However, the margin for distortion that does exist is useful because, as we will see later, pulses do become shortened, lengthened, or delayed slightly if the equipment on the line is not in perfect adjustment.

Fig. 6.9. A.T.&T. No. 33 ASR teletypewriter station, operating at 100 words per minute. It can transmit directly from keyboard or paper tape. It receives either by page printing or punching paper tape. Tape can be punched from the keyboard for transmission later. It uses the U.S. ASCII code (Fig. 6.3). *Courtesy of A.T.&T.*

Fig. 6.10. A.T.&T. No. 37 KSR teletypewriter for operation on 150-baud lines (150 words per minute). It uses the U.S. ASCII code (Fig. 6.3) with an eighth bit for parity checking. *Courtesy of A.T.&T.*

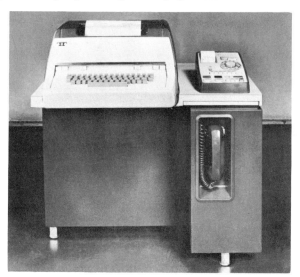

RELAY OPERATION

The relatively small current received on a teletype line can be used to operate a *relay* such as relay, D, in Fig. 6.3. This is an electromagnetic device by means of which a small current can cause a circuit to be opened or closed. The small received current can thus cause a larger current to flow.

Figure 6.11 illustrates the essential parts of a relay. This consists of a soft iron core with electrical winding around it. One end of the core is enlarged and is close to a soft iron armature which is pivoted as shown. When a small current flows in the winding, the core is magnetized and attracts the armature. The other end of the armature pushes together the contacts shown. These contacts form a switch which permits a larger current to flow through the wires attached to them. When the original current ceases, the armature is released; the springs separate the contacts, and the circuit thus becomes open again.

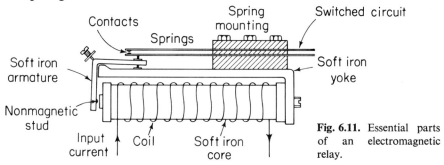

Fig. 6.11. Essential parts of an electromagnetic relay.

The magnetic material of the armature does not quite touch the core. It is kept apart from it by a small nonmagnetic stud as shown. This is designed to ensure that when the initial current ends, the armature will, in fact, move away and not be held by the slight residual magnetism. The contacts on the springs are made of a material of high electrical conductivity and resistance to corrosion. This ensures, better than would the metal of the springs themselves, that contact will be made and broken cleanly. Many relays have more than one set of contacts, so that many circuits can be opened or closed at the same time. When the relay operates, some of its contacts may be closed, others opened.

Electromagnetic relays such as that in Fig. 6.11 are the most common type of telephone relay. Other types with greater reliability are being used increasingly in applications such as line switching. These include "mercury-wetted" relays in which the contacts are encapsulated in glass which tilts so that a globule of mercury can ensure that electric contact is made. In electronic exchanges, a "reed relay" is being used. A typical form of this is sketched in Fig. 6.12. Here the contacts are two magnetic reeds sealed in a glass tube and so free from external influences such as dust, grease, and corrosive atmospheres. The mating surfaces are plated with gold, silver, or some other metal or

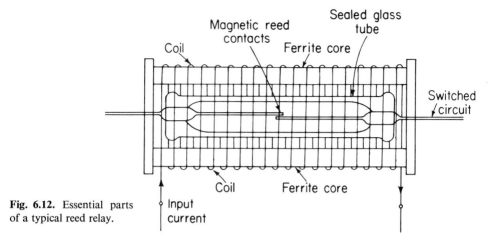

Fig. 6.12. Essential parts of a typical reed relay.

Labels in figure: Coil, Magnetic reed contacts, Sealed glass tube, Ferrite core, Switched circuit, Input current, Coil, Ferrite core

alloy which enables good contact and no sticking. The winding which moves the contacts magnetically together or apart is outside the glass on a ferrite core.

TELEGRAPH REPEATERS

The signals traveling down the telegraph lines become weaker the further they are transmitted, and as will be discussed in the next chapter, become increasingly distorted. The signal needs to be amplified at intervals as it travels down the line. In some cases, it is not only amplified but also reshaped. If it travels too far without being amplified and reshaped, it will fail to operate the machinery at the receiving end correctly. On modern circuits, electronic amplifiers (discussed in Chapter 9) are used to "repeat" the signal at intervals down the line. Before electronic circuits came into use, the relay was employed for this.

Figure 6.13 illustrates a line on which two relay repeaters are used. At each of these locations there is a source of direct current: a bank of storage batteries. The weak signal received operates a relay, and this switches the current from the batteries onto the next line segment. In this way a new square-edged set of pulses is retransmitted by each relay.

The relay converts the misshapen pulses it receives into new square-edged pulses. It thus corrects much of the shape distortion but does not correct time distortion. Each pulse relayed will be delayed slightly, in a manner that will be made clearer in the next chapter. A relay which is not perfectly adjusted may shorten or lengthen pulses. When a negative voltage changes to a positive voltage, this change may be always 8 milliseconds late, for example; and when positive voltage changes to a negative, this may be always 4 milliseconds late. The result is that the positive pulses are all 4 milliseconds too short, and the negative ones 4 milliseconds too long. This in itself will do no harm, as the "receive contacts" in Fig. 6.6 are shorter than the "send contacts." However, other factors can also cause this "bias" distortion. An accumulation of such distortions may cause error.

121

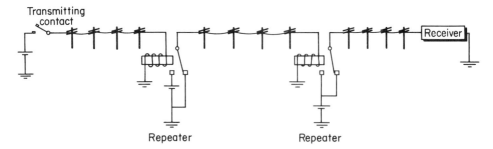

Fig. 6.13. The principle of relay repeaters.

Because the timing error is passed on, cumulatively, by relay repeaters, longer telegraph links were constructed with another form of electromechanical repeater which used some form of timing mechanism to regenerate correctly timed pulses. A constant speed motor drives a cam or a rotating brush contact to generate exactly timed pulses, which are either sent or not, depending upon whether the input is an on or off pulse.

This type of regenerative repeater (commonly called a "regen") is *speed and code sensitive*. It is designed to operate with standard telegraph codes and speeds. If a code is sent which does not have five data bits, an equal length START bit, and a STOP bit of the requisite length, it will not be transmitted correctly. Similarly transmission at speeds other than that of the repeater will not be possible. Such equipment will cause a problem when it is desirable to use a line for transmission of data from machines which do not use standard telegraph codes, as is true with many of the common low-speed data-processing devices. The repeaters on most of today's telegraph links are not code and speed sensitive; those regenerative repeaters still exist on some lines, especially outside the United States and Canada. Devices in central offices exist which convert code and speed during transmission.

The electromechanical devices had one advantage that the amplifier did not have. They could reconstruct the shape of the pulses and hence eliminate at least some of the effects of noise and distortion. The amplifier merely amplifies the noise. Later in the book, when we talk about pulse-code modulation, we will see this advantage return.

TELEGRAPH
CIRCUITS

At one time most telegraph circuits were carried on overhead wires like those seen in the Western movies. In Wall Street the sky used to be filled with overhead wires. As the number of circuits grew, underground wires were used for long distance links. Later it became common to send telephone and telegraph signals over the same path. When telephony grew up it soon outgrew telegraphy, and when there were many more telephone circuits than telegraph it became economic to send the telegraph signals over telephone links. Today this trend has gone much further and many telegraph signals can travel together over one path, being manipulated by all of the complex electronics that are part of today's telephone plant. The simple electromagnetic repeaters have been largely replaced by the amplifiers and modulation and multiplexing equipment described in the following chapters.

A circuit designed for telegraph (not telephone) often had only a single wire spanning the distance. This is called an earth-return circuit. As in the diagrams in Fig. 6.1, each end of the line was connected to earth and this completed the circuit. One pole of the power supply at each station was connected to earth. This was done by making a connection to the protective lead sheaths of underground signal cables, or to a metal main water pipe, or by burying plates, lead strips or driving spikes into the earth. The resistance of such an earth-return path is very small.

Other telegraph circuits were obtained as a byproduct of telephone circuits. Telegraph signals may be sent down any two telephone channels by a process called "superposing." Each telephone channel ends on a transformer winding. The midpoints of these windings were taken and used as an extra pair of wires down which telegraph signals could be sent without either interfering with the telephone signals, or the telephone signals interfering with the telegraph. The extra circuit obtained this way was called a "phantom circuit."

Over a single wire it was common to use equipment which could not transmit in both directions at the same time. The signals would travel either east to west or west to east. With double-current signaling, relays could be used to separate the east-to-west and west-to-east signals. This was referred to as "simplex" transmission in England, and "half duplex" in America. A more ingenious arrangement of relays would permit "full duplex" operation, i.e., transmission in both directions at the same time.

**DUPLEX,
QUADRUPLEX, AND
MULTIPLEX SYSTEMS**
It was realized early in the history of telegraphy that the capacity of telegraph lines was such that more than one signal could be sent over one line if a method could be devised for packing together the input bits and then sorting them out at the receiving end. The possible speed of the line, in other words, could be considerably higher than the rate of 50 bits per second, or thereabouts, at which the teleprinters operated. The term "diplex working" was used to mean the sending of two signals together over one common circuit.

One of the first techniques for doing this used four signal levels instead of the two levels shown in Fig. 6.1. Two relays were used in the detection of these. One relay was operated by small currents and the low amplitude double-current signals caused it to work. The other was unaffected by the low currents and came into operation only on receipt of the high-amplitude double-current signal. The combination of their operation was used to separate the two signals.

The lines, however, were still not filled to capacity. It was not practical to extend the preceding principle to four or more simultaneous signals because the relays were not sensitive enough to separate the signal levels, and so the "multiplex" system illustrated in principle in Fig. 6.14 was used. A system using this principle was constructed by Baudot and a similar one by Edison. The armatures shown on the sending and the receiving devices rotate at the same speed. The sending armature, in effect, samples the four input signals, sending the samples down the line one after another. The receiving armature, being exactly in synchronization, separates them onto the four output circuits. The devices in Fig. 6.14 are called "distributors." On a more common type of Baudot distributor, 20 segments are used for sending four five-bit signals, with four more segments for maintaining synchronization. As with other telecommunications devices discussed later in the book, the success of this system depends upon maintaining accurately the synchronization between the two armatures. This was done by deliberately running one of the distributors slightly faster than the other and correcting it once per revolution on receipt of a synchronizing pulse.

Today, electronic repeaters and multiplexers are used on telegraph lines. Telegraph signals are commonly sent over the *telephone* lines with electronic

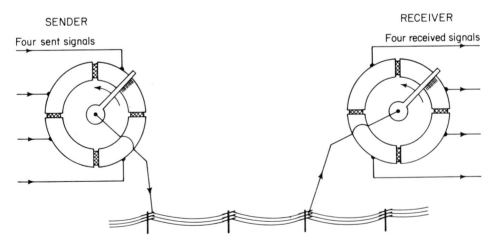

SENDER

Four sent signals

RECEIVER

Four received signals

Fig. 6.14. The principle of quadruplex telegraph transmission.

multiplexing equipment so that several (usually 12 or 24) telegraph signals can be sent simultaneously over one voice line as is described in later chapters. They are spaced sufficiently close for overall distortion to be low. Long-distance telegraph circuits in the United States and Europe always use the voice lines in this way. Regenerative repeaters are found where a multiplicity of connections between segments of telegraph lines increases the noise and distortion to an unsuitable level.

Each interconnecting link of a network is assigned a circuit coefficient indicating the expected level of distortion. When the sum of these coefficients reaches ten, a regenerative repeater is inserted. This figure corresponds to an error rate of about one character error in 44,000. The implications of this and other error rates found in data transmission are discussed in later chapters.

7 DC SIGNALING

There are two ways in which signals are sent down a communication line. They may be sent as they are, without modification, or they may be superimposed upon a higher frequency waveform which "carries" them. This chapter is concerned with the former, in which the current on the line contains relatively low-frequency components. The transmission of signals at their originating frequencies is sometimes called "baseband" signaling to differentiate it from the carrier frequency transmission discussed in the following chapters.

The main telecommunication "highways" which used to carry baseband signals over long distances now use higher frequency carrier transmission. Links from individual locations carrying the human voice to these highways use voice-band signaling. In less densely populated or underdeveloped areas the voice-band links may be many miles, or hundreds of miles, in length.

In this chapter we will discuss the relatively simple links in which baseband pulses travel along wires in the form shown in Fig. 6.1; in other words, direct current (DC) signaling. The wires may be open overhead wires hanging from the insulators on the cross arms of telegraph poles, or they may be inside a thicker cable, grouped with many other wires. They may be wires laid down privately within a factory or laboratory.

As the squared-edged pulses travel along the communication line they are distorted by the line. The pulses received at the other end are far from square edged, and if the line is too long, the signals too weak, or the transmitting speed too great, the received signal may be unrecognizable and wrongly interpreted by the machine at the other end. The factors that cause this distortion in direct-current signaling will still be at work with the more sophisticated alternating-current signaling, dealt with later.

The factors mainly responsible for the distortion are the *capacitance*,

126

Fig. 7.1. Some time-sharing computer systems have large numbers of data sets (modems) on lines to the users' terminals. It is possible to avoid this expense in some cases where the terminals are in the same locality by designing the line control with DC signaling. *Photo by author.*

inductance, and *leakage* associated with the line used for transmission. There are other factors such as the noise impulses that interfere with signaling, but these will be discussed in later chapters. There is one advantage to sending signals in a DC form as in Fig. 6.1: it is simple and inexpensive. If the signals from a data-processing machine are converted to an AC form in which they are "carried" by higher frequencies, this needs a device called a modem or data set (Chapters 10 and 13) at each end of the line to convert the signals to AC form and then convert them back again after transmission. Such a device for low-speed transmission typically costs about $20 to $40 monthly rental. A time-sharing system with 500 low-speed terminals (only a few of which are in use at any one time) would be likely to pay, then, about $20,000 to $40,000 per month for modems. Figure 7.1 shows a rack of such modems for a typical time-sharing system. If DC signaling were used, this cost could be avoided.

It is possible to send DC signals over wire pairs of a few miles in length at speeds of up to 300 bits per second. The distortion of the signals makes it impractical to send data in this form at speeds much higher than 300 bits per second, except over very short distances. This, however, is a useful speed for many computer applications. The speed could be increased enormously by using small coaxial cables rather than wire pairs or by having a regenerative repeater every thousand feet or so on a wire pair. In many systems a large number of typewriter-speed terminals within a localized area, say three miles across, could be connected to a time-sharing system or to a concentrator without modems. While today most common carrier lines require modems, it is possible that the wire pairs which connect to all locations with a telephone could be used over a limited area for DC signaling as in the earlier days of telegraphy. A low-cost exchange for data signals used in this way has been developed.

LINE CAPACITANCE   Let us first discuss the capacitance of the line. This is the main cause of distortion. As we raise the voltage at one end of the line there is some delay before the voltage at the other end rises by an equivalent amount. The cable acts rather like a water hose. Because of its "capacity," when electricity is applied at one end, a certain amount is needed to fill it up before the result is detectable at the other end. Let us suppose that a short section of line may be represented by the resistance, R, and electrical capacity, C, in Fig. 7.2.

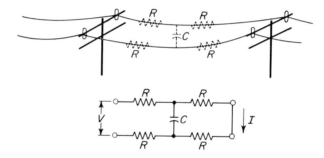

Figure 7.2

As is shown in the elementary electricity books, when a battery of voltage V is connected across a capacitor of capacity, C, and resistance, R, the current, I, flows until the condensor is fully charged. It starts at a high value, momentarily ($I = V/R$) and falls until it approaches zero, at which time the capacitor is fully charged.

The equation for the current at a time, t, after the voltage was applied is

$$I = \frac{V}{R} e^{-t/RC}$$

Similarly, the current, I, received in Fig. 7.2, is

$$I = \frac{V}{R} (1 - e^{-t/RC})$$

If the voltage at the sending end is now suddenly replaced by a short circuit, the current at the receiving end does not cease instantly, but dies slowly because of the discharge of the capacitance. The equation for the falling current is

$$I = \frac{V}{R} e^{-t/RC}$$

Time Constant

This buildup and decay of current is shown in Fig. 7.3. The square-edged pulse transmitted is nothing like square edged when it is received at the other end.

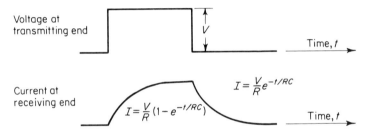

Fig. 7.3. Distortion of a DC pulse due to line capacitance.

The constant RC in the preceding equations is referred to as the time constant of the circuit, and is a measure of the time taken for the current to build up to $(1 - 1/e) = 0.6321$ of its final value, or to decay to $1/e = 0.3679$ of its original value. The time of buildup or decay on these levels is thus proportional to both the resistance and capacitance of the line.

Where the transmission line consists of an open pair of wires hanging from telegraph poles, the capacitance in question is between these two conductors separated by several inches of air. As in the case of an ordinary electrical capacitor, the capacitance is larger if the size of the conductors is larger, and also when the distance between the conductors is smaller. If the wires are in a cable, as is now often the case, the capacitance will be much greater because the wires are closer together and the insulating material has a higher dielectric constant than air. When the first submarine cables were laid in the sea they had a much poorer performance than was anticipated because the presence of seawater increased the effective capacitance of the cable.

The preceding illustration is, of course, grossly oversimplified. However, it serves to illustrate the point that if the pulses representing data are too short in duration, if there are too many pulses sent per second, then the pulses become indistinguishable when they are received, as illustrated in Fig. 7.4.

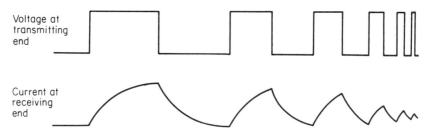

Fig. 7.4. The effect of capacitance in the communication line. The faster the pulse rate, the more difficult it becomes to interpret the received signal.

In practice, there will be resistance across the receiving end, such as the resistance of the relays or electromagnets of the receiving equipment. The transmitting end will also have some resistance. Both of these increase the time constant.

LINE INDUCTANCE   In addition to capacitance and resistance, there is also inductance associated with the line, although this is generally of less importance than the capacitance.

Inductance in a circuit resists the sudden buildup of current. Current in an inductive circuit produces a magnetic field. A coil of wire in a circuit is an inductance; it is a much stronger inductance if it surrounds magnetic material. Large inductances which form part of electronic circuits are constructed by wrapping many thousands of turns of fine wire around a heavy, laminated, highly magnetic core.

When a battery of voltage, V, is applied across a circuit with resistance, R, and inductance, L, the current grows as shown in the equation:

$$I = \frac{V}{R}(1 - e^{-(R/L)t})$$

When the battery is replaced by a short circuit the current does not cease immediately, but dies away slowly as the magnetic field built up by the current collapses. The energy stored in the magnetic field is dissipated in the circuit. The current falls as shown in the equation

$$I = \frac{V}{R}e^{-(R/L)t}$$

The time constant here is L/R.

The reader might think of the communication line as being something like a fireman's hose. Suppose that the fireman wishes to send data down his hose. (He is not really a fireman, but an espionage agent who has an accomplice inside the building which the hose goes into.) He attempts to send the data by means of a piston. As he pushes and pulls the piston at one end of the hose, the pulses are transmitted to a receiving piston at the other end. If the hose were absolutely rigid and the water in it absolutely incompressible, the movement of the receiving piston would follow the movement of the transmitting piston exactly. Again, if the water had no viscosity and moved completely without friction, the piston would be able to transmit at a very high speed. However, the hose is not rigid. It is slightly elastic and the water with air bubbles in the hose is slightly compressible, so the receiving piston does not follow the movement of the transmitting piston exactly. Furthermore, there is viscosity and friction; therefore the piston cannot move and transmit at limitless speed. These properties are very loosely analogous to the capacitance and inductance of a communication line.

If our James Bond fireman were to attempt to transmit at a fairly slow speed, say one pulse every five seconds, the receiving piston would follow the movement of the transmitting piston faithfully enough to recognize each pulse. As he increased his transmission speed, however, the signal distortion would become greater. If he were to transmit at two pulses per second his accomplice might be able to receive this correctly. At ten pulses per second it would need sensitive and sophisticated receiving equipment to detect the pulses without error. On a communication line, the natural capacitance and inductance of the line would have a more serious effect, the higher the frequency of transmission. The longer the line, the worse the effect. In addition, there is noise of the line. Suppose that the fire hose is vibrating due to the motion of the pump nearby. At high-transmission speeds the strength of the received pulses becomes comparable in magnitude with this "noise," and errors in the interpretation of the data will occur.

ARRIVAL CURVE   The properties of a given DC telegraph line are somewhat more complex than would be suggested by the preceding simple equations, and the transient effects of resistance, capacitance, inductance, and also leakage from the line due to not quite perfect insulation, may be summarized in an "arrival curve." Such a curve is illustrated in Fig. 7.5.

This shows the growth of current at the receiving end of a line when a steady voltage is suddenly applied across the transmitting end. The right-hand side of the diagram shows the decay of current when the voltage is then suddenly removed. There is an interval between the switching on of the voltage and the start of the current growth at the other end. This is

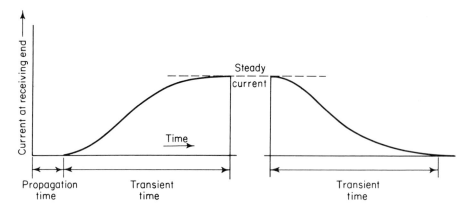

Fig. 7.5. Arrival curve for a typical telegraph line (unloaded).

referred to as the propagation time, and is in effect the time the signal takes to pass down the line. The periods during which the current is building up, or decaying, are called the "transient times." From the shape of the arrival curve for a particular line, its response to any voltage change may be evaluated. The exact shape of the arrival curve is difficult to calculate theoretically for a particular line but may be measured experimentally. It can be recorded with an oscillograph.

Knowing the shape of the arrival curve for a given line, the distortion that a bit pattern will suffer may be plotted, by adding and subtracting the arrival curve for the various input voltage changes. This is done in Fig. 7.6. The resulting current at the receiving end may be used to operate a relay. The threshold current for relay opening and closing is the dotted line through the curve of received current in Fig. 7.6. When the current is greater than this, the relay closes, thus reconstructing a sharp voltage change equivalent to the input.

If the bit rate transmitted were twice as great as that in Fig. 7.6, it would not be possible to set a threshold level for relay operation that would give the resulting correct bit pattern. The input pulse duration would be too small relative to the transient time of the line.

This was a condition which prevented the correct operation of some of the early submarine cables. The first cable from England to France was laid in 1850 after some difficulty. A receiving device was connected to it by an excited group on the French coast, and a message was sent from the founder of the cable-laying company to Prince Louis Napoleon Bonaparte. The transient time of the cable in water was greater than had been anticipated, however, and to the group's bewilderment the receiver produced gibberish. Before the

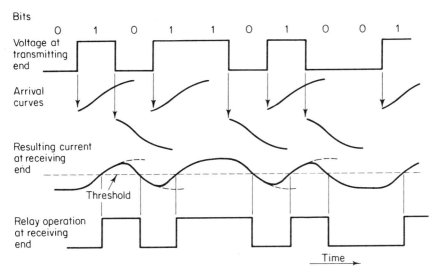

Fig. 7.6. Transmission over a telegraph line. The received current operates a relay which reforms the original bit pattern. If the transmission rate over the same line were doubled, the relay at the receiving end would not correctly reconstruct the bit pattern.

reason for the trouble was discovered moreover, a fisherman's anchor pulled on the line, and he hauled it aboard his ship in astonishment and cut out a section to show his friends!

**KELVIN'S
LAW**
The transient time is affected mainly by the capacitance, resistance, and length of the line.

In 1855 Kelvin produced a famous law of telegraphy saying that for a line of negligible inductance and leakage, and negligible terminal impedances, the maximum operating speed is inversely proportional to CRl^2, where C is the capacitance per unit length, R is the resistance per unit length, and l is the length.

To transmit at a given rate, therefore, a given line must not exceed a certain length. If it is desired to transmit over a distance greater than this, a repeater must be inserted in the line.

Any device which reconstructs and retransmits a teletype or other data signal is called a *regenerative repeater*. This is true of modern electronic circuits, as well as of the older relay circuits. A repeater which is not regenerative simply amplifies the signal and corrects certain types of distortion that have occurred, but does not reconstruct a new, sharp-edged pulse train.

BIAS
DISTORTION

Because of the shape of the arrival curve, distortion can occur in the length of the bits received. This is illustrated in Fig. 7.7. As a "mark" changes to a "space" there will be a slight delay in the falling off of the received voltage, and so the receiving machine will begin its "space" slightly late. Similarly the buildup of voltage when a "space" changes to a "mark" will not be instantaneous, and so the receiving machine will begin its "mark" slightly late. Let us suppose that the sampling threshold of the receiving circuit is set slightly too high. As shown in Fig. 7.7 this will cause the space-to-mark transition to be slightly later than the mark-to-space transition. Hence the received spaces will be longer than the marks. Similarly if the threshold is set too low, the marks will be elongated at the expense of the spaces.

This effect will be greater the higher the transmission speed and the higher the value of (CRl^2). It may also become bad when there are several telegraph

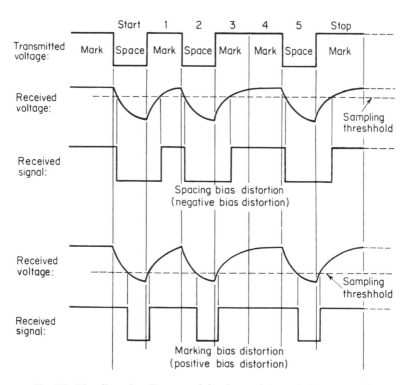

Fig. 7.7. Bias distortion. Because of the shape of the arrival curve, an ill-adjusted receiver threshold can cause "bias distortion." Either the marks (1 bits) become elongated and the spaces (0 bits) shortened or vice versa.

links in tandem. If the bias distortion becomes too bad, this will result in the incorrect reception of data.

LOADING   The losses of the type described are much higher in cable circuits than in open-wire lines because the capacitance is greater. There are a number of ways of reducing CR, and hence reducing the loss. The resistance can be decreased by using larger cable conductors. The capacitance can be decreased by increasing the separation of the conductors. Both of these approaches are used on wires strung between telegraph poles, but there is a practical limit as to how far apart the wires can be, and how heavy or expensive they can be. In cables, enlarging the conductor or the spacing between conductors decreases the number of separate circuits that can be carried in one cable, and so again there is a limit to what can be done.

Heaviside in 1887 proved that the distortion can be minimized by causing the relationship between the inductance and capacitance of the line to satisfy the equation:

$$RC = LG$$

where L is the inductance per unit length,

R is the resistance per unit length,

C is the capacitance per unit length,

and G is the shunt conductance per unit length, sometimes known as the leakance, a measure of the leakage between conductors on the line.

RC has already been made as small as possible, but it is still large compared with LG on a conventional telegraph or telephone line. The inductance and leakage are both very small. It is undesirable to increase the leakage of the line as this would diminish the signal; therefore, to satisfy the equation $RC = LG$, the inductance is increased.

The first important application of Heaviside's work was to submarine cables. These had no repeaters and so distortion was a severe problem. To increase their inductance, iron wire was wound around their core. At a later date, materials with better magnetic properties were discovered, and today more modern cables have a thin permalloy or mumetal tape wrapped helically around the conducting core. This has a high magnetic permeability. By this means, cable-transmission speeds can generally be increased by a factor of four. Some of the early cable designs were speeded up eight or ten times.

Adding inductance to a cable is referred to as "loading" it. Wrapping magnetic tapes or wires around a cable is too expensive for most purposes, and it is found satisfactory to insert loading coils at intervals along the cable. The inductance of, and the distance between, loading coils are chosen to minimize the distortion on the line and so permit high-speed transmission over it. Often the loading coil consists of a ring of powdered permalloy of high magnetic permeability wrapped around with copper wire. Such coils may be fitted at intervals of a mile or so on cable circuits. Open-wire pairs are never normally loaded because their capacitance is much smaller, and because their characteristics tend to change with adverse weather conditions.

Loading will be discussed again in connection with alternating current (AC) circuits which carry a much higher data rate than those discussed in this chapter. If the reader would like to steal a glimpse ahead to Fig. 9.12, he will see how the attenuation constant of an unloaded line varies with frequency. Loading can make the attenuation almost constant over a limited but usable range of frequencies, as shown. Figure 9.11 shows some typical loading coils on telephone lines.

In general, for both AC and DC circuits, a lessening of distortion on the line means that a higher transmission rate can be achieved, and likelihood of errors is less.

8 AC TRANSMISSION MEDIA

As we saw in Chapter 1, during the last hundred years a series of inventions have enabled telecommunication links to be built with ever increasing capacity. The early telegraph links carried signals at speeds up to about 30 words per minute, or about 15 bits per second. Now we are laying down cables which carry many thousands of voice channels, each with a capacity of over 5000 bits per second (with sufficiently good modems).

The ability to combine several channels in one physical link came into operation in 1874 with a scheme produced by Baudot, which permitted six users to transmit simultaneously over a single line—a dramatic improvement giving speeds up to about 90 bits per second.

In 1876, Alexander Graham Bell spoke the first sentence over his new invention, the telephone. In the years to follow, telephone lines, switchboards, and later automatic exchanges were built. "Loading," discussed in the previous chapter, was applied to telephone lines in 1899. Prior to this the longest commercial line stretched from New York to Chicago. By 1911, it was possible to speak from New York as far as Denver, a distance which today seems an amazing achievement when one realizes that amplifiers had not been invented.

In 1913, a great step forward was made when the vacuum tube repeater was first used. A coast-to-coast service with such tubes was operating in the United States by 1915. The development of electronics followed fast, and by 1918, the first *carrier* system was in use, enabling several voice channels to be sent over a single pair of wires. The number of voice channels that can be sent over a single cable has steadily increased through the years. Coaxial cables replaced wire-pair cables for high-capacity links, and today these carry thousands of telephone channels.

In 1897, Marconi formed the Wireless Telegraph and Signal Company.

In 1899, he succeeded in sending radio messages across the English Channel and in 1901, across the Atlantic. Lodge developed means of radio tuning. Radio telegraphy grew fast.

In 1902, Fessenden developed a system for modulating radio frequencies by the human voice, but radio telephony on a commercial scale awaited the coming of vacuum tube amplifiers and modulators. The first commercial radio stations were installed to connect two land telephone networks in 1920, between Santa Catalina Island, off California, and the mainland. By 1927 telephones in Europe and the United States were linked commercially.

Microwave radio links began to be installed after the war, and today have become a major feature of telephone systems. Towers, large and small, with a collection of microwave antennas, have sprung up in cities and across the countryside. The chains of microwave relays, which now span the industrialized countries of the world, carry up to 11,000 telephone channels, and will probably carry more in the future.

The 1960's brought satellites, lasers, and high-speed waveguides, all of which are taking their place in today's telecommunication picture. Long-distance communication links are fast growing in capacity. As the number of circuits carried by a link increases, the cost per circuit falls. The Bell Laboratories helical waveguide system, already working but not yet commercially installed, can carry as many as 200,000 voice channels.

In a hundred years, the capacity of communication systems, taking the equivalent number of bits per second, has risen from 15 to about a billion (10^9).

This chapter discusses the various types of physical transmission media that are in use. Subsequent chapters will describe in more detail how they are used for voice, television, and other signals, and what is involved in sending data over them.

The media will be contrasted by discussing the frequency at which signals are sent over them. Microwave links, for example, operate at a very high frequency, coaxial cables at a lower frequency, and wire pairs still lower. We are all familiar with the frequencies on the dial of a domestic radio. Stations on the FM band are picked up at between about 88 and 108 megacycles. (Stations of the AM broadcasting band in the United States are between 500 and 1600 kilocycles. These frequencies, along with the frequencies at which other media operate, are shown in Fig. 8.1. This is a small part of the total electromagnetic spectrum that was shown in Fig. 1.2.)

The word "hertz" has now come into common usage to mean "cycles per second." "Kilocycles per second" becomes "kilohertz," "one million cycles per second" (often written simply "megacycles") becomes "megahertz," and so on. "Hertz" and "cycles per second" are found interchangeably in the literature, the latter being retained, often, because it is self-explanatory.

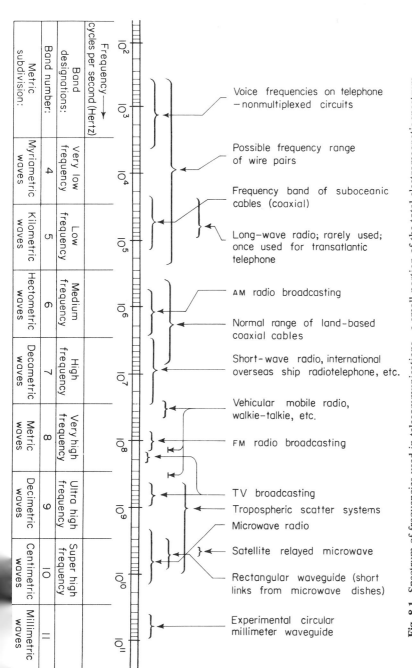

Fig. 8.1. Spectrum of frequencies used in telecommunications—a small portion of the total electromagnetic spectrum shown in Fig. 1.2. Note: the allocation of radio frequencies to different uses is much more complicated than on this chart which has been simplified to show the main categories discussed in this book.

The chart labels (top to bottom as marked on the frequency scale):

- Voice frequencies on telephone —nonmultiplexed circuits
- Possible frequency range of wire pairs
- Frequency band of suboceanic cables (coaxial)
- Long—wave radio; rarely used; once used for transatlantic telephone
- AM radio broadcasting
- Normal range of land-based coaxial cables
- Short-wave radio, international overseas ship radiotelephone, etc.
- Vehicular mobile radio, walkie-talkie, etc.
- FM radio broadcasting
- TV broadcasting
- Tropospheric scatter systems
- Microwave radio
- Satellite relayed microwave
- Rectangular waveguide (short links from microwave dishes)
- Experimental circular millimeter waveguide

Frequency—→ cycles per second (Hertz)	10^2	10^3	10^4	10^5	10^6	10^7	10^8	10^9	10^{10}	10^{11}
Band designations:		Very low frequency	Low frequency	Medium frequency	High frequency	Very high frequency	Ultra high frequency	Super high frequency		
Band number:		4	5	6	7	8	9	10	11	
Metric subdivision:		Myriametric waves	Kilometric waves	Hectometric waves	Decametric waves	Metric waves	Decimetric waves	Centimetric waves	Millimetric waves	

What is going to be of particular interest to us is not absolute frequency of operation, but the range of frequencies which can be sent over the facility. As will be discussed in Chapter 10, the quantity of data, or in general the amount of information that can be transmitted, is proportional to the bandwidth or *range* of frequencies that can be sent. On Fig. 8.1, the range of frequencies shown for microwave radio is much greater than that for FM broadcasting, for example. The former stretches from about 2000 to 12,000 megahertz, a range of 10,000 megahertz. The latter stretches from about 80 to 150 megahertz, a range of about 70 megahertz. Wire pairs transmit frequencies up to about 200 or 300 kilohertz normally. One could, then, transmit far more information over microwave than over the FM broadcasting frequencies, and far more over the latter than over wire pairs.

The following are the media of main interest today:

1. *Open-Wire Pairs*

In earlier years most telephone connections were made by means of wire

Fig. 8.2. This telephone pole crossbar was designed to carry open-wire pairs, two of which are shown. For convenience a group of twisted-wire pairs have been slung beneath the same bar. The twisted-wire pairs here have an amplifier and the open-wire pairs do not. Open-wire pairs transmit signals 30 miles or more without amplification. Twisted-wire pairs normally have amplifiers every 2 to 4 miles. *Photo by author.*

pairs stretched between telephone poles. The pairs of wires shown in Fig. 8.2 are suspended from insulators on the cross bars of the poles. The wires are copper, or steel coated with copper—steel for strength, copper for conductivity. At frequencies above 1000 cycles, most of the current flows on the outside "skin" of the wire, in the copper coating. The wires in a pair are about 0.128 inch in diameter, and spaced by about 8 to 12 inches.

A wire pair can carry telephone conversations a long way without amplification. It was on such wires, for example, that New York could speak to Denver before vacuum-tube amplifiers were invented. Today it is often desirable to send several voice channels together over the same pair of wires. This needs a higher frequency, and at higher frequencies the attenuation is greater. Therefore amplifiers are placed closer together in the line.

Wire pairs are susceptible to *cross talk*. Electromagnetic or inductive coupling produces interference, and a conversation on one pair could become faintly audible on the next. Large separation of the adjacent pairs and periodic reversal of the wires reduce this to an almost negligible level. Weather conditions affect the loss or *attenuation* on open-wire lines. Leakage occurs at the insulators when they are wet. The electrical resistance of the wires rises with temperature, and wet and humid conditions increase the attenuation.

Open-wire pairs have now largely been replaced by cables, but are still seen in rural districts and in less highly developed countries. They are fast becoming part of the romantic past and as such form the setting in songs like "Moonlight in Vermont."

2. *Wire-Pair Cables*

In the cable lines which have replaced open-wire pairs, the conductors are insulated, and brought close together. Many of them may be packed into one cable. This would tend to increase *cross talk* considerably. The conductors are twisted in pairs to minimize the electromagnetic interference between one pair and another. Different twist lengths are used for nearly pairs. The group of conductors is wrapped in a sheath of lead or aluminium. Cables laid in cities have many hundreds of wire pairs in one cable, as shown in Fig. 8.3. Figure 8.2 shows a smaller twisted wire-pair cable slung, for convenience, beneath the bars of telephone poles already carrying open-wire pairs. The wires in cables are much smaller than wires for open pairs. Short cables use wires about 0.015 inch in diameter. Longer cables use thicker wires up to about 0.056 inch. Because of this the resistance of the wires is higher, and the signal needs to be amplified more frequently than with open-wire pairs. The amplifiers, or "repeaters," are in manholes or attached to the poles carrying the cable at intervals along the cable route, commonly every three or four miles. Similar repeaters are used with open-wire pairs but these might be, say, 40 miles apart; less for some systems.

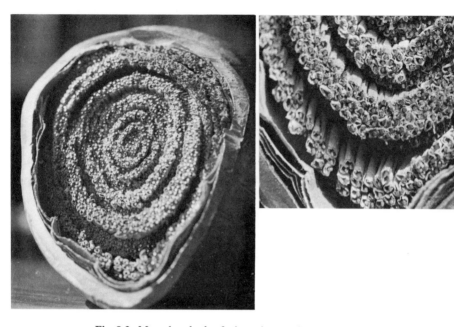

Fig. 8.3. Many hundreds of wire pairs may be grouped together in a lead-sheathed cable like this. Such cables are laid under the streets of cities, and take pairs of wires from subscribers' telephones to their local central office (exchange). *Photo by author.*

Twisted wire cable, as with the other media we will discuss, can carry more than one voice channel. The frequencies of the human voice are raised to higher frequencies. Different channels are raised by different amounts, and in this way the frequency range available (shown in Fig. 8.1) is filled. This is a form of *multiplexing*, called "frequency division multiplexing," and it is discussed further in later chapters. It is common for such cables to carry 12 or 24 voice channels simultaneously in two directions using frequencies up to about 268 kilohertz. Because of the desire to pack many channels into one cable, it is required that the cable should operate at the highest possible frequency. Unfortunately, however, the loss of signal strength, or "attenuation," becomes great at high frequencies. Figure 9.7 is an illustration of the different signal attenuation encountered at different frequencies.

Recent developments in repeater design permit frequencies of one megahertz to be transmitted over wire pairs. Such repeaters would be spaced at intervals of about one mile. This capability will permit Picturephone signals to be sent over wire pairs. Three wire pairs will be used for one Picturephone unit, one for vision in each direction and one for sound in both directions.

The *capacitance* between conductors is much greater in a cable pair than in open-wire lines, because the conductors are much closer together. This has a more serious effect at high frequencies than at low frequencies. For this reason, when multiplexing was first developed it was used only on open-wire lines. The capacitance of a cable could be reduced by increasing the separation between the wires, but this would increase the cost and substantially reduce the number of wires a cable could carry.

3. Coaxial Cable

As the frequencies become higher, the current flows more on the outside edge of the wire. It uses an increasingly small cross section of the wire, and so the effective resistance of the wire increases. This is called the "skin effect." Furthermore, at higher frequencies an increasing amount of energy is lost by radiation from the wire. Nevertheless, it is desirable to transmit at as high a frequency as possible so that as many separate signals as possible can be sent over the same cable. The skin effect limits the upper frequencies.

A coaxial cable can transmit much higher frequencies than a wire pair. It consists of a hollow copper cylinder, or other cylindrical conductor, surrounding a single wire conductor. The space between the cylindrical shell and the inner conductor is filled with an insulator. This may be plastic or may be air, with supports separating the shell and the inner conductor every inch or so. A coaxial cable is shown in Fig. 8.4.

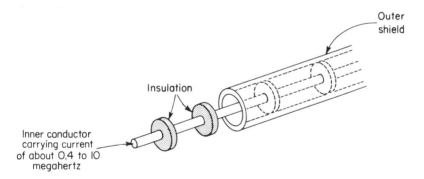

Fig. 8.4. Coaxial cable construction.

Several coaxial cables are often bound together in one large cable as in Figs. 8.5 and 15.2. At higher frequencies there is virtually no cross talk between the separate coaxial cables in such a link because the current tends to flow now on the inside of the outer shell, and the outside of the inner wire. Because of this shielding from noise and cross talk, the signal can be dropped to a lower level before amplification.

A very large number of separate telephone calls can be transmitted together down a coaxial cable system. Whereas a single-wire pair commonly carries 12 or 24 voice channels, one single coaxial cable commonly carries 1800, and the highest capacity ones carry 3600. A group of coaxials bound together in one cable as in Fig. 8.5 carries more than this. In a high-capacity link, 20 coaxials are bound together. Two of these are reserve links in case of failure. The remaining 18 could carry $9 \times 3600 = 32,400$ two-way voice conversations.

The main reason for this higher capacity is that the signal loss, or attenuation, does not

(A)

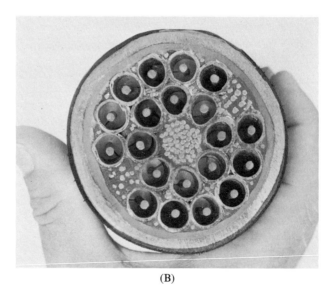

(B)

Fig. 8.5. A cable with 20 coaxial units, which can carry 18,740 telephone calls at once, or the equivalent in television signals or data. *Courtesy AT&T.*

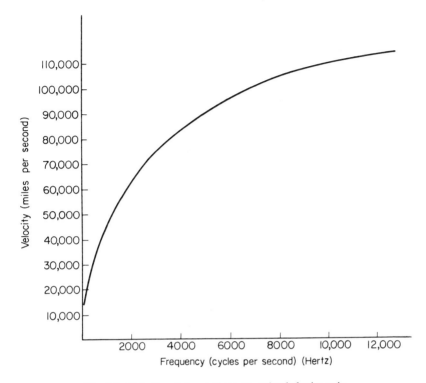

Fig. 8.6. Velocity of signal along an unloaded wire pair.

become severe until very high frequencies. Figure 9.8 illustrates this and should be compared with Fig. 9.7.

Furthermore, other forms of distortion are much less. On a wire pair carrying voice frequencies, the velocity of propagation of the signal varies widely with frequency. This is illustrated in Fig 8.6. The lower frequencies of the human voice will arrive later than the higher frequencies. The longer the line, the greater the delay will be, and so the greater the distortion will be. This is referred to as "delay distortion," and is further discussed in Chapter 12. It can have a more serious effect when the line is used for data rather than for voice. Coaxial cable circuits give a higher velocity of propagation which varies only very slightly with frequency, thus giving very little delay distortion. The propagation velocity along a coaxial cable at frequencies above about four kilohertz is approximately equal to the velocity of light, or if the space inside the conducting cylinder is filled with plastic, then to the velocity of electromagnetic waves in that material, which might be 25 to 45% lower than in air.

A *loaded* wire pair *gives* less distortion, but the transmission velocity is lower. It is normally about 10,000 to 20,000 miles per second at voice frequencies. The signal in a coaxial cable can thus travel at ten times the speed of an equivalent signal in a loaded voice-frequency wire pair. This is of value because, as will be discussed in the next chapter, it often removes the need for *echo suppressors*.

The additional expense of coaxial cables is justified by the following advantages; the first is by far the most important.

1. A *much* larger number of channels can be sent over one cable.
2. Negligible cross talk between cables.
3. Lower delay distortion and variation of amplitude with frequency.
4. Higher propagation speeds, which can remove the need for echo suppressors on many long lines, because the interval between the speech and its echo becomes very small.

Not surprisingly, many thousands of miles of coaxial cable links have been installed as intercity trunks throughout the world.

4. *Microwave Radio*

The main contender with coaxial cable circuits for bulk transmission is microwave radio. This medium has been used even more extensively than coaxial cable in recent years for the building of long-haul trunks. Like coaxial cable, microwave links today carry thousands of voice channels, and are in widespread use for the transmission of television.

Many cities of the world now have their skylines proudly dominated by a tower carrying microwave antennas. Tokyo has a tower like the Eiffel Tower, but 40 feet higher. East Berlin has one 1185 feet high. One of London's most expensive dinners can be eaten in a revolving restaurant just above the microwave antennas, and Moscow, outdoing the rest, has one 250 feet higher than the Empire State Building.

As can be seen from Fig. 8.1, microwave radio is at the high frequency end of the radio spectrum. Unlike long-wave radio, it is not reflected by the ionosphere, and its scattering by hills and other objects is less. It needs line-of-sight transmission and the antennas which relay it, forming chains across the country, are all on towers within sight of one another. Figure 8.8 shows typical microwave antennas in a city, and Fig. 8.7 shows a relay tower in the country. Relay towers are usually spaced about 30 miles apart. On a long-distance telephone conversation, or television transmission, the signal is picked up every 30 miles, amplified and retransmitted.

A long-distance microwave circuit has fewer amplifiers than a coaxial cable link of the same length. The microwave link has amplifiers at each relay point, in other words about 30 miles apart. The coaxial cable has amplifiers every 2 to 4 miles. A coaxial cable circuit coast-to-coast across the United States therefore has a thousand or so amplifiers. The equivalent microwave circuit has only 100. It is a disadvantage to have too many amplifiers because a slight defect in them may be cumulative. For television transmission, for example, the amplification needs to be held constant within narrow limits for parts of the signal at different frequencies. If it has to pass through 800 amplifiers with similar characteristics this means that each one of the 800 must be very exact indeed in this respect. This is difficult and expensive to engineer. Therefore, microwave links have come into wide use for television transmission. Fortunately, the television peak hours do not coincide with the peak usage of telephones, and so the same facility can be used by day for telephones. As will be seen in a later chapter, one television channel can carry 1200 telephone channels.

During the night hours these high-capacity links are underutilized.

Figure 8.8

Figure 8.7

Town & Country Microwave Relay Towers. London's GPO tower with a small, older tower on a building nearby; and an AT&T tower in New Mexico. Chains of microwave relays carrying television or several thousand telephone channels are today's main alternative to coaxial cable links for long-distance traffic. *Figure 8.7 courtesy of AT&T; Fig. 8.8 courtesy of IT&T.*

Furthermore, many computers stand idle on their third shift. As the night hours are at different times traveling east to west, it would make economic sense to link computers at different longitudes and fill some of the idle time on both the machine and the transmission facilities.

Unlike lower-frequency radio, microwave antennas are fixed rigidly in order to focus a beam of the narrowest angle possible on their distant associated antenna. It is common for a beam of about a 1° angle to be used, and a typical antenna size is about ten feet across. Microwave radio is scattered by hills and other objects. The beams from the antennas must clear trees and buildings, otherwise their reflections may cause echoes.

Different moisture and temperature layers can cause the beam to bend and vary in amplitude, just as we sometimes see light shimmering over a hot surface or causing minor mirages along a road surface in the sun. Occasionally these effects can cause fading. Rain can change the attenuation slightly, especially at the higher microwave frequencies, and occasionally trouble is caused by reflection from unanticipated objects such as helicopters or new skyscrapers in a city. To a limited extent automatic compensation for changes in the radio attenuation is built into the repeaters.

In addition to the long-haul trunks, many short microwave links of lower capacity are in use. The telephone companies find it convenient in some locations to use them as feeders to the main exchanges. Television companies use them for outside broadcasting. The army uses a portable microwave receiver–transmitter as a field telephone.

Privately owned microwave links have been set up by some corporations. The American Electric Power Service Corporation, for example, has more than a thousand path-miles of private microwave links used mainly for voice. Other corporations have set up shorter links. In some cases, they have been set up primarily for data where there was a large amount of data to transmit —as, for example, when part of a programming team is remote from the computer being used.

5. Satellites

A communication satellite provides a form of microwave relay. It is high in the sky and therefore can relay signals over long distances that would not be possible in a single link on Earth, because of the curvature of the Earth, mountains, and atmospheric conditions.

The first communication satellites were in relatively low-altitude orbits, and consequently speeded around the Earth in a few hours. This was bad because the ground antennas had to move constantly to beam signals to them, and they were only overhead for a brief period. Transatlantic television transmission was born, but was confined to five-minute sessions of Walter Cronkite or Richard Dimbleby. In 1965, the Early Bird satellite was launched into a

Fig. 8.9A. This 160-foot inflated dome in Raisting, Germany houses a 28-ton parabolic satellite antenna controlled by a computer-prepared magnetic tape. Microwave radio links connect the station to the German telephone and television networks. *Photograph from Communications Satellite Corporation.*

Fig. 8.9B. Inside a large dome at Andova, Maine, this horn antenna weighing 380 tons, built by AT&T, can communicate via satellite with stations such as that above. The 14-foot disk antenna seen perched on top of the horn is designed to send commands to transmitting equipment on the satellite. *Photograph from Communications Satellite Corporation.*

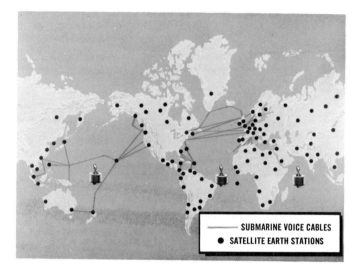

Fig. 8.10. Satellites and submarine cables in use in 1968. The first satellite had a capacity of 240 voice channels and cost $7 million. The 128-channel transatlantic cable cost $50 million. Submarine cables planned for the 1970's have 720 voice channels. However, satellites of the 1970's will have at least 100 times the 1968 capacity and will cost relatively little more to orbit. *Photograph from the Communications Satellite Corporation.*

much higher orbit (22,300 miles), so that it traveled around the Earth in 24 hours. This is very convenient because the earth itself rotates in 24 hours and so the satellite appears to hang stationary over the Earth. Small jets make adjustments to its position to keep it as exactly stationary as possible. There are now a growing number of "stationary" satellites for military and civilian uses.

The satellites are powered by solar batteries. Like microwave links on Earth they can be built to handle several thousand voice channels. Satellites today handle international traffic. It is likely that in the 1970's they will be used as an alternative to the other media discussed for long distance traffic *within* a country such as the United States (Fig. 8.10). Satellites are discussed in Chapter 20.

6. *Submarine Cable*

Satellites have spectacularly increased the potential for overseas communication. Prior to the launching of satellites the main means of communication across the sea was by cables on the ocean bed. The laying of telegraph cables across the sea was a major triumph of engineering in the 1850's, starting with an unsuccessful cable across the English Channel in 1850, and progressing to the transatlantic cable of 1858 which had a spectacular but short life. After immense difficulties and frustrations in the laying of the first transatlantic cable, it fired the public imagination when it finally worked. But the signals that trickled through it were so minute that only the most sensitive mirror galvanometer of the day could detect them. The submarine cables of that era had no repeaters. The first message, from Queen Victoria to President Buchanan, was of only ninety words but took sixteen and a half hours to transmit. Sixteen days later the cable failed and never worked again.

It was 1956 before the first voice cable was laid under the Atlantic. The difficulty of building underwater amplifiers of the immense reliability needed prevented this from being done earlier. The cable needed amplifiers every 38 miles. It was 0.62 inch in diameter and surrounded by heavy armor to give it strength and protection from corrosion. Even so the cables were occasionally broken near the coast by trawlers. The probability of the cables breaking or failing in deep water has to be very low as they would be prohibitively expensive to repair. The amplifiers on the first American cables are cased in a tubular section seven feet long and two inches in diameter, and can be coiled up on the large drums which hold the cables. The amplifiers on the first British cables are in much wider, heavier casing. They were consequently more difficult to lay on the seabed, but have duplicated components for reliability. The second generation of American cables also have rigid duplex amplifiers. Surprisingly, both the American and British amplifiers laid on the ocean bed up to the mid-1960's, rather than transistors, used vacuum tubes, as these had reliability proven over a longer period. Today transistor amplifiers are used.

The cables are coaxial, but with a larger spacing between the inner and outer conducters than for cables on land. Figure 8.11A shows the construction of the third generation of Bell System cables.

Because of the long spacing between amplifiers the upper frequency at which the cables can be operated is lower than with land cables. The capacity of the first cables was therefore only 48 voice channels and two cables were used for two-way talking. A.T.&T.'s second generation cables carry 128 two-way voice channels on one cable. By the end of the 1960's it is expected that a cable carrying 720 simultaneous conversations will be in operation. Table 8.1 shows the main characteristics of the three generations of Bell System cables.

Today's cables have their capacities increased about 90% using an ingenious technique called TASI, described in Chapter 15. The future of such cables, however, is uncertain as it now seems clear that satellites will span the oceans at much lower cost. On many of today's transatlantic calls,

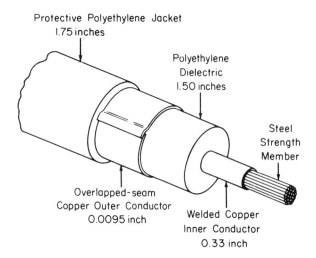

Protective Polyethylene Jacket
1.75 inches

Polyethylene
Dielectric
1.50 inches

Steel
Strength
Member

Overlapped-seam
Copper Outer Conductor
0.0095 inch

Welded Copper
Inner Conductor
0.33 inch

Fgi. 8.11A. Bell Laboratories third Generation of submarine cable, laid down in 1969, carries 720 simultaneous two-way voice channels. This is made possible by using a larger diameter dielectric to reduce transmission losses which increase rapidly at high frequencies, and by using a closer spacing of repeaters. *Reproduced with permission from the Bell Laboratories Record, May 1967.*

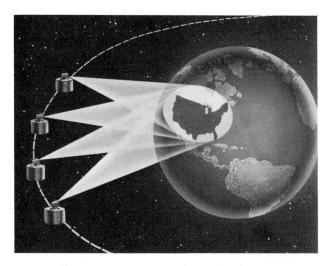

Fig. 8.11B. A domestic satellite system in the United States has been proposed by COMSAT. Such a system in the early 1970's could use four satellites operating with more than 150 Earth stations. It would provide 16 commercial TV channels, 4 educational TV channels, and 28,000 message channels. Within the United States, long-distance transmission may become cheaper by satellite than by land facilities. *Photograph from the Communications Satellite Corporation.*

transmission in one direction is by satellite and the return path is by cable. This makes the overall delay in obtaining a response less than the delay of half a second that is encountered if a satellite is used for both directions.

Table 8.1. THREE GENERATIONS OF SUBMARINE CABLES*

	First Generation 1956	Second Generation 1963	Third Generation 1969
Capacity (3 kHz Channels)	48	128	720
Top Frequency On Cable	164 kHz	1.1 MHz	5.9 MHz
Cable	Two-0.620″ Armored	One-1.00″ Armorless	One-1.50″ Armorless
Repeater Type	Flexible Vacuum Tube	Rigid Vacuum Tube	Rigid Transistor
Components Per Repeater	67	205	161
Repeater Spacing	38.7 Nautical Miles	20 Nautical Miles	10 Nautical Miles
Maximum System Length	2200 Nautical Miles	3500 Nautical Miles	4000 Nautical Miles

*Reproduced with permission from the *Bell Laboratories Record*, May 1967.

7. High-Frequency Radio Telephone

Before 1956 almost all transatlantic telephone traffic was carried by high-frequency radio telephone. It is still used for international telegraphy and for telephone to ships at sea and to countries not connected by cable and with no satellite antenna.

As will be seen from Fig. 8.1 the *high-frequency* band is of much lower frequency than that of microwave. High-frequency (HF) radio transmission is reflected by the ionosphere. Because of the movement of and changes in the ionosphere, it is subject to fading, distortion, and periodic blackouts. It is used for short-wave worldwide broadcasting, and can be picked up on some domestic radio sets. Long-distance HF telephone or telegraph circuits rarely form part of a computer-data transmission system, except for transmitting telegraph signals from remote parts of the world. The data error rate is extremely high, and elaborate means of error detection and automatic retransmission are needed. Nevertheless some such links have been successfully used. A 20-megahertz link was used successfully between computers in

Poughkeepsie, New York and Santiago, Chile in a recent winter athletic competition.

8. *Tropospheric Scatter Circuits*

The troposphere is much lower than the ionosphere and more stable. It extends up to about 6 miles. The ionosphere is above 30 miles. The troposphere scatters radio waves, and this is used for telecommunication links of up to about 600 miles where it is not possible, or economic, to construct land lines or microwave links. There are tropospheric scatter circuits over the frozen mountains of Alaska, and from the United States to Nassau. There used to be one to Cuba. It is possible that other points in the Caribbean will become linked with such circuits.

Island chains such as these are typical of areas that can benefit from these circuits. The tropospheric scatter circuit is used to transmit beyond the visible horizon. The received signal is the result of a multiplicity of reflections of different paths from the troposphere.

Tropospheric scatter circuits use very large antennas and a higher transmitter power than microwave circuits. The number of channels that can be engineered into such a circuit depends upon its distance. On a link of 100 miles, several hundred voice channels can be sent. A typical number on longer links is 72 channels. Over short links, television has been transmitted. Tropospheric scatter circuits are subject to fading and are affected by atmospheric conditions; however, they are much more dependable than HF circuits using the ionosphere.

Table 8.2 compares the costs of some installed circuits. The tropospheric scatter circuit is here the most expensive; its cost per channel would be lower than submarine cable, however, if it carried several hundred channels as is sometimes the case. It will be seen that microwave relay is the least expensive of the four systems. Today the installed cost per channel is lower than indicated by these figures because more channels can be sent over one link.

Table 8.2. BASIC COSTS FOR VARIOUS INSTALLED COMMUNICATION SYSTEMS*

	Basic Installed Cost per Mile	Number of Channels	Installed Cost per Channel Mile	Annual Operating Cost per Mile	Operating Cost per Channel Mile
Coaxial cable	32,500	600	54	4600	8
Microwave relay	10,000	600	17	2652	5
Submarine cable	10,000	72	139	1584	22
Tropospheric scatter	20,000	72	278	4032	56

*Chipp, R. D., and T. Cosgrove, "Economic Analysis of Communication Systems." *Seventh Communications Symposium of the IRE*, Utica, N.Y. (October 1961).

9. *Short-Distance Radio*

It is possible that short-distance radio links of the type used in taxis, walkie-talkies, and so on, will be used widely for computer input and output. A small mobile radio terminal could have many applications. It could be used in the control of a railroad marshaling yard, for example, in police cars or in aircraft. It may work in conjunction with a nearby transmitter on a device which itself is connected to a computer by landline. It may operate with the public mobile telephone services for vehicles. Figure 8.12 shows a typical terminal in a vehicle connected by radio-to-land telephone links.

Unlike some of the systems discussed earlier, only a small amount of the available capacity of the medium would be made use of. A high degree of

Fig. 8.12. The Kleinschmidt telescripter, a compact page printer designed for mobile installations such as police cars, commercial vehicles, ships, and aircraft. The terminal operates over radio telephone and has error control facilities. Should the operator leave his car, he will receive the message upon his return. *Photograph from SCM Corporation.*

redundancy could be built in to protect the data from the considerable amount of noise that would be encountered.

10. *Waveguides*

All of the media discussed above are in commercial operation today. It seems likely that the next major step forward to expanding the arteries that carry large numbers of voice or other channels across the country may be the use of waveguides.

A waveguide is, in essence, a metal tube down which radio waves of very high frequency travel. There are two main types of waveguide, rectangular and circular. Rectangular waveguides have been in use for some time as the feed between microwave antennas and their associated electronic equipment. It is normal to see a waveguide going up a microwave tower to the back of the dish that transmits the signal. They are not used for long distance communication, and are rarely employed for distances over a few thousand feet. They consist of a rectangular copper or brass tube, 15 inches across or smaller (Fig. 8.13). Radiation at microwave frequencies passes down this tube.

Circular waveguides are pipes about two inches in diameter. They are constructed with pre-

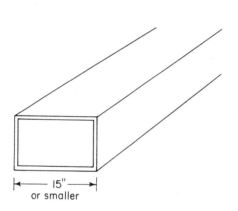

|←——— 15" ———→|
or smaller

Fig. 8.13. Rectangular waveguide.

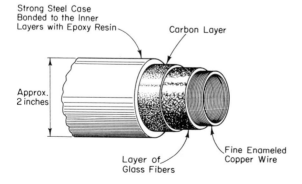

Strong Steel Case
Bonded to the Inner
Layers with Epoxy Resin

Carbon Layer

Approx.
2 inches

Layer of
Glass Fibers

Fine Enameled
Copper Wire

Fig. 8.14. Construction of the helical waveguide.

Fig. 8.15. A circular waveguide under test in England (Standard Telephones and Cables Ltd.). Links of this type may come into commercial use in the 1970's and have a capacity of 100,000 or more voice channels.

cision, and are capable of transmitting frequencies much higher than rectangular waveguides, or the other media discussed. Figure 8.14 [1] shows the construction of a Bell System waveguide. This is referred to as a helical waveguide because a fine enameled copper wire is wound tightly around the inside in a helix. This is surrounded by a layer of thin glass fibers, and then by a carbon layer. The whole is encased in a strong steel case, and bonded to it with epoxy resin. The purpose of this construction is to attenuate undesired modes of wave propagation. Figure 8.15 [2] shows an experimental length of waveguide with bends in it constructed to measure the effect of bends on transmission. It was found that these gentle bends caused little loss of signal strength.

The loss in waveguides built so far actually becomes less as frequency increases up to frequencies of about 100,000 megahertz. [3] This is shown

[1] King, A. P., and Mandeville, G. D., "The Observed 33 to 90 kmc Attenuation of Two-Inch Improved Waveguide." *Bell System Tech. J.* (September 1961).

[2] Young, D. T., "Measured TE$_{01}$ Attenuation in Helix Waveguide with Controlled Straightness Deviations." *Bell System Tech. J.* (February 1965).

[3] Steier, H. H., "Attenuation of the Holmdel Helix Waveguide in the 100–125 kmc band." *Bell System Tech. J.* (May 1965).

in Fig. 9.9. Theoretically, it should continue to lessen indefinitely as frequency increases, though an upper limit is set by today's engineering. Waveguides constructed by Bell Laboratories are capable of carrying no less than 200,000 voice channels in one direction.

Although at the time of writing such a system is experimental and has not been installed commercially, it seems likely that it will be installed in the future using the pulse code modulation techniques described in Chapter 14. Such a system will be excellent for data transmission. The noise level encountered on the Bell System waveguide now operating is low enough for circuits of several thousand miles to be constructed; for example, coast-to-coast links in the United States.

LASERS   Still higher in the electromagnetic spectrum (Fig. 1.2) is the laser, operating at the frequencies of light. Lasers have been used successfully for transmission from space vehicles. For earthbound communications they are still in the realm of the research laboratories. It seems probable, however, that they will eventually provide the means of building channels of enormous capacity—immensely greater even than the helical waveguides. It has been said that lasers portend a revolution in telecommunications as fundamental as the invention of radio.

"Laser" stands for *Light Amplification by Stimulated Emission of Radiation*, and was preceded by "maser," standing for *Microwave Amplification by Stimulated Emission of Radiation*. A laser produces a narrow beam of light which is sharply monochromatic (that is, occupies a single color or frequency) and *coherent* (that is, all of the waves travel in unison like the waves traveling away from a stone dropped in a pond). Normal light, even that of one color, consists of the small spread of frequencies and waves which are incoherent, bearing a random position relative to one another.

An analogy with sound waves is a somewhat inexact analogy, but it will help the reader to visualize the difference between a laser beam and an ordinary light beam. The sound from a tuning fork consists of waves which are of one frequency, and which are reasonably coherent. On the other hand, if I put a hammer through my apartment window the sound waves would be neither monochromatic nor coherent. The former may be compared with a laser beam; the latter with ordinary light. The laser or maser beam is formed by a molecular process somewhat analogous to the tuning fork. It is possible to make certain molecules oscillate with a fixed frequency in much the same manner as the tuning fork.

The electrons in an atom can move only in certain fixed orbits. Associated with each orbit is a particular energy level. The electrons can sometimes be induced to change orbits, and when this happens the total energy associated with the atom changes. The atom can therefore take on a number of discrete energy levels—a fact from quantum mechanics that is well known today. Certain processes can induce the electron to jump from one orbit to another or, to state it another way, to induce the atom to switch from one energy level to another. When this happens the atom either absorbs or emits a quantum of energy. In this way, light, radio waves, or other electromagnetic radiation is emitted in discrete quantums.

When ordinary light is emitted the mass of molecules switch their energy levels at random. A random jumble of noncoherent waves is produced. Under the lasing action, however, the molecules are induced to emit in unison, the substance oscillating at a given frequency, and a stream of coherent waves at this single frequency results. This could be either a microwave frequency (maser) or a light frequency (laser).

When a laser beam produced by certain lasing molecules falls on other molecules of that type it can induce oscillation in them. A form of resonance is set up. The reader might imagine a huge pendulum much too heavy to move far by a single hard push. If he gives a series of relatively gentle pushes, however, he can set it swinging. He may go on pushing at just the right point in the swing, and the length of the swing increases until the pendulum builds up great power. This is resonance. His gentle pushes have been amplified into massive oscillations. In a similar manner (and again the analogy

Fig. 8.16. The potential information-carrying capacity of the laser is much higher than the other media discussed in this chapter. Certain problems have yet to be solved before public laser communication links can be built. Here a gas lens invented at Bell Telephone Laboratories is being tested. The gas lens may be used to focus the laser beam. *Photograph from AT&T.*

is helpful but not exact), a weak laser beam can fall on a lasing substance and cause resonance in it. It sets the molecules oscillating so that a powerful laser beam is emitted. The laser beam has thus been *amplified*. In this way a very intense beam of a single frequency can be emitted.

A beam of ordinary light, even a beam which we describe as monochromatic, actually consists of a small spread of frequencies, each of which would be bent slightly differently by a prism or lens. A laser beam, however, is not dispersed by a prism and optical arrangements can be built for it so precisely that a beam of laser light can be shone onto the moon and illuminate only a small portion of its surface. A beam can be concentrated with a lens into a minute area, and the intense concentration of energy into such a small area causes very localized heating to occur. A cutting or welding tool is provided of a miniature precision beyond the dreams of Swiss watchmakers. The surgeon has a microscopic scalpel; the General a potential death ray.

For telecommunication use we have a beam of great intensity which is highly controllable and which can be amplified. Whereas today's microwave beams disperse over an angle of about 1°, a laser beam could be almost exactly parallel. However, the most exciting fact about it is that its frequency is about 100,000 times higher than today's microwave and its potential bandwidth almost 100,000 times greater. If we can learn how to superimpose the information on the beam (modulate the beam) at a sufficiently high rate, laser communication links in the future may well carry 100,000 times as much information as today's microwave links.

The big problem that remains is how to modulate the beam. Its intensity or some other property must be varied sufficiently fast to convey the large quantity of information. A variety of different techniques for making the laser beam carry information has been suggested. It is not clear yet which of them will eventually prove to be the best for telecommunications. To give a crude example of what is meant by modulation, the beam could be varied by means of a series of very rapidly moving shutters, diffraction gradings, or mirrors. The variation would be used to convey information. This mechanical process, however, would be extremely slow, compared with the capacity of the beam. The same function must be performed electronically at enormous speed. One possible way of doing this would be to use electric field absorption. The absorption region of a semiconductor can be transferred to a different wavelength when an electric field is applied. Varying the field can thus be used to vary the absorption of a laser beam, and so its amplitude may be varied at rates as high as several billion (10^9) times per second.

Another possibility is to use a phenomenon called "Pockel's effect." Here the beam is shone through a transparent piezoelectric crystal. When an electric field is applied, it strains the crystal and rotates the plane of polarization of the laser beam. Again the beam has been modulated at rates of several billion cycles per second. Considerably higher modulation rates than these are needed to take advantage of the laser's full bandwidth, but it does not seem overly optimistic to assume that they will be achieved.

Although the laser beam is sometimes visualized as being shone through the air as a pencil-thin beam of light, this would have many disadvantages. It could be interfered with by anything that would disturb ordinary light—fog, snow, boys with kites, or flocks of pigeons. Instead the beam is more likely to be sent through a pipe containing a bundle of optically transparent fibers.

If a fiber is surrounded by a substance of lower refractive index, such as air, light passing down it will be totally reflected by the edges of the fiber. This *total internal reflection* occurs in a similar manner at the surface of a pond. If you put your head under the water and look at the surface some distance away it will appear to be a totally reflecting mirror. The ray of light is not refracted out of the pond at all because of its low striking angle, but totally reflected back into the water. The laser beam travels down a transparent fiber, and is confined within the fiber by total internal reflection. It will be absorbed somewhat by the fiber, and it will have to be periodically amplified. Lasers of many different frequencies could travel together down the same fiber, and a bundle of such fibers could occupy one pipe.

It has been said that such a laser system has the potential ability to carry all the information carried by all of the telephone lines in the world today at the same time.

9 ATTENUATION AND REPEATERS

The strength of the signal transmitted by any transmission medium falls off with distance. Therefore, if it is transmitted more than a few miles, it must be amplified. Most transmission systems have amplifiers at intervals to restore the signal to its former strength. The amplifier is broadly similar to that used in a domestic radio or hi-fi unit for amplifying those signals. There are, however, other electronic circuits associated with the transmission line amplifier which correct the various forms of distortion that occur during the transmission. The amplifier and its associated circuits are referred to as a *repeater*.

The distance between the repeaters depends upon the degree of *attenuation* or falling off in strength of the signal. The signal strength cannot be allowed to fall too low, otherwise it becomes increasingly difficult to distinguish it from the noise that is always present. If noise is mixed with the signal, the amplifier amplifies this as well as the signal.

REGENERATIVE REPEATERS If the signal consists of a series of discrete steps or on/off pulses, such as the teletype signals in Figs. 6.1 and 6.5, a repeater can be built which *reconstructs* the signal in its original form. Each repeater will then transmit a new, clean, sharp-edged signal free from distortion and the effects of thermal noise. If a noise burst is bad enough to destroy pulses, and the data become unrecognizable by the repeater, then errors will be passed on down the line. Otherwise, the signal passed on will be substantially as clean and sharp as when it was new.

A repeater of this type is called a *regenerative* repeater. Its effect is illustrated in Fig. 9.1. Regenerative repeaters were used generally on the early teletype lines. They were in use long before the invention of electronic amplifiers. A teletype signal could be reconstructed simply by using a battery and a make-and-break contact. A relay opened and closed according to whether the incoming signal was a "1" or a "0," and was used to form new pulses to travel down the next line segment, as in Fig. 9.1.

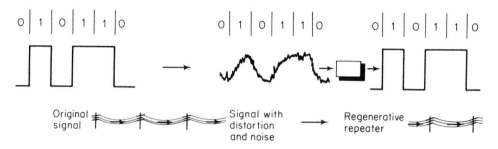

Fig. 9.1. Transmission in the form of pulses can be reconstructed at intervals down that line with regenerative repeaters. This cannot be done with transmission in an analog form.

Regenerative repeaters could clearly be of great value on any line which is designed to transmit digitized data. However, few of the world's telecommunication lines today are designed for transmitting baseband digital data. They are designed primarily to carry the human voice, and this is transmitted almost universally in an analog form, that is, that signal occupies a continuous range of amplitudes rather than a few discrete levels. Therefore, *regenerative* repeaters cannot be used—only repeaters which amplify the signal and correct some of its distortions in an analog fashion. These, unfortunately, amplify the noise along with the signal and cannot separate the two as in Fig. 9.1.

Even telegraph signals, which once enjoyed this form of reconstruction, are often today crammed together into a voice channel. The engineers have traded the ability to regenerate them for the much greater advantage of high utilization of the communication line's capacity.

A new form of transmission called *pulse code modulation* is being introduced. This is discussed in Chapter 14. With it signals are once again transmitted in the form of pulses which can be regenerated. Furthermore, analog signals like those representing the human voice are converted into a digital form and sent as reconstructable pulses. Pulse-code modulation will revolutionize the world's communication links. However, today's multibillions of dollars worth of installed telephone plant is almost all analog, and this is what most of our computers will have to transmit over for the time being, using amplifiers as repeaters.

TWO-WIRE AND
FOUR-WIRE CIRCUITS
Most communication links have two amplifiers in their repeaters, one for each direction of transmission. Long-distance lines usually consist of four wires or their equivalent, two for each direction as in Fig. 9.2. This is referred to as a *four-wire circuit*.

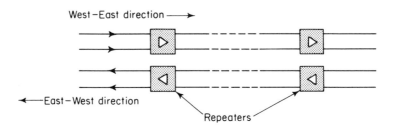

Fig. 9.2. A four-wire circuit.

A telephone conversation with voice traveling in either direction can also be transmitted over a *two-wire circuit*. There are two voice-carrying wires leaving your telephone and disappearing into the wall plaster. A two-wire circuit may have one amplifier which serves both directions. This is made possible by suitably arranged coils which act like transformers. Figure 9.3 shows a simple two-wire repeater. Whichever direction the signal travels in, it is amplified and the amplified signal fed back into the line. The circuit in Fig. 9.3 is rarely used; most two-wire repeaters use two amplifiers, one for each signal direction.

A four-wire circuit, used for long-distance trunks, may not necessarily have four actual wires. Many of them do and these are referred to as *physical four-wire circuits*. However, two conductors can form an *equivalent four-wire circuit*, by separating the two directions of transmission into different frequency bands. The east–west and west–east signals are changed in frequency by different amounts and can then travel on the same two physical wires without interfering with each other. Similarly, in data transmission,

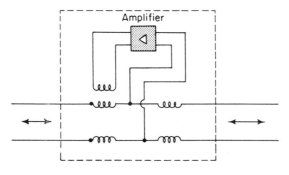

Fig. 9.3. A simplified diagram of an amplifier on a two-wire circuit (seldom used today).

signals can be made to travel over two wires if their frequencies are changed so that they do not interfere with each other. The two directions are separated in frequency rather than space.

Where it is desirable to minimize the number of physical channels, two-wire or *equivalent* four-wire circuits will be used. Two-wire circuits are commonly used where the transmission takes place at voice frequencies, as with the wires leaving your telephone. A two-wire circuit probably goes all the way from your telephone to your local telephone exchange ("local central office"). When several voice channels are packed onto one pair of wires, however, four-wire transmission is normally used.

Whether they are physical four-wire or equivalent four-wire circuits depends on how important it is to minimize the number of physical paths. With open-wire pairs, for example, a physical four-wire circuit would mean doubling the number of wires stretched between the telephone poles. This is undesirable, and usually equivalent four-wire transmission is used, needing one pair of wires only. On the other hand, high-capacity intercity trunks carrying large numbers of conversations at once, usually separate the directions of transmission physically. The electronic equipment is designed to pack many channels all going in the same direction into one coaxial cable or microwave facility.

HYBRID COILS   Where the two-wire line from your telephone joins the four-wire trunk, a connecting circuit is needed. An outgoing signal on the two wires is transferred to the appropriate pair of the four-wire line by this, and an incoming signal on the other pair of the four-wire line is transferred to the two-wire line.

The essence of this junction circuit is the *hybrid coil* shown in Fig. 9.4. The signal on the two-wire line traveling west-to-east in the diagram is picked up by the coil entering the upper amplifier, amplified and transmitted down the west–east half of the four-wire line. A signal traveling east-to-west is amplified by the lower amplifier and enters the two-wire line. It enters the hybrid coil at its center, and hence the signals induced into the uppermost part of the coil cancel out. If the hybrid coil were perfect, and the balancing network precisely duplicated the line section it faces, no signal would enter the upper amplifier.

On a two-wire line, two amplifiers are often used rather than the one in Fig. 9.3. Two hybrid coils take the signals into these—one for each direction.

ECHOES   Unfortunately, the hybrid circuit is not perfect. When a signal travels east-to-west in Fig. 9.4 a small portion of it *does* find its way into the upper amplifier. The signals induced into the two halves of the upper coil do not cancel out

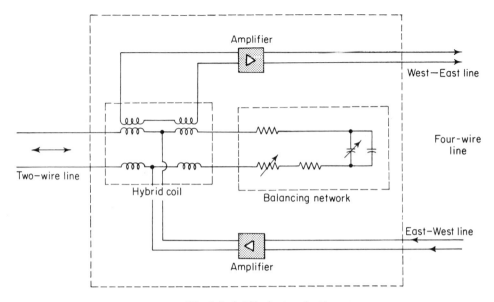

Fig. 9.4. A 2/4-wire terminating set.

exactly. The balancing network shown in Fig. 9.4 is chosen to minimize this unfortunate effect. However, the line characteristics vary somewhat with ambient temperature and different telephone handsets are connected to the network. The circuit cannot be balanced perfectly for all of these conditions.

When a small fraction of the east-to-west signal goes into the upper amplifier, it is amplified and travels back west-to-east. There is thus an *echo* on the line. Other circuit components can cause echoes also. In fact, whenever the transmission line has a sharp change in impedance a small portion of the signal is reflected and travels back down the line.

Echoes have varying psychological effects on persons making a telephone call. The effects are sometimes not unpleasant, but sometimes they are annoying. An echo coming 0.005 second after the speaker's voice is not necessarily objectionable. It sounds rather like speaking in a bathroom. (People might even be tempted to sing.) Echoes coming a few tenths of a second after the speaker have a serious effect. Experiments show that they cause many people to stutter or repeat words. Many people speak in a disconnected manner. Some stop entirely.

ECHO
SUPPRESSORS

On most of the world's telephone systems it is considered that echoes with a round-trip delay of more than about 0.045 second cannot be tolerated. Where the echo reaches the speaker after this period or longer an *echo suppressor* is employed to reduce it to a negligible level. Many circuits with less delay than this also use echo suppressors. An echo suppressor is a circuit which reduces the return transmission by inserting a large amount of loss into the return path.

The echo suppressor is activated by a circuit which detects the human voice. A *speech detector* on the east–west channel operates the echo suppressor of the west–east channel and these echoes are attenuated for the duration of the east–west speech. Likewise, a speech detector is also needed on the opposite direction of travel. If *A* is talking to *B* on the telephone, and *B* wants to speak, *B* cannot be heard, except perhaps very faintly, until *A* stops talking. In a fast conversation with *A* and *B* interrupting one another, they may hear the echo suppressors switching on the other's voice, sometimes in midsentence. This does not usually impair conversation seriously.

With today's telephone plant only long lines need suppressors. On loaded wire-pair telephone cables, signals of voice frequency travel along the line at speeds of the order of 20,000 miles per second. This will vary considerably depending upon the characteristics of the line and its loading coils, but roughly a signal would have to travel about 500 miles and back before its propagation time reaches 0.045 second. When coaxial cables or microwave radio is used, or if the wire pairs carry the higher frequencies used when they transmit several channels together, then the velocity of propagation will be nearer to the speed of light. Over such media the signal could travel nearer 4000 miles and back before the 0.045-second delay occurs; however, there is another cause of delay where many signals travel together down one link. Normally, they are not all going to the same destination, and so must be separated for switching purposes. As will be explained in a later chapter, this involves dropping them down to voice frequencies to carry out the switching operation and then packing them together again. This introduces a small delay, and so the total delay will depend upon the number of such "terminals" on the link. As a result of this we find echo suppressors in all terrestrial telephone circuits over 1500 miles in length, and often on shorter circuits. Longer alternate routes are used to bypass a busy group of trunks, and often a connection as short as 300 miles contains an echo suppressor. Care is taken to have more than one echo suppressor switched into a connection because of the degradation they cause to the transmission of speech.

A "stationary" satellite is 22,300 miles from the earth. The propagation delay to and from it is therefore about 0.25 second (186,000 miles per second is the velocity of the signal to and from it). Echo suppressors are thus needed when such a satellite is used.

Echo suppressors designed for voice cannot be used when *data* are transmitted over a voice circuit. If they exist, they must be disabled. There are two main reasons for this. First, the speech detector is designed to detect *only* speech. It must be insensitive to noise, whistles, or other extraneous sounds or the false operation could play havoc with the conversation. Digital data would not necessarily operate it satisfactorily. Second, the means of detecting speech causes it to listen for a short time before it operates. On a two-wire path the first syllable of a sequence can be clipped due to the echo suppressors being this slow in reversing their direction. This would not be satisfactory with data signals, and so time has to be allowed for the echo suppressors to reverse their direction of operation.

To achieve the most efficient use of a full-duplex line for data transmission it is desirable to transmit in both directions at the same time. Data signals may flow in one direction, while control signals and error retransmission requests flow in the opposite. Or, on a line with many data machines attached to it, data may be flowing from one of them to the computer at the same time as the computer is replying to another. This, however, cannot be the case on a line with an echo suppressor. Echo suppressors unless disabled prevent simultaneous two-way transmission over the public network.

ECHO SUPPRESSOR
DISABLERS
In some countries, however, when dial-up telegraph transmission was introduced using the existing voice lines, echo suppressors were built which could be disabled by a specific control tone. These disablers are now being used for higher-speed data transmission and they permit bidirectional transmission. When the echo suppressors are out of action it is possible to use either simultaneous two-way transmission or half-duplex transmission, with relatively fast reversal of transmission direction.

Typical echo suppressor disablers require that a single-frequency tone in the band 2000–2250 cycles per second be transmitted from either or both ends of the line. This tone must last for approximately 400 milliseconds and there must be little or no energy at any other frequency. The echo suppressor will then stay out of action until there is no signal being transmitted from either end of the line for a period of approximately 50 milliseconds. The data machines must be designed in such a way that they do not leave the line silent for 50 milliseconds, or the echo suppressor will have to be redisabled. A "carrier" signal, explained in Chapter 13, ensures the line does not become silent. Once the suppressor is re-enabled, it again functions normally until another disabling tone is sent.

The disabling tone can be *heard* on the telephone as a continuous high-pitched whistle. It is therefore used as a signal to the person dialing that he has established the connection he desires to the computer. The girl in Fig. 2.3, for example, wishes to establish a connection between her data terminal and a computer. She dials the number of the computer—a conventional telephone number. She may briefly hear a conventional ringing tone, and then a high-pitched whistle comes down the line—referred to as the *data tone*. This whistle will disable any echo suppressors. When she hears the whistle she knows that she is in contact with the computer and she then presses the key labeled "DATA" on her data set. This switches the set to operate as required for data, and her terminal machine is now connected to the distant computer.

What happens to the echoes, then, if the echo suppressor is disabled? They will still be present as they would be on a line which, like the majority, has no echo suppressor. Faint echoes reach the receiving machine as unwanted noise. As will be seen in subsequent chapters, this, along with other noise, limits the maximum speed at which we can transmit. Note that it is the receiving machine we are now worried about, not the transmitting one, whereas in speech telephony it was the *talker* who was disturbed by the echoes. The echoes, in general, are not sufficiently strong to cause substantial errors in the interpretation of the data signals when data are transmitted at 600 or 1200 bits per second over a voice line. When the speed is increased, however, more ingenious means of transmitting are required (Chapter 13), as all noise becomes more significant.

DECIBELS   The unit which is normally used for expressing differences in signal strengths in telecommunications is the *decibel*. The decibel is a unit of power ratio, not an absolute unit. Signal-to-noise ratio is normally quoted, for example, in decibels.

However, it is not directly the power ratio, but is ten times the logarithm of it (to base 10).

$$\text{Number of decibels} = 10 \log_{10} \frac{P_1}{P_2}$$

where P_1 is the larger power (normally) and P_2 is the smaller. This is sometimes confusing to newcomers to the field.

The decibel also used to be defined as the unit of attenuation caused by one mile of standard No. 19 gage cable at a frequency of 866 cycles, though this definition is now regarded as obsolete.

Amplitude ratios are also quoted in decibels. Power is proportional to the square of the amplitude of a signal. A power ratio of 100, say, is equivalent to an amplitude ratio of 10. Therefore, where the two amplitude levels are A_1 and A_2, we have

$$\text{Number of decibels} = 20 \log_{10} \frac{A_1}{A_2}$$

Decibels are used to express such quantities as gain in amplifiers, noise levels, losses in transmission lines and also differences in sound intensity.

It made sense to refer to sound levels by a logarithmic unit because the response of the human ear is proportional to the logarithm of the sound energy, not to the energy itself. If one noise sounds twice as great as another, it is not in fact twice the power, but it is approximately 2 decibels greater. The sound energy reaching your ears in the New York subway may be 10,000 times greater than in the room where you are reading this book, but it does not sound 10,000 times greater. It sounds about 40 times greater—you have to shout 40 times harder to make yourself heard to a person the same distance away. Ten thousand times the sound energy is called "40 decibels greater."

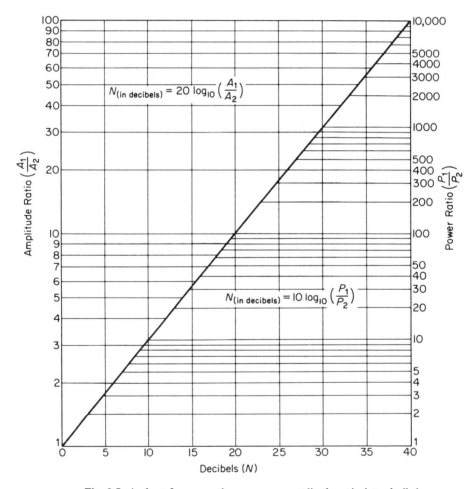

Fig. 9.5. A chart for converting power or amplitude ratio into decibels.

In electrical circuits, power losses or gains may be added or subtracted arithmetically if they are referred to in decibels. Thus suppose a signal is transmitted over a line and that this reduces it in power in a ratio 20 to 1. It then passes over another section of line which reduces it in a ratio 7 to 1. The net reduction is in the ratio 140 to 1. Expressing this in decibels: the first reduction is $10 \log_{10} 20 = 13.01$ decibels; the second reduction is $10 \log_{10} 7 = 8.45$ decibels. The net reduction is the sum of these: 21.46 decibels ($10 \log_{10} 140 = 21.46$ decibels).

Similarly, if we say that line loss is 2 decibels per mile, then the loss at the end of 25 miles of line is 50 decibels. We therefore need an amplifier of gain 50 decibels to produce a signal of the original power. This is a useful way to express such values.

Figure 9.5 is a graph to enable the reader to quickly convert power or amplitude ratios in decibels and vice versa.

NEPERS
The unit of power ratio was originally the *bel* named after Bell, the inventor of the telephone. One bel is equal to a power ratio of 10 to 1. This is too large a unit for most purposes and so the decibel, one tenth of the bel, had come into common usage.

Another unit in common use is the *neper*. This is also a logarithmic unit but uses logs to the base e. Amplitude ratios are expressed in nepers as

$$\text{Number of nepers} = \log_e \frac{A_1}{A_2}$$

and therefore power ratios are expressed by

$$\text{Number of nepers} = \frac{1}{2} \log_e \frac{P_1}{P_2}$$

It follows that 1 neper = 8.686 decibels and that 1 bel = 1.151 nepers. In this book we will use decibels exclusively.

ATTENUATION CONSTANT
The attenuation of a cable is usually described in terms of an attenuation constant which is related to the decay of signal strength.

Consider a short section of cable of length Δl as shown in Figure 9.6. The voltage of the signal entering this section is V and that of the signal leav-

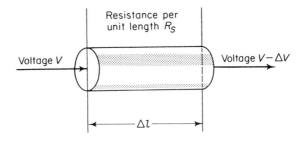

Figure 9.6

ing is $V - \Delta V$. The loss of voltage,

$$-\Delta V = IR_s\Delta l$$

where I is the current flowing in the section and R_s is the resistance, per unit length. However, $I = V/R$, where R is the resistance relative to earth where the voltage is zero.

$$\therefore \quad \frac{\Delta V}{V} = -\frac{R_s}{R}\Delta l$$

In the limiting case

$$\frac{1}{V}dV = -\frac{R_s}{R}dl$$

Integrating:

$$\log_e V = -\frac{R_s}{R}l$$

$$\therefore \quad V = e^{-(R_s/R)l}$$

The voltage ratio between two points distance l_1 and l_2 down the line is therefore

$$\frac{V_1}{V_2} = e^{-R_s/R(l_1-l_2)}$$

In general,

$$\frac{V_1}{V_2} = e^{-\alpha(l_1-l_2)}$$

where α is a constant characteristic of the line and called the attenuation constant.

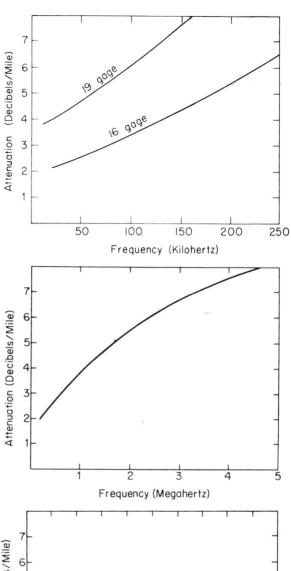

Fig. 9.7. Typical attenuation on twisted-wire-pair cables.

Fig. 9.8. Attenuation in a coaxial cable ($\frac{3}{8}$-inch outside diameter).

Fig. 9.9. Attenuation in a helical waveguide (2-inch diameter). *Redrawn from "The Attenuation of the Homdel Helix Waveguide in the 100–125 kMc Band,"* by William H. Steier, *Bell System Technical Journal,* May 1965.

For alternating currents one must take the capacitance and inductance of the line into consideration and the expression for α becomes complex.

The attenuation constant is usually expressed in decibels per mile. Some typical values of attenuation constants are given in Table 9.1. Figures 9.7 to 9.9 show how the attenuation varies with frequency on wire pairs, coaxial cable, and helical waveguide. This characteristic determines bandwidth and hence the capacity of such links.

Table 9.1. TYPICAL ATTENUATION CONSTANTS

Transmission Medium	Frequency	Typical Attenuation Coefficient (decibels per mile)
Wire pairs on poles	1000 cps	0.1
Twisted wires in cable, 16 gage	48 kc	2
16 gage	140 kc	3.5
22 gage	48 kc	6
22 gage	140 kc	8
Coaxial cable, $\frac{3}{8}$ inch o.d.	300 kc	2
	2000 kc	6
	8000 kc	10
Transatlantic coaxial cable	160 kc	1.4
Rectangular waveguide	5×10^9 cps	9
Helical millimeter waveguide	5×10^{10} cps	2

LOCATION OF REPEATERS

The repeaters are spaced at intervals sufficiently close to prevent the signal from being attenuated to a level at which it will be too small relative to the possible sources of noise. For voice transmission it is generally desirable to maintain an overall signal-to-noise ratio of 30 decibels or better.

On many good quality circuits, when the signal has traveled a distance such that it has fallen in power by a factor of the order of 100, in other words 20 decibels, it is boosted back to its original value. Thus on a coaxial cable system with an average attenuation coefficient of 5 decibels per mile, repeaters may be installed every 4 miles. On the other hand, on open-wire pairs with an average attenuation of, say, 0.4 decibel per mile, the repeaters may be placed at distances of about 50 miles.

On the transatlantic cables with vacuum-tube repeaters, the repeaters are spaced about every 40 miles. The attenuation on this cable is about 1.4 decibel per mile, which gives an attenuation of 56 decibels between repeaters. This greater figure is used on the submarine cable in order to minimize the number of repeaters. This reduces the DC power that must be transmitted down the cable to the repeaters and also reduces the probability of the cable failing. The longer distance between repeaters is acceptable because the noise encountered is less, due to shielding from the seawater.

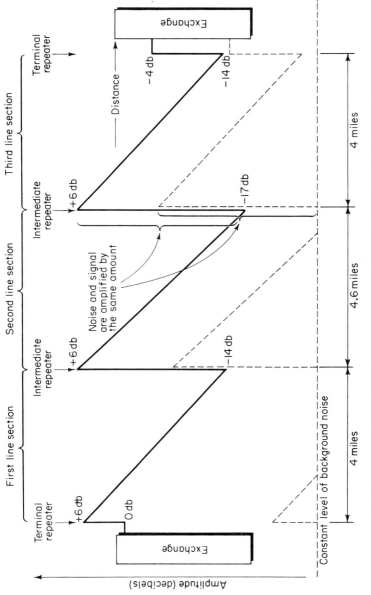

Fig. 9.10. Attenuation and amplification on a line with a coefficient of 5 decibels per mile.

Construction of loading coils manufactured by L. M. Ericsson, Sweden. *From L. M. Ericsson, Sweden.*

(A)

Bell System Loading coils for telephone lines on the assembly line at the Western Electric plant. *From AT&T.*

(B)

Fig. 9.11. Loading coils.

Figure 9.10 illustrates the use of repeaters on a 12.6-mile length of cable with an attenuation constant of 5 decibels per mile. If there were no repeaters on this line the total drop in signal amplitude would be 63 decibels. This is too great a drop as the signal level would fall below the level of the background noise. When the signal is amplified *the noise is amplified with it*, as shown by the dotted line in Fig. 9.10. If the signal falls too low then the ratio of signal strength to that of background noise becomes low and never improves because the two can never be separated. On the second line section of Fig. 9.10 the repeater spacing is slightly greater than on the first section. This allows the signal to fall slightly closer to the background noise level. This closer spacing of signal and noise remains until the signal reaches the exchange. It can be seen from Fig. 9.10 that if the repeaters had been closer together, the signal-to-noise ratio would have remained at a better figure. The one repeater interval that is greater than the others causes more than its fair share of degradation of the signal, and so it is advisable to have all of the repeaters the same distance apart.

LOADING
Loading, as was discussed in Chapter 7 is a means of decreasing the attenuation of a transmission line and holding it more nearly constant over a given frequency range. Its main purpose is to combat the effect of the capacitance between the wires. Local loops from subscriber to central office commonly have loading coils about every 6000 feet, sometimes 3000 or 9000 feet.

Figure 9.11 is a photograph of typical loading coils. Figure 9.12 shows the difference in attenuation between a loaded noncarrier wire pair (operating at voice frequencies) and the same line unloaded. It will be seen that for a certain band of frequencies the attenuation on the loaded line is less than on the unloaded line and also is fairly constant. Above a certain frequency, however, the attenuation rises fast. The combination of the capacitance of the line and the inductance of the loading coil causes the line to act like a low-pass filter, that is to say, it transmits signals of frequencies up to a given cutoff point, and above that, attenuation increases greatly. The loading coil must be selected for the particular frequency band that is to be transmitted. It would be quite different on a line that is to carry one voice channel than it would be on a line that carries several.

The data-processing designer may have to take loading into consideration on short lines. Some computer manufacturers' specifications for short-distance line equipment state that the lines must be nonloaded. This is generally intended for lines installed by a computer user within his own premises over a distance not greater than about eight miles. If privately installed lines are used for high-speed data, then the lines usually need to carry load coils if the distance is greater than about a mile.

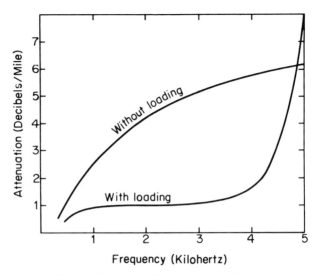

Fig. 9.12. The effect of loading on a wire-pair circle using voice-frequency transmission (24-gauge cable).

ATTENUATION IN RADIO TRANSMISSION

A signal transmitted by radio does not decay exponentially as is the case with transmission lines. Instead it obeys an inverse square law, the power falling off inversely as the square of the distance transmitted.

Suppose that a microwave antenna transmits with a power P_1, and that a similar antenna at a distance l receives the signal, the received signal having a power P_2.

Suppose that the transmitting antenna is designed so that it radiates a beam which is square in cross section and radiates in a solid angle θ by θ radians (Fig. 9.13). At distance l the cross-sectional area of the beam is $(\theta l)^2$. Let the area of the antenna be a. Then only $a/(\theta l)^2$ of the transmitted power is received:

$$\frac{P_2}{P_1} = \frac{a}{(\theta l)^2}$$

It can be shown that for an antenna with a square transmitting aperature the angle θ is given approximately by the following relation:

$$\theta = \frac{\lambda}{\sqrt{a}} \qquad (9.1)$$

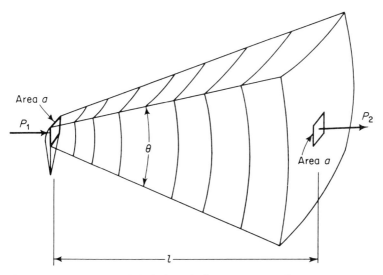

Fig. 9.13. Calculation of microwave attenuation.

where λ is the wavelength transmitted. Therefore

$$\frac{P_2}{P_1} = \left(\frac{a}{\lambda l}\right)^2 \tag{9.2}$$

The amplitude ratio is therefore

$$\frac{A_2}{A_1} = \frac{a}{\lambda l} \tag{9.3}$$

where A_1 is the transmitting amplitude and A_2 is the amplitude received. λ is inversely proportional to the frequency f of the wave:

$$\lambda f = C$$

where C is the velocity of light. We may then write (9.3) as

$$\frac{A_2}{A_1} = \frac{af}{lC} \tag{9.4}$$

THE SPACING OF MICROWAVE LINKS

Let us substitute figures into Eq. (9.4) for a typical system. A frequency band in common use is 5925–6425 megahertz. The midpoint of this is $f = 6175$ megahertz. The velocity of light is 186,000 miles per second. A typical antenna for such transmission might have an aperture 8 feet × 8 feet. Therefore, substituting, the attenuation ratio per mile is

$$\frac{(\frac{8}{5280})^2 \times 6.175 \times 10^9}{1 \cdot 86 \times 10^5} = 0.0762$$

Thus if the microwave antennas are situated 30 miles apart,

$$\frac{A_2}{A_1} = \frac{1}{30} \times 0.0762 = 0.00254$$

which is a loss of 52 decibels.

It will be seen that the signal strength does not fall off exponentially as in the case of wire systems. It falls off much more slowly. The preceding system has an attenuation of 32 decibels over 3 miles, 52 decibels over 30 miles, 72 decibels over 300 miles, and so on. Contrast this with a cable system having an attenuation of 16 decibels over 3 miles. This would suffer an attenuation of 160 decibels over 30 miles, 1600 decibels over 300 miles, and so on. The microwave systems would thus need far fewer amplifiers, but each requires large antennas and the tower to support them.

Equation (9.4) shows that A_2/A_1 can be improved by increasing the frequency, f. For this reason the highest frequencies practical are used in microwave links. However, above about 10 gigahertz (10,000 megahertz), the effect of rain and snow in attenuating the signal becomes increasingly and prohibitively serious. Also the refraction of the beam by different moisture and temperature layers becomes serious and can cause deep fading of the signal. Therefore microwave systems operate at frequencies between 3000 and 12,000 megahertz.

A_2/A_1 can also be decreased by increasing the size of the antennas' apertures, a. There is also a limit to this set by the economics of the system; however, where for some reason the microwave antennas *have* to be a long distance apart, the antenna size can be increased. This is sometimes the case in mountains or links across large expanses of water. Communication via satellite uses microwave frequencies, and here the ground antennas are very large, and specially designed.

As will be seen from Eq. (9.1), increasing the frequency or enlarging the transmitting antenna narrows the angle of the beam transmitted, and this is the reason why these two factors are effective in reducing the signal loss. When the beam becomes too narrow it becomes more expensive to build antennas that will keep it rigidly on its target 30 miles or so away. This is particularly so as microwave dishes are fixed on the top of tall towers subject to high gales. In the typical example we have just cited, the angle of the beam is approximately 1°.

A major limitation on the separation between microwave relays is often,

Fig. 9.14. The curvature of the Earth sets a limit to the spacing of microwave repeaters. If they are more than 30 miles apart and not on hills, very large and expensive towers are needed. Also, fading becomes a serious problem above 30 miles.

however, the curvature of the earth. They must normally be built within line of sight of one another. Microwave antennas, even on the top of towers a few hundred feet high, often cannot be more than 30 miles apart. Sometimes large antennas are placed on mountain ridges to transmit greater distances.

Above 30 miles separation, *fading* effects become markedly more severe. This effect, combined with the others, has led to the building of microwave systems in which most of the towers are of the order of 30 miles apart. When it becomes necessary to extend microwave transmission into higher frequencies—the 10- to 18-gigahertz range—then fading effects will be more significant. Rain will cause much more severe fading and this may over-ride other tower-spacing considerations, and cause the towers to be built much closer together.

COMPANDORS   One of the problems in the design of amplifiers and repeaters is that the signal to be amplified can vary widely in strength. Sometimes the person telephoning may shout. Another person may talk very softly with his mouth a long way from the telephone mouthpiece. After going through the long chain of amplifiers both of these signals must emerge at a reasonable volume, and noise free.

The problem can be understood by looking at Fig. 9.10. This illustrates the passage of a signal of one particular amplitude. After this has been transmitted it remains about 10 decibels above the level of the noise that was amplified with it. Some of the signal will be of greater strength and so better off than this, but some will be of lower strength. Suppose that a weak signal is 15 decibels lower than the one illustrated. When this reaches the repeaters in the diagram it will be only about the same amplitude as the noise level, or even lower. The noise will be amplified with it and the weak signal will be drowned in noise.

To overcome this problem, it is desirable that the very strong and very weak signals are adjusted in amplitude so that they are closer together. The repeaters can then be more effective in keeping them above the noise level. This is done with a device called a *compandor*. The compandor com-

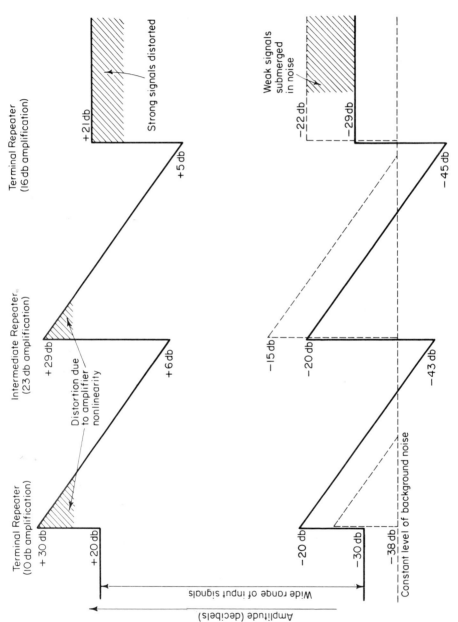

Fig. 9.15A. Transmission of signals of a wide range of amplitudes without a compandor.

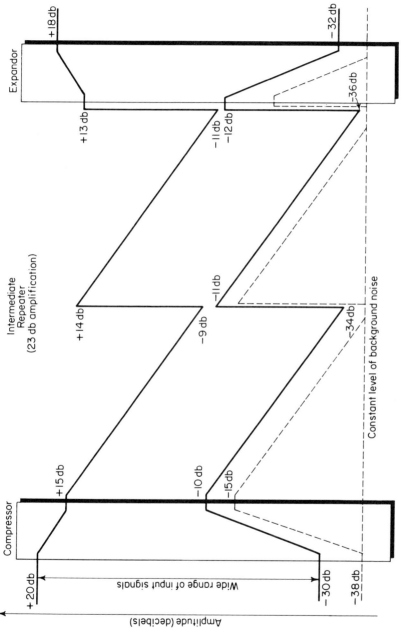

Fig. 9.15B. Transmission of the same range of signals, with a compandor.

presses the range of signal amplitudes before transmission, and then, after transmission, restores them to their former levels. Thus there are two parts of the compandor circuits, a *compressor* at the transmitting end and an *expandor* at the receiving end.

There may be as much as 50 decibels difference between a loud voice input and a weak voice input. On a typical circuit this is "compressed" so that the difference is reduced to about 25 decibels. The compressor raises the level of the weak signals so that when transmitted they do not sink below the noise level, and it lowers the level of the loud signals so that they do not overload the amplifiers. The transmission of speech within this limited range of volumes gives much clearer results than if the range were greater.

Figure 9.15 illustrates the transmission of signals of a wide range of amplitudes. They are transmitted over a link which has one intermediate repeater. Figure 9.15A shows the transmission without using a compandor. The weakest signals drop below the level of the thermal noise. After amplification they are still submerged in noise. The stronger signals, on the other hand, overload the amplifier which does not have a linear response over such a large range. When the compandor is used on these signals (Fig. 9.15B), they do not fall below the noise level or overload the amplifier. The expandor lowers the amplitude of noise and so the channel is more silent when no one is speaking.

Compandors do not, of course, improve the signal-to-noise ratio for steady power signals. The improved clarity is a result of the wide variation in human speech amplitudes. Data signals are transmitted at a steady power and so will not be improved by compandors. They may, in fact, fare somewhat worse on compandored channels than on noncompandored channels because the former may be engineered for a smaller signal-to-noise ratio, knowing that the compandor would make this acceptable for speech.

10 FREQUENCY AND BANDWIDTH

Light, sound, radio waves and AC signals passing along telephone wires are all described in terms of *frequencies*. In all of these means of transmission the instantaneous amplitude of the signal at a given point oscillates rapidly, just as the displacement of a plucked violin string oscillates. Rate of oscillation is referred to as the frequency and described in terms of *cycles per second*.

With light we see different frequencies as different colors. Violet light has a higher frequency than green; green has a higher frequency than red. With sound the higher frequencies are heard as higher pitch. A flute makes sounds of higher frequency than a trombone. Normally, the light and sound reaching our senses do not consist of one single frequency, but of many frequencies or a continuous band of frequencies all traveling together. A violin note has many harmonies higher than the basic frequency with which the violin string is vibrating. The human voice consists of a jumble of different frequencies. When we see a red light it is not one frequency but a collection of frequencies which combine to give this particular shade of red. The same is true with the electrical and radio signals of telecommunications. We will not usually be discussing one single frequency but a collection, or a band, of frequencies occupying a given range.

THE SPEECH SPECTRUM
The human ear can detect sounds over a range of frequencies; in other words, it can hear sounds of different pitch. A sensitive ear can hear sounds of frequencies ranging from about 30 cycles per second up to 20,000 cycles per second, though most people have a range somewhat less than this.

When we refer to a sound of a given frequency, we mean that the air is vibrating with that number of oscillations per second. In order to transmit this sound the microphone of a telephone converts the sound into an equivalent number of electrical oscillations per second. The telephone channels over which we wish to send data are, then, designed to transmit electrical oscillations of a range equivalent to the frequencies of the human voice, although these frequencies are often changed for transmission purposes.

In fact, the telephone circuits do not transmit the whole range of the human voice. It was found that this was unnecessary for the understanding of the speech and the recognition of the speaker. Figure 10.1 illustrates the characteristics of human speech and shows that its strength is different at different frequencies. Most of the energy is concentrated between the frequencies 300 and 3400 cycles per second, and each telephone channel is designed to transmit only this range. This is a decision based upon economics. It permits the maximum number of telephone conversations to be sent at one instant over the various physical media discussed in Chapter 8. while still making the human voice intelligible and the speaker recognizible.

Figure 10.1 may be described as a *spectrum diagram*. The reader should become familiar with such a form of diagram as it will be used several times subsequently in explaining the techniques used in data transmission.

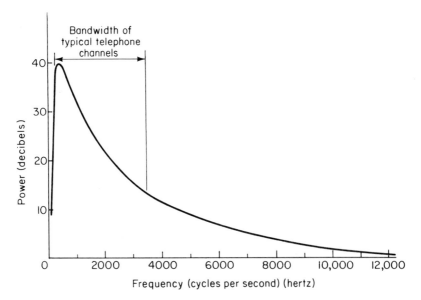

Fig. 10.1. Spectrum of human speech, In order to transmit speech so that the speaker is recognizable and understandable only the range indicated need be sent.

Figure 10.1 relates to audible frequencies. Diagrams used on later pages of this book refer to frequencies of electrical signals. Frequencies much higher than the audible range are often used to carry the *lower* frequency signals in a way that is explained below. Sound spectra or electrical signal spectra are broadly equivalent to light spectra with which the reader may, perhaps, be more familiar. A light beam may be split up into several different frequencies by a spectrometer to produce a band of different colors in the same way that sunlight is split up by rain to form a rainbow. Sometimes the spectrum may contain a continuous band of color, and other times, sharp spectral lines. The spectral diagrams we shall use for purposes of explanation do the same to the jumble of frequencies in an electrical signal, and some diagrams, such as those in Fig. 13.11, show sharp spectral lines rather than a continuous spectrum.

A spectral line (of light or electrical waves) relates to transmission at one frequency only. For a frequency of the transmission may be represented by the equation

$$a = A \sin 2\pi ft$$

where a is the instantaneous amplitude which is a function of time t, and A is the maximum amplitude.

We shall refer many times to this *sine wave*. It is illustrated in Fig. 10.2.

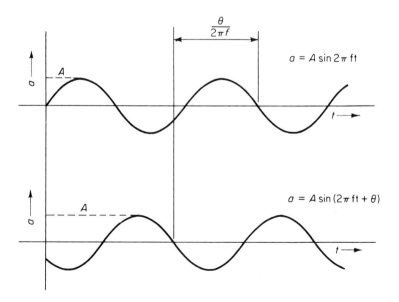

Fig. 10.2. Two sine waves of frequency f with phase difference θ.

There are f peaks of the type in this diagram occurring every second—that is what we mean when we say the "frequency" is f cycles per second.

PHASE

Figure 10.2 shows two sine waves both of frequency f, which are displaced from each other in time so that their peaks do not occur simultaneously. They are therefore said to be different in *phase*. If one wave is described by $a = A \sin 2\pi ft$, then the other is described by $a = A \sin (2\pi ft + \theta)$, where θ is said to be the *phase difference*.

The time for one cycle of a sine wave, in other words, time $1/f$, is equivalent to a phase difference or angle of $\theta = 360°$ (or 2π radians). Two waves of the same frequency, but differing in phase by $360°$, are identical. One of the methods of sending digital information that will be discussed in Chapter 13 is to transmit it as variations in phase. The maximum that the phase can be varied for this purpose is less than $360°$ because a $360°$ change would be indistinguishable from the original.

Two sine waves differing in time by Δt have a phase difference of $\theta = 2\pi f \Delta t$. The time difference Δt, therefore, as indicated in Fig. 10.2, is $\theta/2\pi f$.

BANDWIDTH

While the frequency range 300 to 4000 or even 300 to 3000, is satisfactory for voice transmission, music would sound poor because it would be clipped of the higher and lower frequencies which give it its quality. To faithfully reproduce the deep notes of percussion or double bass we need to go down to 60 or even 30 cycles per second, and to reproduce the high harmonics which make instruments sound realistic, a frequency up to 15,000 or better, 18,000, is desirable. It is toward these extremities that the high-fidelity enthusiasts strive.

AM radio transmits sound frequencies up to 5000 cycles per second and thus it is capable of reproducing music that does not sound too distorted, but is not high fidelity. FM radio can produce the whole range needed for high-fidelity reproduction. We say that AM radio uses a *bandwidth* of 5000 cycles per second, whereas FM has a bandwidth of 18,000. Bandwidth means the *range* of frequencies which are transmitted. A telephone channel capable of sending signals from 300 to 3300 cycles per second has a bandwidth of 3000.

The waves of FM radio do not actually travel at frequencies 30 to 18,000. The transmission occurs, as shown in Fig. 8.1, at frequencies of the order of 100,000,000. A similar consideration is true with AM radio, and with high frequency media used as carriers of telephone channels or data transmission.

The transmission media may work efficiently only at frequencies of, say, 70 to 150 megahertz (1,000,000 cycles per second is referred to as one megahertz). This high frequency must therefore in some way be made to *carry* the lower frequencies. Stated in another way, the low frequencies must *modulate* the *carrier frequencies* to produce a signal which can be transmitted efficiently and from which, after transmission, the lower frequencies can be recovered.

Let us suppose that a bandwidth of 4000 is to be used for voice transmission, and the carrier frequency is 30 kilohertz. The conversion process may change the frequency band from 0–4000 to 30,000–34,000 cycles per second. The bandwidth is still 4000 and will still carry the same quantity of information, be it voice or data.

The term bandwidth, therefore, says nothing about the frequency of transmission; it only indicates the size of the range of frequencies.

A bandwidth of more than 4000 may carry more than one voice channel. Suppose that the transmission media handles the frequency range 30,000 to 42,000. The process of converting the original low frequencies may be done for three voice channels so that they form bands at 30,000–34,000 as before, and also 34,000 to 38,000 and 38,000 to 42,000. Packing several channels into one bandwidth so that they are transmitted simultaneously is referred to as *multiplexing* and will be discussed in Chapter 15.

For data transmission the wider the band, the greater is the number of bits that can be sent over that channel. However, it also has a special significance because all channels have a certain amount of *noise and distortion* on them. The greater the bandwidth the greater the probability of transmitting a given amount of data without error in the presence of noise and distortion.

**BANDWIDTH ON
A TYPICAL
TELEPHONE SYSTEM**
Figure 10.3 illustrates the relative signal strength received on a typical telephone system. The reader may compare this with the spectrum of human speech in Fig. 10.1. It will be seen that between about 300 and 3400 cycles per second, different frequencies are attenuated roughly equally. Above 4000 virtually no signal is received. The strongest human voice frequencies fit into this range.

Where multiplexing is used the wide bandwidth available may be divided up into slices of 4000 cycles. The signals like that in Fig. 10.3 fit into these slices leaving a comfortable gap between separate channels. The gap is needed to minimize interference or "cross talk" between channels. The electronics of the telephone plant have deliberately chopped the signal into the shape in Fig. 10.3 so that it fits completely into the 4000 cycle slices, but nevertheless gives a "flat response," i.e., equal attenuation, over the range 300 to 3400 cycles, which is the important range for voice transmission.

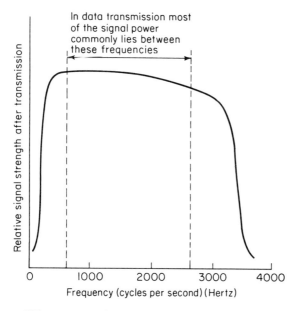

Fig. 10.3. The variation of amplitude with frequency of a signal received on a typical telephone system.

When we send data over the telephone, this will be similarly chopped, so we must make sure that it can survive this butchery without losing bits. If we employ a private leased line, the whole of the bandwidth in Fig. 10.3 will be ours to use—a bandwidth of about 3100 cycles.

If we use the public network the band available may be very slightly less than that in Fig. 10.3, especially if there are several channels in tandem. Also the public link cannot be as free from distortion as a private leased link, and so the maximum data transmission speed over it is lower. Furthermore, the telephone company uses part of the bandwidth in Figure 10.3 for signaling, and our data must be sent in such a form that they will not interfere with this and cause their automatic devices to take incorrect action. This is explained in Chapter 17.

Another way of presenting the information in Fig. 10.3 is to plot against frequency the attenuation suffered by the signal in being transmitted on that particular line. This is done in Fig. 10.4. The average attenuation over the bandwidth in which the majority of the signal strength is concentrated is somewhat less than 30 decibels. Below 400 and above 3000 cycles per second the attenuation becomes much greater. The region between the horizontal dotted lines in Fig. 10.4 is important in the design of data transmission equipment, as we shall see later in the book. On most telephone lines the attenuation does not vary more than about 10 decibels between 400 and 3000 cycles per second. The lines are engineered so that this part of the curve is relatively flat, but the drop at the edges of the 4000 cycle per second block of bandwidth is fast.

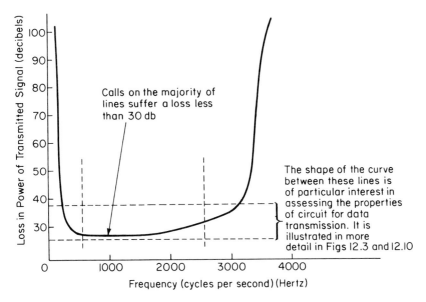

Calls on the majority of
lines suffer a loss less
than 30 db

The shape of the curve
between these lines is
of particular interest in
assessing the properties
of circuit for data
transmission. It is
illustrated in more
detail in Figs 12.3 and 12.10

Frequency (cycles per second) (Hertz)

Fig. 10.4. Attenuation at different frequencies.

MODULATION   The process of modifying a carrier so that it carries a signal of lower frequency, is referred to as *modulation*. The process of converting it back again so that the original signal is recovered is called *demodulation*.

AM and FM radio transmission stand for "amplitude modulation" and "frequency modulation," respectively, two techniques of carrying sounds at the frequencies to which we tune a domestic radio. "Tuning" is the process of selecting one channel from the many that are received simultaneously at slightly different frequencies. Amplitude and frequency modulation, and other variations, are also used for sending data over telecommunication links. Different modulation systems have different advantages depending upon the system needs, and the system planner may be faced with having to choose between modulation methods. This is discussed in Chapters 13 and 21.

In data transmission, modulation methods are used in two separate ways. *First,* they are used by the common carriers in their plant to change the frequencies of the voice bands as required. (This is illustrated in Fig. 10.5.) The modulation techniques and equipment for this are entirely part of the engineering of the transmission media. A computer system designer cannot change this in any way, but must merely use the channels provided for him and note any properties that may affect the data transmission.

Second, given a channel with certain properties, designed perhaps for voice rather than data, modulation is used to facilitate and improve the sending of bits over it. Modulation enables the maximum speed to be obtained

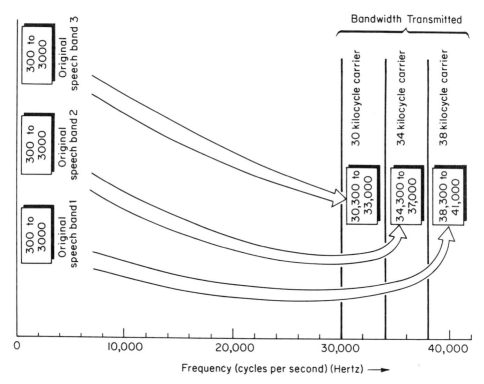

Fig. 10.5. Three voice bands modulate higher frequency carriers and are transmitted together.

from a given channel, and the modulation technique is designed so that it gives the maximum protection from the noise and distortion on the channel.

In order to hook a data-processing machine up to the telephone or telegraph channel provided, a small box of electronics is needed which converts the bits from the machine into a waveform suitable for the channel in question, and also converts the waveform received back into bits. This device is refered to as a *data set* or *modem*, the latter being a contraction of the words "modulation" and "demodulation" (Fig. 10.7 shows some typical modems; Fig. 10.6 illustrates their use).

Modems such as these are designed and manufactured both by the common carriers and by the manufacturers of the data-processing equipment. There are a variety of different designs of modems.

The basic function of the modulation process is to convert the data to be sent into a waveform tailored to the characteristics of the channel. Figure 10.4 shows the loss on a channel at different frequencies. The stream of data bits must here be converted into a signal having its energy mainly between 500 and 3100 cycles per second, and preferably evenly spread within this range. This is then transmitted down the channel, and at the other end the signal will be converted back into bits by the demodulation process. A baseband signal

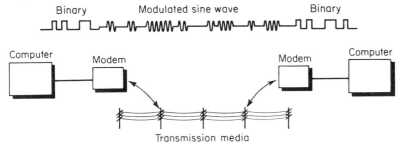

Fig. 10.6. The use of modems.

Fig. 10.7. Typical modems.

The GPO Datel Modem No. 2 for transmitting up to 200 bits per second over Datel 200 lines in the United Kingdom.

The Bell System Dataphone Modem No. 202A for transmitting at speeds up to 1200 bits per second over public dial-up voice lines.

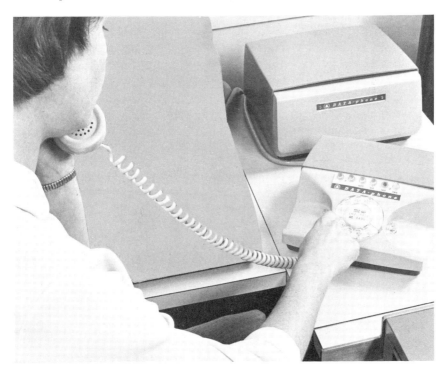

may have a substantial part of its energy at frequencies below about 200 cycles per second. This could not be transmitted without conversion over the channel in Fig. 10.4 (though it is usually possible to send it over the base-band channel from your telephone to the local central office).

A variety of different modulation processes are possible, and these are further discussed in Chapter 13. There is much scope for ingenuity in the design of modems, and the increasing speed at which data can be sent over telephone lines is largely due to improving modem design. Often the data-processing system designer is faced with a choice of modems he may use. A further function of the modem is to protect the common carrier lines from undesirable signals which might cause interference with other users, or with the network's signaling system.

It will be seen that in their passage between data-processing machines, the bits may undergo two quite separate modulation processes. In fact, there may be more than two because the transmission media may, for example, build channels into channel groups, channel groups into super groups which contain several channel groups, these into basic master groups, and then fit three or more basic master groups into one transmission system, as shown in Fig. 16.1. The waveform then has to be subjected to successive processes of modulation or other means of multiplexing, which are generally done so adroitly that one cannot distinguish a channel that has undergone one translation from one that has undergone a hundred (Chapter 15).

THE EFFECT OF LIMITED BANDWIDTH

The reader may imagine the electrical signals we discuss as being a jumble of sine waves like those in Fig. 10.2, differing in frequency, f, and amplitude, A. The spectrum diagrams we will use plot A against f and so analyze this jumble.

It was proven by Fourier that any periodic function can be represented by a sum of simple sinusoidal functions. Any function with a period, T, (and hence a frequency $f = 1/T$) can be considered as a sum of sine functions whose frequencies are integral multiples of f.

Fourier's theorem can be written as follows:

$$
\begin{aligned}
F(t) = A_0 &+ A_1 \sin(2\pi\, ft + \theta_1) \\
&+ A_2 \sin(2\pi \times 2ft + \theta_2) \\
&+ A_3 \sin(2\pi \times 3ft + \theta_3) \\
&\quad \vdots \\
&+ A_n \sin(2\pi \times nft + \theta_n) \\
&\quad \vdots
\end{aligned}
\tag{10.1}
$$

The function in question is here represented by a series of sinusoidal components (spectral lines) of differing amplitudes at frequencies f, $2f$, $3f$, and so on. These may be referred to as "harmonics." A plucked violin emitting a "middle C" note of frequency 200 cycles per second has harmonics at 400, 600, 800 cycles per second, and so on.

In practice, as with the case of the violin string, the amplitudes, A_n, of the higher harmonics are quite small, and become smaller as n becomes larger.

If we wish to transmit the original signal with absolute accuracy we must transmit all those harmonics that are of significant magnitude and preserve their phase relationships. If we do not transmit all of those harmonics the resulting signal will then be only an approximation of the original.

The middle C violin note sounds realistic when reproduced over a hi-fi unit with a frequency range up to 18,000 cycles per second. It is recognizable over an AM radio with an upper frequency of 5000 cycles per second. If somebody played the violin to you over the telephone, the 3000 cycle bandwidth would make it almost unrecognizable as a violin. And if you listened only to the first few harmonics up to, say, 600 cycles per second, the note would definitely not be recognizable as a violin, but *would* be recognizable as "middle C."

This is the situation in data transmission also. We have a limited bandwidth available and we want to transmit the maximum number of bits per second over it. We do not therefore transmit all of the harmonics, but only enough for the bits to be recognizable as such.

This is illustrated in Fig. 10.8, which shows how "bits" are likely to become distorted on an actual transmission system. Suppose that we transmit pulses such as those shown at the top of the figure. The data rate is 2000 bits per second. If we transmit the fourth harmonic, as shown at the bottom of the figure, the resulting pulse shape is reasonably close to the original. It would be much closer if we transmitted, say, the eighth harmonic. To transmit the fourth harmonic a bandwidth slightly over 8000 cycles per second is needed, and for the eighth harmonic, over 16,000. With a bandwidth of 4000 cycles per second the pulses are reasonably like the original, and with 2000 could certainly be detected as being bits or not bits with good equipment. At 1000 cycles per second the pulses bear little resemblance to their original shape, but skillfully designed detection equipment might recover the original bits. At 500 cycles per second there is no hope of reconstructing the original.

Figure 10.8 does not show the effects of noise and distortion. These will further change the shape of the pulses, sometimes severely, as discussed in subsequent chapters. The probability of error in the recognition of bits will be greater with the misshapen bits transmitted over smaller bandwidths.

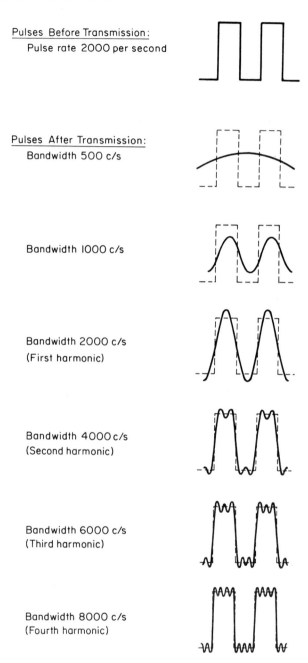

Pulses Before Transmission:
 Pulse rate 2000 per second

Pulses After Transmission:
 Bandwidth 500 c/s

Bandwidth 1000 c/s

Bandwidth 2000 c/s
(First harmonic)

Bandwidth 4000 c/s
(Second harmonic)

Bandwidth 6000 c/s
(Third harmonic)

Bandwidth 8000 c/s
(Fourth harmonic)

Fig. 10.8. The effect of bandwidth on the quality of pulse transmission.

FOURIER
ANALYSIS

To understand the functioning of data transmission equipment and modems it is useful to analyze the signals transmitted into their component frequencies.

A relatively simple piece of Fourier analysis can be applied to a repetitive bit pattern with rectangular bits as shown in Fig. 10.9.

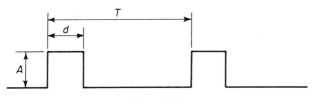

Figure 10.9

A bit represented by a rectangular increase in voltage, A, is transmitted once every T seconds. In other words, the pattern is repeated with a frequency f, where $f = 1/T$. The duration of the bit is d seconds. It was shown by Fourier that this increase in voltage is a sinusoidal function of time, $V(t)$, as follows:

$$V(t) = \frac{Ad}{T} + \left(\frac{2Ad}{T}\frac{\sin \pi d/T}{\pi d/T}\right) \cos 2\pi ft$$
$$+ \left(\frac{2Ad}{T}\frac{\sin 2\pi d/T}{2\pi d/T}\right) \cos 2\pi \cdot 2ft$$
$$+ \left(\frac{2Ad}{T}\frac{\sin 3\pi d/T}{3\pi d/T}\right) \cos 2\pi \cdot 3ft + \cdots$$
$$\cdots + \left(\frac{2Ad}{T}\frac{\sin n\pi d/T}{n\pi d/T}\right) \cos 2\pi \cdot nft + \cdots \qquad (10.2)$$

This consists of sinusoidal (cosine) components at frequencies f, $2f$, $3f$, and so on, up to infinity. In other words, it is a collection of sine waves superimposed on top of each other. These are referred to as "harmonics" of the basic frequency, f. The amplitudes are the terms in parentheses. For high harmonics (large n) these amplitudes will be small.

For the case where $d = T/2$, the resulting square wave may be regarded as a 0 1 0 1 0 1 ... bit pattern, and the resulting spectrum is plotted in Fig. 10.10.

In Fig. 10.11 the first three harmonics are plotted: $2A/\pi \cos 2\pi ft$, $-2A/3\pi \cos 2\pi \cdot 3ft$ and $2A/5\pi \cos 2\pi \cdot 5ft$. The sum of these waves is shown as the dotted line, and it will be seen that this roughly approximates to the square wave that is being transmitted.

The 0 1 0 1 0 1 ... square wave is a highly repetitive pattern, and so

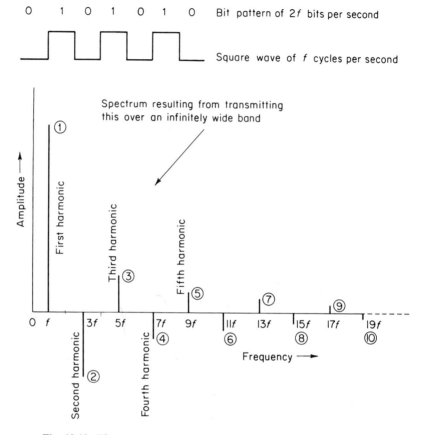

Fig. 10.10. The spectral components of a square wave representing a bit pattern 0 1 0 1 0 1 . . . Over a limited bandwidth only the lower harmonics can be transmitted.

gives the relatively few spectral lines in Fig. 10.10, which are fundamentals of the frequency of repetition of the basic square wave. If the bit pattern is less repetitive than this, the number of spectral lines increases.

This may be seen still using the simple analysis of Eq. (10.2) by increasing the distance between the pulses. Suppose that the bits 1 0 0 0 0 are repeated so that T/d is now 5. The spectral components then become

$$\frac{2A \sin \pi/5}{\pi} \cos 2\pi ft$$

$$\frac{A \sin 2\pi/5}{\pi} \cos 2\pi \cdot 2ft$$

$$\frac{2A \sin 3\pi/5}{\pi} \cos 2\pi \cdot 3ft \quad \text{and so on} \quad (10.3)$$

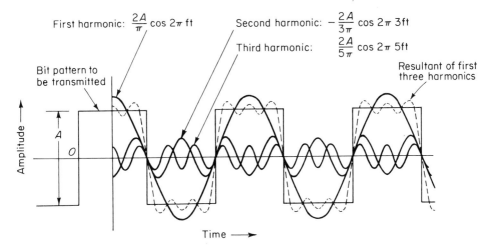

Fig. 10.11. The first three harmonics composing a bit pattern 0 1 0 1 0 1 .... The sum of the first three harmonics only approximately represents the bit waveform transmitted.

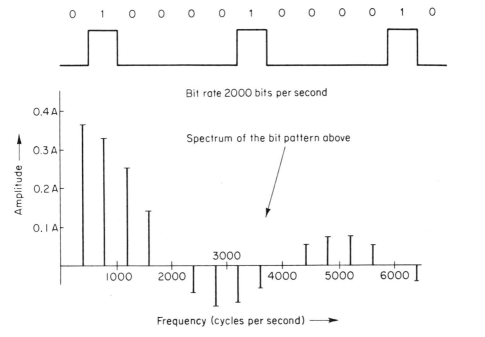

Fig. 10.12. Spectrum of rectangular pulse with a separation of five times the pulse width.

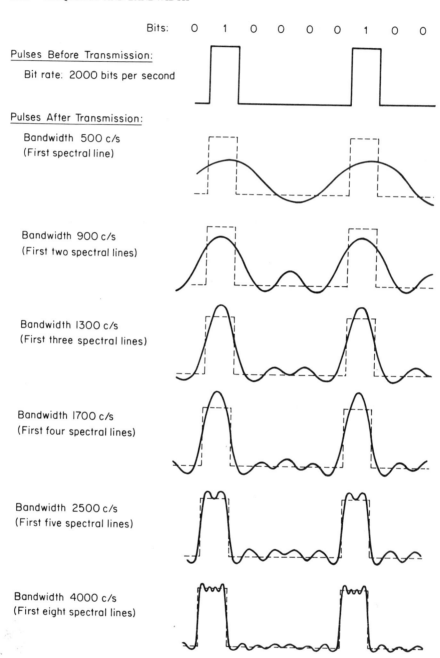

Fig. 10.13. The effect of transmitting the pulses in Fig. 10.12 over differing bandwidths.

These are plotted in Fig. 10.12. Figure 10.13 shows the resulting wave-shapes of such a pulse train when different bandwidths allow different numbers of spectral lines to be sent.

If the transmission rate is 2000 bits per second, the first spectral line will be at 400 cycles per second, the second at 800, and so on. As is shown in Fig. 10.13, the first two spectral lines are barely sufficient to recover the original signal. When three spectral lines are transmitted, the bit pattern becomes more recognizable. A bandwidth of twice the signaling rate in bits per second gives a reasonably squared-off pulse, but the bit pattern could be recovered with less bandwidth than this.

A large number of lines occur when the pulse width, d, is one twelfth of the repetition frequency. The amplitudes of the spectral lines form an envelope shape $\sin x/x$ where $x = n\pi d/T$ or in this case $x = n\pi/12$. Figure 10.14 is drawn, like Fig. 10.12, for a bit rate of 2000 bits per second, and a bit width, d, of 1/2000 second, assuming that the presence of a pulse represents a 1 bit and its absence a 0 bit.

If the bit pattern is irregular rather than strictly repetitive, as in the preceding examples, the number of spectral lines will increase until for a random bit pattern, or for one bit on its own, the lines become merged into a continuous spectrum.

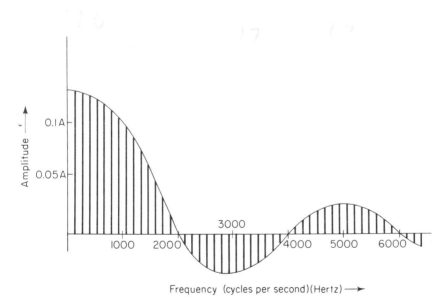

Fig. 10.14. Spectrum resulting from a pulse of width d repeated at intervals T, where $T/d = 15$. Pulse width is 1/2000 second. Bit rate is 2000 bits per second.

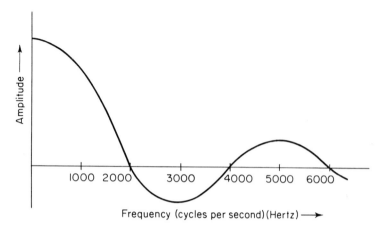

Fig. 10.15. Continuous spectrum of a solitary pulse with width 1/2000 second.

Figure 10.15 extends the ratio T/d further than in Figs. 10.14 and 10.12, making T infinite. In other words, Fig. 10.15 represents one solitary pulse, of the same width as those in Figs. 10.12 and 10.14. The spectrum is now continuous. The energy is spread throughout the spectrum rather than concentrated into single spectral lines. The zero points in the spectrum, however, still occur at the same points as in Figs. 10.14 and 10.12, and the relative amplitudes of the envelope containing the spectral lines are similar. Roughly the same bandwidth considerations still apply as those illustrated in Fig. 10.13.

11 THE MAXIMUM CAPACITY OF A CHANNEL

The capacity of a channel may be described as the maximum rate at which information can be sent over it without error, and this, for data transmission purposes, may be measured in bits per second.

The rate at which we can send data over a channel is proportional to the bandwidth of the channel. Hartley[1] proved in 1928 that a given bandwidth × time is required to transmit a given quantity of information. This can be pictured by imagining a phonograph record with data recorded on it in the dots and dashes of Morse code. If we double the speed of play of the record we halve the time needed to relay this coded data. Doubling the speed of the record doubles the frequencies of the sound, as well as the bandwidth used. Similarly, we may increase the record speed and relay the data very fast providing there is some way of interpreting the squeaks that result. When we exceed a certain speed the sounds will no longer be audible because we have exceeded the frequencies detectable by the human ear. The human ear thus has a limited bandwidth.

In 1924 and 1928, Nyquist[2] published papers also concerned with the capacity of a noiseless channel. He showed that if one sends $2W$ different voltage values (or other symbols) per second, these can be carried by a signal with no frequencies greater than W. If frequencies greater than W are sent, they are *redundant*, unnecessary for the reconstruction of the series of signal values at the receiver.

In other words, a bandwidth W can carry $2W$ separate voltage values per second. If one is sending binary signals as in the telegraph signaling

---

[1] Hartley, R. V. L., "Theory of Information." *Bell System Tech. J.*, **7** (1928).

[2] Nyquist, H., "Certain Factors Affecting Telegraph Speed" (1924), and "Certain Topics in Telegraph Transmission Theory" (1928). *Transactions A.I.E.E.*

discussed in Chapter 7, the sending voltage has one of two separate values. One can therefore send $2W$ bits per second. However, if one sends two bits simultaneously by having *four* possible voltage levels at any one instant, then the $2W$ voltage values per second are used to code $4W$ bits per second. Eight alternative voltage values at one instant can be used to code three bits and achieve a signaling rate of $6W$ bits per second.

In general, n bits can be sent at any one instant by using one of 2^n possible signal levels. Therefore with 2^n possible and distinguishable signal levels, a signaling rate of $2nW$ bits per second can be transmitted through a channel with W cycles per second of bandwidth.

If L is the number of signaling levels:

$$2^n = L$$

$$\therefore \quad n = \log_2 L$$

Therefore the channel capacity, C, in absence of noise, is given by

$$C = 2W \log_2 L$$

The question thus arises: How many signaling levels can be transmitted and be separately distinguishable at the receiver? Noise and distortion on the line, fluctuations in the attenuation, and a limit on the signal power which can be used obviously restrict this.

BAUDS   The speed of a transmission line is often quoted as being a certain number of "bauds." This term is usually used to relate to the signaling speed actually used on a line, not to the capacity of the line. It refers to *the number of times the line condition changes per second*. If the line condition represents the presence or absence of *one* bit, then the signaling speed in bauds is the same as bits per second. If, however, the line can be in one of four possible states, that is $L = 4$, then one line condition represents a "dibit," that is, two bits instead of one ($n = 2$). x bauds will then be the same as $2x$ bits per second. The Bell 201 data set, for example, transmits data in dibits; each pair of bits is coded as one of four possible combinations. If the signals are coded into eight possible states then one line condition represents three bits. One baud equals three bits per second, and so on.

The reader should note that the term "bauds" is sometimes taken to mean "bits per second." While this is true with many lines because they use two-state signaling, it is not true in general. For any line not using two-state signaling, it is wrong. *The term bauds has sometimes therefore proven confusing, and will not be used again throughout this book, except when discussing telegraph services which have the word normally associated with them.*

SIGNALING ON
A CHANNEL
WITH NOISE

Shannon,[3] twenty years later, proved again mathematically that a channel has a finite maximum capacity. He discussed a continuous channel as well as one transmitting discrete values. His work relates first to a noiseless channel, and then, more interestingly in our case, to a channel with noise.

Shannon proved that if signals are sent with a signal power S, over a channel perturbed by white noise (random, i.e., Gaussian, fluctuations) of power N, then the capacity of the channel in bits per second is

$$C = W \log_2 \left(1 + \frac{S}{N}\right) \tag{11.1}$$

where W is the bandwidth of the channel.

This formula gives the maximum signaling rate over a communication channel, in terms of three parameters which are known or measurable. It is of fundamental importance, and is sometimes referred to as the *Shannon–Hartley law*. According to this law, the maximum number of data bits that can be sent over a channel in time T seconds is

$$WT \log_2 \left(1 + \frac{S}{N}\right)$$

Shannon's law relates to transmitting bits the sequence of which is *completely unpredictable*. As will be discussed later in this chapter, if there were some way of anticipating a nonrandom bit sequence the transmission rate might be increased. However, for an unpredictable bit sequence Shannon's proof shows that there is *no possible way* of exceeding this quantity of information for these channel parameters. An engineer can design very ingenious modulation techniques and elaborate coding systems, but try as he might he will never send more than this number of bits over the channel, unless he increases either the bandwidth available or the signal-to-noise ratio.

Let us suppose that a certain section of telephone line is known to have a signal-to-noise ratio of 20 decibels. In other words, the noise power from the line is $\frac{1}{100}$ of the signal power transmitted (as shown in Fig. 9.5). We wish to use this line to transmit data and the bandwidth available is 2600 cycles per second. Using these in Eq. (11.1) we find that the capacity of the line is

$$C = 2600 \log_2 \left(1 + \frac{100}{1}\right)$$

$$\log_2 x = (\log_2 10)(\log_{10} x) = 3.32 \log_{10} x$$

$$\therefore \quad C = 2600 \times 3.32 \, x \log_{10} 101 = 17{,}301$$

[3] Shannon, Claude E., "Mathematical Theory of Communication." *Bell System Tech. J.* (July and October 1948).

The *maximum possible* rate at which data could be transmitted over this voice line is thus about 17,300 bits per second.

If the signal-to-noise ratio were 30 decibels—a more typical figure—then we would have

$$C = 2600 \log_2 \left(1 + \frac{1000}{1}\right) = 25,900 \text{ bits per second}$$

The only way to improve upon this is to make fundamental changes in the construction of the line which would increase the transmitting power of the amplifiers, increase the bandwidth, or reduce the noise. There is nothing that can be done by way of ingenious terminal equipment design that would give a bit rate higher than these figures. If the common carrier provides a line of these characteristics the figures above give the maximum transmission rate that we could ever achieve.

It is not unknown for an ingenious inventor to propose a scheme that would do better than Eq. (11.1). However, so fundamental is Shannon's law that any such plausible scheme may be treated with the same attitude as inventions for perpetual motion machines. Somewhere in the scheme there is a flaw, and one can say with assurance that it will not work.

In fact, systems used in practice on voice lines work at speeds very much lower than those above. It is common to find transmission schemes operating at 600 and 1200 bits per second on such lines. Sometimes the part of the bandwidth that can actually be used for transmitting is less than 2600 cycles per second because of signaling considerations. But even on a good quality line with the full bandwidth available, 2400 bits per second is the speed commonly used today, although 4800 is sometimes used and we can expect to see 7200 bits per second soon. Part of the reason for this is that as one approaches closer to the Shannon maximum, the encoding necessary becomes very complex with longer and longer word lengths and therefore more and more delay in encoding and decoding.

Over the communication line described, the maximum speed that is likely to be achieved with tolerable error rates with today's modulation equipment is about 10,000 bits per second, or somewhat over one third of the Shannon limit. At present it seems doubtful whether speeds much higher than this will be achieved economically over working systems using a line such as that described.

WHITE GAUSSIAN NOISE The noise referred to in Shannon's equation is Gaussian noise. This means that the amplitude of the noise signal varies around a certain level in a purely *random* fashion with respect to time. The amplitude of the noise signal follows a *Gaussian* distribution. Shannon's equation was proved using this assumption.

This may seem a somewhat unjustified assumption to make. How do we know that the noise amplitude follows a Gaussian distrubution? The noise I hear in my New York apartment certainly does not follow any such pattern. It consists of the television next door, a rhythmic banging from the plumbing, and the wail of police cars screaming through the night. However, if I open my window and listen to the sounds from far away, the hum of the big city, this infinite jumble of diminutive sounds does approximate that of Gaussian distribution.

In telecommunication circuits there will certainly be much noise that is not Gaussian, such as the clicks and whistles we sometimes hear on the telephone. However, in all electronic circuitry there is a steady continuing background of random noise. This is sometimes referred to as *thermal* noise.

The atoms and molecules of all substances vibrate constantly in a minute motion which causes the sensation of heat. The higher the temperature the greater this vibration. As the atoms vibrate they send out electromagnetic waves, and as there are many atoms, we have a chaotic jumble of electromagnetic waves of all frequencies. The electrons in electrical conductors move in a similar random fashion. These motions form the ultimate unavoidable noise background to all electronic processes. It is a continuous Gaussian noise like the hum of a distant city.

We thus have to send data signals against this background of a ceaseless random variation in amplitude, usually of low intensity. When one can hear it, it sounds like a hiss. If the volume of an FM radio is turned up full when there is no program being received, one can hear the hiss of this noise.

This Gaussian noise in electronic circuits is referred to as *white noise*. It is called "white" because it contains all spectral frequencies equally on average just as white light contains all the colors of the rainbow equally. It sounds like a hiss, different from the hum of diminutive sounds from a distant city because these, although Gaussian, are not "white" because they contain more low frequencies than high frequencies. High frequencies are absorbed more than low frequencies as sound travels through the air and is reflected off buildings and off the ground.

Figure 11.1

Figure 11.1 illustrates Gaussian noise. As its random variations occur there are occasional peaks several times the average amplitude. Normally, however, the data transmission equipment will be designed so that these are not large enough to interfere with the data.

If the electronic equipment were perfect, and *perfectly* insulated from external interference, there would still be white noise. Any electrical conductor is a source of white noise of power, N, where

$$N = kTW \tag{11.2}$$

where T is the temperature in degrees Kelvin,
W is the bandwidth, and
k is Boltzmann's constant: 1.37×10^{-23} joule/degree.

The power of the white noise is thus proportional to the absolute temperature. This fact is of little value on Earthbound communication links, but is important in receiving very long-distance transmissions from space. The transmitter can operate at much reduced power in the icy depths of space when shielded from sunlight.

Thermal noise, caused by the random motion of electrons, is the inescapable minimum. Practical circuitry in amplifiers and modulators will typically generate noise, however, which exceeds thermal noise by some 5 to 25 decibels. Large numbers of such devices are encountered on a long circuit and so the Gaussian noise at the end of the channel exceeds thermal noise by many decibels. Signal-to-noise ratio in well-maintained telecommunications channels will seldom be better than 30 decibels.

The power of thermal noise, unlike some other types of noise discussed in the next chapter, is proportional to bandwidth. For a given transmitting power, therefore, as will be seen from Eqs. (11.1) and (11.2), *the channel capacity is not quite proportional to bandwidth.* Doubling the bandwidth of the channel does not quite double its capacity. A 40,000 cycles per second channel will not carry quite as much data as ten 4000 cycles per second channels. Figure 11.2 sketches the relationship. An infinite bandwidth would carry a finite, maximum number of bits per second.

THE TRANSMISSION RATES ACHIEVED IN PRACTICE   Shannon's equation sets a theoretical maximum on the performance of the communication link, in the presence of white noise. The telephone company provides two wires coming out of a wall socket in the computer room, and these are one end of a channel of bandwidth, W. If perfect equipment could be designed to connect the computer to these two wires, it would be able to transmit to a distant and similarly equipped machine at a bit rate

$$W \log_2 \left(1 + \frac{S}{N} \right)$$

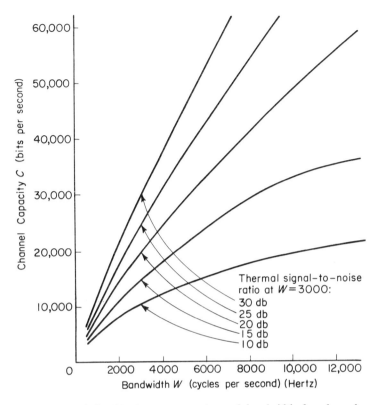

Fig. 11.2. Relationship between capacity and bandwidth for channels with differing levels of Gaussian noise.

However, with today's equipment, only a considerably lower speed than this can be obtained. The modulation process needed to convert signals for transmission cannot achieve the efficiency needed to give bit rates as high as Shannon's theoretical figure.

Chapter 13 discusses modulation more fully. There are a variety of different methods for modulating data to be transmitted, and these give different grades of performance over a given bandwidth. Making the best use of the bandwidth available is, in fact, to a large extent dependent on the design of the modems, and herein lies scope for much ingenuity.

Again assuming purely white and Gaussian noise, the signaling speed at a given bandwidth can be evaluated theoretically for each type of modulation. This can be established as a function of signal-to-noise ratio and probable error rates.[4] Expressions for the maximum signaling rate can be obtained

---

[4] Bennett, W.R. and Davy, J.R., *Data Transmission*. New York: McGraw-Hill, 1965.

which, as would be expected, give lower rates than the Shannon formula.

Figure 11.3 plots the Shannon formula, showing the speed per cycle of bandwidth in terms of signal-to-noise ratio. The shaded area below this curve gives an indication of the speeds that are achieved in practice today. It will be seen they are very much less than the Shannon limit. In fact, if one fifth of the Shannon limit were achieved, it would be regarded today as a fast and sophisticated system.

Figure 11.3 shows the maximum signaling speeds with two common types

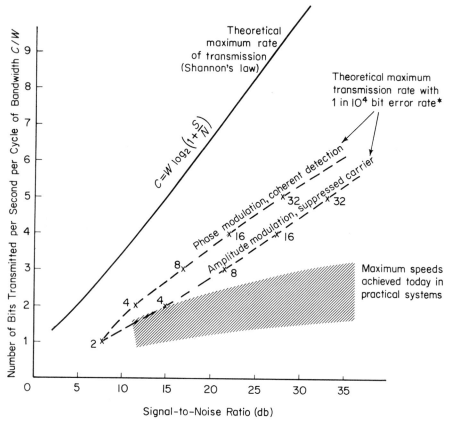

Fig. 11.3. The maximum data transmission speeds achieved in practice today are considerably lower than the Shannon theoretical maximum. These speeds fall into the shaded area above. The dotted lines are the theoretical maximum speeds with two common types of modulation (Chapter 13), in the presence of Gaussian noise, and calculated for an error rate of 1 error bit in every 10,000 transmitted. *Curves reproduced from Data Transmission by Bennett and Davey, McGraw Hill, 1965.*

of modem, assuming that they are operating in the presence of Gaussian noise with an error rate of one bit in 10^4. This is a somewhat larger error rate than is acceptable in practice, and hence these speeds are not found on actual systems. The figures on these dotted curves refer to number of states the signal can be in at any one instant. A binary signal, for example, can be in one of *two* states, as in Fig. 6.1. However, if there are four possible voltage levels rather than two, then these can represent two bits at one instant instead of only one. Eight levels can represent three bits. 2^n levels can represent n bits at one instant. However, as the number of voltage levels that must be distinguished increase, their spacing decreases, and the randomly fluctuating noise amplitudes are more prone to do more damage. In practice, more than four levels are rarely used because of this. This will be discussed further in Chapter 13.

It is clear that one way to increase the capacity of a channel is to raise the signal-to-noise ratio. As we have seen, the level of white noise is determined by natural phenomena which are beyond our control. Other types of noise *can* be controlled, although not entirely, and many measures are taken to do this. However, there is a level below which N cannot be pushed. If the distance between the repeaters is great, then the signal strength falls substantially, whereas the noise level generated at all points of the line remains the same. Too great a repeater separation gives too low an S/N ratio. The telephone companies can thus improve S/N by increasing the number of repeaters, though beyond a certain point it is not economic to do this.

How about increasing S, then? This is also largely a question of economics. Beyond a certain level it becomes expensive to increase the signaling power.

More than a hundred years ago the communications industry learned a bitter lesson about making S too large. After some of the toughest financial wrangling of the nineteenth century, and more than a year of heartbreaking failures on the high seas, the first transatlantic telegraph cable was laid—a magnificently impressive feat for its era. As was mentioned in Chapter 8, it worked appallingly slowly, taking half a day to transmit data that we can send over today's voice cable in a second. However, the press headlines were sensational beyond precedent. Dr. Whitehouse, a telecommunication scientist in England, decided that higher voltages were needed. His colleague, Dr. William Thomson (Lord Kelvin), disagreed. Whitehouse, however, insisted on using large induction coils which he had built. The line insulation gradually broke down and the 2500 tons of cable became useless. It was eight years before another cable was laid. One American newspaper claimed that the cable had been a hoax and an English writer "proved" that it had never been laid at all!

Today the maximum signal power is dominated more by questions of multiplexing. Where many channels, some data and some voice, travel over the same facility, the signal power of the data channels cannot be increased beyond a certain level; otherwise they would degrade the voice service. The common carrier is obliged to provide good service to all of his customers and so he uses the highest signal power for data that will not interfere significantly with telephone users obliged to share common facilities at the peak hour traffic load. As we will see in the next chapter, data signals that might contain periods of single-frequency transmission of a few seconds or more are particularly prone to cause interference on systems using multiplexing, and so must be further limited in power.

The economics of the engineering of modern telecommunication lines dictate that S can be a certain level and steps can be taken to decrease N, but beyond that point it is cheaper to engineer a greater bandwidth, W.

ENTROPY

The preceding Shannon formula relates to data in which when one bit or character is sent we have no clue as to what the next bit or character will be. This is normally the case with the computer techniques in use today. It is either not possible, or if it is possible the machine makes no attempt to estimate the probability of the next bit being 1, or the next character being A or 6.

This is not true with human communication. Here there is often a good chance of guessing what the next letter or next word will be. If I send the characters E L E P H A N, a human recipient will feel that there is a high probability of the next character being a T. When a telegram begins "CHRISTMAS COMES BUT ONCE A," it is reasonable to guess that the next word will be "YEAR."

If we can guess what the next bit, character, or word will be, the information is to some degree redundant, and so we may be able to devise a coding scheme which enables us to send more information than the channel capacity would otherwise allow.

The same applies to noise. We have discussed only white noise, in which we have no clue as to what the instantaneous noise amplitude at any point in time will be. We know that it is likely to lie in a certain range, with a Gaussian probability distribution. There may be other noise situations, however, in which we could make a more knowledgeable estimate of the likelihood of a certain noise pattern.

This informed guesswork constitutes an important part of the newly developed mathematical discipline of *information theory*. In Shannon's paper, "The Mathematical Theory of Communication," long before he reached his memorable $C = W \log_2 (1 + S/N)$ formula he had discussed the question of choice and uncertainty in the coding of information. To do this he used the concept of *entropy*.

Entropy is a measure of uncertainty or randomness. It is a concept which physicists have used for some time, largely in connection with thermodynamics, and it is intriguing to find it turning up again in a quite different discipline.

In the physical world the degree of randomness constantly increases. A parallel beam of light striking a wall is scattered in millions of random directions. Heat in a machine, organized into areas of high temperature and areas of low temperature tends to flow from the high to the low temperature. Similarly, on a communication line, voltages organized into square-edged 1 and 0 pulses become distorted and, if not regenerated by external means, they eventually become so distorted that they are inseparable from the noise background. In other words, entropy, the measure of randomness, increases. This appears to be one of the most fundamental laws of the universe, and it is sometimes quoted as an alternative way of stating the Second Law of Thermodynamics.

The temporary strivings of an intelligent agent can increase the degree of order in a small corner of the physical world, but left to its own devices, nature restores the chaos and entropy increases. All seems condemned in the long run to approximate a state akin to Gaussian noise.

The entropy associated with a message is, in effect, a measure of the uncertainty of what is to follow in the message. If the next symbol to be sent consists of six bits, then the entropy associated with that symbol can vary from zero bits to six bits. If it is certain, before it is sent, what each of the bits in the symbol will be, then the entropy associated with that symbol is zero. If it is completely uncertain what it will be—in other words, each bit has an equal probability of either being a 0 or 1—then the entropy is six bits per symbol.

The six-bit symbol can have $2^6 = 64$ possible different states. Let us number these 1 to 64, and let the probability of the symbol in the ith state be P_i. The 64 states are the only possible states, therefore,

$$P_1 + P_2 + P_3 + \cdots + P_{64} = 1$$

The entropy, H, of such a symbol is defined as the sum of the factors $P_i \log_2 P_i$ for each possible state the symbol can be in.

$$H = -(P_1 \log_2 P_1 + P_2 \log_2 P_2 + P_3 \log_2 P_3 + \cdots + P_{64} \log_2 P_{64})$$

When it is certain what the value of the symbol will be, then one of the values of P is 1, and all of the others are zero. Therefore,

$$H = -\log_2 1 = 0$$

The entropy is zero because there is no uncertainty as to what the symbol will be.

It can be shown that the maximum value of the preceding expression occurs when $P_i = P_2 = P_3 = \cdots P_{64} = \frac{1}{64}$. In other words, there is an equal probability of the occurrence of any state. Then

$$H = -64 \times \tfrac{1}{64} \log_2 \tfrac{1}{64} = 6$$

In general, if the symbols consist of x bits each of which could be a 1 or 0, then the entropy will range from zero to x.

For a symbol, word, or message of n possible states, the entropy is defined similarly as

$$H = -\sum_{i=1}^{i=n} P_i \log_2 P_i$$

and this ranges from a minimum of zero to a maximum of $\log_2 n$.

As an example of this, consider the throwing of a die. If it is a normal six-sided die this gives an equal probability of producing any number from one to six. The entropy associated with the throw is then

$$-(6 \times \tfrac{1}{6} \log_2 \tfrac{1}{6}) = 2.58$$

If, however, three of the sides are the same—let us say three sides read 1, 2, and 3, respectively, and the other three read 4—then the entropy would be

$$-(3 \times \tfrac{1}{6} \log_2 \tfrac{1}{6} + \tfrac{1}{2} \log_2 \tfrac{1}{2}) = 1.79$$

Similarly, with data transmission, if the symbols, words, or messages contain some measure of redundancy or predictability, then the entropy associated with them will be less than if they were random.

Shannon,[5] having defined entropy in this way, went on to prove that *for a noiseless channel with some discrete method of signaling such that its maximum capacity is C bits per second, the maximum rate at which data can be transmitted is C/H.*

Shannon went on to show that for a continuous signal the entropy of a Gaussian distribution is

$$H = W \log_2 2\pi eS \qquad \text{bits per second}$$

where W is the bandwidth used and S is the average power of the signal.

If N is the average white noise power, and $H_{(N)}$ is the entropy of this noise,

$$H_{(N)} = W \log_2 2\pi eN$$

---

[5] Theorem 9 in Shannon's "Mathematical Theory of Communication," *Bell System Tech. J.* (July and October 1948).

If the signal and noise on a continuous channel together form a Gaussian ensemble of average power $(S + N)$, then the entropy of this $H_{(S+N)}$ is

$$H_{(S+N)} = W \log_2 2\pi e(S + N) \qquad \text{bits per second}$$

Shannon showed that the maximum capacity of such a channel is given by

$$\begin{aligned} C &= H_{(S+N)} - H_{(N)} \\ &= W \left[\log_2 2\pi e(S + N) - \log_2 2\pi eN\right] \end{aligned}$$

And so the equation $C = W \log_2 (S + N)/N$ is obtained.

We thus see that the Shannon formula $C = W \log_2(S + N)/N$ applies to bit patterns which are completely unpredictable, and to noise which follows a Gaussian distribution. If the bit pattern is to some extent predictable, a coding scheme might, theoretically, be devised which removes the predictability or redundancy. The message would therefore be sent in fewer bits and the original bit pattern restored on reception.

Similarly, if the noise has less entropy than Gaussian noise, a theoretically higher bit rate would be possible.

The noise that is encountered in practice often has short sharp spikes of much greater amplitude than the white noise background. These destroy or add bits, and result in an error rate much higher than would be expected from a theory assuming constant Gaussian noise. Noise is discussed in the next chapter.

Information theory sets a maximum on what we might expect to achieve over given channels. In a sense it provides a target for the engineers to work toward. It goes on to produce theorems about the nature of signal coding, and error detection and correction codes which might aid in achieving the maximum transmission rate over a given bandwidth.

12 NOISE AND DISTORTION

On any telecommunication link there will be noise and distortion of some degree. A variety of techniques can be used in engineering the link to reduce this to an acceptable minimum.

Unfortunately, however, the acceptable criteria for data transmission are in certain ways different from those for other uses of the link such as voice. There can be a considerable degree of impulse noise and distortion on a voice line without the speech becoming unintelligible, annoying, or even too unnatural. Similarly, teletype lines can be noisy but when a telegram arrives with a few incorrect letters, it is still basically readable and understandable to a human being.

The systems engineer can rarely obtain a link which is specifically designed for data transmission, though this will become more common in the years to come. However, the immense value of the development of computers using telecommunications is that the present vast network of lines and exchanges, which has taken so much work to build up, can be used today to bring the power of the machines to all places where it can be made use of. Therefore we often have to use lines with noise and distortion to carry a signal for which they were not designed. Means have to be devised for overcoming this inadequacy.

Voice transmission differs from data transmission in two fundamental ways. First, with voice transmission we have an intelligent agency at each end of the line. If a burst of noise or other failure prevents the listener from hearing a word he can either guess what the word should have been, or else ask the speaker to repeat it. If he cannot hear he will ask the speaker to speak louder. This highly flexible intelligence does not exist when machine talks to machine, so control procedures must be devised which are as fail-safe as possible. Second, the information conveyed by the human voice is at a very much slower rate than that at which we want the machines to "talk." The normal rate of speaking is equivalent to something like 40 bits per second of written words, and this is "coded" with a very high degree of redundancy. We can usually follow the meaning of what is being said if we hear only about half of the words. Data transmission, on the other hand, over voice channels can take place at 2400 bits per second and higher. It is because of the low rate of information in speech, and because of the adaptability of the human ear, that distortions and noise levels damaging to data transmission have been quite acceptable in the engineering of the world's telephone lines.

This chapter outlines the types of noise and distortion that are common, and the effects they have. Some types can be overcome or minimized by suitable design of the terminal equipment, or by slower rates of transmission. Others cannot be prevented, but must be faced up to in the design of systems by means of error detection and correction, and retransmission techniques. Tight controls on the accuracy of data transmitted must be built into the computer programs.

SYSTEMATIC AND FORTUITOUS DISTORTION

We may classify the disturbances into two types: systematic and fortuitous. *Systematic distortion* is that which occurs every time we transmit a given signal over a given channel. Knowing the channel we can predict what is going to occur. The pulses may be *always* narrower or *always* distorted in a certain way. Given frequencies will *always* have a certain minimum phase delay. *Fortuitous distortion* is something which occurs at random, and so is not predictable, except in terms of probability. Examples of fortuitous distortion are white noise, impulse noise, chatter from the switchgear, cross talk, atmospheric noise, and so on.

Systematic distortion is then something which might possibly be compensated for electronically so that its effects are eliminated. Fortuitous distortion is more difficult to compensate for, though steps can be taken to minimize its effects and repair the damage it does. It may be possible to correct systematic distortion so that it never actually damages data. Fortuitous distortion, on the other hand, is occasionally going to produce an extra large noise burst or impulse which destroys or creates one or more data bits at random.

Let us first discuss the various types of fortuitous distortion.

WHITE NOISE

White noise was described in the last chapter. This is the random hiss that forms a background to all electronic signaling. It cannot be removed and so it sets a theoretical maximum on the performance of any communication link, and on the various modulation methods. The amplitude of the signal after attenuation must be kept sufficiently far above the white noise background to prevent an excess of hiss on radio or telephone circuits, or an excess of errors in data transmission. On the majority of lines the signal-to-white-noise ratio is better than 30 decibels although occasionally a dialed call will encounter a much worse ratio than this.

Occasionally there will be spikes of white noise higher than the majority, and peaks of other noise types such as cross-talk which may add on to the white noise. The error rates in the various types of equipment due to white noise alone can be calculated theoretically.

If white noise were all we had to worry about, the design of data transmission systems would be more straightforward. Unfortunately, there are other types of noise and distortion which are far less predictable and more disastrous in their effects.

IMPULSE NOISE   Unlike white noise and the various types of systematic distortion described later, *impulse noise* can have peaks of great amplitude which saturate the channel and blot out data. Impulse noise is the main source of errors in data. The duration of the impulses can be quite long relative to the speed of data transmission—sometimes as long as 0.01 second, for example. This would be heard merely as a sharp click or crack to a human listener and would not destroy any verbal intelligence, but if data were being transmitted at 75 bits per second, one bit might be lost. For speeds of 1000 or 2000 bits per second a group of ten or more bits would be lost.

Often a noise impulse removes or adds two or more adjacent data bits, and this means that conventional *parity checking may not detect the error.* A more sophisticated form of error detection code is needed, as discussed in a later chapter.

Figure 12.1 gives an illustration of the effects of a burst of noise. In this example the signal-to-noise ratio is low, as is indicated by the amplitude of the white noise relative to that of the signal. In this diagram the sampling is shown taking place at one instant. Some systems take a series of samples throughout the intended duration of the pulse, and thus lessen the probability of short noise spikes giving incorrect results.

There are many causes of impulse noise, some of which can be controlled, but most of which cannot without a complete re-engineering of the telecommunication facilities. Some impulse noise is audible during telephone conversations and some goes unnoticed. Stray clicks and crackles are all too familiar. Impulse noise comes from a variety of different sources. It may come from within the communication channel itself or from a source external to the channel.

External noise is picked up by induction or capacitance effects. Sharp voltage changes in adjacent wires or equipment induce noise spikes in the

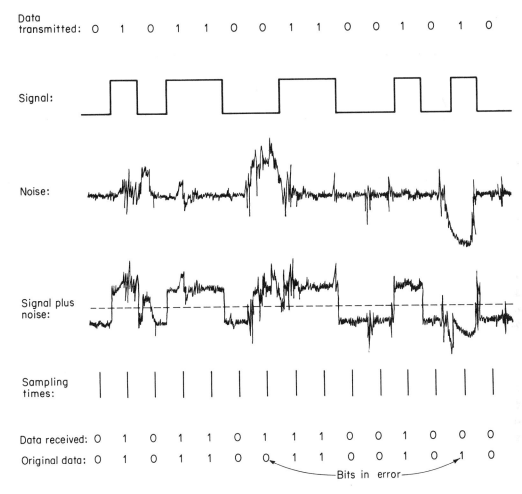

Fig. 12.1. Transmission in the presence of bad noise.

communication channel. Many of the audible clicks which are of high amplitude and which damage one or several adjacent bits come from switch-gear and telephone exchanges. Sometimes one can hear the rapid sequence of clicks generated by another person dialing. All relay operation is a poten-tial source of noise if the shielding or suppression is not adequate. Any switches or relays which make or break circuits carrying current cause a sharp voltage change and so can induce an equivalent voltage change in near-by sensitive circuits. Sometimes the power supply may induce hum or higher frequency components into the communication channel.

The inductive or capacitive coupling through which noise is induced may be in the exchange. It may be coupling between adjacent cable pairs which are physically close. The noise generated by relays and switches may travel down wires a long way before reaching the low-level transmission signals, and may come from plant in separate buildings.

Dial switching offices usually generate more noise than manual exchanges because there are many relay and switch operations, and large offices generate more noise than small ones—although switch manufacturers go to great pains to provide noise suppression. In some manual exchanges, particularly private branch exchanges, trouble has been experienced due to operators plugging into the data connection and listening to see whether the connection is free, as they might do with voice. Many large exchanges in cities, especially outside the United States, contain much old plant and this can cause more noise than the newer exchanges. Exchanges with step-by-step switches (Chapter 18) are worse than those with cross-bar switches. Often these switches are the most important noise source on a line. Figure 12.2 shows characteristics of a typical noise burst caused by step-by-step selection switches. Amplitudes of 100 millivolts are common in such disturbances. They can occur at points where the signal strength is low and may last up to several hundred milliseconds. The periodicity is caused by the step-by-step motion of the selector (see Fig. 18.3).

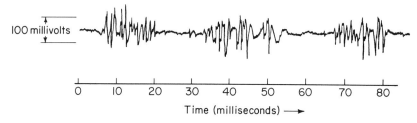

Fig. 12.2. Typical example of impulse noise caused by step-by-step selection switches (Fig. 18.3) in a public exchange.

Noise of the type in Fig. 12.2 usually causes errors in data to occur in a cluster rather than singly. Chapter 21 gives some statistics on the quantities of data errors and the degree of clustering that is found.

In years to come, when the present exchange equipment is largely replaced by electronic exchanges, the noise from this source will probably be much less. Today, however, lines going through public switching offices are more prone to noise than private lines. Other sources of impulse noise on public lines are the various ringing tones that are used, and the devices used during maintenance such as breakdown test sets and buzzers.

External noise can also come from atmospheric sources. As might be expected, open-wire pairs hanging between telegraph poles can easily pick up atmospheric static. They are affected by distant lightning flashes, and sometimes by contacts with trees or other foreign objects. Sometimes power lines or radar transmitters can cause interference. Radar interference has caused trouble with computer systems installed at airports, sometimes with the transmission of data and sometimes with the computer.

Impulse noise also originates from *within* the communication channel itself. This may be caused by circuit faults such as poor quality soldering and dirty relay contacts and jacks. Nonsoldered twisted joints may cause noise due to changes in temperature and slight movements of the joint. In all of these cases a variation in the contact resistance causes a fluctuation in voltage.

Many circuits carry more than one channel as explained in Chapter 15. In such systems there is usually a small amount of cross talk between one channel and another. The parameters of the multiplexing scheme for voice are chosen so that the effect of this is very small, and it is unlikely to affect data. However, an extra strong signal or impulse on one channel will exceed an overload point in the amplifiers and other devices, and various effects of this will be felt in the other channels. The signal which causes the overload may be a noise impulse, or it may result merely from the fact that all of the signals being transmitted by the same multiplex device happen to be at a peak at that instant. The sum of the peaks exceeds the capacity of the channel for distortion-free transmission. This fortuitous adding together of peaks occurs in most multiplex systems, especially during busy periods. Harmonics and modulation products (described in the next chapter) spill into other channels.

Large impulses in any communication system tend to overload the amplifiers, repeaters, and other electronic equipment they pass through on their journey. If an impulse is very large it will momentarily render each amplifier or repeater inoperative, and this will tend to prolong the disturbance. It will tend to generate resonant frequencies characteristic of each amplifier and filter in its path. These frequencies are usually close to the maximum frequency the system is designed to handle, and so again will tend to add to the disturbance. Amplifiers tend to convert severe amplitude disturbances into frequency disturbances so that they interfere with frequency modulation, as well as amplitude modulation (see next chapter).

There are many different means of reducing the effects of impulse noise. First, good screening can be used and careful planning of the circuit paths to minimize induction especially from switching equipment and relays. Second, multiplex systems are designed so that cross talk and peak overloads are minimized. Third, the amplifiers, filters, repeaters, equalizers, and other equipment on the line are designed to lessen the noise effects sufficiently for voice. As will be discussed later, further improvement of equalization can be carried out for data transmission. Fourth, the choice of modulation method can have an effect on the accuracy of transmission.

The computer systems designer cannot change the properties of the line he is given. Choice of the most suitable modem, however, is sometimes in his hands. He can lease a line with "conditioning" to minimize distortion, as discussed later, and he can ensure that the cabling and equipment on the user's premises are located and designed so that noise is not picked up there (as has often been the case).

CROSS TALK   "Cross talk" refers to one channel picking up some of the signal that is traveling on another channel. It occurs between cable pairs carrying separate signals. It occurs in multiplex links in which several channels are transmitted over the same facility (Chapter 15). It occurs in microwave links where one antenna picks up a minute reflected portion of the signal for another antenna on the same tower. In both of the latter cases the level of cross-talk noise is very small, because the system is designed with strict criteria for the maximum allowable cross talk.

Often the strongest source of cross talk is induction between separate wire circuits. Any long telephone circuits running parallel to each other will have cross-talk coupling unless they are perfectly balanced which is not the case in practice. Cross talk between wire circuits will increase with increased length of circuit, increased proximity, increased signal strength, or increased signal frequency.

Cross talk may originate in exchanges or switching centers where large numbers of wires run parallel to each other around the exchange. It may originate in a subscriber's building. It can be caused by capacitive as well as inductive coupling.

However, on most systems it is barely greater, and often less, than the level of white noise and so, like white noise, it does not normally interfere with data and is not annoying during speech. Occasionally, sometimes due to faults in the exchange, cross talk becomes louder and it is possible to hear another person's voice on the telephone. There will also be momentary peaks in cross talk which do interfere with data. With these exceptions, however, the level of cross talk is known or measurable, and can be treated like white noise for the purposes of selecting transmission parameters so that no interference with data will normally occur.

INTERMODULATION   There are certain undesirable types of data
NOISE   signals which can *cause* bad cross talk. On a
                             multiplexed channel, many different signals
are amplified together, and very slight departures from linearity in the equipment cause "intermodulation" noise. The signals from two independent chan-

nels intermodulate with each other to form a product which falls into a separate band of frequencies, just as two sound waves may "beat" to form a sound oscillation of a different frequency. The result of this may fall into a band of frequencies reserved for another signal. Such products arising from large numbers of pairs of channels combine to form low-amplitude babble which adds to the background noise in other channels. However, if one signal were a *single frequency*, then when it modulates a voice signal on another channel, this voice might become clearly audible in a third independent channel. One telephone user in this case would hear the conversation of one other. Privacy is important on the telephone and so the telephone company attempts to restrict the power of any single-frequency signal to a suitably low level.

The guilty single frequency could arise from data transmission in one of two ways. First, a repetitive code in a data signal could cause it unless the modem was specifically designed to prevent this. Many data-processing machines send repetitive codes to each other as part of their "line control" procedures; for example, to keep machines in synchronization while data are not being transmitted. Second, the modem itself, if not designed to avoid doing so, might transmit a single frequency when not transmitting data. Often one can hear this when dialing a computer. When the connection is established the apparatus at the other end will send a single-frequency "data tone" down the line to tell you that the connection is established. On some modems this frequency will always be present when there are no data. Such techniques could cause severe intermodulation cross talk unless the signal strength is restricted. If it is restricted then we are effectively reducing the capacity of the channel as seen from Shannon's equation

$$C = W \log_2 \left(1 + \frac{S}{N}\right)$$

This problem can be overcome by good modem design. When there are no data, the modem must not transmit a fixed-frequency tone, unless it is of very low amplitude. Further, the data must be randomized so that repetitive data patterns are not converted into a signal in which a single frequency dominates. Modems with these properties are now available and place no code restriction on the user. When they are used they can be permitted to send a high-strength signals over the carrier network and do not cause undesirable intermodulation cross talk.

This is especially important for transmission over bandwidths wider than a single telephone channel. The power of the signal, and of the noise, are both proportional to the bandwidth. The limitation imposed upon single-frequency transmission is, however, independent of bandwidth. Therefore, with this restriction, the signal-to-noise ratio will be lower for such signals, the higher the bandwidth.

ECHOES   Echoes on transmission lines are similar to cross talk in their effects on data transmission. Where there is a change in impedance on the transmission line a signal will be reflected so that it travels back down the line at reduced amplitude, thus forming an echo. The signal-to-echo power ratio can occasionally become less than 15 decibels though it rarely falls below 10 decibels. It can however be greater than white noise or cross talk.

Echo suppressors are used on long lines as was discussed in Chapter 9. They are not generally of value, however, in the problem of echoes in data transmission. Their action is triggered by the detection of human voice signals, and they are normally disabled when the circuit is used for data. In voice telephony, talker echoes become annoying when they are heard with a time delay measured in tens of milliseconds. In data transmission, however, delays of a fraction of a millisecond are significant, and it is the listener rather than the talker who is affected by them. Multiple reflections down a two-wire path, or echoes formed by the loop path of a four-wire circuit, reach the receiving machine or modem. If they are of sufficient volume they can cause errors in data.

SUDDEN CHANGES   Sometimes also the amplitude of the signal
IN LEVEL   changes suddenly. This may be due to faults in amplifiers, unclean contacts with variable resistance, added load or new circuits switched in, maintenance work in progress, or the switching to a different transmission path. Similar *phase* changes may occur suddenly, though there are fewer factors that can cause this.

These sudden changes can have an effect on certain data transmission systems which could result in the loss or addition of a bit. The effect they have depends upon the type of modem in use.

LINE   Occasionally a communication circuit fails
OUTAGES   to be operational for a brief period of time.
These "outages" may be caused by faulty exchange equipment, storms, temporary loss of carrier on a multiplex system, or other reasons, giving a brief period of open or short circuit. Often maintenance work on the lines, repeaters and exchanges is the cause of brief interruptions. This gives rise to two concerns. First, the data may be damaged by signal losses of a few milliseconds. Second; signal losses of 10 seconds or more may cause a serious break in system availability.

Tables 12.1 and 12.2 show some measurements of the frequency of line outages of different durations. Table 12.1 is for a private leased G.P.O.

voice line in England of 200 miles[1] routed through three coaxial cables on a "Supergroup" (see Chapter 16). The distribution of interruptions listed in Table 12.1 was recorded during two weeks of continuous operation.

Table 12.1

Duration of Interruption, milliseconds	Number of Interruptions	Relative Frequency, %
< 10	4	4
10–20	16	16
20–50	21	21
50–100	7	7
100–300	20	20
300 to 1 minute	25	25
> 1 minute	7	7

Table 12.2, made independently, is for a private leased voice line from London to Rome.[2] This was approximately 1220 miles long and routed over three tandem carrier systems using coaxial cable and wire pairs, with a short (approximately 30-mile) microwave link across the English Channel. During a total test time of 822 hours the following interruptions were recorded:

Table 12.2

Duration of Interruption	Number of Interruptions	Relative Frequency, %
6 to 60 milliseconds	685	69.68
60 to 600 milliseconds	83	8.44
600 milliseconds to 6 seconds	105	10.68
6 seconds to 1 minute	68	6.92
1 to 10 minutes	23	2.34
> 10 minutes	19	1.93

In voice transmission, a break as long as one second might not be considered too serious. For data, however, it is much more serious especially at the higher transmission speeds for which it might represent the loss of one or more complete messages. It may cause certain types of modems to lose synchronization. Thus again, what is satisfactory for voice is not so satisfactory for data.

It will be seen from these tables that the majority of interruptions are not long enough to cause a serious gap in the availability of the system, although

---

[1] Williams, M. B., "Characteristics of Telephone Circuits in Relation to Data Transmission," *Post Office Electrical Engineers' J.*, London (October 1966).

[2] *Data Transmission Test on a Multipoint Telephone Network in Europe*, from CCITT Contribution COM Sp. A/No. 64 by IBM World Trade Corporation in CCITT *Blue Book:* Geneva, International Telecommunications Union, 1964.

occasional long breaks occur. They will however cause loss of data. Retransmission will be necessary. But with good line-control procedures a high efficiency of transmission will still be possible.

FADING
Radio links are subject to fading. Many long-distance telephone circuits travel over microwave paths, and fading sometimes occurs. Small fades are compensated for by the radio automatic gain control. Large fades, however, may cause a serious degradation of the signal-to-noise ratio. Heavy rain and snow may cause fading. Violent gales may cause slight movement of the microwave dish. On rare occasions objects such as helicopters or flocks of birds may come into the transmission path. Sometimes microwave paths have been interfered with by new buildings which may cause microwave reflections.

Other radio transmission is not very often used for data links to computers (at the time of writing) although there are certain applications for which it is invaluable, and certain locations where it is the most economic form, or even the only possible form, of transmission. High-frequency radio is subject to many variations and sudden changes which are not found in wire transmission or microwave, such as deep and variable fading.

On local walkie-talkie radio transmission, the signal passes directly from the receiver to the transmitter. Long-distance radio, including the normal AM radio in the home, relies on reflection by the ionosphere. In the latter case, the path variations are very much greater. There are many propagation paths, and these suffer large daily and seasonal variations. The different propagation paths interfere with each other, and so cause severe amplitude and phase variations. Different frequencies will suffer these effects in different amounts, and the effects constantly change so that they cannot easily be compensated for. Long-distance radio with ionospheric reflection is normally not regarded as good enough for data transmission, although, where it is the only facility available, it is used at a low-transmission rate with special modems.

SYSTEMATIC DISTORTION
The types of noise and distortion discussed above were all "fortuitous." Those below are "systematic" and so can be compensated for partially or completely in the design of the electronics.

In general, as the speed at which data are to be transmitted increases, so the need for uniformity in the transmission characteristics becomes greater. On private leased lines, steps can be taken to ensure that this uniformity measures up to certain standards. When dialing for a connection, however, it is not certain which path the call will take and there are likely to be certain connections in the network on which the distortion will be high. Loaded cables, for example, which are not properly terminated or which have discontinuities, give very undesirable transmission characteristics. It is possible that a short section of a nonloaded cable can be switched into the link, again increasing its distortion level. Some of the loading coils may be faulty or missing. The proportion of faulty or poor quality sections in a public network differs from one area to another. Some networks still have a high proportion of old telephone plant in them. Some of the early cables used very heavy loading; this gives bad delay distortion which is discussed below. In most of the major industrial countries this old plant is being rapidly replaced with modern equipment having more suitable characteristics for data transmission.

When dialing for a connection on the public network, then, there is small probability that a line with several nonuniform characteristics might be obtained. This would give a higher proportion of errors than normal, and especially so if a high transmission speed was being used. Redialing might establish a different route between the two points, and avoid the bad segment. Often, however, the error rate is not high enough to indicate to the user at the time that he has a bad line. He may never know that he is experiencing twice, three times, perhaps even ten times the normal error rate.

ATTENUATION-FREQUENCY DISTORTION   The attenuation of the transmitted signal is not equal for all frequencies, as ideally one would like it to be. This was shown in Chapter 10 in the discussion of bandwidth. The increase in attenuation at the edges of the band is indeed what demarcates the bandwidth as shown in Fig. 10.3.

The attenuation of a typical cable pair, *within* the voice band, is approximately proportional to the square root of the frequency. To compensate for this variation in amplitude and to reduce attenuation as discussed before, the cable may be loaded by adding inductance at intervals. Similarly, on multiplex systems carrying many voice channels, filters are designed to yield a flat amplitude-frequency curve. However, some variation in amplitude across the band remains, and this is referred to as amplitude-frequency distortion. The effect of this is to distort the receivable signal slightly.

The solid line in Fig. 12.3 shows the attenuation-frequency curve of a typical telephone line. Attenuation relative to that at 1000 cycles per second is shown. It is common that, as in this case, the attenuation level does not vary more than 10 decibels between 400 and 3000 cycles per second. This line would probably be satisfactory for transmission at 600 or 1200 bits per second. If, however, it were desirable to transmit data on the line at speeds greater than that, say 2400 or 4800 bits per second, a further flattening of the attenuation-frequency curve would probably be needed, and to do this an

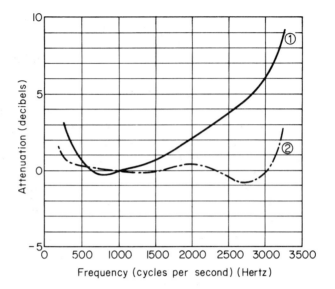

① Is a typical attenuation-frequency curve for a leased telephone line (without equalization). With today's modems this line would typically be used for transmission at 600 or 1200 bits per second.

② Is for the same line with equalizers. This line could now be used for transmission at speeds up to 4800 bits per second. See also Fig. 12.6.

Fig. 12.3. Variation of attenuation with frequency on modern telephone lines.

equalizer might be used at each end of the line. The equalizer would give a somewhat greater overall attenuation but a flatter frequency-attenuation curve. The dotted line in Fig. 12.3 shows the effect of the equalizer. Here again attenuation is shown relative to that at 1000 cycles per second.

Circuits differing widely in their physical nature are today engineered to have an attenuation-frequency curve similar to that of Fig. 12.3. Figure 12.8, for example, shows measurements made on a tropospheric scatter circuit in Alaska. The attenuation varies slightly from day to day but still remains close to the curves in Fig. 12.3.

Much worse results than these, however, are sometimes obtained on old telephone plant or equipment that is not functioning correctly. In some areas this might be encountered on the switched public network. Figure 12.9 shows a bad example. Here the dotted line shows an attenuation variation of about 20 decibels between 800 and 2000 cycles per second, and much more than would be encountered between 800 and 3000 cycles per second. The

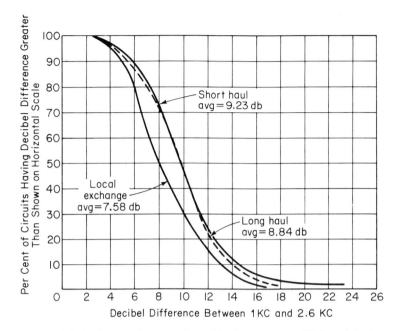

Fig. 12.4. *Variation of attenuation with frequency on AT&T switched public network.* The curves relate to the difference in attenuation between 1000 and 2600 cycles per second, and show the percentage of lines having different values. About 70% of the local exchange lines, for example, have a difference less than 10 decibels. *AT&T contribution A.T. 43, No. 13 in* CCITT Red Book, *1961, published by the International Telecommunication Union, Geneva.*

General Post Office in Britain advised designers of data-transmission systems to assume the line characteristics of Fig. 12.9.[3] This assumption would restrict the maximum transmission speed attainable. However, the old plant on the public network of most countries is rapidly being replaced. Carrier operation is replacing lengthy lines with heavy loading, and this gives a much flatter attenuation frequency curve.

Figure 12.4 shows results of measurements made on the AT&T switched public network in the United States.[4] These measurements were made on over 1100 test calls. About 25% of these were local calls not involved with the long-distance switching plan. About 25% were short-haul long-distance calls with distances up to 500 airline miles. The remaining 50% were long haul, 400 to 3000 miles long. Figure 12.4 shows the difference in attenuation

---

[3] Williams, M. B., "Characteristics of Telephone Circuits in Relation to Data Transmission," *Post Office Electrical Engineers' J.*, London (October 1966).

[4] From AT & T Contribution G.T. 43, No 13 in CCITT *Red Book*: Geneva 1961, International Telecommunications Union.

between frequencies of 1000 and 2600 cycles per second. It indicates that about half of the local exchange calls have a variation of 8 decibels and the other half about 10 decibels. A variation in attenuation as bad as that in Fig. 12.9 would be a rare occurrence.

PHASE-FREQUENCY DISTORTION   The phase of the signal likewise is not transmitted linearly. The signal is delayed more at some frequencies than at others. This is referred to as phase-frequency distortion or *delay distortion*. Some frequencies reach the receiver ahead of others.

It is a serious form of distortion in data transmission. It has only been corrected to a limited extent on the voice channels that we may wish to send data over, because the human understanding of speech is not greatly affected by it. The ear is a relatively slow acting organism. It is normally necessary for a sound to exist for 0.2 second in order to be recognized. If we have delay distortion of 0.05 second, the speech is still intelligible, though normally the distortion is not nearly that great.

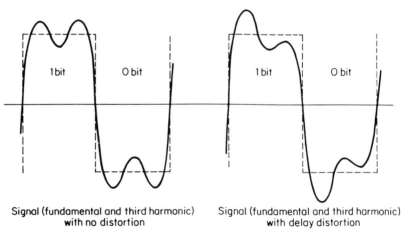

Signal (fundamental and third harmonic)
with no distortion

Signal (fundamental and third harmonic)
with delay distortion

Figure 12.5

Figure 12.5 shows the effect of delay distortion on the transmission of a square-edged pulse. As was noted in Chapter 10, a square-edged pulse train is in effect composed of many frequencies, and so the edges of the pulses begin to distort as the wave travels to its destination. Again, if parallel transmission were used on the line, as is described in Chapter 23, in such a way that one bit of a character were transmitted at 800 cycles per second, the next at 1000, and so on, then, because of delay distortion, some of these bits would reach the receiver before others. The main effect of delay distortion, however, is on the more elaborate forms of modulation described in the next chapter. Delay distortion must be kept below a certain level in order that the fastest and most efficient types of modem work correctly.

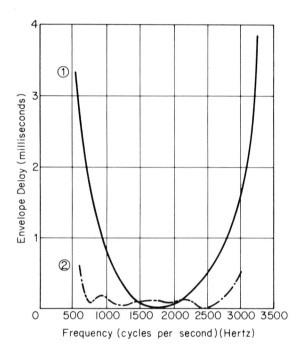

① Is a typical envelope delay curve for a leased telephone line (without equalization). With today's modems this line would typically be used for transmission at 600 or 1200 bits per second.

② Is for the same line with phase equalization. This line could now be used for transmission at speeds up to 4800 bits per second. See also Fig. 12.3.

Fig. 12.6. Variation in envelope delay with frequency on modern telephone lines.

Figure 12.6 shows the delay distortion encountered on a typical telephone line. The solid curve shows the delay of different frequencies, in milliseconds, relative to that at about 1800 cycles per second which arrives first, in this case. Just as *equalizers* are used to compensate for attenuation distortion, so a form of equalizer can be added to the line to compensate for delay distortion. The signal at 1800 cycles per second is slowed down to the speed of those at the outer frequencies. A typical result of this compensation is shown by the dotted line in Fig. 12.6.

As with the curves for attenuation in Fig. 12.3, an unequalized circuit with the characteristics of the solid line would be likely to be used for transmission at 600 or 1200 bits per second; probably no faster. If a leased telephone line is to be used for transmission at 2400 or 4800 bits per second, it will be equalized beforehand. To do this, the line has attached to it small networks adjusted to give equal attenuation and equal delay as far as is possible.

Again, as with attenuation distortion, circuits differing widely in their physical nature are today engineered to have a delay curve similar to that in Fig. 12.6. Figure 12.8 shows measurements made on the same tropospheric scatter circuit for delay distortion. Again it differs from day to day but remains close to the curves in Fig. 12.6.

Bad delay distortion, much worse than in Fig. 12.6 can be found on old telephone plant, and in some areas this is encountered on the public telephone network. In Fig. 12.9 the delay distortion is bad as well as the attenuation distortion. It could be worse than this on long-wire pair circuits. Long-wire pairs are usually heavily loaded to correct attenuation distortion which is discernible in speech, but delay distortion has been neglected. On the other hand, very little delay distortion is found on coaxial cables and microwave links. The high-frequency medium has virtually no effect on voice channel characteristics. More and more long-distance calls are today being transmitted over coaxial cable links and microwave relays, and so the incidence of bad delay distortion on long-distance links is diminishing.

Figure 12.7 shows delay distortion measured on the AT&T switched public network. The measurements relate to the same 1100 dialed connections as those in Fig. 12.4. It will be seen that 90% of the calls there is not too great a variation in delay characteristics.

STANDARD PROFILES
FOR LINE
DISTORTION

CCITT makes recommendations that certain types of lines should have delay and attenuation distortion characteristics lying within given profiles. To a large extent, national telecommunication organizations accept these recommendations and attempt to engineer their lines to the specifications laid down. In addition, national bodies lay down distortion specifications for certain tariffs. A data transmission user with a leased line can, if he wishes, check that his line does lie within the laid-down profiles. Where a voice line is to be used for speeds higher than 2000

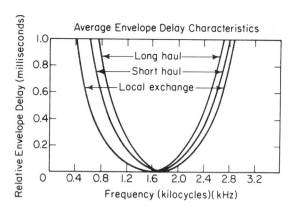

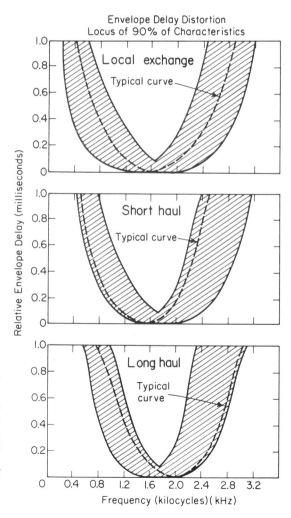

Fig. 12.7. Envelope delay distortion on typical AT&T switched, public voice lines (USA). *Redrawn from AT&T contribution A. T. 43, No. 13 in CCITT Red Book, 1961, published by International Telecommunication Union, Geneva..*

233

Fig. 12.8. Modern circuits of widely differing physical nature are engineered to have characteristics close to those of Figs. 12.6 and 12.7. Here, for example, are curves showing the attenuation and phase distortion on a tropospheric scatter circuit in Alaska. *Redrawn from Transmission Testing on Alaska Forward-Propagation Tropospheric Scatter Circuits, M.I.T., Lincoln Laboratory, June 1963. Published by International Telecommunication Union, Geneva.*

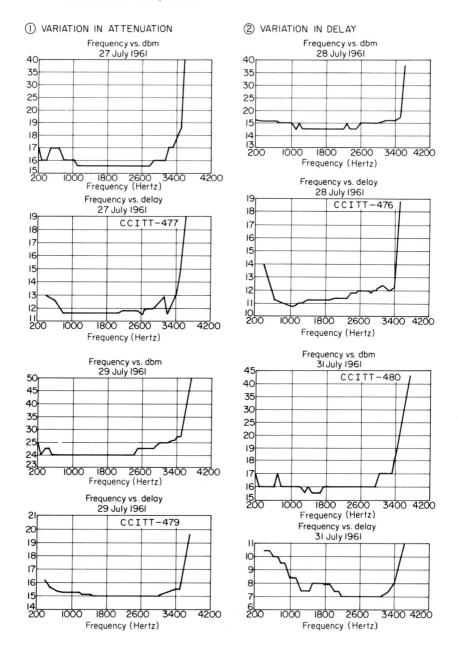

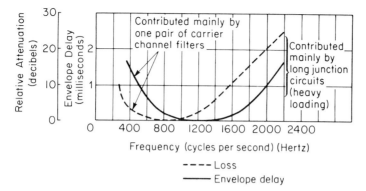

Fig. 12.9. Example of attenuation and delay distortion on a switched public telephone network. Some old telephone plant has properties much worse than Figs. 12.3 and 12.4 *Redrawn from The Characteristics of Telephone Circuits in Relation to Data Transmission by M. B. Williams, The Post Office Electrical Engineer's Journal, London, October 1966.*

bits per second, this has been done, because here a low bit error rate could only be achieved if the line did in fact meet its objectives for distortion-free operation.

Figures 12.10 and 12.11 give the FCC profiles for the maximum distortion permissible on lines with type C2 conditioning in America (Schedule 4B). The former figure shows the attenuation variation, and the latter the delay distortion. *Line conditioning* means the adding of equalizers to the line to bring its performance within the limits shown in Figs. 12.10 and 12.11. See Table 5.2 on page 99.

The curves for the line with equalization from Figs. 12.3 and 12.4 are drawn on Figs. 12.10 and 12.11. It will be observed that both of these fall within the limits. The equalized lines thus satisfy the tariff for type C2. The curves for unequalized lines from Figs. 12.3 and 12.6 would both cut across the FCC profiles and so would not quite meet the conditioning requirements.

FREQUENCY OFFSET   Signals transmitted over some channels suffer a frequency change. That is, if 1000 cycles per second are sent, 999 or 1001 might be received. This is sometimes caused by the use of multiplex systems for carrying each voice band at a different frequency. The oscillators used for generating the carrier supplies for modulation and demodulation are not precisely at the same frequency. When demodulation occurs the entire band suffers a frequency change because the carrier used for demodulating does not have exactly the same frequency as that which was used for modulating. Frequency shift is overcome by transmitting a subcarrier with the signal on

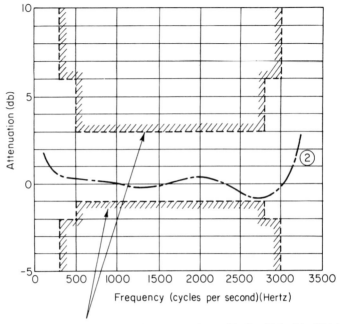

FCC Limit for lines with Type C2 conditioning (Schedule 4B Lines).
Curve ② from Fig.12.3 is redrawn above. It will be seen that
this meets the FCC standard whereas the line without equalization
in Fig. 12.3 would not.

Fig. 12.10. Standardized limits for attenuation variation on a high
quality line.

the same channel as will be discussed in Chapter 15. A change of about 20
cycles per second could be permitted without causing unpleasant distortion
of the human voice. However, the CCITT recommendation is that frequency
offset should be limited to ± 2 cycles per second, per link, and most circuits
conform to that. A circuit with five links in tandem might then have a frequency shift up to ± 10 cycles per second. Under faulty conditions, this
value may be exceeded for short periods, but rarely exceeded by enough to
interfere with data transmission.

**BIAS AND
CHARACTERISTIC
DISTORTION**

Repeaters are sometimes used to reconstruct
pulses, producing a new, clean, square-edged
pulse out of what by that time had become a
distorted pulse. Similarly, the output of modula-
tion systems are "sliced" to give square-edged pulses. A form of systematic
distortion that occurs can result in all the pulses being lengthened or short-

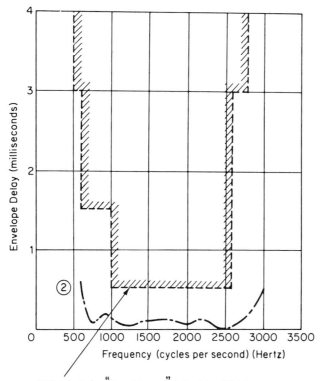

FCC Limit for "Conditioned" Schedule 4B Lines
Curve ② from Fig. 12.4 is redrawn above. It will be seen that
it meets the FCC standard, whereas the line without equalization
in Fig. 12.3 would not quite meet it.

Fig. 12.11. Standardized limits for envelope delay on a high quality line.

ened. This was illustrated in Fig. 7.7 and is referred to as bias distortion. If
all of the one-bit pulses are lengthened it may be called "positive bias," or
"marking bias," and if they are shortened it may be called "negative bias,"
or "spacing bias." Bias distortion changes sign when the 1 and 0 bits are interchanged, or, in other words, does the opposite to a 1 to what it does to a 0.
Bias distortion may be caused by a decision threshold for the pulse regeneration being set at the wrong value, and thus can usually be adjusted.

A similar type of systematic distortion is called "characteristic" distortion. Here the effect is not reversed when the 1 and the 0 are interchanged,
but is similar for either of them. For example, a single 1 or 0 may be shortened
in transmission, whereas a long mark or space representing adjacent 1's or
0's may lengthen. This may be caused by some nonlinear characteristic of the

transmission, possibly caused by bandwidth restriction or intersymbol interference.

GENERAL CONCLUSIONS

To summarize, a major cause of data errors is impulse noise. On the public network this is often caused by electromechanical exchange equipment. The *speed* at which data can be transmitted, basically limited by the bandwidth available, is further affected by attenuation distortion, and more so by delay distortion. On private lines these can be compensated for by equalizers. The long-distance leased line is subject to brief line interruptions, as are switched circuits, and these can lose data.

With the noise and distortion that exists it is common to transmit at speeds of 1200 bits per second over switched voice lines. Over specially "conditioned" private voice lines speeds of 2400 are common. Both of these figures may soon be tripled by better modem design. Some leased voice lines transmit at 4800 or 5600 bits per second today. A summary of the error rates found on the various types of circuit is given in Chapter 21. It is clear that data must be protected by error-correcting codes, or error-detecting codes and retransmission, for most data-transmission applications.

13 MODULATION AND DEMODULATION

When we wish to transmit music, or the human voice, or data signals, it often happens that their frequency spectra are unsuited to the medium we must use for transmission.

Take the case of radio broadcasting, for example. You wish to listen to a violin concerto on the radio so you tune your radio to the station on which it is playing—96.3 megacycles. This is the frequency, the midpoint of the frequency band at which this communication system is then operating. Waves of this frequency travel through the atmosphere and are picked up by your radio set. However, the violins are not being played at this frequency. You would not hear them if they were. The sound of the violins is in the range 30 to 20,000 cycles. This sound must therefore be used to modulate the waves of very much higher frequency which the medium uses for transmission. The same is true in the transmission of data.

Modulation methods were first used almost exclusively in radio transmission. However, their use in line transmission soon followed because it was realized that communication lines had a bandwidth greater than that needed for speech. Consequently, several telephone conversations could be sent together down one telephone line. The way to do this was to change the frequencies so that several sound channels could be packed into one wider bandwidth, as was shown in Fig. 10.4. Modulation was needed to achieve this "frequency division multiplexing."

As the telephone business grew, channels of wider and wider bandwidth were developed. Coaxial cable links became available, and later microwave links. This trend to channels of greater bandwidth is still going on today. Communication facilities are being laid down which carry more and more telephone circuits. To pack these circuits into the one physical facility, more and more modulation is needed—modulation upon modulation, as will be described in the following chapters.

This is a problem exclusively for the telephone companies. Now, however, with the advent of data transmission, new attention has been focused on modulation, not only by the telephone companies but by manufacturers of computers, office copying equipment, instrumentation, and by a variety of other concerns. Modulation has become the key to using the world's communication links for sending information they were not designed to handle.

If we wish to send *data* over a telephone circuit we must use a *carrier frequency* somewhere near the middle of the voice band and superimpose the data upon it in much the same way that the violin concerto was superimposed upon the broadcasting frequency of 96.3 megacycles. The carrier selected is *modulated* with the data to be sent. The output of the modulation process needs to have a spectrum resembling the spectrum of the human voice (Fig. 10.1), or at least that truncated part of the voice spectrum which fits the telephone bandwidth. The signal has to be fitted into the shape shown in Fig. 10.4.

In order to make a voice circuit carry data efficiently, the modulation technique is designed to tailor the waveform to the characteristics of the channel. This tailoring process gives rise to much ingenuity. The modulation technique must be devised to maximize the quantity of data transmitted and minimize the effects of noise and distortion. Whatever bandwidth or media we use, modulation enables us to convert our data signals so that we transmit them with maximum efficiency. It matches the characteristics of the signal sent to the characteristics of the transmission medium.

THE SCOPE OF THIS CHAPTER   There are, then, two quite different types of modulation equipment. First, that used by the telephone companies in multiplexing voice and other signals onto higher frequency transmission media; and second, the modems that the computer planner is concerned with to make his data travel over the voice channel.

The basic principles of modulation are the same for both of these types of equipment. The reader, however, is presumed to be more interested in data transmission, and so the main emphasis of this chapter is placed on the modulation of data rather than on modulation in the telephone plant. Amplitude modulation and frequency modulation, described below, are in regular use by the common carriers for handling telephone circuits. Phase modulation is not in common use for voice transmission. It is becoming the most favored, however, for digital transmission. In the following discussion, we describe how amplitude and frequency modulation are applied to transmitting data;

basically the same theory could be applied also to the transmission of voice. These are the two methods that are used for "frequency division multiplexing," described in Chapter 15.

A new and different means for building telecommunication plant is coming into use which employs pulse techniques. Everything is converted to pulses that look remarkably like computer data. These techniques are described in the following two chapters.

THREE
DIFFERENT
TYPES OF
MODULATION

When we employ a *sine wave carrier* to convey data, it has three parameters which we could modulate: its amplitude, its frequency, and its phase. There are thus three basic types of modulation in use: *amplitude modulation, frequency modulation,* and *phase modulation.* Each of these methods is in common use today. The sine wave carrier may be represented by

$$a_c = A_c \sin (2\pi f_c t + \theta_c) \qquad (13.1)$$

where a_c is the instantaneous value of carrier voltage at time t,
   A_c is the maximum amplitude of carrier voltage,
   f_c is the carrier frequency, and
   θ_c is the phase.

The values of $A_c, f_c,$ or θ_c may be varied to make the wave carry information.

This is illustrated in Fig. 13.1. A sinusoidal carrier wave of, say, 1500 hertz (cycles per second), a midfrequency of a voice channel band, is modulated to carry the information bits 0 1 0 0 0 1 0 1 1 0 0. In this simplified diagram the channel is being operated inefficiently because far more bits could be packed into the carrier oscillations shown. The tightness of this packing determines the speed of operation.

Furthermore, here we modulate the carrier by placing it in one of two possible states in each case. With amplitude modulation we could send several different amplitudes as in the case illustrated in Fig. 13.8. Similarly, with frequency modulation, we could use several frequencies rather than just the F_1 and F_2 shown. With phase modulation Fig. 13.1 illustrates only 180° phase changes; we could use phase changes which are multiples of 90°, giving four possible states, or 45° giving eight, and so on. Increasing the number of states of the carrier that are used increases the complexity of the decoding or demodulation circuits, and considerably increases the susceptibility of the transmission to noise and distortion. If distortion can change the carrier phase by $\pm30°$ for example, four-phase modulated signals can still be correctly detected, but not eight-phase.

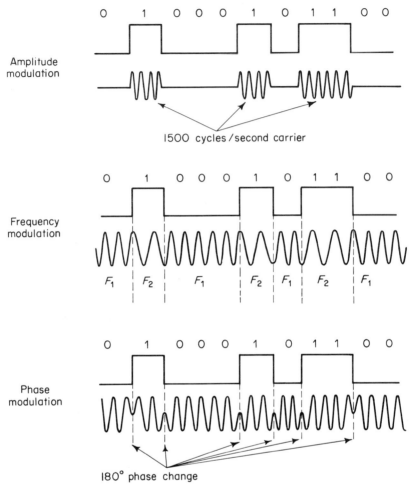

Fig. 13.1. The three basic methods of modulating a sine wave carrier (a simplified diagram showing only binary signals).

We are therefore seeking a workable compromise between the quantity of data that can be packed into the transmission, and the ability of the modem to decode it correctly in the presence of noise and distortion.

For correct decoding an accurate replica of the original carrier must be given to the demodulating circuit. There are a number of ways of obtaining this. In some cases it is sufficient to generate the replica independently in the demodulating equipment. A reference frequency may be generated by a high-precision quartz oscillator and used for decoding frequency modulation. It is in phase modulation that it is most difficult to obtain a reference. The demodulator can have no absolute sense of phase.

The original carrier may be reconstructed from information in the signal. This may be done by transmitting a separate tone of narrow bandwidth along with the signal, or it may possibly be obtained from the modulated signal itself. Sometimes the signal is briefly interrupted at intervals to give information about the carrier.

Let us examine the three main modulation methods in more detail.

1. AMPLITUDE MODULATION

In amplitude modulation the *amplitude* of the carrier wave is varied in accordance with the signal to be sent. In its simplest form the carrier is simply switched on and off to send 0 and 1 bits as in Fig. 13.1.

In general, the signal to be sent is multiplied by the carrier wave,

$$a_c = A_c \sin (2\pi f_c t + \theta_c)$$

This results in a signal which contains the original carrier plus two *sidebands*, one higher in frequency than the carrier, and the other lower. If the signal being transmitted has a frequency f_m (modulation frequency), this will give an *upper sideband* with frequency $f_c + f_m$, and a *lower sideband* with frequency $f_c - f_m$. It is in these two sidebands that the information is carried.

Any signal that is to be sent—voice or data—can be represented by a series of sine waves using Fourier analysis. It was shown on page 196 how an on–off pulse square wave such as the 1's and 0's of data transmission can be represented as a series of sine curves [Eq. (10.2)]. We are then modulating a sine wave carrier by another sine wave or series of sine waves. This can be represented mathematically as follows:

Let us assume, for simplicity, that the phase constant of the carrier is zero. The carrier $a_c = A_c \sin 2\pi f_c t$ is to be modulated by a wave we represent by $a_m = A_m \sin 2\pi f_m t$. The resultant wave is

$$
\begin{aligned}
a_{mc} &= (A_c + a_m) \sin 2\pi f_c t \\
&= (A_c + A_m \sin 2\pi f_m t) \sin 2\pi f_c t \\
&= A_c \sin 2\pi f_c t + A_m (\sin 2\pi f_m t) \sin 2\pi f_c t \\
&= A_c \sin 2\pi f_c t + \frac{A_m}{2} \cos 2\pi (f_c - f_m) t - \frac{A_m}{2} \cos 2\pi (f_c + f_m) t \\
&= A_c \sin 2\pi f_c t + \frac{A_m}{2} \sin \left[2\pi (f_c - f_m) t + \frac{\pi}{2} \right] \\
&\quad + \frac{A_m}{2} \sin \left[2\pi (f_c + f_m) t - \frac{\pi}{2} \right]
\end{aligned}
$$

(13.2)

This contains the three components, the carrier at frequency f_c which contains no information, and the two *sidebands* at frequencies $(f_c - f_m)$ and $(f_c + f_m)$ which do contain information because their amplitude is proportional to A_m. Thus:

$$\text{Carrier:} \quad A_c \sin 2\pi f_c t$$

$$\text{Lower sideband:} \quad \frac{A_m}{2} \sin \left[2\pi(f_c - f_m)t + \frac{\pi}{2} \right]$$

$$\text{Upper sideband:} \quad \frac{A_m}{2} \sin \left[2\pi(f_c + f_m)t - \frac{\pi}{2} \right]$$

A_m/A_c is referred to as the *modulation factor* or *modulation index*.

The maximum practical value of the modulation index is 1 and often it is less. If the amplitude of the modulating wave became greater than that of the carrier, giving a modulation index greater than 1, the resultant wave would have an envelope with more peaks than the modulating wave, and the original signal would not recovered. This is shown in Fig. 13.2 and it is referred to as *overmodulation*.

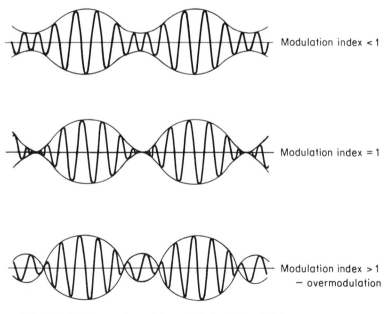

Fig. 13.2. Different values of the modulation index A_m/A_c.

If the modulating signal consists in effect of *several* sine waves, then we shall have that number of frequencies both in the upper and lower sidebands.

In voice transmission, for example, if a carrier of 60 kilohertz is modulated by speech filling a band of 300 to 3000 hertz, the resulting transmission will be of an upper sideband of 60,300 to 63,000 hertz, a lower sideband of 57,000 to 59,700, and the original carrier of 60,000 (Fig. 13.3).

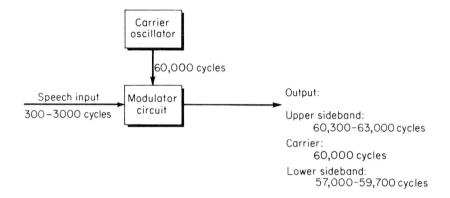

Figure 13.3

The Fourier series representing a square wave of frequency f_m, in other words a 1 0 1 0 1 0 bit pattern being sent at a rate of $2f_m$ bits per second (ignoring phase) is

$$\frac{4A_m}{\pi}\Big(\sin 2\pi f_m t - \frac{1}{3}\sin 6\pi f_m t + \frac{1}{5}\sin 10\pi f_m t$$
$$- \frac{1}{7}\sin 14\pi f_m t + \frac{1}{9}\sin 18\pi f_m t \ldots\Big) \tag{13.3}$$

The results of using this to modulate the preceding carrier will be the following products (ignoring phase):

$$\text{Carrier:}\quad A_c \sin 2\pi f_c t$$

$$\text{Upper sideband:}\quad + \frac{2}{\pi}A_m \sin 2\pi(f_c + f_m)t$$

$$- \frac{2}{3\pi}A_m \sin 2\pi(f_c + 3f_m)t$$

$$+ \frac{2}{5\pi}A_m \sin 2\pi(f_c + 5f_m)t$$

$$- \frac{2}{7\pi}A_m \sin 2\pi(f_c + 7f_m)t$$

$$+ \frac{2}{9\pi}A_m \sin 2\pi(f_c + 9f_m)t, \ldots, \text{etc.}$$

Lower sideband: $+\dfrac{2}{\pi}A_m \sin 2\pi(f_c - f_m)t$

$$-\dfrac{2}{3\pi}A_m \sin 2\pi(f_c - 3f_m)t$$

$$+\dfrac{2}{5\pi}A_m \sin 2\pi(f_c - 5f_m)t$$

$$-\dfrac{2}{7\pi}A_m \sin 2\pi(f_c - 7f_m)t$$

$$+\dfrac{2}{9\pi}A_m \sin 2\pi(f_c - 9f_m)t, \ldots, \text{etc.}$$

This is illustrated in Fig. 13.4 for a modulation index of 1.

The more general case is likely to produce a spectrum with more lines on it than this. It can be shown, for example, that a regular train of square

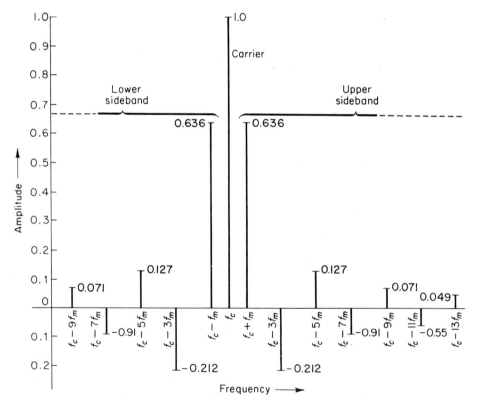

Fig. 13.4. Spectrum resulting from amplitude modulation of a square wave representing bits 0 1 0 1 0 1 0 1 . . . .

pulses, each of width d seconds and sent at a speed of S pulses per second, are represented by the following frequency lines:

$$2A_m Sd + \sum_{n=1}^{\infty} 4A_m Sd \frac{\sin \pi nSd}{\pi nSd} \cos 2\pi nSt \qquad (13.4)$$

The lines are thus at frequencies S, $2S$, $3S$, $4S$, ..., and are bounded by an envelope of the form $\sin x/x$ where $x = n\pi Sd$.

When these pulses modulate a sine wave of frequency f_c the resulting transmission is at frequencies $f_c + S$, $f_c - S$, $f_c + 2S$, $f_c - 2S$, $f_c + 3S$, etc., with again a large component at f_c carrying no information.

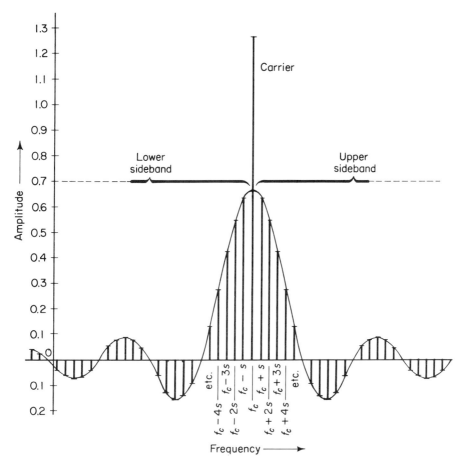

Fig. 13.5. Spectrum resulting from amplitude modulation of a train of pulses. Interval between pulses is six times pulse width.

This is illustrated in Fig. 13.5, again for a modulation index of 1 and a value of Sd equal to $\frac{1}{6}$. (Interval between pulses = 6 × pulse width.)

The question now becomes apparent: *How much of the spectra like those in Figs. 13.4 and 13.5 do we in fact want to transmit?*

The carrier wave contains no information and may be suppressed. The lower sideband duplicates the information that is in the upper sideband, and therefore some systems transmit only one sideband. Further, not all of the components shown are needed to extract the information. It could be extracted from a relatively narrow band of frequencies where the sideband amplitude is largest.

To transmit all of the spectrum shown would consume an unnecessarily wide bandwidth, or, given a fixed line or channel, it would restrict the signaling speed. Also it would need more power to transmit. As energy must be limited to values that will not be harmful to other users sharing the common facility, it is desirable to use all of the power in transmitting that part of the spectrum which contains the most information content. This gives the best chance of separating the signal from the noise picked up.

The power is proportional to the square of the amplitude. Therefore, referring back to Eq. (13.2), the power transmitted in the carrier is proportional to A_c^2, and the power in each sideband is proportional to $(A_m/2)^2$.

For a modulation factor of 1, $(A_c = A_m)$, it needs four times as much power to transmit the carrier, which contains no data, as to transmit either sideband. In practice, modulation factors of less than one are used and so the carrier may need six or eight times as much power as the sideband.

It is common, therefore, to find *suppressed carrier amplitude modulation* in which the carrier has been removed by a filter and only the sidebands transmitted, and also *single-sideband amplitude modulation* in which one sideband has been removed. It can be shown that this latter improves the signal-to-noise ratio over full amplitude modulation by 4 decibels or more. It also halves the bandwidth required.

DETECTION   When the modulated waveform reaches the demodulator, a "detection" process must convert it back to the original signal. For amplitude modulation there are two main types of detection: "Synchronous," "coherent" or "homodyne" detection, and "envelope" detection.

Synchronous, coherent or homodyne detection, which will be referred to below by the term "synchronous" detection, involves the use of a locally produced source of carrier which has the same frequency and phase as that bringing the received signal. The transmission is multiplied by this carrier and this enables the signal to be extracted. Some additional components appear with it consisting of sidebands centered around $2f_c$, $4f_c$, $6f_c$, and so on. These are filtered off with a low-pass filter.

The result is now close to the original but is not yet a rectangular or accurately synchronous waveform, so it may be trimmed up. If the signal is binary the receiver interprets each pulse as being either a 1 or 0, and produces a new, clean rectangular pulse similar to the original. This may be done simply by a "slicer" which straightens up the edges of the pulse, or by a means for regenerating the waveform. In the latter case a local source of timing may be used so that a newly timed synchronous wave is generated.

Envelope detection involves rectifying and smoothing the signal so as to obtain its envelope. This is again combined with "slicing" or regenerating new pulses. After rectification, two threshold levels as illustrated in Fig. 13.6 will tell the slicer when to start a "0" and when to start a "1."

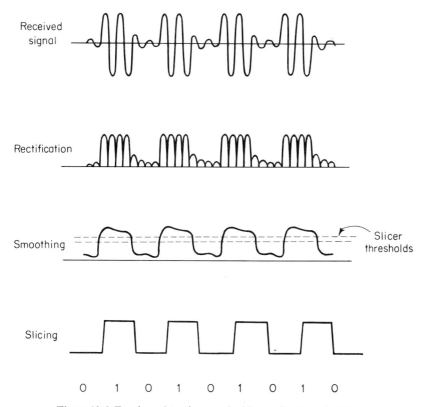

Figure 13.6. Envelope detection, used with amplitude modulation.

In synchronous detection, in order to produce the reference wave of the same frequency and phase as the carrier, it is normally necessary to transmit some information with the signal for this purpose. Such a wave can be extracted from the carrier and so the carrier may not be completely suppressed. It is usually partly suppressed because of its relatively high energy content. We now have a form of transmission in which one sideband is suppressed and only enough of the carrier is sent to give a reference frequency and phase for synchronous detection.

Elements used with amplitude modulation

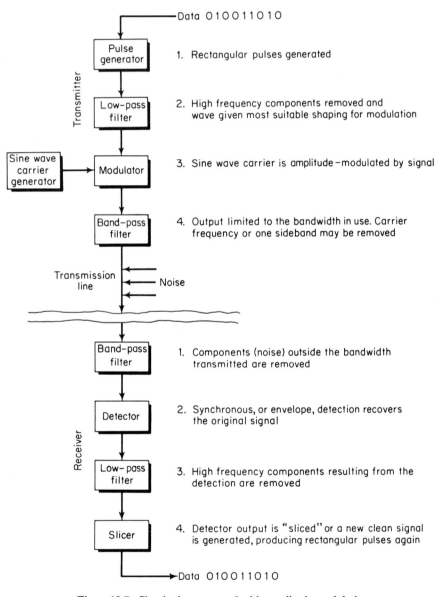

Figure 13.7. Circuit elements used with amplitude modulation.

Envelope detection does not require the reference wave to be produced, and so is considerably less expensive, as producing it is one of the main problems of synchronous detection. Envelope detection does however need both sidebands and full-amplitude carrier. Suppressed sideband amplitude modulation would lead to an envelope shape which differs from that of the original signal.

In choice of detection method we thus have a compromise between speed and cost. Envelope detection needs twice the bandwidth of synchronous detection because both sidebands must be transmitted. Synchronous detection, however, is considerably more complex and expensive.

These various functions of an amplitude modulation modem are illustrated in Fig. 13.7.

MULTIPLE-LEVEL TRANSMISSION   The preceding discussion relates to two-level amplitude modulation. The carrier is transmitted at two relative amplitudes as in Fig. 13.1. It is possible to transmit with more than two levels of amplitude. If four levels are used as in Fig. 13.8, the levels can be made to represent the bit pairs or "dibits" 00, 01, 10, and 11, respectively. This gives a lower margin for error in the threshold decision of the slicer or regenerator. Theoretically, the number of single bits carried by the signal can be twice as great; however, the susceptibility to noise is greater. The ratio of the level difference that must be detected to the noise level is substantially lower. Similarly, eight levels would permit three bits to be carried per level, and so give three times the speed of two-level transmission, but the level difference that must be detected would be still less.

Unfortunately, amplitude modulation is already vulnerable to the common types of noise. Multilevel amplitude modulation has not often been

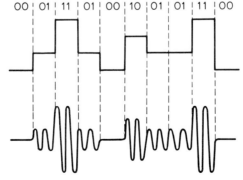

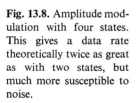

Fig. 13.8. Amplitude modulation with four states. This gives a data rate theoretically twice as great as with two states, but much more susceptible to noise.

used; however, the same principle applied to phase modulation is now becoming common over good lines.

The A1 Data System modems developed by the Bell System in connection with SAGE, the USA air defense network, used three-level amplitude modulation, but only two levels carried binary information; the third contained a framing signal. This was a synchronous transmission system and the framing signal was used to maintain this synchronization.

2. FREQUENCY MODULATION

When frequency modulation was developed it was used to replace amplitude modulation where better performance in the presence of impulse noise and voltage level changes was needed. The signal is transmitted at constant amplitude and so is resistant to changes in amplitude. However, a larger bandwidth is needed. Although amplitude modulation techniques are still used extensively in the common carrier's plant, frequency modulation is now being used more and more for *modems*. It has been adopted by the Bell System in the United States for their Dataphone 200 service and by the GPO in the United Kingdom for their Datel 200 and 600 service.

In frequency modulation, the frequency of the carrier wave varies in accordance with the signal to be sent. This is illustrated in a simplified form in Fig. 13.1. The frequency of the carrier assumes one value for a "1" bit and another for a "0" bit. This type of on-off modulation is sometimes called *frequency-shift keying or carrier-shift keying*.

The modulation can also be a continuous analog process, the input signal being any waveform, which again we may regard as a collection of sine waves.

The unmodulated carrier, as before, may be represented by

$$a_c = A_c \sin 2\pi f_c t$$

If its frequency f_c is modulated by a sine wave of frequency f_m we have

$$a_{cm} = A_c \sin 2\pi (f_c + \Delta f_c \sin 2\pi f_m t)t \qquad (13.5)$$

where Δf_c is the maximum frequency deviation that can occur.

The ratio $\Delta f_c / f_m$ is now referred to as the *modulation index*.

In general, the spectrum resulting from frequency modulation is much more complex than the equivalent amplitude modulation, with many more components. If the modulating waveform is a simple sine wave it can be shown that the resulting wave will contain sidebands at frequencies $f_c + f_m$ and $f_c - f_m$, as before, and also at $f_c + 2f_m$, $f_c - 2f_m$, $f_c + 3f_m$, $f_c - 3f_m$,

$f_c + 4f_m, f_c - 4f_m$, and so on. In other words, there are *an infinite number of sidebands spaced at intervals equal to the modulating frequency.* The further they are from the carrier frequency the lower their amplitude.

It can be shown that the spectrum is as follows:

$$a_{cm} = A_c J_0\left(\frac{\Delta f_c}{f_m}\right)\sin 2\pi f_c t$$

$$+ A_c J_1\left(\frac{\Delta f_c}{f_m}\right)[\sin 2\pi(f_c + f_m)t - \sin 2\pi(f_c - f_m)t]$$

$$+ A_c J_2\left(\frac{\Delta f_c}{f_m}\right)[\sin 2\pi(f_c + 2f_m)t + \sin 2\pi(f_c - 2f_m)t] \qquad (13.6)$$

$$+ A_c J_3\left(\frac{\Delta f_c}{f_m}\right)[\sin 2\pi(f_c + 3f_m)t - \sin 2\pi(f_c - 3f_m)t]$$

$$+ A_c J_4\left(\frac{\Delta f_c}{f_m}\right)[\sin 2\pi(f_c + 4f_m)t + \sin 2\pi(f_c - 4f_m)t]$$

$$+ \cdots \text{ etc.}$$

where $J_0(\Delta f_c/f_m)$, etc., are Bessel[1] functions.

The Bessel functions giving the relative amplitudes of these spectral components are shown in Fig. 13.9.

Using this diagram Fig. 13.10 was drawn for the case of a carrier of frequency 10,000 being modulated to carry a sine wave of frequency 1000. Fig. 13.10 compares the spectrum for amplitude modulation with those for frequency modulation using modulation indices of 1, 2, and 5.

It will be seen that the spectrum lines carrying information are concentrated into a narrower range of frequencies when $\Delta f_c/f_m$ is small. The transmission f_m can therefore occur over narrower bandwidths.

The spectra could be considerably more complicated for actual data transmission because, as we have discussed above, the data consist in effect not of one sine wave but of many. One relatively simple case may be considered, however, and that is where data bits are sent strictly at two frequencies f_c and $f_c + \Delta f_c$. This is analogous to two amplitude modulated signals, one of frequency f_c and one of $f_c + \Delta f_c$, which fit together exactly. We may thus consider two square waves such as that in the spectrum of Fig. 13.4. If these are sent and with the same amplitude the spectrum will contain two sets of lines such as those in Fig. 13.4, separated by Δf_c. This is drawn in Fig. 13.11 for different values of Δf_c, and here again the information is concentrated into a relatively narrow bandwidth when Δf_c is small.

The bulk of the signal is in fact carried in the frequencies between $f_c + (\Delta f_c + f_m)$ and $f_c - (\Delta f_c + f_m)$. This may be the range transmitted, with other

---

[1] For values of Bessel functions see, for example, Jahnke, E., and Emde, F., *Tables of Functions*: New York, Dover Publications, 1945.

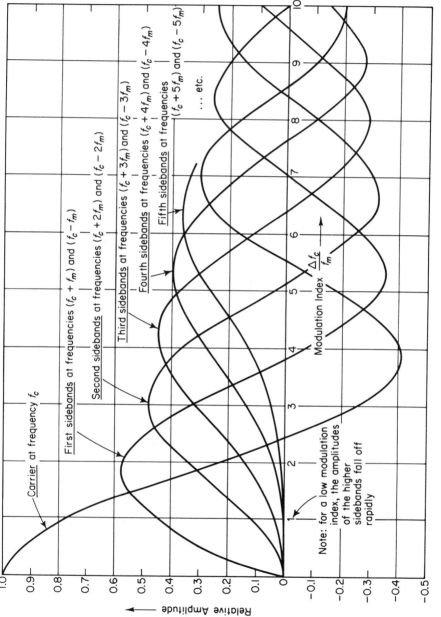

Fig. 13.9. Spectral components of a carrier of frequency f_c, frequency modulated by a sine wave of frequency f_m.

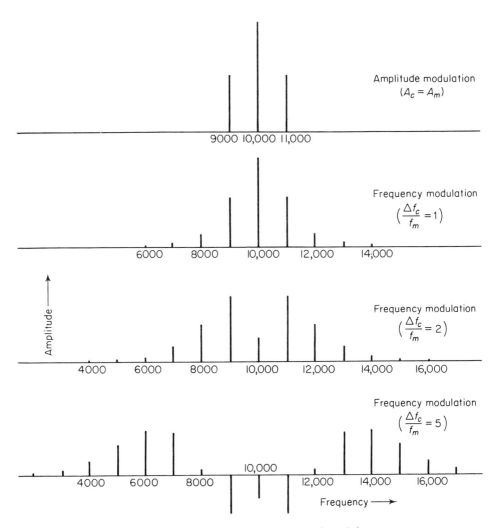

Fig. 13.10. Spectra resulting from modulating a carrier of frequency 10,000 with a sine wave of frequency 1000; a comparison of amplitude modulation and frequency modulation with different modulation factors.

frequencies removed. If it is necessary to keep distortion to a very low figure a wider bandwidth may be employed, for example,

$$f_c + (\Delta f_c + 3f_m) \qquad \text{to} \qquad f_c - (\Delta f_c + 3f_m)$$

It will be seen in Figs. 13.10 and 13.11 that the carrier amplitude is not as large relative to the sidebands as for amplitude modulation. In some cases the

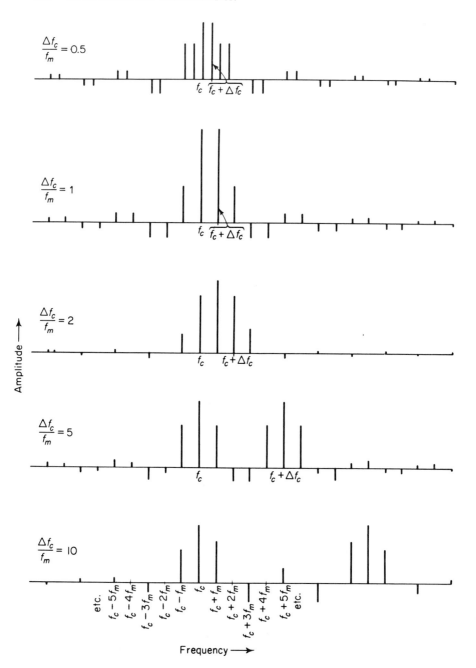

Fig. 13.11. Spectra resulting from frequency modulation of a square wave representing bits 0 1 0 1 0 1 0 1 ... (equivalent to Fig. 10.3 for amplitude modulation).

carrier disappears completely. The information, however, is spread over the carrier and sideband frequencies. The carrier is therefore not suppressed in frequency modulation as it may be in amplitude modulation. However, it becomes smaller and smaller as the modulation index is increased. One set of sidebands may be suppressed, as the upper and lower side bands are again mirror images of one another.

Multiple-level transmission can be used in a similar manner to that with amplitude modulation, and again this packs more bits into a given bandwidth but increases the susceptibility to errors. Dibits, for example, as in Fig. 13.8, may modulate the carrier so that it uses four different frequencies. This will double the data rate, but the signal-to-noise ratio needed to achieve the same error rate will be much greater; or for the same signal strength, there may be many more errors.

DETECTION   The frequency-modulated signal is transmitted at constant amplitude. The noise it encounters will occasionally change its frequency, but will more commonly have amplitude modulation effects. The latter can be ignored by the detection process. To do this only a narrow amplitude slice is used for the detection. This is centered around zero amplitude. Ideally, only the instant the received wave crosses zero should be used in the detection process. In the detection circuit a device called the "limiter" converts these zero crossings into a square wave. This has then removed any amplitude distortion.

The output of the *limiter* can then be converted by different types of circuits to produce the original bit pattern. A frequency-sensitive circuit may be used to produce an amplitude variation proportional to the instantaneous frequency. Alternatively, pulses may be generated corresponding to each zero crossing and these pulses passed through a low-pass filter to produce a wave with an amplitude variation equivalent to the bit pattern transmitted. This is illustrated in Fig. 13.12. As with amplitude modulation in Fig. 13.6, a *slicer* is used to generate a rectangular waveform according to certain threshold values, and thus the modem produces a clean output.

3.   PHASE MODULATION

Just as frequency modulation for data transmission to a large extent replaced amplitude modulation because of its better resilience to noise, so phase modulation is now to some extent replacing the others; though at the time of writing it is still less used than amplitude and frequency modulation. It is not used for multiplexing in telephone plant except in certain isolated cases.

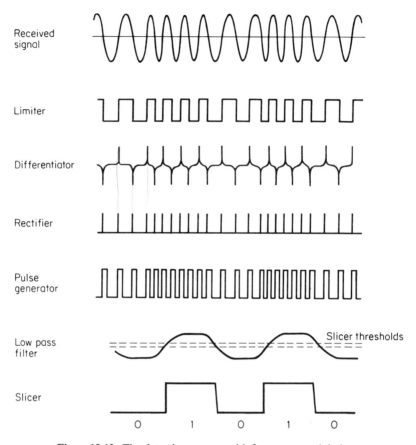

Figure 13.12. The detection process with frequency modulation.

In phase modulation the phase of the carrier is varied in accordance with the data to be sent. A sudden phase change of $+180°$ cannot be differentiated from a change of $-180°$. Therefore the maximum range over which the phase can be varied is $\pm 180°$. As small changes in phase cannot be transmitted and detected with accuracy, phase modulation is not normally used for the transmission of speech and music, for which frequency and amplitude modulation are commonly used. The small range of variations can be used, however, to code the two bits of binary transmission, or four bits, eight bits or possibly even more when multiple-level codes are used. With four phases in use each interval carries two bits of information (a "dibit") and with eight phases, three bits.

The unmodulated carrier may, as before, be represented by

$$a_c = A_c \sin 2\pi F_c t$$

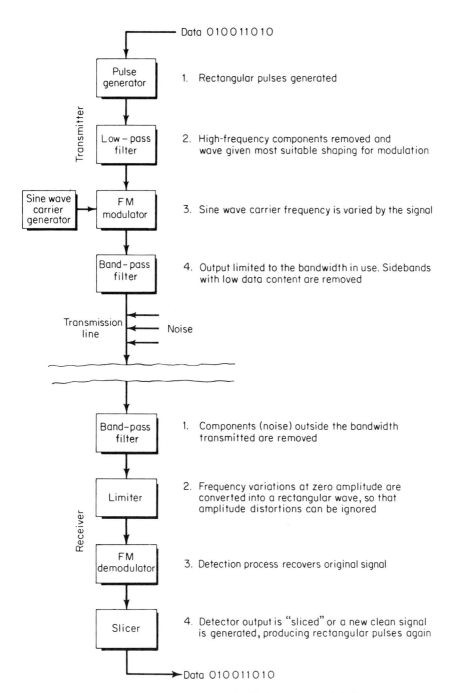

Fig. 13.13. Circuit elements used with frequency modulation.

If its phase is modulated by a sine wave of frequency f_m we have

$$a_{cm} = A_c \sin (2\pi F_c t + \Delta\theta_m \sin 2\pi f_m t) \qquad (13.7)$$

where $\Delta\theta_m$ is the maximum change in phase and is here called the *modulation index*.

The instantaneous frequency of the wave is $(1/2\pi) \times$ (the rate at which its angle is changing at that instant), in this case:

$$\frac{1}{2\pi} \times \frac{d}{dt}(2\pi F_c t + \Delta\theta_m \sin 2\pi f_m t) = F_c + f_m \Delta\theta_m \cos 2\pi f_m t \qquad (13.8)$$

Thus the instantaneous frequency is F_c, the carrier frequency + a term $f_m \Delta\theta_m \cos 2\pi f_m t$. This is equivalent to frequency modulation of the carrier frequency f_m by a wave of frequency f_m.

Δf, the maximum frequency deviation is $f_m \Delta\theta_m$.

Phase modulation is thus equivalent to frequency modulation with a modulation index $(f_m \Delta\theta_m/f_m) = \Delta\theta_m$. (This holds only when the modulation is sinusoidal.)

Thus again the resulting wave will contain an infinite number of sidebands spaced at intervals equal to the modulating frequency, i.e., sidebands at frequencies $F_c \pm f_m$, $F_c \pm 2f_m$, $F_c \pm 3f_m$, and so on.

It can be shown that the spectrum is as follows:

$$
\begin{aligned}
A_{cm} = {} & A_c J_0(\Delta\theta_m) \sin 2\pi\, F_c t \\
& + A_c J_1(\Delta\theta_m)[\sin 2\pi(F_c + f_m)t - \sin 2\pi(F_c - f_m)t] \\
& + A_c J_2(\Delta\theta_m)[\sin 2\pi(F_c + 2f_m)t + \sin 2\pi(F_c - 2f_m)t] \\
& + A_c J_3(\Delta\theta_m)[\sin 2\pi(F_c + 3f_m)t + \sin 2\pi(F_c - 3f_m)t], \\
& + \cdots \text{ etc.}
\end{aligned}
\qquad (13.9)
$$

where $J_0(\Delta\theta_m)$, etc., are Bessel functions, again. These are illustrated in Fig. 13.14.

The spectra resulting from phase modulating a carrier with a sine wave would thus be similar to those for frequency modulation in Fig. 13.10. Because of the greater modulation index possible with frequency modulation it is possible to spread the data content over a greater bandwidth than with phase modulation. Generally phase modulation uses a smaller bandwidth than frequency modulation, or, conversely, more information can be sent in a given bandwidth. The highest transmission speeds on a given bandwidth have thus often been obtained with phase modulation.

As is illustrated in Eq. (13.8) the instantaneous frequency is the derivative of the angle or phase. A sine phase variation therefore is equivalent to a cosine frequency variation. A nonsinusoidal phase variation, on the other hand, would not produce a similar frequency variation.

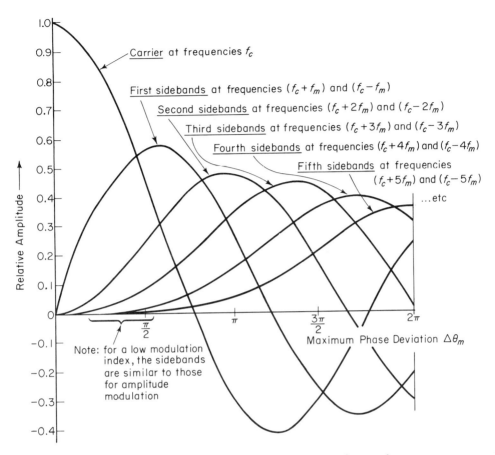

Fig. 13.14. Spectral components of a carrier of frequency f_c, phase modulated by a sine wave of frequency f_m

One relatively simple case is where a 0 bit and a 1 bit are transmitted as two identical signals differing only in that they are 180° apart in phase. This is equivalent to two amplitude modulated signals which fit together exactly. Unlike the equivalent case illustrated in Fig. 13.11 for frequency modulation, the two signals would have components at the same frequencies. Those modulation systems transmitting bit patterns in this way, in general, exhibit more resemblance to amplitude modulation than to frequency modulation.

DETECTION   There are two basically different methods of detection in phase modulated systems: *fixed-reference detection* and *differential detection*.

The receiver has no absolute sense of phase. It is therefore necessary either to use the signal in some way to generate information about the phases at the source, or else to manage without it, and operate by examining the *changes* in phase that occur.

The former approach needs a *fixed reference* giving the source phase. To achieve maximum efficiency it is desirable to transmit this carrier information with the minimum power. There are a number of ingenious methods of obtaining the reference phase from the carrier frequency. Alternatively, a separate tone may be sent: a very narrow band outside the data band, harmonically related to the carrier frequency so that it may contain information about the phase of the latter. Unfortunately, delay distortion may change the phase of this tone by a different amount to the carrier, because of its different frequency. This then has to be compensated for.

Again, a phase reference may be sent in bursts at intervals in the transmission. Data are often organized into words or records, separately sent and checked. Each of these may be preceded by a burst of carrier reference.

Figure 13.15 illustrates the generation of a four-phase signal and its subsequent detection using a fixed-reference phase. The data are divided into pairs of bits, called *dibits*. In this illustration the first bit of each pair is used to modulate a sine wave carrier, and the second bit is used to modulate the same carrier delayed in phase by 90°. Similarly, two sine waves are used for detection, one being 90° in phase later than the other, and both having been generated by some means or other from the signal itself.

Differential detection does not attempt to generate a fixed-reference phase at the receiver. Instead, the data are coded by means of *changes* in phase. Thus in two-phase transmission a 1 bit may be coded as a $+90°$ change in the phase of the signal, and a 0 bit as a $-90°$ change, In four-phase transmission (similarly, with eight-phase transmission) the changes might be as follows:

Bits	Phase Change
0 0	$-135°$
0 1	$- 45°$
1 1	$+ 45°$
1 0	$+135°$

The detector now merely looks for changes in phase and does not need a reference-phase signal. There is no need to have the coding start at any specific phase. If the phase of the signal slips or drifts because of interference, the system recovers without aid.

In order to carry out the detection, the signal received is delayed one symbol interval and compared with the signal then being received. This comparison indicates the phase change that has occurred between the symbol intervals. The phase change detected is then converted into bits, dibits, etc., as appropriate.

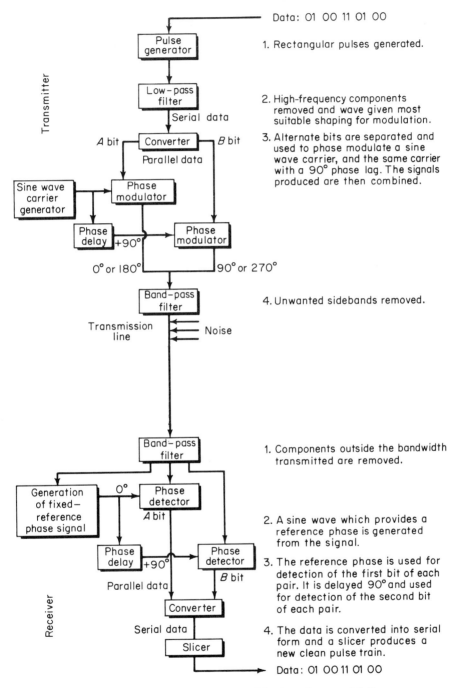

Data: 01 00 11 01 00

1. Rectangular pulses generated.

2. High-frequency components removed and wave given most suitable shaping for modulation.

3. Alternate bits are separated and used to phase modulate a sine wave carrier, and the same carrier with a 90° phase lag. The signals produced are then combined.

4. Unwanted sidebands removed.

1. Components outside the bandwidth transmitted are removed.

2. A sine wave which provides a reference phase is generated from the signal.

3. The reference phase is used for detection of the first bit of each pair. It is delayed 90° and used for detection of the second bit of each pair.

4. The data is converted into serial form and a slicer produces a new clean pulse train.

Data: 01 00 11 01 00

Fig. 13.15. Possible circuit elements used for four-phase modulation.

Because of this mechanism for delaying by one symbol interval, the speed of the transmission cannot easily be varied. Furthermore, it is difficult to use this type of detection for other than synchronous transmission in which the bits of characters or words are sent in a continuous, equally spaced stream, with no start–stop bits or gaps between characters, as in telegraphy.

14 PULSE TECHNIQUES

The last chapter was discussing a compromise: How to send digital data over communication links which were not designed for digital transmission, but for analog.

Almost all of the world's telephone plant today uses analog transmission with frequency division multiplexing, which needs analog modulation as described in the last chapter. In most countries it is likely to remain so for years to come because of the multibillions of dollars tied up in such equipment. However, the technology is evolving rapidly, and if the telecommunication companies were to start afresh today in building the world's communication channels, it is doubtful whether frequency division multiplexing would be generally used, or indeed any of the forms of analog modulation described in the last chapter. A new and different form of plant would be installed using a technique called *pulse code modulation*, in which the voice and other analog signals would be converted into a stream of bits looking remarkably like computer data. Some developing countries with a less massive investment in today's equipment are installing pulse modulated systems, and lines of this type are already in extensive use in the United States.

A variety of pulse techniques are theoretically possible for the transmission of information. If pulses form the basis of a telecommunication link, then digital information no longer needs to be modulated in the way described in the last chapter. However, analog information, such as the sound of the human voice, needs to be coded in some way so that it can be transmitted in the form of pulses, and then decoded at the other end to reconstitute the voice sounds. It seems certain that the circuits of decades to come will be designed to transmit very high-speed pulse trains into which voice, television, facsimile, and data will all be coded, and sent in a uniform manner. By an irony resulting from electronics, the compromise will have swung the other way. Instead of manipulating data so that they can be squeezed into channels designed for voice, the voice will be coded so that *it* can be sent over channels which are basically digital.

There is one major advantage in using digital techniques for transmission. Oddly enough, we had this advantage in the early teletype links, but when several teletype channels were multiplexed into one voice circuit the advantage was lost. Now the changing economics are bringing it back. With analog transmission such as that discussed in the previous chapter, whenever the signal is amplified, *the noise is amplified with it*. As the signal passes through its many amplifying stations, so the noise is cumulative. With digital transmission, however, each repeater station *regenerates* the pulses. New, clean pulses are reconstructed and sent on to the next repeater where another cleaning up process takes place. And so the pulse train can travel through a dispersive noisy medium, but instead of becoming more and more distorted until eventually parts are unrecognizable, it is repeatedly recarved, and thus remains impervious to most of the corrosion of the medium. Of course, an exceptionally large noise impulse may destroy one or more pulses so that they cannot be reconstructed by the repeater stations.

The main disadvantage of pulse transmission is that a much greater bandwidth is required. To send a given quantity of telephone conversations, for example, we would need a much higher bandwidth than with the analog systems in use today. However, because the signal is regenerated frequently, the pulse code modulation signal can operate with a lower signal-to-noise ratio. There is thus a tradeoff between bandwidth and signal-to-noise ratio, in the transmission of a given quantity of information. Furthermore, it can be shown that the greater the bandwidth of the channel the better the improvement in signal-to-noise ratio of pulse code modulation over analog modulation of a sinusoidal carrier.

The cost of the electrical equipment, referred to as terminal equipment, at each end of the communication link can be made considerably cheaper with pulse code modulation than with frequency division multiplexing. Three factors are swinging the economics further in favor of pulse code modulation. First, the trend to much wider bandwidth facilities; second, the decreasing cost of logic circuitry which would be used in coding and decoding, and packing many different signals together for simultaneous transmission; and third, the rapidly increasing need to transmit data and signals other than voice.

Possibly the most important of the advantages is the fact that all signals, voice, television, facsimile, and data, become a stream of similar-looking pulses. Consequently they will not interfere with one another and will not make differing demands on the engineering of the channels. Today, television and data, are much more demanding in the fidelity of transmission than speech, and create more interference when transmitted with other signals.

TYPES OF With pulse transmission a train of pulses is
PULSE employed to "carry" information just as a sinus-
MODULATION oidal carrier was used in the schemes discussed
in the last chapter. The information to be sent
will be used to modulate or change the pulse train in some manner. There are
several means of accomplishing this.

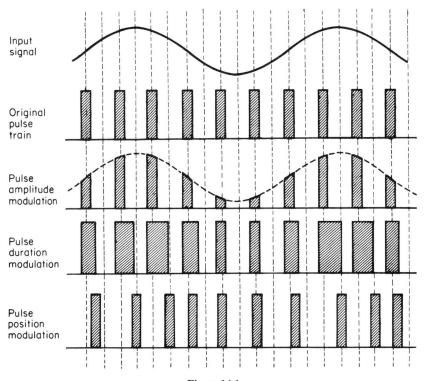

Figure 14.1

Pulse modulation techniques fall into two main categories. First, some physical characteristic of each pulse may be modified in accordance with the input signal. Its amplitude might be changed, or its width, or its position. These three possibilities are illustrated in Fig. 14.1. Here the signal is represented by the sinusoidal wave which is used to modulate the pulse train shown. The *Pulse Amplitude Modulation* is commonly referred to by the initials PAM, *Pulse Duration Modulation* by PDM, and *Pulse Position Modulation* by PPM.

The second category is *Pulse Code Modulation*, PCM, in which the signal to be sent is converted into a series of digits or characters, and is sent in a coded form of on/off pulses in much the same way that information transfers occur within a computer. It is pulse code modulation that is the exciting candidate for the communication plant of the future.

Fig. 14.2. A pulse code modulation coding tube used in the Bell T1 carrier system. *Courtesy AT&T.*

Compare the PAM illustration in Fig. 14.1 with that for amplitude modulation of a sine wave carrier in Fig. 13.2. There is much similarity and *envelope detection* can be used for demodulating the PAM signal in much the same way as that described in the last chapter for amplitude modulation.

SAMPLING　　　The pulses illustrated in Fig. 14.1 are, in effect, sampling the input signal at a limited number of points in time. The same is true when pulse code modulation is used. The question therefore rises: How often do we need to sample the signal in order to be able to reconstruct it satisfactorily from the samples? The less frequently we can sample it, the lower the number of pulses we have to transmit in order to send the information, or, conversely, the more information we can transmit over a given bandwidth.

It can be shown mathematically that *if the signal is limited so that the highest frequency it contains is W cycles per second, then a pulse train of 2W pulses per second is sufficient to carry it and allow it to be completely reconstructed.*

The human voice then, if it is limited to frequencies below 4000 cycles per second, can be carried by a pulse train of 8000 pulses per second, Any of the types of modulation illustrated in Fig. 14.1 can be used for this. The original voice sounds, below 4000 cycles per second, can be *completely* reconstructed.

PAM, however, operated as is illustrated in Fig. 14.1, is still basically an analog modulation system. The amplitude of the pulse can take on a continuous range of values from zero to the maximum amplitude. An infinite number of pulse amplitudes are possible.

It is normal with pulse modulation to transmit not an infinitely finely divided range of values but a limited set of specific discrete values. The input signal is "quantized." This is illustrated schematically in Fig. 14.3. Here the signal amplitude can be represented by one of the eight values shown. The amplitude of the pulses transmitted will therefore be one of these eight values. An inaccuracy is introduced in the reproduction of the signal by doing this, analogous to the error introduced by rounding a value in a computation. Figure 14.3 shows only eight possible values of the pulse amplitude. If there were more values the "rounding error" would be less. In some systems in actual use today 128 pulse amplitudes are used, or, to be exact, 127, as the zero amplitude is not transmitted.

PULSE CODE   After a signal has been *quantized* and then
MODULATION   *samples* taken at specific points, as in Fig. 14.3,
the result can be coded. If the pulses in Fig. 14.3 are coded in binary, as shown, three bits are needed to represent the amplitude of each sample. A more accurate sampling with 128 quantized levels would need seven bits to represent each sample. In general, if there were N quantized levels, $\log_2 N$ bits would be needed per sample.

The process producing the binary pulse train is referred to as *pulse code modulation*. The resulting train of pulses passes through frequent repeater stations which reconstruct the pulse train, and is impervious to most types of telecommunications noise other than major impulses or drop outs. The mere presence or absence of a pulse can be recognized easily even when distortion is present, whereas determination of pulse magnitude would be more prone to error.

On the other hand, the original voice signal will never be reproduced exactly, because of the quantizing errors. This continuous deviation from the original signal is sometimes referred to as "quantizing noise." It is of known magnitude and can be reduced, at the expense of bandwidth, by increasing the

① The signal is first "quantized" or
made to occupy a discrete set of values

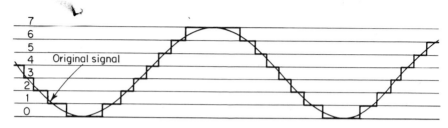

② It is then sampled at specific points. The
PAM signal that results can be coded
for pulse code transmission

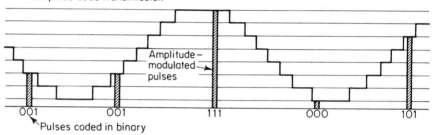

③ The coded pulse may be transmitted
in a binary form

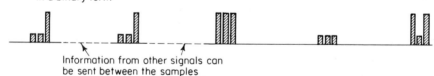

Information from other signals can
be sent between the samples

Figure 14.3

number of sampling levels; 128 levels, needing seven bits per sample, are enough to produce telephone channels having a signal-to-noise ratio comparable to that achieved on today's analog channels.

THE COMPANDOR   If the signal being transmitted were of low amplitude, then the procedure illustrated in Fig. 14.3 would not, of itself, be so satisfactory. The quantizing noise, still the same absolute magnitude, would now be larger relative to the signal magnitude.

The quantizing error is a function of interval between levels and not of the signal amplitude; therefore the signal-to-quantizing noise ratio is lower for smaller signals. For this reason a *compandor* is normally used.

A compandor is a device which, as discussed in Chapter 9, compresses the higher amplitude parts of a signal before modulation, and expands them back to normal again after demodulation. Preferential treatment is therefore given to the weaker parts of a signal. The weaker signals traverse more quantum steps than they would otherwise, and so the quantizing error is less. This is done at the expense of the higher amplitude parts of the signal for these cover less quantum steps.

This is illustrated in Fig. 14.4. The effect of companding to move the possible sampling levels closer together at the lower amplitude signal values, is

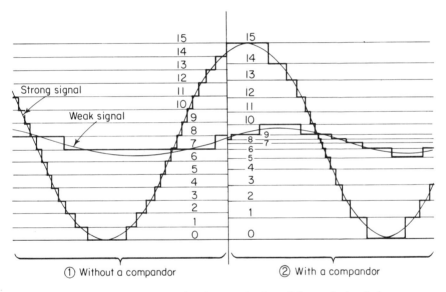

Fig. 14.4. With a compandor the quantization of the weak signal gives more separate values, and therefore a better ratio of signal to quantizing noise.

sketched on the right-hand side of Fig. 14.4, which shows the quantizing of a weak signal and a strong signal. The right-hand side of the diagram is with companding, the left-hand side without. It will be seen that on the left-hand side the ratio of signal strength to quantizing error is poor for the weak signal. On the right-hand side it is better. Furthermore, the strong signal is not impaired greatly by the use of the compandor. In practice, the PAM pulses are companded and one equipment serves all of the channels, which are being multiplexed together.

REGENERATIVE REPEATERS   One of the most attractive features of digital, as opposed to analog, transmission is the ability to place repeaters at intervals down the communication link to completely reconstruct the signal. In most PCM systems working today the repeaters are placed at intervals of about a mile. The Bell T1 System, operational since 1962, uses repeaters at intervals of 6000 feet.[1] These repeaters reconstruct 1,544,000 pulses per second. A higher bandwidth coaxial link was operated experimentally by the Bell Laboratories in 1965,[2,3] which transmits 244 million pulses per second with repeaters every mile. A ten-mile link had an error rate below 10^{-10}, and this will be good enough for a 4000 mile link coast-to-coast in the United States.

A regenerative repeater has to perform three functions, sometimes referred to as the 3 R's: reshaping, retiming, and regeneration. When a pulse arrives at the repeater it is attenuated and distorted. It must first pass through a preamplifier and equalizer to reshape it for the detection process. A timing circuit provides a signal to sample the pulse at the optimum point and decide whether it is a 1 or 0 bit. The timing circuit also controls the regeneration of the outgoing pulse and ensures that it is sent at the correct time and is of the correct width.

As with the phase modulation discussed in the previous chapter, there is a problem in keeping the timing signals in the repeaters exactly in synchronization. Normally, timing information must be sent with the pulse train in some way. For this purpose the pulses may have three permissible levels rather than two. A sine wave is generated from the input signal and this may be used to produce the timing pulses. In addition, a "framing" signal may be sent to indicate which is the start of a "frame" of information. The framing signal for the Bell T1 PCM system is described in the next chapter.

MULTIPLEXING   As with other modulation schemes, more than one voice channel is carried over operational PCM links. As is indicated at the bottom of Fig. 14.3 there is normally much space between the coding of each separate sample. Therefore the bits from many different voice channels are all packed together.

In the Bell T1 System, for example, each "frame" occupies exactly 125 microseconds. The frame contains one sample from each of 24 separate voice channels. Each channel is thus sampled in turn every 125 microseconds. The logic of the terminal equipment packs these bits together and sorts them out when they are received.

Multiplexing is the subject of the next chapter.

---

[1] Mayo, J. S., "A Bipolar Repeater for Pulse Code Signals," *Bell Sys. Tech. J.*, Jan. 1962.

[2] Mayo, J. S., "Experimental 224 MG/S PCM Terminals," *Bell Sys. Tech. J.*, Nov. 1965.

[3] Dorros, I., Sipress, J. M., and Waldhauer, F. D., "An Experimental 224 MG/S Digital Repeatered Line," *Bell System Tech. J.* (September 1966).

PULSE RATE   If pulse code modulation is used to transmit the human voice frequencies below 3000 cycles per second, then, as previously stated, a theoretical minimum of 6000 samples per second are needed. If each sample codes one of 128 permitted signal levels, thus needing seven bits for each sample, then not less than $6000 \times 7 = 42,000$ bits per second will be needed to convey this telephone voice. If the systems transmit the voice channel with frequencies up to 4000 cycles per second, then at least $8000 \times 7 = 56,000$ bits per second are needed.

To transmit 42,000 pulses per second, we require a bandwidth of not less than 21 kilohertz. Fifty-six thousand bits per second needs at least 28 kilohertz. In practice, the bandwidth needed for the pulses to be recognizable and reconstructable is somewhat more than half the pulse rate. The bandwidth needed for this type of modulation is thus a minimum of seven times the sum of bandwidths of the individual signals, and practical systems commonly need as much as twice this bandwidth. This could be reduced by having a smaller number of quantizing levels, as in Figs. 14.3 and 14.4, but the reduction in bandwidth would give a corresponding increase in quantizing noise. In general, if N is the number of quantum levels, so that $\log_2 N$ is the number of bits required per sample, then the theoretical minimum bandwidth required will be $\log_2 N$ times that of the signal. This is much worse than, for example, single-sideband amplitude modulation in which a bandwidth only very slightly higher than the signal bandwidth is needed. In typical voice systems, seven bits per sample are used and so it will be normal for PCM to use a bandwidth seven or more times that of the voice signal transmitted. In practice the Bell T1 system transmits 24 voice channels each of 4 kilohertz; and for this a system bandwidth of 1.5 megahertz is used—over 15 times the sum of the signal bandwidths.

In spite of this extravagance in bandwidth, the economics of the future lie with time-division multiplexing rather than with today's frequency-division multiplexing. This is mainly because the "terminal" costs are lower. Terminal costs dominate telecommunication economics especially at short distances, and are likely to do so even more strongly as wider bandwidth circuits are introduced.

The circuitry needed for PCM, although complex, is cheaper than that for AM or FM of comparable transmission quality. Considerable logic circuitry is needed and as everyone in the computer business knows, logic circuitry is fast becoming cheaper. The band-pass filters used in frequency-division mutliplexing are expensive, whereas the low-pass filters for PCM are less so. Perhaps most important, frequency-division multiplexing costs are almost proportional to the number of channels transmitted together over one transmission link. Little of the circuitry is common to the separate channels. With time-division multiplexing, much of it is common and so the terminal cost goes up only slowly as the transmission capacity increases. As we have seen, transmission capacities have been rising rapidly in the last decade or so, and this trend is almost certain to continue. Furthermore, as mentioned earlier, all manner of different signals, such as data, facsimile, and television, can be mixed together in PCM form without mutualinterference. In the future, then, it appears likely that much telephone plant will be PCM.

This is good news for the data-processing man. The 56,000 bits per second that are needed to carry a telephone conversation could equally well be used for data. With synchronous transmission of 7-bit characters, this gives about 8000 characters per second over a single telephone channel.

There are very few links in operation today giving more than 600 characters per second over a voice line, and it is more common to find speeds in the region of 100 to 200 characters per second.

Those readers who have had reason to complain that the printer they can have on the other end of a telephone line is slow, can take heart in the thought that over a PCM telephone line they could print at about 4000 lines per minute, or fill a very large screen full of data in a second.

REFERENCES

1. Davies, G. G., "An Experimental Pulse Code Modulation System for Short-Haul Trunks," *Bell System Tech. J.* (January 1962).

2. Mayo, J. S., "A Bipolar Repeater for Pulse Code Signals," *Bell System Tech. J.* (January 1962).

3. Aaron, M. R., "PCM Transmission in the Exchange Plant," *Bell System Tech. J.* (January 1962).

4. Shennum, R. H., and Gray, J. R., "Performance Limitations of a Practical PCM Terminal," *Bell System Tech. J.* (January 1962).

5. Mann, H., Straube H. M., and Villars, C. P., "A Companded Coder for an Experimental PCM Terminal," *Bell System Tech. J.* (January 1962).

6. Dorros, I., Sipress, J. M., and Waldhauer, F. D., "An Experimental 244 MG/S Digital Repeatered Line," *Bell System Tech. J.* (September 1966).

7. Fultz, K. E., and Penick, D. B., "The T1 Carrier System," *Bell System Tech. J.* (September 1965).

8. Travis, J. F., and Yaeger, R. E., "Wideband Data on T1 Carrier," *Bell System Tech. J.* (October 1965).

9. Mayo, J. S., "Experimental 244 MG/S PCM Terminals," *Bell System Tech. J.* (November 1965).

10. Edson, J. O., and Henning, H. H., "Broadband Codes for an Experimental 244 MG/S PCM Terminal," *Bell System Tech. J.* (November 1965).

11. Witt, F. J., "An Experimental 224 MG/S Digital Multiplexer-Demultiplexer Using Pulse Code Stuffing Synchronization," *Bell System Tech. J.* (November 1965).

15 MULTIPLEXING

All of the transmission media discussed in Chapter 8 have a capacity great enough to carry more than one voice channel. In other words, their bandwidths are considerably greater than the approximately 3400 cycles per second needed for transmitting the human voice. Each open-wire pair hanging from telegraph poles may carry about 12 telephone channels. The thicker cables with many twisted-wire pairs that hang from poles or lie under the ground carry many more telephone channels. Coaxial cable and microwave systems commonly carry bands of 600 to 1860 voice channels, or many more, and circular waveguide systems that could be constructed now if it were economically desirable will carry as many as 100,000 or 200,000 voice channels. At the lower end of the scale, each voice channel may be split into 12 or 24 telegraph channels (see Table 15.1).

Where a facility is set up, such as a chain of microwave links, which has a broad bandwidth, it is very desirable to make the maximum use of this bandwidth by making it carry as many channels as possible. The worldwide demand for communication facilities of all types is increasing at a tremendous rate and economics and the need to conserve precious radio-frequency space demands that the common carriers devise means of increasing the capacity of their facilities. Building new communication links is expensive. It is often desirable, therefore, to construct a communication link with as wide a bandwidth as possible and then divide the bandwidth between as many users as possible.

The technique of carrying several channels over one telecommunication facility is referred to as *multiplexing*. In a multiplex system, two or more signals are combined so that they can be sent together as one signal. The original signals may be voice, telegraph, data, or other types of signals. The

Table 15.1 FREQUENCIES USED FOR SUBDIVIDING A VOICE CHANNEL
INTO 24 TELEGRAPH CHANNELS, EACH 50 BAUD. CCITT
RECOMMENDATION NO. R. 31.

Channel Number	Lower Frequency of Band (cycles/second) (hertz)
1	420
2	540
3	660
4	780
5	900
6	1020
7	1140
8	1260
9	1380
10	1500
11	1620
12	1740
13	1860
14	1980
15	2100
16	2220
17	2340
18	2460
19	2580
20	2700
21	2820
22	2940
23	3060
24	3180

resulting combined signal is transmitted over a system with a suitably high bandwidth. When it is received it must be split up into the separate signals of which it is composed.

The word "multiplexing" is also used in other connections in data processing. For example, a "multiplexing channel" on a computer is one on which several devices can operate at the same time. Several printers, card readers, or paper tape punches may be operating simultaneously, and the bits which are sent to them, or received from them, are in some way intermixed as they travel along the single channel. Also, a "multiplexer" is sometimes used as the name of a device which receives, transmits, and controls data on several communication links at the same time. The bits arrive or are transmitted at a rate which is slow compared with the machine's scanning speed and, therefore, the machine is capable of overlapping its handling of many links. Again, word multiplexing has also been used in connection with time-sharing systems to refer to the use of one computer handling in real-time the communication with several terminal or console operators. The computer, working at much faster speed than its human operators, switches its attention rapidly from one to another, and one operator need not know that the computer is in fact interleaving the conversations of many such people.

The word "multiplexing," then, in general means the use of one facility to handle in parallel several separate but similar operations, and in particular, in telecommunication language, means the use of one telecommunication link to handle several channels of voice or data. Multiplexing is possible, and of economic value, because the operations that are multiplexed take place at a considerably slower speed than the optimum operating speed of the facility in question.

As will be discussed in the next chapter, communication channels are normally grouped together in "packages" which fill the bandwidth available on different types of plant. Twelve voice channels may be multiplexed together, for example, to form a signal of bandwidth 48 kilohertz. Much telecommunication plant is built to handle this bandwidth. Other transmission media handle a far higher bandwidth than this, and five 48-kilohertz links may be taken to a point where they feed a facility of 240-kilohertz bandwidth. In this case the original voice-channel signal has passed through two multiplexing processes. It may pass through more than two. Ten of the 240-kilohertz links may meet at a point where they are again multiplexed together to travel on a facility of a bandwidth of 2400-kilohertz (in fact, slightly higher because the packing is not 100% efficient). Yet again three of these "packages" may occupy an 8-megahertz bandwidth. The communication routes spanning the countries of the world thus carry large numbers of channels that were themselves grouped together stage by stage.

The original signal often goes through as many as four multiplexing stages and equivalent demultiplexing. It is thus worked upon by a variety of electronic conversion processes before it ultimately arrives at its destination, little the worse for these multiple contortions.

TWO METHODS OF
MULTIPLEXING

There are two basic methods of transmitting more than one signal over one path: *frequency-division multiplexing* and *time-division multiplexing*. The former separates the signals in frequency, as was shown in Fig. 10.5. The latter separates the signals in time by taking very short samples of the separate signals and combining them. In both cases, one wideband transmission medium is employed to transmit a number of different signals in parallel.

The information to be transmitted may be thought of as occupying a

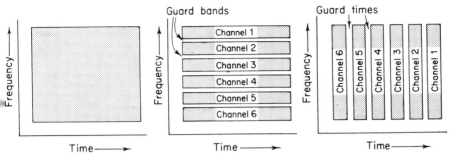

Fig. 15.1. (Left) The space available for communication. (Center) Frequency-division multiplexing. (Right) Time-division multiplexing.

two-dimensional continuum of frequency and time as illustrated in Fig. 15.1 (left). The quantity of information that can be carried is proportional to the period of time used, and to the range of frequencies, the bandwidth, used. If the quantity of information required from one channel is less than that which the physical facilities could carry, then the space available can be divided up either in frequency slices, or time slices, as in Fig. 15.1 (center and right).

In either case the engineering limitations of the devices employed prevent the slices from being packed tightly together. With frequency division, a *guard band* is needed between the frequencies used for separate channels, and with time-division, a *guard time* is needed to separate the time slices. If the guard bands or guard times were made too small, the expense of the equipment would increase out of proportion to the advantage gained.

Sometimes the term *space-division multiplexing* is also used in the telecommunications industry to mean packing separate physical channels into one cable. Cables have been constructed carrying many hundreds of pairs of wires (Fig. 8.3). The cable in Fig. 15.2 contains twelve separate coaxial cables, and this is in common use to give a high total bandwidth.

Fig. 15.2. Space-division multiplexing, Twelve coaxial units are grouped with one cable. Each coaxial unit carries 1800 one-way voice channels combined by frequency-division multiplexing. The entire cable carries about 11,000 two-way voice channels, or the equivalent.

1. FREQUENCY-DIVISION MULTIPLEXING

A familiar example of frequency multiplexing is radio broadcasting. The signals received by a domestic radio set contain many different programs traveling together, but occupying different frequencies on the radio bandwidth. The speech and sounds from each radio station *modulate* a carrier of a frequency allocated to that station, in the manner discussed briefly in Chapter 10. The tuning circuits in the radio set allow one such signal to be separated from all the others.

Frequency-division multiplexing on a telephone line is basically similar. The signal, for example the human voice, is used to modulate a carrier which may have a much higher frequency. The signal thus occupies a relatively narrow bandwidth which is a part of a much wider bandwidth transmitted. Other signals modify carrier frequencies that are spaced from each other by a given interval, typically 4 kilohertz. These modulated carriers are all amplified and transmitted together over the channel. The spacing between the carrier frequencies is slightly greater than the bandwidth needed to transmit the signal in question. This was illustrated in Fig. 10.3.

Figure 15.3 illustrates the principle of the equipment for frequency-division multiplexing. Here twelve signals each needing a bandwidth of not more than 4 kilohertz are combined so that they can be sent together over one physical channel.

At the sending end there are twelve modulators and at the receiving end twelve demodulators. In fact, the modulators and demodulators are combined into twelve single units to permit two-way transmission to take place. For simplicity, Fig. 15.3 illustrates only one-way transmission. The signals pass through twelve low-pass filters to remove any high-frequency components, and are then used to modulate twelve separate carrier signals each 4 kilohertz apart. The frequencies resulting from each modulation process must be restricted to their own band. If they spill over into the bands occupied by other signals, the signals will not be separated correctly at the receiving end. As was shown in Chapter 13, the modulation process—whether it be amplitude, frequency or phase modulation—produces components spread over a frequency range wider than that of the original signal. Frequency and phase modulation spread their products over a wide spectrum (Figs. 13.9, 13.10, and 13.14). Therefore, the outputs of each of the twelve modulators must be filtered again to stop them from interfering with each other. Band-pass filters are used to restrict each signal to the allocated 4-kilohertz band shown.

When the signal is received a converse process takes place. Twelve band-pass filters let through the frequencies of one signal only, as shown. These then pass into twelve demodulating circuits and the original signal is recovered.

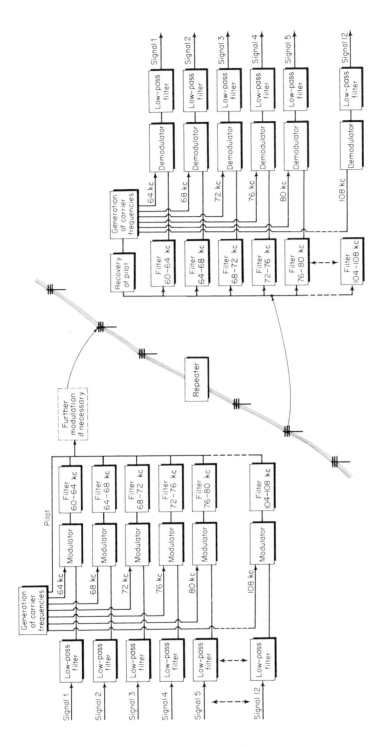

Fig. 15.3. Frequency-division multiplexing. A diagram illustrating the principle.

It is desirable that the twelve carrier frequencies used for modulation are accurately separated by 4 kilohertz and that those used for demodulation are *identical*. As we are packing as many separate signals as practicable into one physical channel, there is little room for error in the carrier frequencies used. For this reason the carrier frequencies may all be generated from the same source. In Fig. 15.3 a sine wave may be used to produce carriers at 60, 64, 68 kilohertz, and so on. The reference frequency which is the source of the carriers may be transmitted along with the twelve channels so that it can be used for controlling the frequencies used for demodulation at the other end, as shown.

The reference frequency transmitted is referred to as the *pilot*. Generating the carriers needed for modulation and demodulation is simplified if these are all harmonically related to the pilot.

If the carrier used for the demodulation is slightly different in frequency to that used for modulation this results in distortion of the signal and *frequency offset* mentioned in Chapter 12. Frequency offset is disturbing in the case of music transmission. A note and its harmonics are offset by the same amount, and consequently the harmonic is no longer a multiple of the base frequency. This results in "inharmonic" music in which the distortion is particularly noticeable.

When the modulation has taken place as described, the resulting band of twelve signals still may not be suitable for the transmission link in question. The link may be designed to carry a different range of frequencies in which case the newly formed band may be changed as a unit to the requisite frequency band. In other words, it has to undergo a further modulation process. Also it may be combined with other similar groups of signals so that several groups occupy a still greater bandwidth. In this case it has to undergo a further multiplexing process and in many systems there are several multiplexing processes combining different groups of signals so that they travel over a high capacity facility.

To achieve efficient use of a bandwidth, one set of sidebands resulting from the modulation process is usually removed. This is "suppressed sideband" modulation as described in Chapter 13. The "N" type carrier system in use in the United States uses both sidebands and has a channel spacing of 8 rather than 4 kilohertz. This, however, is not common practice and in other countries is generally regarded as too expensive in bandwidth.

Unfortunately, the filters that can be constructed at a reasonable cost do not have a sharp cutoff at the edges of the band of frequencies they pass. Instead their attenuation varies with frequency in a manner somewhat like that illustrated in Fig. 15.4. This curve could relate to the filtering of a 4-kilohertz band after modulation of a carrier at 64 kilohertz, or very slightly less than that.

When several such filtering processes are packed together the result will be as in Fig. 15.5. It will be seen that the bands the filters pass overlap in the regions of high attenuation. To minimize this, multiplexing schemes define a "guard band" as illustrated; and the system is designed so that as far as possible the required data occupy only those frequencies shown between the dotted lines. The useful bandwidth for each channel in the illustration is somewhat less than 4 kilohertz.

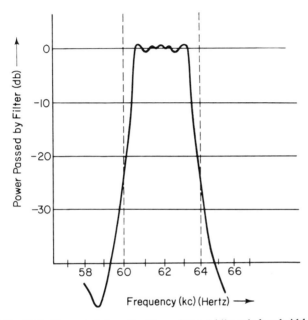

Fig. 15.4. Characteristics of a filter using a 4-kilocycle bandwidth.

Even with a "guard band," there will still be some low amplitude interference between channels, illustrated by the shaded portions of Fig. 15.5. The system must be designed so that this cross-talk is of sufficiently low amplitude not to cause annoyance or, if possible, not to be discernible. The "guard bands" or the overlapping of the filter attenuation curves cause the total useful bandwidth to be less than the total transmission medium bandwidth. The ratio

$$\left(\frac{\text{total useful bandwidth}}{\text{total transmission medium bandwidth}} \right)$$

is sometimes called the *frequency efficiency* of the system. We may find that into a 48-kilohertz bandwidth we are packing twelve channels, but they have a usable bandwidth of only about 3400 hertz each. The frequency efficiency is then $(12 \times 3400)/48,000 = 0.85$. It will be seen that the frequency efficiency depends first upon the width of the guard band and hence upon the filter characteristics, and second upon the degree to which the modulation products are dispersed in frequency. If, for example, we transmitted both sets of sidebands, or used frequency modulation with a modulation index that scatters the products over a wide frequency range, we would be increasing the bandwidth needed for each channel and so lowering the frequency efficiency of the multiplexing process.

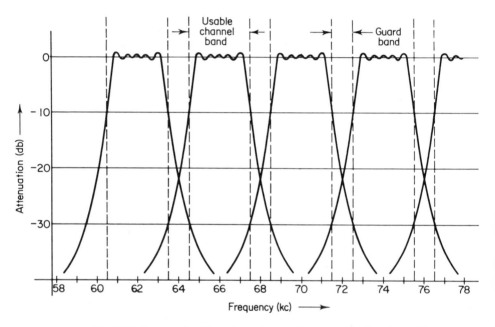

Fig. 15.5. Because the filters do not have a sharp cutoff at the edges of the bands they pass, the usable channels must be separated by a guard band. Even so there is some slight cross talk as illustrated by the shading. A high-amplitude noise impulse in one channel will make itself felt in the adjacent channels.

To carry out multiplexing the transmission medium used must be linear. Amplitude-frequency distortion or phase delay on the medium as a whole will have a serious effect on the individual channels transmitted. Equalizers are applied to the overall transmission rather than to individual channels. The amplifiers and, if a higher level of multiplexing is carried out, the modulators which operate on the group of channels must be made with a good linearity.

Even though the group transmission is carefully equalized the effect of filters on individual channels is to produce some amplitude-frequency distortion over the channel band. This can be seen from Fig. 15.5. This use of filters in multiplexing is partially to blame for the channel characteristics of amplitude-frequency distortion that were illustrated in Fig. 12.3, and discussed in Chapter 12.

The economics of multiplexing arise partly from the fact that one repeater amplifies many channels. In Fig. 15.3 all frequencies from 60 to 108 kilohertz are amplified together. If no multiplexing were used, a separate repeater would be needed for each channel. This saves expense especially on long-distance transmission on which many repeaters would be used.

Figure 15.3 shows schematically transmission in one direction only. In actual systems two-way transmission is necessary. At each end of the link modulators and demodulators would be needed, and these may have some circuitry in common, particularly the oscillator. A *hybrid* circuit splits the two-way transmission so that outgoing signals are fed to the modulator and received signals from the demodulator are sent to the appropriate receiving equipment.

2. TIME-DIVISION MULTIPLEXING

The major alternative to frequency-division multiplexing is *time-division multiplexing*. Here the time available is divided up into small slots and each of these is occupied by a piece of one of the signals to be sent. The multiplexing apparatus scans the input signals in a round-robin fashion. Only one signal occupies the channel at one instant. It is thus quite different from frequency multiplexing in which all of the signals are sent at the same time, but each occupies a different frequency band.

Time-division multiplexing may be thought of as being like the action of a commutator. Consider the commutator sketched in Fig. 15.6. The mechanically driven arm of this device might be used to sample the output of eight instruments. Providing the values of the voltages from the instruments are not varying too rapidly compared with the rotation time of the arm, the individual inputs can be reconstructed from the composite signal. Such a device is used in telemetering. To separate the signals when they are received, a commutator similar to that illustrated might be used, but with the input and output reversed. The receiving commutator must be exactly synchronized with

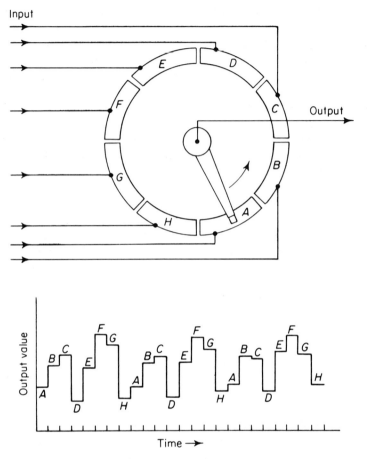

Fig. 15.6. A commutator can be used as a simple form of time-division multiplexing.

the transmitting commutator. The time multiplexing devices we meet in telecommunications today are normally electronic and of much higher speed, but in principle are similar to the commutator.

How fast can the signal be changing? This question was answered in the previous chapter. If the highest frequency in the signal (Fourier analysis) is f_s cycles per second, then at least $2f_s$ samples per second are required. With $2f_s$ samples per second the signal can be reconstructed completely. If then we "multiplex" voice signals with frequencies up to 4000, the commutator or its electronic equivalent must rotate at 8000 times per second. If n signals are to be multiplexed together, then $2nf_s$ samples per second must be transmitted.

Figure 15.7 illustrates the multiplexing of four signals, to give a train of

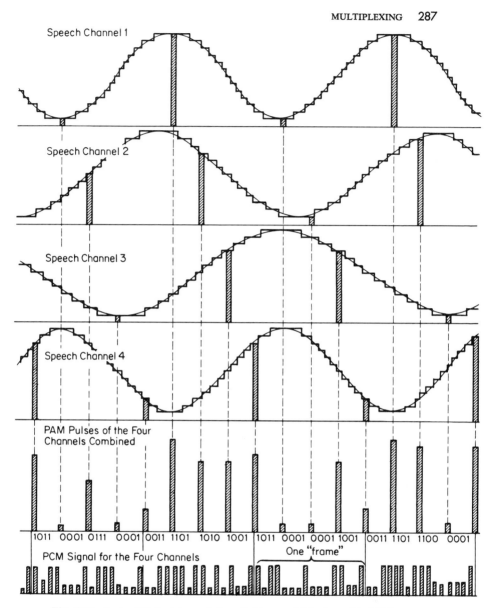

Fig. 15.7. A simplified picture of time-division multiplexing with PCM transmission.

PAM pulses. The result is then coded, as in Fig. 14.3 of the last chapter, into a PCM signal. For simplicity, only a four-bit code is shown in the diagram, and no compounding is used. It will be seen that the result is a series of "frames," each of 16 bits. Every frame contains one sample of each signal.

In order to decode the signal it is necessary to be sure where each "frame" begins. With this knowledge, the signals can be reconstructed. The first four bits relate to signal 1, the second four to 2, and so on.

SAMPLING   The sampling of the signal prior to coding is done by a series of accurately timed switches, or sampling gates, shown schematically in Fig. 15.8. Here the signals are first put through low-pass filters which restrict them to 4 kilohertz or somewhat below this. They are then sampled by passing through a series of gates which open for a very brief period of time. This creates PAM pulses which are fed together through a compandor which gives preferential gain to the low-level signals, and then coded in binary, giving the type of result illustrated in Fig. 15.7.

At the receiving terminal, the reverse process takes place. The signal is decoded, "expanded" by a compandor, and amplified by a wideband power amplifier which raises it to the level of the original signal. It then again passes through a series of very accurately timed sampling gates. These separate the channel and the result is a set of pulse amplitude modulated signals. A low-pass filter on each channel then integrates the samples, and the original is recovered, or at least that part of it below about 4 kilohertz. An actual system would have signals traveling in both directions and so would be somewhat more complicated than Fig. 15.8.

There is clearly a problem in this. The sampling gates must open and shut at *exactly* the right instants in time. The gates at the receiving end must *exactly* correspond to those at the transmitting end, and must take into consideration any transmission delay. Furthermore, because the pulses tend to spread out slightly as they travel down the line, the samples cannot be packed tightly together. A *guard time* is needed between them.

The sampling gates are controlled at each terminal by a pulse train from an oscillator of precise frequency. The frequency of sampling can be maintained and the sample time "tuned" so that it is made at the center of the incoming pulses. In addition to this, it is necessary to establish synchronization so that the receiving terminal can identify which pulse is which.

SYNCHRONIZATION   There are a variety of ways possible for the establishment of synchronization, and detecting where the "frame" begins. Where PCM is used with binary coding, the bits must be either 1 or 0, and no different amplitude can be used to indicate the beginning of the frame. Wide pulses or differently positioned pulses cannot be used either, because this would upset the repetitive way in which the regenerative repeaters work. Therefore, special binary coded information is included in the frame for synchronization.

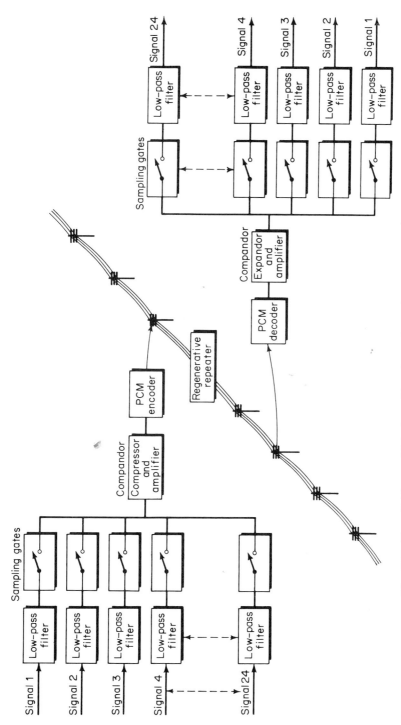

Fig. 15.8. Time-division multiplexing with pulse code modulation. A simplified diagram.

289

The Bell T1 PCM system multiplexes together 24 voice channels. Seven bits are used for coding each sample. The system is designed to transmit voice frequencies up to 4 kilohertz, and therefore 8000 samples per second are needed. 8000 frames per second travel down the line. Each frame, then, takes 125 microseconds. A frame is illustrated in Fig.15.9.[1] It contains eight bits for

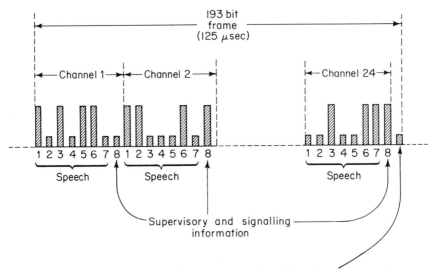

Framing code. The 193rd bits on successive frames follow a pattern which is checked to ensure synchronization has been maintained. If synchronization is lost this pattern is scanned for to re-establish it.

Fig. 15.9. The bit pattern used to multiplex 24 voice channels on the Bell T1 system.

each channel. The eighth is used for supervisory reasons and signaling, for example, to establish a connection and to terminate a call. There are a total of 193 bits in each frame and so the T1 line operates at $193 \times 8000 = 1,544,000$ bits per second.

The last bit in the frame, the 193rd bit, is used for establishing and maintaining synchronization. The sequence of these 193rd bits from separate frames is examined by the logic of the receiving terminal. If this sequence does not follow a given coded pattern then the terminal detects that synchronization has been lost. If synchronization does slip then the bits examined will in fact be bits from the channels—probably speech bits—and will not exhibit the required pattern. There is a chance that these bits will fortui-

[1] Davis, C. G., "An Experimental Pulse Code Modulation for Short-Haul Trunks," *Bell System Tech. J.* (January 1962).

tously form a pattern similar to the pattern being sought. The synchronization pattern must therefore be chosen so that it is very unlikely that it will occur by chance. If the 193rd bit was made to be always a "1" or always a "0," this *could* occur by chance in the voice signal. It was found that an alternating bit pattern, 0 1 0 1 0 1 . . . , never occurs for long in any bit position. Such a pattern would imply a 4-kilohertz component in the signal, and the input filters used would not pass this. Therefore, the 193rd bit transmitted is made alternately a 1 and a 0. The receiving terminal inspects it to ensure that this 1 0 1 0 1 0 . . . pattern is present. If it is not, then it examines the other bit positions which are 193 bits apart until a 1 0 1 0 1 0 . . . pattern is found. It then assumes that these are the framing pulses.

This ingenious scheme works very well with speech transmission. If synchronization is lost the framing circuit takes 0.4 to 6 milliseconds to detect this. The time required to reframe will be about 50 milliseconds in the worst case if all the other 192 positions are examined, but normally will be much less, depending upon how far out of synchronization it is. This is quite acceptable on a speech channel. It is more of a nuisance when data are sent over the channel. When data are transmitted there certainly is a chance that a 0 1 0 1 0 1 . . . pattern could exist fortuitously, and this could lead to false framing. Probably a different method of framing is needed when such a link is used for data, but there are many possible ways of doing this.

TASI   An ingenious technique is used on some of today's very long-distance, frequency-division multiplexed lines for packing extra voice conversations into these expensive links. This is called *Time Assignment Speech Interpolation*, or TASI.

On a link carrying a conversation, both parties do not normally speak at once, and for a small proportion of the total connection time (usually about 10%) nobody is speaking. The long-distance link is normally a four-wire line, and so any one-way path is in use only about 45% of the total time. In other words, for 100 talkers only about 45 on average will be talking simultaneously. TASI aims to use less than 100 channels to carry these 45 voices. There is a spread about this average and so it cannot suffice with only 45 channels. There is a possibility that most of the talkers at one instant will be talking in the same direction. As the number of talkers becomes large, however, the ratio of talkers to channels required becomes close to 1/0.45.

The TASI equipment is designed to detect a user's speech and assign him a channel in milliseconds after he begins to speak. An almost undetectable amount of his first syllable is lost. He retains the channel until he stops speaking; a short time after then, if the channel is needed for another talker, it will be taken away from him. If the traffic volume is high, the speaker's path may be snatched away as he pauses in midsentence, and when he utters his next words a different path is given to him. If, on the other hand, there are few users he will retain his path. TASI can sometimes be heard in operation by a user if he knows what to listen for. On the transatlantic cable there are relatively few paths, and a caller during a peak period can detect a slight change in the noise amplification which indicates that a channel has been given to his called party in the nick of time to catch his next word. There is a small but finite chance that a TASI circuit will be unable to find enough free paths, and for a very brief period of time words will be lost.

The cost of TASI switching equipment is high, but less expensive than the long channels which it saves. As bandwidth availability becomes less costly, as is the trend, gimmicks like TASI may be less sought after, and indeed the relative inefficient (for voice) time-division multiplexing will probably replace frequency-division multiplexing.

It is interesting to reflect that many real-time *data* connections have a substantially lower line utilization than voice connections. The user of a time-shared system holds his telecommunication line while he thinks and then slowly keys in data. For brief periods only the computer replies at high speed to his screen or terminal. In this case, some form of "time assigned data interpolation" would be worthwhile if there are many such users, and would give a proportionately bigger saving than TASI.

16 TRUNKS AND
WIDEBAND FACILITIES

We have seen how a large number of signals can be multiplexed together to travel over a single path. The main telecommunication highways of the world are wideband facilities carrying many signals in parallel. Today, they are microwave and coaxial links; tomorrow they will be waveguides, satellites, perhaps lasers. From these, lesser pathways branch out, like feeder roads joining a throughway. They have narrower bandwidths but still carry many signals. Yet smaller pathways link into these, and so on, until eventually we reach the cul-de-sacs taking the telephone to individual homes.

It is desirable to standardize the bandwidths and frequencies used. Then equipment from different manufacturers can work together. A multiplexed group of signals can travel over the network of one common carrier and pass on to that of another without expensive demultiplexing and remultiplexing. Standards were laid down within the United States and within other countries. To a major extent international standardization has been achieved and this today is assuming much greater importance. However, there are still incompatibilities between national networks.

Figure 16.1 shows how channels are multiplexed together to form standardized "packages." The frequencies shown on the diagram are those of the Bell L3 coaxial system which may be regarded as typical. This is an eight-megahertz bandwidth, coaxial cable system widely installed throughout the United States. It can carry 1860 voice channels, or 600 voice channels plus a 4.2-megahertz television channel.

The massive growth of commercial television in the United States has been a spur to building of such wideband facilities to carry the programs across the nation. Fortunately, television peak broadcasting periods do not coincide with the time of day when people are using their telephones the most, and so the same bandwidth which carries a television program cross country in the evening can handle 1260 telephone conversations by day. In Britain, although the BBC operated a television service as long ago as 1938, the growth of television was slow, probably because the medium was not used for advertising until the mid-50's, and then there was only one channel with restricted advertising. Today there are still only three channels. In most European countries there are less than this. Consequently, there are less wideband communication facilities in Europe than in the United States or Japan, and this may possibly hamper the growth of data transmission to some extent.

GROUPING The voice channel itself might be regarded as the first building block for packaging signals. Computer and other data are tailored to fit the voice channel, and telegraph messages are multiplexed together to fill this frequency band. In a typical system,[1] 12 telegraph signals are combined into one composite signal. Twelve frequencies or "tones" in the voice-frequency range are each modulated, using FM, by one of the telegraph signals. The result is a signal in the range 200 to 3200 hertz (300 to 3400 in Europe, the CCITT recommendation), which can travel over voice channels anywhere in a telephone network. In Europe 24 signals of 50 bands are multiplexed into one voice channel using the frequency bands shown in Table 15.1. The baseband telegraph signal by itself could not have been transmitted without modification over voice channels in general because its important frequency components lie below 200 hertz.

The next building block, referred to in Fig. 16.1, is the *channel group*. A number of voice channels are multiplexed together to travel as a unit in a band of 60 to 108 kilohertz. This frequency band is used throughout most of the world as a standard. The band 12 to 60 kilohertz is also used. Many of the world's telephone *wire lines* and their associated plants are designed for 60 to 108 kilohertz. Without this standardization, international telephony on its present scale would have been much more expensive and could have become almost impossible. Before the war there was much controversy as to whether the voice channels in this band should be separated by 3 or 4 kilohertz. The choice of 4 kilohertz became standard and is now in common use, giving 12 voice channels in a channel group. There are some exceptions to this, however. Six-kilohertz spaced channels are used in the Netherlands. Much of the Bell plant in the United States (the N-type short-haul carrier system)[2] uses double sideband AM, and consequently needs a bandwidth greater than 4 kilohertz. Eight-kilohertz spacing is used. Because system lengths are short, AT&T

---

[1] Hysko, J. L., Rea, W. T., and Roberts, L. C., "A Carrier Telegraph System for Short Haul Application," *Bell System Tech J.* (July 1952).

[2] Caruthers, R. S., "The Type N-1 Carrier Telephone System: Objectives and Transmission Features," *Bell System Tech. J.* (January 1951).

found that economy results from this in the terminal design that offsets the halving of line capacity. Cheaper filters and simpler demodulators are used, and the signal-to-noise ratio is better. Oddly enough these economies were not found in Europe and 4-kilohertz spacing, with single sideband modulation, is generally installed there.

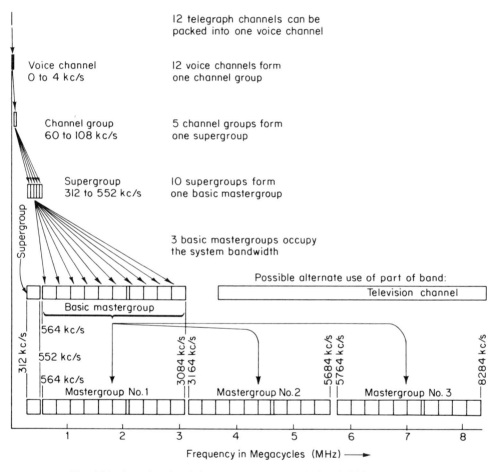

Fig. 16.1. A typical breakdown of an 8-megacycle bandwidth to carry 1860 voice channels, or 600 voice channels and a television channel—the Bell L3 system.

The intercontinental satellite systems that are becoming a major feature of world communications use 4-kilohertz channel spacing, and are further emphasizing the need for international standardization.

Five channel groups are multiplexed to form a *supergroup*. This occupies frequencies 312 to 552 kilohertz. The telephone companies thus manufacture another subdivision of transmission facilities to carry this band of $5 \times 12 = 60$ telephone channels. The frequencies 312 to 552 kilohertz are generally agreed upon internationally. However, several different pilot frequencies are used by different countries.

The next step up in bandwidth is the *basic mastergroup*. Ten supergroups are multiplexed together to form one mastergroup, which carries $10 \times 5 \times 12 = 600$ voice channels. This is suitable for the bandwidth available on a coaxial cable or microwave link.

Still wider bandwidths became available both on coaxial cable and microwave systems. They were needed to carry television cross country. Television requires a bandwidth of at least 4.1 megahertz, and normally rather more than that is allocated to it. The Bell L3 system illustrated in Fig. 16.1 can carry either one supergroup, one mastergroup and a television channel, or one supergroup and three mastergroups, giving a grand total of 1860 voice channels.

Even this is not the ultimate. The Bell L4 system carries six mastergroups with the frequency allocation shown in Fig. 16.2, and so has a capacity of

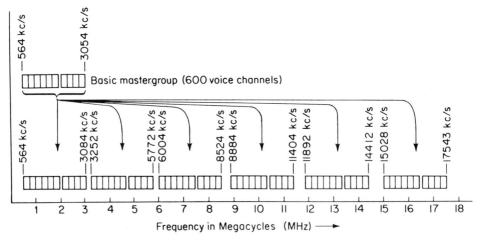

Fig. 16.2. Frequency allocation in the Bell L4 system (3600 voice channels).

3600 voice channels. The coaxial cable shown in Fig. 15.2 handles 10,800 ($= 3 \times 3600$) telephone conversations simultaneously, and thus has the capacity of three L4 systems. Similarly, today's microwave links can transmit several times the L4 capacity and the helical wave guide system which Bell Labs have built experimentally—but not, at the time of writing, installed commercially—will transmit 200,000 voice channels.

International standardization above the supergroup level has been poorer than that below it. The CCITT standard mastergroup is different from the Bell standard mastergroup. It contains five supergroups as opposed to the latter's ten supergroups. The CCITT gives three allocations for a 12 megahertz system, each composed of combinations of blocks of 5 or 15 supergroups. Neither the Bell L3 nor L4 system has this. The pilot frequency allocations vary considerably from one country to another.

This has not been too serious so far. The largest blocks of circuits transmitted between countries with different standards have been accommodated at the supergroup level, and here it has been necessary to convert the pilot frequencies. However, global telecommunications will probably increase on a vast scale in the years to come, especially with high-capacity satellites becoming available, and the mastergroup incompatibilities will give rise to considerable expense and inefficient use of facilities.

One of the exciting prospects for the late 1970's is the direct pickup of television programs from satellites. It is now clear that satellite transmitter power sufficient for this will be achieved. This could become a significant force in world affairs. However, it will be seriously impeded by the differences that exist between different national television systems. The United States uses 525 lines per frame; Europe uses 625; and Britain uses 405 and 625. Europe uses 50 frames per second and the United States 60. More recently, different systems for color television have been introduced.

The telecommunications industry has lessons to teach about the value of looking imaginatively to the future and setting standards accordingly. It is a lesson which is largely being ignored in the computer industry. Today's proliferation of incompatible languages, systems and codes will have expensive and damaging repercussions in the future now that we are moving into an era of data transmission, computer utilities, communal data, and program banks, and terminals for everybody.

LINKING OF DIFFERENT FACILITIES   Figure 16.3 shows, figuratively, three small towns, one of which is at the junction of a coaxial system carrying a mastergroup, and a microwave chain carrying three mastergroups. The towns may be many hundreds of miles apart.

If a subscriber A telephones subscriber B, the call will travel over A's *local loop* to the town's small telephone exchange (*local central office*). From there the call will be switched to travel to B over B's *local loop*. The word "loop" means that this line is permanently associated with a particular subscriber. In contrast a "trunk" is a line with common usage on to which the call of any of several subscribers can be switched. Both the local loops connecting A to B are wire lines carrying one call only. The telephone conversation, then, undergoes no multiplexing. The signals travel at voice frequency.

Three Small Towns, Many Miles Apart

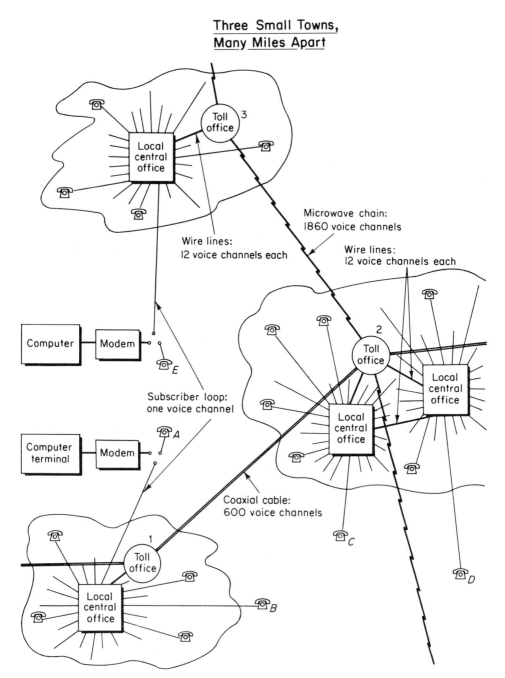

Fig. 16.3. The linking of telecommunication facilities carrying different numbers of channels.

Now consider what happens when C telephones D. These two are not connected to the same exchange. The call must therefore be routed from one central office to another on an *interoffice trunk*. Most of the time this trunk route will be handling several calls from people in that town talking to each other. Therefore, multiplexing equipment could be used. The interoffice trunk might be one or more wire lines carrying a *channel group* of twelve voice channels, or it could be a number of nonmultiplexed pairs in a cable if that is more economical.

When A telephones C, the situation is more complex as there is no direct connection between the local control offices to which they are attached. This is often the case even within one town. A large town with several central offices would have an additional exchange called a "tandem office" for switching lines between central offices. In Fig. 16.3 A's call will travel to the town where C lives over a channel of the coaxial cable system. This is connected in both of these towns to a *toll office*. A's call goes over his local loop to his local central office and this routes it to the toll office on a *toll-connecting trunk* (or *terminal* trunk). Like the interoffice trunk, this trunk may be one of a channel group. The toll office multiplexes the call into a mastergroup of 600 voice channels. The connection from one toll office to another is called an *intertoll trunk*. The toll office of the receiving town demultiplexes it, sends it to the appropriate central office on a toll-connecting trunk in a channel group. From there is goes at voice frequency on to C via his subscriber's loop.

When A telephones E, there is yet another stage in the process because the link to E's town goes over a microwave system which carries 1860 voice channels (when there is no television). The call is taken from the coaxial cable mastergroup and switched to the microwave terminal at the toll office 2. It leaves the microwave link at the toll office in E's town, and reaches him via a toll-connecting trunk, his local central office, and local loop.

The same complex route would be taken if A were using a computer terminal for communicating with a computer in E's town. Suppose that A has a terminal like that in Fig. 16.3. He dials the distant computer to use a program in its files. The computer sends a message which is displayed on the terminal telling him to identify himself. The data that travels in the ensuing work undergoes the same multiplexing processes as a voice conversation would. The data, however, may be more seriously affected by delay distortion, frequency offset, and other systematic distortions. The design of the modem is the key to tailoring the signal so that it can travel over this network without errors other than those caused by unavoidable fortuitous noise.

Let us examine the process which the signal from A must undergo with typical equipment or order to reach E. First, pulses from the terminal modulate a voice frequency carrier in the modem that is used. This might, perhaps, be phase modulation, befitting them to travel down the subscriber loop at voice frequencies and avoid interfering with any signaling equipment in the local central offices.

The local central office then amplitude modulates the already phase modulated data signal to send it in the channel group to the toll office, where channel groups are again amplitude modulated to form a supergroup. The supergroups are modulated to form the mastergroup which is then amplified and transmitted down the coaxial cable.

Probably only a small number of the signals (up to 600 signals) traveling down the coaxial cable will be routed onto the microwave chain. The signal may therefore go through three stages of demodulation at toll office 2 before it can be switched to travel to toll office 3.

It then enters another multiplex terminal and undergoes modulation to channel group, supergroup, mastergroup, and finally to the radio system baseband allocation ranging from perhaps 0.1 to 8 megahertz. It is still not at a suitable frequency for microwave transmission, however. The frequencies used for microwave transmission range from about 2 to 12 gigahertz (10^9, i.e., billion, cycles per second). The bandwidths allocated in the United States by the Federal Communications Commission for common carrier use are shown in Table 16.1.

Table 16.1

Band (megahertz)	Bandwidth (megahertz)
2110–2130	20
2160–2180	20
3700–4200	500
5925–6425	500
10,700–11,700	1000

In this case it is likely that the 3700–4200 or 5925–6425 band will be used. Note that the bandwidth available is much higher than the 8 megahertz of Fig. 16.1 or the 17 megahertz of Fig. 16.2, and in fact, several such channels could be transmitted over one microwave route. The Bell TH system has six active channels, each capable of handling up to 1860 telephone channels, and thus a route capacity comparable to the L4 system discussed earlier.

Our band of 1860 channels, at radio baseband allocation from 0.1 to 8 megahertz, is now frequency modulated as a unit onto a carrier of "intermediate frequency," about 60 to 80 megahertz. This band is shifted again to the correct transmitting frequency in the gigahertz group and amplified. A waveguide carries it to the antenna where it is radiated.

At toll office 3, the converse process takes place, and a channel group takes the signal to the local central office. Here it travels to E, once more at voice frequency, where it is demodulated and fed into the computer.

It is certainly a triumph of modern electronics to pass a voice signal through all these manipulations and then produce it, unharmed, at a telephone hundreds of miles away.

The reader might wonder next time he makes a long-distance call at the multiple contortions his voice is suffering.

WIDEBAND
CHANNELS
Most common carriers lease their channel groups and supergroups, as well as leasing individual channels, to provide a wideband service. Three grades of wideband services in the USA are listed in Table 16.2.

Table 16.2

	Equivalent Bandwidth (kilohertz)	Equivalent Number of Voice Channels
Series 8000 channel	48	12
Type 5700 channel	240	60
Type 5800 channel	1000	240

The Series 8000 channel is thus equivalent to one channel group, the Type 5700 channel to a supergroup, and the Type 5800 to four supergroups.

When an organization leases a wideband channel such as these, it will also lease appropriate channel terminals. A variety of terminating equipment is possible. The channels may be used as wideband channels or may be subdivided by the user into private channels of low bandwidth such as telephone, teletypewriter, or data-transmission channels. The channel group, for example, can have terminating equipment from AT&T which will enable it to be used for one of the following:

a. 12 telephone channels between two points.
b. 48, 150-baud channels between two points.
c. 144 teletypewriter channels between two points.
d. Equivalent combinations of the above.
e. Data transmission at 40,800 bits per second, plus one telephone channel for coordination purposes.
f. Two-level facsimile signals in the frequency range of approximately 29 to 44 kilohertz, plus one telephone channel for coordination purposes.
g. Two-level facsimile signals requiring up to 50,000 bits per second, plus one telephone channel.
h. A channel of bandwidth up to 20 kilohertz of high quality, i.e., only minor deviations in gain and delay characteristics.

Similarly, a supergroup can have terminating equipment that will enable it to be used for one of the following:

a. Seven-level magnetic tape transmission at approximately 105,000 bits per second, plus a control channel and a telephone channel for coordination purposes.
b. Two-level facsimile requiring up to 250,000 bits per second, plus four channels of teletypewriter grade for control and coordination.
c. A channel of bandwidth up to 100 kilohertz having only minor deviations in gain and delay characteristics.

A mastergroup or a standard television channel is capable of transmitting data at rates up to several million bits per second, but standard tariff offerings are not (yet) available for such uses.

Providing wideband transmission facilities can be made difficult by the fact that most installed wideband systems link only the toll offices. It is usually the case that, as in Fig. 16.3, there are no facilities wider than the channel group on the subscriber side of the toll office, and no facilities wider than the voice channel linking the subscriber to his local central office. Special arrangements, therefore, have to be made. In some cases AT&T is using the T1 PCM system, discussed in the last two chapters, as an economical means of providing a high-speed data link over wire lines. Baseband analog repeater systems are also available for use on the wire pairs which go from the central office to a customer's premises. In other situations, short-haul microwave systems have been used.

The telephone companies are planning to introduce a switched network for wideband facilities. When it is working, this, along with PCM techniques, will make many computer applications much more economical.

HIERARCHY OF DIGITAL CHANNELS   As pulse code modulation systems increasingly replace frequency-division multiplexing, a hierarchy of digital facilities will be built analogous to those described. AT&T has plans for a nation-wide network of PCM channels using wire-pair, coaxial cable and microwave transmission media similar to those discussed above. On this network, voice, television, facsimile, Picturephone®, and computer data will all travel intermixed.

We have already described the T1 system which will be part of this network. The other facilities planned are shown in Fig. 16.4. The T1 system carries a "channel bank" of 24 voice channels with time-division multiplexing as was shown in Fig. 15.9. It transmits 1.544 million bits per second and a wideband data terminal can be connected to it. This system, now coming into widespread use, must be a component of any larger time-division multiplexing hierarchy.

The next level up is the T2 line. This carries a pulse stream of 6.3 million bits per second. An M12 multiplex unit combines the bits from four T1 lines to travel over one T2 line. The T2 line is of the capacity required for a Picturephone signal. The Picturephone image when digitized needs about six

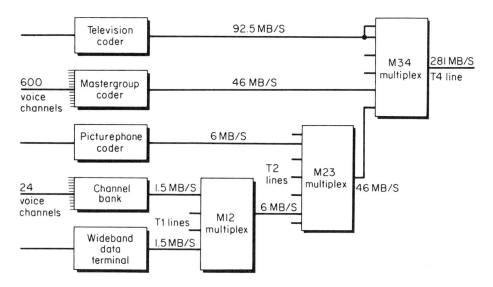

In the proposed digital hierarchy, signals will be multiplexed in several stages. For example, four T1 signals will be combined into a 6 megabit T2 signal. Seven T2 signals then will be multiplexed, forming a 46 megabit pulse stream. This intermediate rate matches that of a coded mastergroup. Six 46 megabit signals will be multiplexed, forming a 281 megabit T4 signal. Other combinations are possible. For example, two television and two mastergroup signals form a T4 signal.

Fig. 16.4. Copyright, February 1967, Bell Telephone Laboratories, Inc. Redrawn and reproduced by permission of the editor, *Bell Laboratories Record.*

million bits per second. If the Picturephone service sells as is hoped there will probably grow up a network of such lines with switching centers. People who eventually have a Picturephone in their home, or businessmen who have them in their offices, will also have a communication link capable of carrying six million bits per second—a very high data rate by the standards of today's computer world; faster indeed than the highest data transfer rate from today's magnetic tapes and disks. What could this do for our time-sharing problems? Certainly the potential uses of such a link are enormous and could bring great changes in business methods.

Seven T2 lines, carrying voice data, Picturephone, or any other signals that are devised, can feed into an M23 multiplex unit. Their signals are interleaved to form a signal at 46 million bits per second. It is planned that today's analog master group can be digitized as a unit to form a signal of 46 million bits per second. Color television needs twice this bit rate and could be carried over two such pulse streams.

At the next level up, the M34 multiplex unit combines six 46-megabit signals to form a signal at 281 million bits per second. This signal would travel over a T4 link. At present there is no transmission facility planned between the T2 and T4 to carry the 46-megabit stream.

The T4 or T2 pulse stream will travel over microwave or coaxial cable links similar to those in use today but redesigned with digital repeaters. Such a means of transmission seems well suited to the new media, helical waveguides, and laser beams, and AT&T has proposed a satellite system employing digital transmission and interconnectable with the preceding network.

A system using such techniques will be able to send *far* fewer voice conversations over one physical link than the analog multiplexing described earlier. However, voice traffic is likely to increase relatively slowly in the years to come, whereas data traffic can be expected to increase at a very high rate. The great advantage of such a system is the ability to carry all types of signals together without problems of them interfering with each other. The terminals and multiplexing equipment are likely to be built

Fig. 16.5. Terminals for the Bell System pulse code modulation T1 carrier system. More than a thousand telephone circuits terminate here, in a typical central office in New Jersey. *Courtesy Bell Telephone Laboratories.*

at lower cost than today's equipment with "large-scale integration" technology in which microminiaturized circuitry can be etched once the appropriate masks have been produced. A characteristic of LSI circuitry is that it becomes low in cost if a sufficiently large quantity can be made to offset the initial design and production of the masks. Before PCM systems are introduced, they must show improvements in cost and performance over existing technology. The Bell T1 system has done this. It seems likely that the T2 and T4 systems may do so also, and it is widely expected that such systems will eventually predominate. This is an exciting prospect for the computer world.

17   SUPERVISORY SIGNALS

The signals traveling over telecommunication networks must perform two functions. The first is the transmission of information. The second is the relaying of supervisory signal to enable the network equipment to take the correct actions. Many supervisory functions are needed to set up a communication path between two points and maintain it in operation.

A correct path must be found through the switching centers. The telephone at the far end must be made to ring. A free channel in a multiplexed group of channels must be found, and when the signal reaches the far toll office it must leave this group. The complex path over which the signal travels must be maintained and not broken into by other signals. However, when the communication ends, the circuit must then be freed for other use. The originating end must be informed of the status of equipment at the distant end. Is the telephone busy or the channel full? When the channel is full alternate pathways to the same destination will be sought. A record must be kept of the distance and time of long calls so that the customer is billed correctly.

For purposes such as these, a variety of supervisory signals must travel on the networks as well as the voice, or other information-conveying signals. The network is like a gigantic nervous system with the supervisory signals carrying sensing and control impulses throughout the system. Where data-processing machines intercommunicate there will be *another* range of supervisory signals to control *these*, but such signals are treated by the communication network equipment as information signals. The supervisory signals discussed in this chapter are those that have been devised primarily for voice transmission.

The human voice itself in some cases acts as a supervisory signal and switches have been devised to operate depending upon whether or not the human voice is present. The voice, for example, switches echo suppressors on and off on very long circuits, and the fact that it is used for this often causes the weak parts of the first syllable to be lost, as the switch does not work until it has detected this first syllable.

Most of the supervisory signals are some form of code, however, that is sent separately, either over the same bandwidth that the voice channel uses, or over a separate signaling band outside the voice band, or in some cases over a separate channel. Much of the supervisory information is transmitted before the conversation, as for example, dialing and ringing. Some, however, as for example, detecting when a telephone receiver is replaced, must be sent at the same time as the information transmission. The sending of these supervisory signals is referred to generally by the term "signaling." A variety of signaling practices have grown up on different telephone systems. There is considerable incompatibility, again, between one country and another, and sometimes incompatibility within one country.

Signaling systems, invented, as they mostly were, for voice communication, have usually not taken the advent of data transmission into consideration. As we shall see there are certain ways in which data could interfere with the telephone networks' supervisory signals. Computer equipment used on a public network has both to make use of the signaling arrangements of that network, otherwise it cannot establish and maintain a call, and at the same time it has to tailor its transmission so as to avoid interfering with the signaling and accidentally triggering any circuit that it should not. This can be quite complex, especially in countries where some old plant is still in use, and could conceivably be reached by the computer transmission. Much of the old telephone equipment was built to last, and it has. Often data-transmission devices designed for one country have met with trouble when exported because they are not compatible with the signaling arrangements of the other country. Some excellent American equipment has failed to find a market in Europe for this reason.

SUBSCRIBER-TO-CENTRAL OFFICE SIGNALING

In general, the signaling methods can be subdivided into those in use between the subscriber's telephone and his local central office, and those on trunks between one automatic office and another. The methods used for these two classes of lines are normally different and independent. The methods in use between the telephone and central office are to a large extent determined by considerations of the telephone itself, and its human user. Similar methods were once used between switching offices, especially those manually operated. The signals between automatic offices, on the other hand, are entirely machine-to-machine signals. They are related to the multiplexing and carrier methods that are in use. With modern central offices the office often acts as a buffer between the customer and the trunks, and the trunk signaling uses its own independent methods. In this way the best form of signaling technique can be chosen for the trunk circuits.

Between the subscriber and the central office, fewer signaling requirements exist. The need for cheap and reliable devices in the telephone set is the dominating factor.

Years ago the switching was manual and the caller attracted the attention of the operator by cranking a magneto handle. This generated a buzzing or ringing sound at the switchboard and worked an indicator telling the operator which line needed attention. The method is still in use in the less developed countries. With a modern plant, however, the caller merely lifts the telephone and DC current flows on the line, lighting a lamp on the switchboard if manual switching is in use, or operating a relay if it is automatic. The automatic exchange puts a "dial tone" frequency on the line. The dial tone is one of a set of *audible signals*, like the ringing and "busy" signals, which are supervisory signals for the human listener. Most of the others are not for human ears, but trigger automatic actions in the telephone plant.

DIALING   The introduction of the telephone dial led the way to automatic switching. As the dial rotates back counterclockwise to its stop, it sends a train of DC pulses down the line. Each digit sends a different number of pulses. This is illustrated in Fig. 17.1. In the earlier telephone exchanges and the smaller ones still being

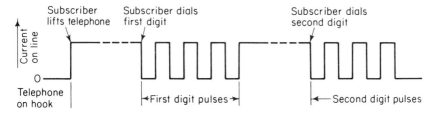

Fig. 17.1. Hand-set dialing pulses.

installed in some countries, each of the pulses in Fig. 17.1 moves a rotary switch by one step. The switches are arranged in wafers which have ten settings, so each digit controls the setting of one such switch. Banks of rotary switches form a path through the exchange which is selected step-by-step as the pulses are received. Switching of this type is called a *step-by-step* system.

Today, and especially with large offices, it is often not economical to do the switching step-by-step. Instead, the address digits are stored in some way and then used to set up the circuit. The storing of the digits is particularly important with trunk calls. Here the office which originally receives the call is not the office which makes the final connection. The necessary addressing information must be sent from the originating office to any other offices which handle the call. It will probably not be sent in the form shown in Fig. 17.1, but will be transmitted with a different signaling method. Where one trunk joins other trunks as when A talks to E in Fig. 16.3, the addressing digits are used at the interconnection places to route the call correctly. Usually there will be a choice of possible circuits as described in the next chapter, and when one is fully occupied, an alternative will be selected. The digits must travel to whatever center is selected.

The simple make-and-break pulses are produced inside the telephone by a cam. The pulse rate on most systems is nominally 10 per second and varies between 7.5 and 12. The same pulses can be generated by tapping the receiver rest to make and break the circuit. With telephone coin boxes of an earlier design it was possible to obtain a connection without putting money in the box, by rapidly tapping the telephone rest. In this way the appropriate signal could be sent to the central office without using the dial. Today in most countries more ingenious methods are needed!

When a computer is planned to use the public network and "dial up" remote terminal or telephones, an automatic calling unit under control of the computer must generate pulses like those in Fig. 17.1.

On some of the exchanges in which address digits are stored in a register or "sender," a new form of dialing has been introduced using audible tones. This is referred to in the United States as Touch-Tone®[1] dialing. Here the telephone no longer has a dial. In its place is a group of twelve (originally ten) small square keys labeled 1 to 9, 0, * and #. Each key sends a different audible musical note composed of two frequencies down the line. By touching seven or more of them in sequence a number can be quickly dialed. The train of tones is received by special equipment in the central office which interprets them, and stores the digits in a register with the same function as that in which ordinary telephone dial pulses are stored. Thus the major switching equipment of the exchange is no different when Touch-Tone dialing is used, only that part for interpreting the signal. Many central offices in the United States are now equipped for Touch-Tone signaling. Subscribers can have a Touch-Tone telephone installed if they wish for a slight additional cost.

The notes from the Touch-Tone keys each consist of two frequencies, one from the group 697, 770, 852, and 941 and the other from the group 1209, 1336, 1477, and 1633. Thus a self-checking code is produced with $4 \times 4 = 16$ combinations. Only 12 of these combinations (four- and three-frequency groups) are used on the conventional, 12-key telephone. A 16-button dial is reserved for military comunications, for security purposes and for multiple priority preemption. The 16 frequencies are agreed upon as an inter-

---

[1] Bell System copyright term.

national CCITT standard. If a receiving office detects more or less than two of these frequencies, this is an error condition.

This type of signaling is referred to as multifrequency signaling, MF. All of the frequencies transmitted are within the normal voice band. We shall come across multifrequency signaling or different types in the chapter on data transmission. It can give a particularly inexpensive method of sending data over a voice line.

The signaling between the central office and telephone thus consists of a means of dialing, a two-state DC signal to indicate whether the telephone handpiece is on its rest or not, and various audible tones intended for the ear of the user. One more signal is necessary. The office must be able to make the telephone ring. On local loops a 20-cycle voltage is used. Where the signal must travel over a carrier channel, a frequency of 1000 cycles modulated by a frequency of 20 cycles is used.

OFFICE-TO-OFFICE SIGNALING

The signaling between offices which are not step-by-step is normally independent of that between the subscriber and the office. Furthermore, on many systems—as for example, the Bell System—when a telephone call passes over several links, as in Fig. 16.3, the signaling over the separate links is independent. If it proves desirable different signaling "languages" can be used over consecutive links. When A calls E in Fig. 16.3 the signaling on the microwave link may or may not be different from that on coaxial cable. Both of these could be different from the signaling on the wire circuit from the central office to toll office.

Signaling which is independent on each link is referred to as *point-to-point* signaling. Each point relays the signal to the next point. Not all systems have this independence. In Europe a somewhat different system is common, using what is called *end-to-end* signaling. Here when a call is routed via toll offices A, B, C, and D, A sends a signal to B saying that this is not a call terminating at B, but a transit call. B allocates a transit register (only) to A, and tells A to go ahead. A sends the digits giving the address of D. B acknowledges these to A and sends a signal to C again saying that this is a transit call. The logic circuitry of B now takes no further part. C's go-ahead message travels to A over the path that B has set up. A sends D's address. C acknowledges this and sets up a path to D. C, as with B before, then releases its transit register. D now tells A to transmit, by passing the logic of B and C, and A sends the rest of the telephone number to D.

When the telephone call is over, messages must again be sent to B and C telling them to disconnect the circuit.

With *point-to-point* signaling, A would send all the information about the routing to B. The register and logic in A which handles this would then be dismissed. B would send the information to C, and then B's register and logic would be dismissed. C would select the final trunk to D and send to D the local address of the called party (often four digits) dropping the other routing digits. This is somewhat quicker than end-to-end signaling and permits the flexible use of different interoffice addressing schemes.

TYPES OF SIGNAL
There are three main types of signal. First, the *dialing signal*, or an equivalent message, giving the address of the office and telephone to be reached. In a step-by-step system, this can be a set of two-state signals as it is from the telephone dial, and each pulse moves a switch until the correct path is set up. Between offices with a register or "sender" which stores the address, however, faster multistate signaling is used. For example, fast multifrequency tones may transmit the address between offices.

Second, signals are needed which tell the *status* of certain equipment. For example, it is necessary to know whether a called customer has answered or not. On a long-distance call, when the customer picks up his telephone the originating office will start charging. It must therefore know when this status changes from "on hook" to "off hook." Similarly, it is necessary to know the availability of "sender" registers or "transit" registers. In the preceding example of end-to-end signaling the offices send acknowledgments of addresses received. These and other status signals can all be sent with two-state signaling.

Third, it is necessary to *control* certain equipment. For example, a line must be seized for a call. Later, after the connection is made a signal is sent instructing that the path be disconnected. Again these actions require two-state signals. On some telephone systems the signals are continuous. In other words, a voltage or other two-state indication is permanently present. On others, the control signal is a short, specially coded message. These are referred to, respectively, as *"continuous"* and *"spurt" signaling*.

There are a variety of other signals which fit into one of these three categories. For example, signals for returning a coin in a coin box, other signals for coin box control, signals for alerting operators, signals for "ringing forward" or sending a ringing signal to the originating end, auxiliary charging functions, and (in Europe) signals for indicating that a call does not terminate in a country but is merely passing through, and language digits to indicate the language to be used if an operator is called in for assistance on the call.

SIGNALING LANGUAGES
We have already looked at two signaling languages: dial pulsing, as in Fig. 17.1, and multifrequency tones in use with Touch-Tone dialing. Multifrequency signaling was in wide use between offices before it was introduced for the Touch-Tone telephone.

A number of DC pulse systems have long been in use, similar to that in Fig. 17.1, but differing in detail. A system called *revertive pulse signaling* is used which is faster than that in Fig. 17.1. Here a start pulse from the transmitting office causes a pulse generator in the receiving office to start, and this sends its pulses back to the transmitting office. A counter at the transmitting end counts these and sends a stop signal when the required digit is reached. The counter in the receiving office then transfers the digit to a register and the counter is freed for the next digit. Another system called *panel call indicator signaling* sends one of five possible signal levels. Two positive voltages, an open line, and two negative voltages are used. The larger positive voltage is used to mean end of pulsing, and the other four are used to code digits.

Multifrequency signaling uses six frequencies placed in that part of the voice spectrum where different channels have the smallest deviation in loss. On the Bell System the frequencies used are 700, 900, 1100, 1300, 1500, and 1700 cycles per second. Digits are coded as two out of the first five of these frequencies, and special codes as two out of the six. If the receiving equipment detects more or less than two of these frequencies, it sends back a signal asking for retransmission. Table 17.1 shows the combinations of frequencies used on the Bell System.

Table 17.1

Code	Frequencies
1	700 + 900
2	700 + 1100
3	900 + 1100
4	700 + 1300
5	900 + 1300
6	1100 + 1300
7	700 + 1500
8	900 + 1500
9	1100 + 1500
0	1300 + 1500
Start of signaling	1100 + 1700
End of signaling	1500 + 1700

The signals are sent over the normal voice channels and are transmitted like speech. They may be sent either by a switchboard operator or, more rapidly, by automatic equipment. If the switchboard operator accidentally presses two keys at once, her error is detected. The reader may possibly have heard these interoffice signals. On some systems the operator's signaling is occasionally audible, and sometimes the automatic signaling can be faintly heard due to cross talk. The quiet listener may hear a far-away flurry of diminutive discordant notes.

IN-BAND AND OUT-OF-BAND SIGNALING

On a trunk carrying multiplexed channels the status and control signal are connected to an AC signal of suitable frequency to transmit over that trunk. Three possibilities arise. There can either be a separate channel over which all the signaling takes place, or each channel can carry its own signals. If the channel carries its own signals, these can be either inside the band allowed for voice transmission or outside it. Both *in-band* and *out-of-band* signaling is in common use.

Multifrequency signaling carries the address only. The status and control signals are carried by either one or two fixed frequencies, depending upon the system. The Bell System uses a single signaling frequency of 2400 or 2600 hertz. Some European circuits use a single frequency of 2280. Others use two frequencies at 2040 and 2400.

These frequencies are in the transmitted voice band. This raises an important problem. The circuit which is triggered by the signal frequency must not be affected by the human voice itself or it might be triggered at the wrong time. In-band signals are, of course, audible and so are not transmitted while conversation is taking place. The detection circuiting must, however, "listen" during the conversation so that it is ready to respond to the signals when the conversation ends. There is a danger that it might be fooled and pick up a sound which it thinks is a signal, during the conversation.

The signals cannot be discriminated from speech by transmitting them at a higher level because this would overload the amplifier. They are therefore detected by transistor circuits which listen for the signal frequency and exclude the human voice.

Two safeguards are commonly used. First, the signal must last for a given period, called the "recognition time." It is very improbable that a frequency of 2600 hertz, or whatever is used, will last for that duration in human conversation. Second, the detection circuit is inhibited by voice frequency sounds other than at the signaling frequency. An alternative safeguard can be employed when two signaling frequencies are used. A signal can be composed of the two frequencies followed by a single frequency. It is virtually impossible that this could be imitated by the human voice.

On some systems *out-of-band signaling* is employed, though *in-band* signaling is the usual system. Out-of-band signaling takes place at a frequency of 3700 hertz thus avoiding the voice band which stretches from about 300 to 3200 or 3400 hertz. This runs no danger of interference from speech. It is unaffected by compandors and echo suppressors. Also signaling can take place during the telephone conversation. However, it needs extra bandwidth and extra electronics to handle the signaling band. Signaling rates are slower because the signal has been confined to a narrow bandwidth.

Furthermore, it could be a problem when the circuit was switched to a channel with in-band signaling. If the voice channel is used for signaling, equipment for handling the signals need only be employed at the ends of the call, not at intermediate toll offices. All of the equipment for transmitting the human voice can also transmit the signals.

SIGNALING AND DATA TRANSMISSION   Because of the economic advantages of in-band signaling, this is the system that is normally used. With some data-transmission machines this has caused a problem.

Data must be sent over the communication line in such a manner that it does not interfere with the signaling system. The communication system recognizes a signal by the fact that it has substantial energy at the signaling frequency and little at other frequencies. This would not be true of the human voice which is smeared across a range of frequencies different from that of the signals. To transmit data we must either ensure that it avoids the signaling frequency completely, which would limit the usable bandwidth; or else that it is smeared across the band so that when there is energy at the signaling frequency there will always be sufficient energy at other frequencies to prevent it from being mistaken for a signal. The latter will make the best use of channel capacity and will be accomplished in the modem design. Figure 17.2

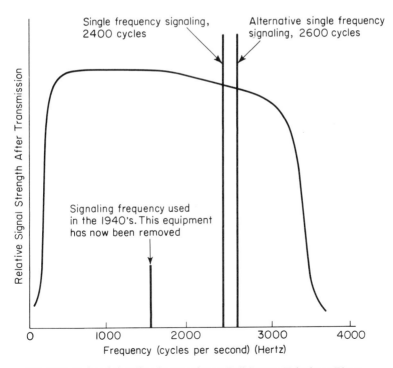

Fig. 17.2. In-band signaling frequencies on Bell System Telephone Plant.

shows the Bell System signaling frequencies. In Britain the Post Office uses a single-frequency signaling band at 2280 hertz, but also there is some equipment with two-frequency signaling at 600 and 750 hertz. This is shown in Fig. 17.3. On the European International Service the frequencies used are again different—a two-frequency system operating at 2040 and 2400 hertz.

The telecommunication companies impose restrictions on users, or manufacturers, of data transmission equipment to ensure that they do not interfere with the signaling. Figure 17.4 shows the relative signaling levels permitted for data by Britain's General Post Office. The two troughs correspond to the signaling frequencies in use. Data transmission machines or modems must be designed so that the relative signal levels cannot exceed those indicated in these troughs, or else so that sufficient energy is sent elsewhere to prevent the automatic devices from assuming that a signal is being sent. A guard tone in the area *ABCD* of Fig. 17.4, for example, could enable signals to be sent in the signaling zone from 2000 to 2430. The use of a guard tone, however,

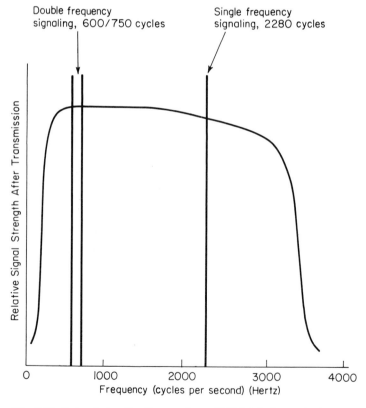

Fig. 17.3. In-band signaling frequencies on British telephone plant.

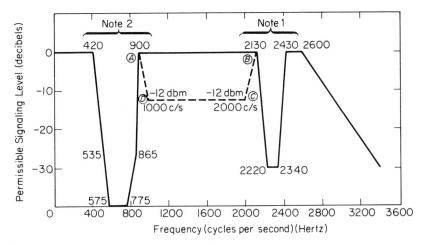

Fig. 17.4. Power level restrictions for data transmission over public switched connections in Britain. Some *private* circuits over carrier channels also need restrictions of this form. *Redrawn from "Characteristics of Telephone Circuits in Relation to Data Transmission," by M. B. Williams, Post Office Electrical Engineers' Journal, London, October 1966.*

Notes:

1. Signal components up to 0 dbm may be permitted within this area if *always* accompanied by signals in area *ABCD*

2. Signals having components within this area may be permitted if characteristics preclude false operation of trunk-signaling equipment

is less efficient than selecting a modulation method which guarantees that the signal is spread across the band. Care also has to be taken that intermodulation products from other channels cannot have strengths greater than those in Fig. 17.4.

Some data sets designed for relatively slow but inexpensive operation transmit data characters by means of combinations of single frequencies. These frequencies would be selected to avoid the signaling frequency zone. However, some such data sets which operate perfectly well in the United States cannot be used on British and other lines without redesign because on these lines they would interfere with signaling. Thus some data sets which work well in one country cannot be used in another.

These restrictions do not apply in general to private lines. However, some private lines over carrier channels may use in-band voice-frequency signaling. On these circuits also, signal imitation by data transmission must be prevented, and this will reduce the available bandwidth. On some private circuits signals are used for providing alternate speech or data facilities. A diagram of the type in Fig. 17.4 may therefore also be issued for some private circuits.

PULSE CODE
MODULATION

When pulse code modulation becomes more widespread for voice communication, the situation will change. Here, as indicated in Fig. 15.7, one bit per channel in each "frame" is used for signaling. There is thus no interference between voice and signaling or between data and signaling. All of the large number of bits per second in a PCM voice channel can be used for data.

18 EXCHANGES AND SWITCHING

There are almost 200 million telephones in the world. Approximately half of them are in North America, but the rest of the world is fast rising in affluence and loquacity. Almost all of the world's telephones must be capable of being interconnected one to another. Clearly they cannot be linked directly as this would need about 2×10^{16} interconnections; and so an enormous network of switching centers has grown up.

Figure 16.3 illustrated two of the main types of offices in which switching takes place. Telephones are connected first to a *local central office*. When a connection is desired to another telephone connected to that office, the switching devices couple it directly. If a longer distance call is made the local central office passes the call on to another exchange.

The switching of calls at the local central office is done automatically in most areas. In other words, the subscriber dials the number he wants and the exchange uses the dialed digits to select the circuit and ring the appropriate telephone. Commonly, the last four digits of the number dialed represent a telephone connected to the local central office. Each such central office can, therefore, handle up to 10,000 telephones, though some handle more than this, using a fifth digit. The two or three digits before these represent an exchange area. The resulting seven-digit telephone number can address up to 9×10^6 telephones (a first digit of 0 is used for special purposes).

To achieve country-wide switching more than seven digits are needed in large countries. In the United States and Canada combined there are more than 20,000 central offices. Each of these needs a unique set of digits in the number. This designation consists of a regional code (or *area code*) and a central office code. The call may, therefore, be first directed to the appropriate regional toll office, and from there to the required central office. Often, however, high usage trunks directly between cities bypass the regional toll offices. Three digits, in the United States and Canada, precede the seven digit local number when a long-distance call is placed—212 MU 9-4196. Here 212 is the New York area code, which would not be dialed if this number was being reached from New York. Similarly, in England, you dial 01 WHI 1212, where 01 is the London area code. WHI reaches the Whitehall central office and 1212 the subscriber on that office. Alphabetic letters such as WHI have a useful mnemonic value but in many countries have been dropped because their use restricts the number of possible combinations. The famous Scotland Yard number has become a mere collection of digits: 01 230 1212.

We are now moving into an era of international dialing. In Europe, as long ago as 1956, Belgium set up a fully automatic link between Brussels and Paris. International dialing in Europe is now in regular use, and limited dialing across the Atlantic has been achieved. For this purpose two *International Code* digits precede the country number, with the series 90 to 99 reserved for intercontinental calls. A *language digit* is also used to indicate the language of the calling party. If an operator is called upon for assistance, the call can then be routed to an operator who speaks that language (when possible). Thus we may have:

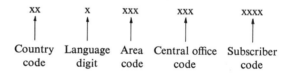

XX	X	XXX	XXX	XXXX
Country code	Language digit	Area code	Central office code	Subscriber code

On a fully automatic system, the subscriber dials the long-distance number. On a *semiautomatic* system the operator dials it. In making a transatlantic call, then, to a known number, the caller may hear one operator only and she is able to dial the number directly. Much of the world's telephone systems have been semiautomatic, and they are fast being changed to fully automatic.

CALL ROUTING

If a call is intended for the city in which it originated, it may be sent by the local central office to another local central office, as with calls from C to D in Fig. 16.3. In a large city, however, there will be many local central offices, therefore it is not economical to have a trunk connecting all of these. If a city has 100 local central offices, for example, it would need 4950 trunk groups to interlink all of them. Instead, another level of switching is used and this exchange is called a *tandem office* (Fig. 18.1). Calls from one local central office to another within a city are routed via the tandem office.

When calls are made outside the city they are routed via a *toll office*, which was shown in Fig. 16.3. Multiplexing equipment here puts the call onto the high-capacity intercity trunks. The exchanges in a city are thus as shown in Fig. 18.1. This diagram also shows privately operated exchanges (PBX's, private branch exchanges) which many organizations have within the city. These are sometimes automatic, but often are operated by a girl at a switchboard.

ALTERNATE
PATHS

Direct dialing between one city and another has now been introduced in many countries. In the United States it is referred to as *direct distance dialing* and in Britain as *subscriber trunk dialing*. Nationwide switching requires a hierarchy of switching centers above that in Fig. 18.1.

It is necessary in developing such a network to employ a number of criteria. First, reliability must be considered. If one trunk is inoperative for some reason, it is desirable to be able to route the same call over alternative

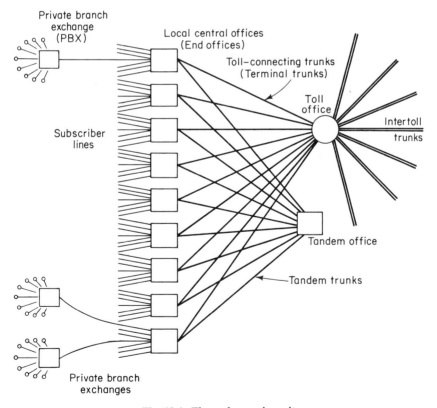

Fig. 18.1. The exchanges in a city.

lines. Second, the load must be considered. What is the probability that the trunk in question will be fully occupied? If it has no spare channels, then again alternative lines must be sought. If the network is built without excessive capacity, several alternatives might be sought before the call is placed. For all of the possible alternatives it is desirable to know the probability of not being able to place the call. Third, the complexity of the switching must be considered. Where alternative routes are sought over a long distance on many links, a number of difficulties could arise. It might be possible for a call to be routed in circles, or to be routed over such a complex path that quality suffers severely. A logical scheme is needed that avoids unnecessary complications.

The toll offices which carry out the long-distance switching are divided into classes for this purpose. The Bell System has four classes of toll office, termed *toll*, *primary*, *sectional*, and *regional centers*. Figure 18.2 shows this hierarchy, the offices being labeled class 4, 3, 2, and 1, respectively. The local central office is shown as a fifth class.

In Fig. 18.2, subscriber Y dials subscriber Z. Y's local central office switches the call to the nearby toll office, A, which in this case is a class 4 office. It could have been any other class. This office has a trunk to a distant class 3 office, G, in the locality of the person being called. This is the best choice of line for this call and so office A tries to switch the call onto that line. That line, however, is not a very high-capacity trunk. It may well turn out to be occupied. If so, A tries its second best choice, a line direct to the class 1 office, D. If this also is full, it will switch the call to its local primary office B.

B also has a range of choices. The best route would be the line direct to G. The longest route that the call can travel is the nine-segment route A-B-C-D-E-F-G-H. It is very unlucky if it does not find a shorter path than this. The longest path for any call is to travel to the nearest regional office (class 1) and from there to the regional office in the neighborhood of the recipient. This path, however, is one in which the lines are built with generous capacity. The lower order trunks, the dotted lines in Fig. 18.2, are fairly tightly engineered. But not so the trunks up to the class 1 office, and those between class 1 offices. These are designed to take the overflow when the lesser circuits are full. The trunks shown as solid lines in Fig. 18.2 are liberally engineered. They are often high-capacity coaxial cables or microwave relays.

The arrangement in Fig. 18.2 is made possible by the use of direct distance dialing. If the exchanges were not automatic the caller would not tolerate going through eight toll offices and two end offices. The call would take too long to establish if all of these routings had to be selected by girls pushing plugs into switchboards. The automatic exchanges, therefore, increase the probability of obtaining a line to the distant party. They increase the efficiency with which the high-capacity trunks are utilized. Even so, occasionally it will not be possible to obtain a line. The lines from the local central office

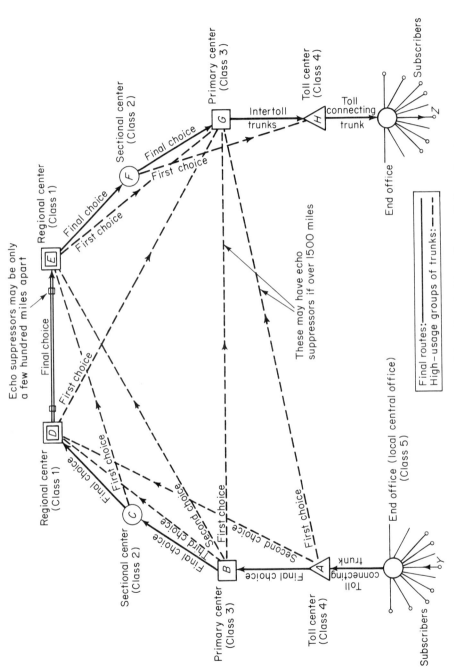

Fig. 18.2. Choice of paths when Y dials Z. A typical long-distance dialing network.

to the toll office may be busy, for example. In Europe the caller can sometimes detect this when dialing as he may hear a "busy" signal before he has dialed all of his digits.

If Y talks to Z at different times, his conversation will probably travel over different paths. It may travel over different physical facilities, one day over microwave, the next over wire-pair cable. He may occasionally obtain a connection with much noise on the line for some reason. Occasionally, people say, "I've got a very bad line. Stay there and I'll redial you." On redialing the noise may have disappeared because now a different line has, by chance, been selected. The same is true with data transmission. If a user at a terminal, such as that in Fig. 5.2, dials a distant computer, he may possibly obtain a "bad" line. A red light on the terminal will indicate a succession of transmission errors, or worse, if the error-detection procedures are not adequate the terminal may print incorrect characters, or the computer program perform unexpected antics. The same is true for batch transmission. The check total may regularly disagree. Here again the user may dial another line. He may send for an engineer who often cannot help except by redialing, himself. In one instance in the author's experience the noise level between two points was always high if the connection was dialed from one end of the link, but low if dialed from the other. Even leased lines may be routed over different paths by the common carrier, and may give different performance on different days.

CONCENTRATORS   If cities A and B each have 500,000 telephone subscribers who might call each other, there are not 500,000 voice channels between the cities. There may be only 600 and this is adequate because only very rarely would more than 600 of these subscribers want to talk to each other at once. It is clearly possible to apply the same principle on the subscriber side of the local central office.

Suppose that 40 two-wire telephone lines go from the exchange to a small community some distance away. The community has 40 telephone subscribers or possibly more than that if some have party lines. The telephone company's statistics indicate that it will be rare that more than 40 lines are in use at any one time. If a small remote switching unit could be used in the community so that only 10 lines went from there to the exchange, then the cost of 30 lines would have been saved.

This is often done, though not universally. The remote switching device is referred to as a *concentrator*.

The use of a concentrator can save money, especially if the lines in question are long.[1] However, switching done remotely in this way is rather more

---

[1] Stagg, U. K., "The 2A Line Concentrator," *Bell System Tech. J.* (October 1965).

expensive than the same switches in the local central office, and by lessening the flexibility with which alternate lines can be substituted, it increases the probability that the caller will not obtain a circuit when he wants one.

**TYPES OF
SWITCHING OFFICE**

There have been three eras in the implementation of switching office or exchanges. Initially they were all manual, and the connection was established by girls plugging cords with jack plugs in appropriate line terminations. Many private exchanges are still manual today. So also are some rural exchanges and many offices for establishing international connections.

Most manual central and toll offices have been replaced by *automatic* exchanges. The subscriber now dials the number he wants and the connection is made by banks of automatic equipment consisting of relays and mechanical switches. Some automatic exchanges have grown to amazing size. In a large-city exchange one can be surrounded by bank upon bank of relays and switches, from floor to ceiling. The multiple clicks as calls are connected are so numerous that the sound approximates to the hiss of white noise, and one can wonder: Is this what the computer would have looked like if we had not invented electronics?

The third category of switching office *uses* the computer. AT&T installed an experimental electronic central office in Morris, Illinois, in 1960. This was successful, and with the knowledge gained, two *Electronic Switching Systems* were designed for quantity manufacture: the No. 1 ESS for local central offices and No. 101 ESS for private branch exchanges. A small number of these were installed successfully and now we are moving fast into the era of computerized control of the telephone networks. This is discussed in the next chapter.

**FUNCTIONS OF
A SWITCHING
OFFICE**

The basic functions performed by a switching office are the same whether it is manual, electromechanical, or electronic. The basic stages that a call must go through are as follows:

1. When the subscriber picks up his telephone the office must *detect that service is needed*. In an automatic office, the dialing tone is switched to that line and the mechanism waits for the subscriber to dial. In a manual office, a lamp lights adjacent to the jack for that line. The operator has a set of cords which have, in effect, two ends with a jack plug on each end. She picks a cord, plugs it into the line in question, flicks a switch so that she can talk on that line, and says "Number please!"

2. The requested telephone number must now be used to *set up an interconnection path*. In the manual office, the girl simply listens to the number requested and plugs her cord into the appropriate output line. She may have the line

to the telephone in question terminating on her plugboard. However, if it is a large exchange she will not, and so she has to route the call to another operator who has. A large office has many operators who communicate in this way.

In the automatic office, the number is received as a train of pulses from the telephone dial, as shown in Fig. 17.1. In the older, *step-by-step* offices each pulse moves a switch position as it is received.

Figure 18.3 shows a *step-by-step Strowger switch*. By means of this, one incoming wire can be connected by 100 possible outgoing wires. The 100 outgoing contacts are arranged in 10 wafers of 10. The moving wiper contact which can complete a circuit with any of these has two possible dimensions of movement. It can slide up and down to select the required wafer, and having positioned itself in the right wafer, it can rotate to select the right contact. It is operated by an address of two digits. The first controls the vertical positioning, the second the rotary movement.

Suppose that the digits 6 and 8 are dialed and reach such a switch, the digits having the form shown in Fig. 17.1. First six pulses reach the switch and cause the contact to move vertically. As the telephone rotates back beneath the finger of the caller, the six pulses it sends activate an electromagnet which operates the vertical lift pawl of the switch. As each pulse arrives the pawl lifts a rack and moves the contact with its shaft up by one step. In this case the contact positions itself at the sixth level.

Then the caller dials the 8. As the telephone dial rotates back, eight pulses are transferred to a second electromagnet in the switch. This moves a second pawl eight times, and a ratchet wheel is nudged around eight times. The contact thus engages outgoing circuit 68. In this way each of the digits dialed moves contacts step-by-step, until the correct path through the office is connected.

The majority of modern offices in North America do not have step-by-step operation, but the incoming pulses operate counters which store the digits in some form of register or memory. The exchange mechanism can then take the digits from this memory as it needs them.

Step-by-step offices have largely been replaced by *cross-bar switches*, although some Strowger switch offices are still being installed in Europe. A cross-bar switch is shown in Fig. 18.4. Like other switches it connects the input wire to one of a number of possible output wires. It consists, in essence, of sets of horizontal and vertical bars which can be moved by electromagnets, in such a way that they cause relay-like contacts to be made at their coordinate intersection. By suitable arrangement of these, a path can be selected through the exchange. Cross-bar switches are faster in operation than Strowger switches, and less prone to create impulse noise. If the call is to go from this office to another, the number will be related from the register. Such a register is sometimes referred to as a "sender."

Another form of exchange common in Europe and South America uses motor driven rotary switches. Rotary switches with up to 500 three-wire outputs are used.

3. The manual switchboard has a number of interconnecting cords smaller than the total number of subscriber connections. If there are several operators, the number of lines between them is also limited. The operator, in effect, *concentrates* the lines into the set of interconnecting cords and lines in a similar manner to the remote concentrator discussed above.

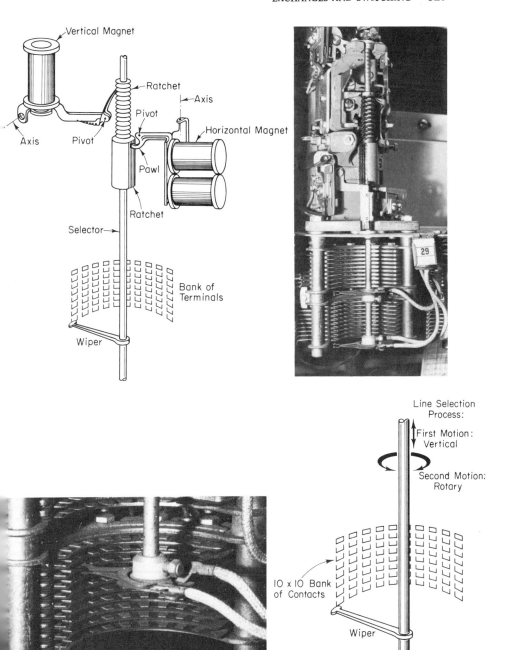

Figure 18.3

(A) An L. M. Ericsson cross-bar exchange in Europe.

(D) The select magnets.

Fig. 18.4. The sequence of operation of a cross-bar switch is as follows: One of the two select magnets associated with the desired horizontal "select" bar is activated. The select bar moves to one of its two positions, operating mechanical interlocks on that level. The hold magnet moves the vertical "hold'" bar. Relay-like contacts at the point of intersection of the horizontal and vertical bars are thus closed. Two select magnets not associated with the same select bar may be activated together. The vertical bar then connects the contacts on the two horizontal bars.

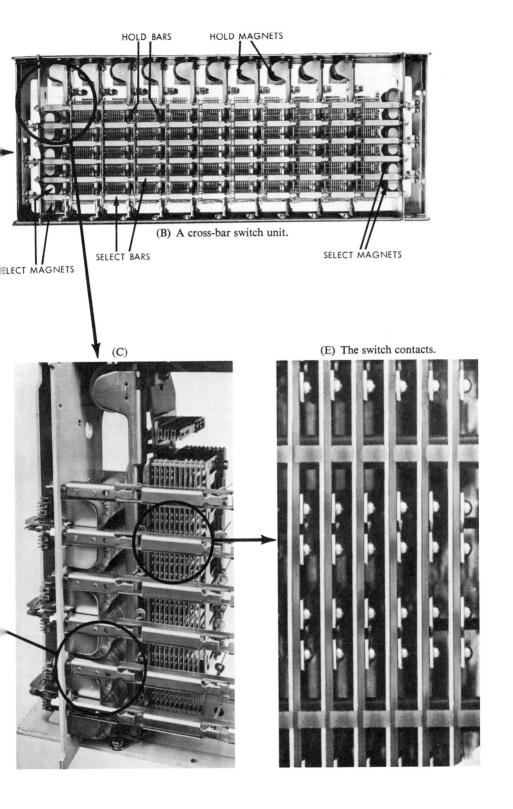

HOLD BARS HOLD MAGNETS

(B) A cross-bar switch unit.

SELECT MAGNETS

SELECT BARS

SELECT MAGNETS

(C)

(E) The switch contacts.

The large automatic exchange does the same. A central office with 10,000 lines would need approximately 50 million interconnections if there were to be a unique path between every input and every possible output. The switches therefore concentrate the calls into a limited number of paths through the exchange. Also, the office will be connected to a limited number of trunks and again the incoming calls are concentrated onto these outgoing lines.

4. The calls, having been concentrated onto the available interconnections, find their way to the requisite part of the exchange and are *switched to the appropriate output lines*. In the manual exchange they reach the appropriate operator, who again selects a cord for the call. When the first operator tells her the number asked for, she plugs the call into the appropriate jack. It has now reached its output line. In the automatic exchange the succeeding digits form a step-by-step circuit selection until, again, the correct output line is reached, or in an exchange with a "sender," the address stored in this is used to select the output line.

5. The required outgoing line might be busy. It is necessary to *detect a busy condition and to notify the caller of it*. Similarly, as there are only a limited number of paths through the exchange, the exchange itself may not be capable of making the connection and again the caller must be notified. If the electromechanical system is unable to make a connection, it will switch a busy tone onto the caller's line. If the call is being connected manually, the girl will observe whether the output line jack is occupied, or if she is connecting with a trunk or a line to another operator, she will make a busy test to see whether it is occupied. She informs the caller verbally.

6. It is necessary to *make the telephone of the called person ring*. The terminating automatic exchange sends a ringing signal down the line when the connection is made. In a manual office the act of plugging the cord into the jack of the outgoing line causes the signal to be sent, either to the called person's telephone or to an outgoing trunk or to the outgoing switchboard where the call will next be handled. In private branch exchanges the girl might have to operate a switch or even wind a handle to send the alerting signal down the line.

7. The telephone of the called party has now rung. The *ringing signal must be removed from the line*, manually or automatically when that person answers. If the telephone goes on ringing unanswered, and the caller does not put his telephone down, the operator may speak to him and tell him that the party does not answer. The automatic exchange may, after a respectable wait, disconnect the call.

8. When the call is successfully established and completed, the parties put their telephones down and *the circuit must then be disconnected*. The exchange circuitry detects that the telephones are back on their rests. The automatic exchange disconnects the circuit, freeing the interconnection paths. The manual exchange has lamps lit by the jack plugs in question to inform the operator or operators that the call is over. They then pull the plugs out. If a caller fails to replace his hand set on its rest, the automatic exchange may send a signal to his telephone in an attempt to alert him. In the U.S.A., a clicking sound is used.

9. Lastly, the caller usually has to be charged. In the manual exchange, the girl can write down the cost of the call. In an automatic exchange there must be

Fig. 18.5. The frame room in a large Bell System central office.

some mechanical way of recording the number of calls each subscriber makes, and the duration and distance of trunk calls. Some exchanges have counters for each subscriber to record this. This must be read periodically. Other exchanges use automatic punch cards or paper tape. *Courtesy New York Telephone Co.*

**BROADBAND
SWITCHING**

A recent development that is of particular interest to computer users is the introduction of broadband switching centers. The Western Union Telegraph Company has placed into operation the first switching centers of a public broadband network. In its initial phase it serves only a small number of cities in the United States, but it will no doubt grow into a nation-wide service.

An interesting feature of the system is that the user can select, *by the number he dials*, the bandwidth of the channel he requires as well as its destination. The equipment is designed to handle bandwidths of 2000, 4000, 8000, 16,000 and 48,000 cycles per second, although initially it provides only the narrower channels. It is anticipated that wider channels will be made available as the demand builds up. As so many circuits throughout the world today are carrier circuits composed of channel groups and supergroups, it is a logical extension of present-day facilities to be able to dial a bandwidth greater than the conventional telephone bandwidth, The channels are there, so why not provide the switching and termination facilities to use them.

On the Western Union system the user keys a seven-digit number to set up the call. The first three digits indicate the distant exchange. The fourth digit indicates the bandwidth required, and the last three digits give the number of the called party on that exchange. Thus

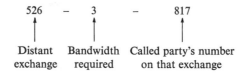

To initiate the call the subscriber picks up the handset and listens for a dial tone as with a conventional telephone call. When he hears it he keys in the number. This is transmitted with multifrequency tone combinations as in Touch-Tone dialing. The exchange receiving the number alerts the called party, using distinctive audible tone rather than a conventional telephone bell. The caller will also receive a signal telling him that the called party is being "rung." When the called party picks up his handset the two persons can talk to each other as in a conventional telephone call. They transfer the call to "data mode" by placing their handsets in a data position. The data machines can then communicate at the selected bandwidth. At the end of the call the subscribers may return to voice mode if they wish. The cost of the call is based upon the distance and time and also on the bandwidth.

The Western Union circuits for this will all be four-wire, and will be appropriately equalized at all switching points. This lessens echo problems and gives a return path for error correction and control functions on the data-handling machines.

19 COMPUTER-CONTROLLED LINE SWITCHING

When one observes and studies the immense complexity of a large switching office it seems clear that computer program-controlled operation would bring a great improvement. For many years engineers have worked on ideas for applying electronics and computer techniques to switching problems. In recent years this research has begun to pay off and several countries are replacing electromechanical central offices with computer-controlled switching systems.

The Bell System No. 1 ESS (Electronic Switching System) shown in Fig. 19.1 is designed to replace economically central offices of a range of different sizes. At its upper limit it can handle 65,000 lines, with a maximum capacity of 100,000 calls in the busy hour.[1] The lower size limit will probably extend economically down to about 4000 lines. No. 1 ESS is now designed for mass production. Electronic exchanges not under computer control have also been designed for smaller exchanges. The TXE2 System installed by the GPO in England provides an exchange with only 200–2000 lines; the TXE3 System handles small exchanges with more than 2000 lines.[2]

The Bell System No. 101 ESS is designed to act as a private branch exchange (PBX), for offices or factories and handles up to 200 extensions. To make such a system economic it was not possible to have a computer in each such exchange, and so a computer at the central office is used which

---

[1] Keister, W., R. W. Ketchledge, and H. E. Vaughan, "No. 1 ESS: System Organization and Objectives," *Bell System Tech. J.* (September 1964).

[2] "Electronic Switching Systems. 1. TXE2 Electronic Exchanges," a booklet published by the GPO, London.

Fig. 19.1. Bell System ESS No. 1. a computerized central office. Computers of extremely high reliability carry out the line switching and associated operations. *Courtesy AT&T.*

controls up to 32 switching units in remote locations, each of which can handle 200 extensions.[3]

Other manufacturers have also been working on computerized switching. It seems likely that as data transmission on dial-up lines becomes increasingly common, exchanges controlled by computers, and probably switching both data and voice lines, will become part of many communication networks.

ADVANTAGES   The economic objectives of the No. 1 ESS are achieved merely in the replacement of existing central offices and on increased capacity in existing buildings. This advance in switching technology comes at an appropriate time as many of the early central offices need replacement. No. 1 ESS needs a fraction of the floor space of its electromechanical equivalent and so, in some cases, the large

---

[3] Higgins, W. H. C., "A Survey of Bell System Progress in Electronic Switching." *Bell System Tech. J.* (July–August 1965).

expansion in switching capacity that is needed today can take place on existing premises.

In addition to these economic benefits, the flexibility of switching under program control has many advantages. Alterations in the exchange can be made by a change in memory contents of the computers, and so, in many cases, can be made very quickly. The manufacturing of the equipment is capable of more standardization because many of the variables that exist on electromechanical equipment are now variables in the program rather than in the hardware. Growth of the exchange is made easier as every No. 1 ESS can handle up to 65,000 lines. New subscriber numbers can be added quickly. In addition, the accounting procedures and traffic measuring procedures can be fully automated. Automatic features can also aid considerably in maintenance.

The computer program can make possible a variety of new features not on today's electromechanical exchanges, which are attractive to the subscribers. It would be possible to set up conference calls with several parties joining in, by dialing. One could dial an extension in one's own home if it were equipped with more than one telephone. Bell System's first experimental electronic central office at Morris, Illinois, gave some subscribers "abbreviated dialing," which enabled them to dial certain selected seven-digit numbers using a two-digit code. This proved very popular. Also various methods were provided to allow the subscriber to have his calls automatically directed to another telephone. The subscriber could, for example, if he went to a friend's house for dinner, dial a special code and then his friend's telephone number. Thereafter all calls could be directed to this number automatically. When he returned home he would cancel the rerouting by dialing another code. Alternatively, he could inform the telephone company of the times and numbers for rerouting.

In addition to some of these facilities the *System AKE*[4] stored program exchange manufactured by L. M. Ericsson in Sweden has an automatic call transfer. Incoming calls may be transferred to another specified number, either when the subscriber is busy, or when he does not answer. Again, if you dial a subscriber on this system and he is busy, you may then dial a code which instructs the computer to dial you as soon as he is free, and then automatically redial him. The need for redialing is dispensed with. System AKE also has an alarm clock service. You dial a four-digit time at which you wish to be woken by the computer. Subscribers may dial directly to private automatic branch exchange extension telephones without the assistance of an operator. System AKE can be set to gather a variety of statistical information about subscribers' calling habits. The system can list particulars of in-

---

4 "Stored Program Controlled Switching, System AKE," manufacturer's booklet from L. M. Ericsson Telephone Company, Stockholm 32, Sweden.

coming or outgoing calls on particular numbers. It has a facility for recording malicious calls. If a subscriber receives a malicious call, he does not replace his handset for a time and system then records his number and the number of the calling party.

Other new facilities are planned. Such is the flexibility of operating under programmed control.

SYSTEM   Figure 19.2 shows, in principle, the general
ORGANIZATION   organization of Bell System's No. 1 ESS.

The subscriber lines, 1, and trunks, 3, enter a switching network, 2, in which the interconnection paths between lines or between lines and trunks can be set up. The switches used are reed switches, called *ferreeds*. Magnetic contacts encapsulated in glass, free from dust and corrosion, are opened and closed by windings outside the glass. They are similar in principle though not in detail to the switch that was shown in Fig. 6.12. They are arranged in unpluggable units containing an 8 × 8 array of switches.

The switches for making the appropriate line connections are opened and closed under control of the program in the computers, 7.

The switching network is organized into frames, and each frame has its own *switching controller*, 5. The controller sets up the appropriate line paths in the frame it controls. Both the switching controllers and the computer are duplicated for reliability reasons, as is much of the remainder of the system. When one such component fails, its counterpart takes over.

The computers have two types of memory unit. *Semipermanent memory units*, 9, contain the programs and fixed data about the lines. This is "read-only" during normal operations and so cannot be accidentally overwritten by a program error or hardware failure. *Temporary memory units*, 8, contain information about the calls in process, and other information which is changing during normal operation. Both types of memory unit, and their contents, are duplicated.

The computer knows the status of the lines, trunks, and signal receivers by means of a continuing scanning operation, carried out by the *line scanners*, 4, which are also duplicated. After each scan the computer writes information about the line status in the temporary store.

Each line and trunk is equipped with a sensing device called a *ferrod*, 13, which can detect telephone on-hook and off-hook conditions. The ferrod is a current sensing device. It consists, in essence, of a ferrite rod with two identically wound solenoid coils through which the line current flows. Two other loops of wire are threaded through two holes in the ferrite rod. These are used for sensing whether or not line current is flowing. The scanner sends an *interrogate pulse* down one loop and detects whether there is a correspond-

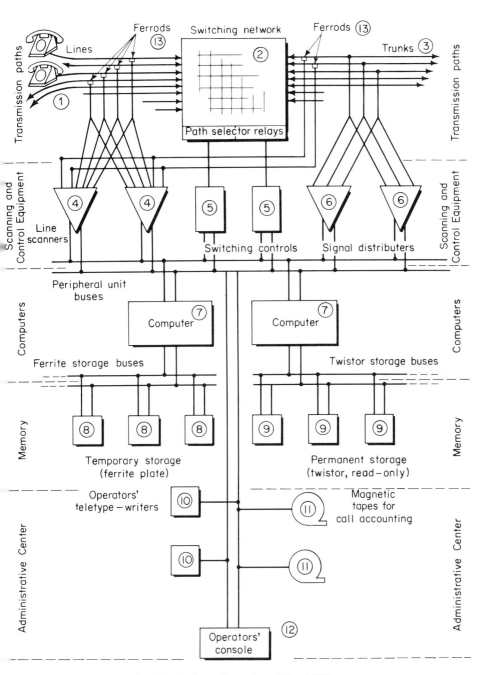

Fig. 19.2. Basic configuration of No. 1 ESS.

ing *read-out pulse* down the other loop. When no DC current is flowing in the line there will be a strong read-out pulse, but when current is flowing, this will be suppressed. The scanners, then, scan these ferrods, and the information they obtain about line status is read into the temporary storage by the computer.

The scanners are provided in modules which scan 1024 lines. A scan takes place every 100 milliseconds, in which each subscriber line is examined to detect call originations. If an origination is detected, that line is connected to a device which interprets the dialing signal, either dial pulses or Touch-Tone. During this period a line is sampled every 10 milliseconds. Once the call is connected, the line is again scanned every 100 milliseconds, the purpose now being to detect when the call is terminated. When the caller hangs up, the line is disconnected by the computer.

As the scanning takes place, the results from the ferrod sensors are sent to the computer, 16 at a time. These are compared with the results of the last scan, stored in temporary storage. If there is a change then the computer branches to the appropriate program to handle it.

As discussed in Chapter 17, it is necessary to send a variety of signals on trunk circuits. No. 1 ESS used a *signal distributor*, 6, again duplicated, for this purpose. Under computer program control this connects the appropriate signals to the trunks as required.

At the bottom of Fig. 19.2 are the devices used by the operating personnel. These include alarms, line test facilities, displays, and control circuitry for maintenance; a teletypewriter, duplicated, allows the operating personnel to communicate with the computer (Fig. 19.3). A magnetic tape unit, duplicated, writes on tape all data related to billing customer calls. This is then processed on an off-line computer. Last, there is a device for changing the information in the semipermanent storage.

THE COMPUTERS   The engineering of the computers in No. 1 ESS is considerably different to that of machines familiar in today's data-processing world. The major factor leading to this difference is the need for extreme system reliability. A design objective was that the sum of the system down times should not exceed two hours over its 40-year life.[5] Furthermore, the system should be left unattended for long periods of time. These criteria seem fantastic by the standards of today's conventional data processing.

While system outage is regarded as catastrophic, however, individual errors are not so bad. Individual errors in conventional data processing may be very serious, but in an exchange they are merely a nuisance. The subscriber

[5] Downing, R. W., J. S. Novak, and L. S. Tuomenoksa, "No. 1 ESS Maintenance Plan," *Bell System Tech. J.* (September 1964).

Fig. 19.3. The master control center of a No. 1 ESS office. The control center permits operating personnel to communicate with and control the system externally. It consists of a teletypewriter for sending and receiving communications, trouble alarm devices, a memory program and writer, and an accounting tape recorder. *Courtesy AT&T.*

must redial his call. One does not want such errors to occur often, but certainly subscribers do have to redial calls occasionally on today's electromechanical plant. Most subscribers, when their dialing fails to reach its destination, blame themselves rather than the machinery the first time it happens—thinking they must have misdialed. This facet of dialer psychology is useful in planning the error and recovery procedures in a computerized exchange.

The computer components have therefore been chosen with breakdown-free operation as the main criteria rather than speed or other factors. All system components other than those concerned with a single line are duplicated. This includes the data buses, shown in Fig. 19.2, in duplicate. The computer is organized and its components designed so that faults can be found and corrected as quickly as possible. When a fault develops it must be corrected rapidly to minimize the probability of a duplex failure. During normal operation one computer is "on-line," carrying out the switching work. The other is in active standby. Both the standby and the on-line machine are automatically monitored continuously so that any fault is signaled as soon as it occurs. When a fault occurs in any of the duplicated components of the system, a switchover occurs to the alternate unit automatically so that the telephone actions are interrupted for only a very short duration.

The instruction word length is 37 bits. In addition to these, each instruction contains seven check bits making a total of 44. The seven check bits enable the circuitry to correct automatically single-bit errors, and to detect double-bit errors. Program instructions are stored in the semipermanent store in this form. The temporary store uses a word length of 24 bits, of which one is a parity bit.

In addition to circuitry for checking parity in transfers to and from the temporary store, and for checking for errors when reading from the semipermanent store, the system contains special circuitry which compares the execution of instructions in the two computers. If a difference is detected, the engineers are notified. Also, all transfers to and from the scanners and other peripheral devices are checked.

The circuitry of the computer is designed very conservatively to give the maximum reliability. It is considerably slower than conventional data-processing machines. The cycle time of the computer is 5.5 microseconds.

To handle the peak-hour traffic of a busy office with 65,000 lines, it was estimated that the system could not spend more than 5000 machine cycles per telephone call.[6] To meet this requirement it was necessary to design an instruction set with powerful instructions that carried out several functions simultaneously. Masking is used; that is, a certain pattern of bits in a word indicated by a key or "mask" are turned to zero when the operation is carried out. For example, a word may be read from the temporary store containing the first dialed digit of a telephone call, and added into an accumulator. The instruction which does this can mask out all information other than the four bits of the digit in question. A wide variety of powerful logic instructions are available. In addition to general-purpose data-processing instructions which are necessary to make the machine flexible enough to handle a variety of possible future demands, it also contains special instructions for reading the

[6] Harr, J. A., F. F. Taylor, and W. Ulrich, "Organization of No. 1 ESS Central Processor," *Bell System Tech. J.* (September 1964).

scanners and performing operations on their information, and for sending output to the switching control equipment and the signal generators. The machine thus has a mix of general-purpose and special-purpose instructions.

Some input–output programs have to be executed at strictly determined times. For example, when a subscriber is dialing, the dial pulses are sampled every 10 milliseconds. This is governed by a clock which interrupts the program being executed, so that control is transferred to the appropriate priority program. When the condition that caused the interrupt has been dealt with, control is returned to the program that was interrupted.

As on more conventional computers, a variety of conditions can cause an interrupt, including the detection of an error by the checking circuitry. The computers have three levels of priority for normal error-free processing. Interrupts can normally occur only at 5-millisecond clock intervals, and snatch control away from lower level programs, giving control to a higher priority program. When the higher priority work is completed, the computer returns to the program that was interrupted. There are *another seven levels of priority*, however, *for error conditions*. These seven levels of interrupt can occur at any instant when a fault is detected. They trigger a variety of procedures designed to give automatic switchover to a fault-free configuration. Duplicate units can be switched in times comparable to the cycle time of the unit. Thus for most of the failures that occur there will be no break in the processing of the majority of the calls.

Perhaps the most unconventional feature of the computers is the design of the storage units. The semipermanent storage employs a large *twistor memory* invented at Bell Laboratories.[7] The temporary storage employs a ferrite sheet memory.

THE TWISTER MEMORY

The twister memory is used to store the programs, and data of a semipermanent nature. Its contents can be read by the computer, but not written. Only the operator can change its contents. The capacity of one memory unit is 5.8 million bits. The programs read between four and five million bits of this. Data about lines and trunks which give the telephone number, class of service, and information about features of the line need between 1 and 14 million bits, depending upon the office size. Each memory unit is organized into 131,072, 44-bit words, and one word is read with a cycle time of 5.5 microseconds.

The data is stored in the form of small magnets attached to aluminium sheets. Such a sheet is approximately $11 \times 6\frac{1}{2}$ inches and it is shown in Fig. 19.4. The spots in this photograph are the magnets, each containing one bit

[7] Bobeck, A. H., "A New Storage Memory Suitable for Larger-Sized Memory Arrays —The Twister," *Bell Systems Tech. J.* (November 1957).

Fig. 19.4. An aluminum sheet with 2816 magnetic spots, which forms part of the high-reliability semipermanent memory of ESS No. 1. Each spot contains one bit of information, a "0" if the spot is magnetized and a "1" if it is not. The spots are read with the twister wire in Fig. 19.5, There are 128 of these cards in a module, and 16 modules in a memory unit. This is a "read-only" memory. Its contents can be written by a separate unit but not by the main computer. *Courtesy Bell Telephone Laboratories.*

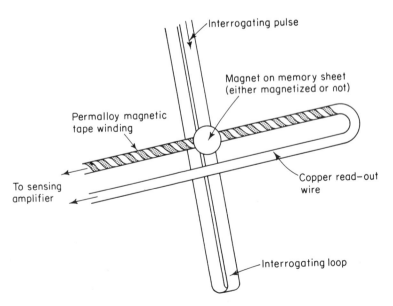

Fig. 19.5. The principle of the twister memory.

of data. The data bit is either 1 or 0, depending upon whether the magnetic spot is magnetized or demagnetized. Each sheet contains 64 words of 44 bits.

The information on the sheet is read by 44 pairs of copper read-out wires, one pair for each bit position in the words. One of these is shown diagramatically in Fig. 19.5. At right angles to these there are 64 interrogating loops, one for each word. To read one word, a pulse is sent through the appropriate interrogating loop. At the intersection of the interrogating loop and the read-out wires lies the magnet (the spots in Fig. 19.4).

One of the pair of read-out wires is wound around with a spiral of permalloy magnet tape. This is the key to the operation of this type of memory. If at the intersection of the interrogating loop there is no magnet, then the pulse in the interrogating loop will cause the magnetization of the permalloy tape to switch direction and then switch back. This will produce a current pulse in the copper pair which will be detected by a sensing amplifier. If, however, there is a magnet at that intersection (Fig. 19.5), this will not happen. The force of the magnet will be sufficiently strong to hold the magnetization of the permalloy tape in its present state, and prevent the interrogating pulse from reversing it. If there is a magnet, then, the sensing amplifier will receive no pulse. If there is not a magnet, it will receive a pulse. In other words, if the spot on the aluminum sheet is magnetized, this is a 0 condition; otherwise, it is a 1 condition.

The program, or the data about lines, can be modified simply by mag-

Fig. 19.6. Memory cards such as that in Fig. 19.4 being inserted into the ESS No. 1 semipermanent store. *Courtesy AT&T.*

netizing or demagnetizing the spots. To do this the aluminium sheets are removed and a special device used. Such a device can be operated by computer itself, the operator keying the relevant information into the teletypewriter. Figure 19.6 shows the sheets being loaded into the computer memory units.

THE FERRITE SHEET MEMORY

The ferrite sheet memory is a read-write memory, also with a cycle time of 5.5 microseconds, and again designed with reliability as the main criteria. It is used to store any data which must be changed by the computer, and particularly, that which must be stored moment by moment as a call is being handled. It also stores data used in administration, maintenance, billing the subscribers, and so on. The amount of temporary storage needed will vary with the number of lines the central office handles. With the range envisaged for No. 1 ESS it will vary from 100,000 to 4 million bits. These stores are built in units of four modules, each unit holding 196,608 bits, and thus being organized into 8192 words of 24 bits each.

Each module consists of 768 ferrite sheets. Each of these magnetic sheets is about one-inch square and contains 256 small holes. It is shown in Fig. 19.7. Each hole can store one bit, like the holes in a conventional core storage.[8] One set of wires needed for this is plated on the ferrite sheets, thus lessening the difficulty of the expensive core threading operation.

Fig. 19.7. This one-inch square ferrite sheet, perforated with 256 tiny holes, is part of the high-reliability temporary memory of ESS No. 1. The ferrite around each hole acts as a "core" and stores one bit of information. Three wires threaded through the holes and a conductor plated onto the sheet are used to write information into and read it out of the memory. Sheets are stacked in a module and four modules make up a Call Store, each holding 196,608 bits of erasable information. *Courtesy Bell Telephone Laboratories.*

[8] Meyerhoff, A. J., *et al.* (Eds.), *Digital Applications of Magnetic Devices*: New York, John Wiley and Sons, 1960, pp. 372–390.

PROGRAMMING   The programs for controlling the central
office operation total about 100,000 instructions
at the time of writing and may well become larger as additional functions
are added. These are stored permanently in the twister memory. The programs are written so as to be the same for all sizes of central office with
the differences all in a parameter table.

The programs fall into a variety of different priority categories. At the
top of the priority hierarchy for *normal* processing would be programs for
sampling the dial tones or pulses. Near the bottom would be programs for
gathering statistics about the number of calls. The machine is equipped with
10 levels of interrupt, of which only the bottom three are used during normal
processing. Most of the programs which are not involved with error conditions are in the lowest of these. Work is allocated to them by the scheduling
loop of a supervisory program illustrated in Fig. 19.8. This supervisory
program also transfers control to subroutines when necessary. When each
program is finished, control is given back to the scheduling routine which
decides what to do next.

The 10 interrupt levels are labeled A to K (I is missed out), as shown in
Fig. 19.8. Levels J and H, if needed, are given control every 5 milliseconds to
ensure that none of the essential tasks are bypassed. An error detected by the
various error detection circuits causes an immediate interrupt to one of the
levels A to G. Any program can be interrupted by a higher level interrupt
condition.

On any real-time system where reliability is important, significant parts
of the programs relate to error detection, switchover to alternate components,
and fallback to a different or degraded mode of operation. On this system,
more than 50% of the 100,000 instructions are used for reliability reasons.
It is easy to design a system which will switch to alternate configurations when
failures occur, but much more difficult to design the programs that will control this switching, and cause the minimum disruption to processing.

When an error occurs, an "interrupt sequencer" circuit transfers control
to the programs in one of the interrupt levels A to G in Fig. 19.8. For example, if an error is detected in the semipermanent memory, an interrupt to
level E programs will occur. If the computers disagree in the execution of an
instruction, an interrupt to level C will occur—providing, of course, that
the machine is not already in a high mode of operation. The purpose of these
programs is to establish as quickly as possible a system configuration that will
still work correctly. It will then operate the appropriate switches to set up
this configuration, and return control to the processing programs.

It is possible that this still might not be good enough because the computer on which the interrupt occurred is itself in trouble. A working processing unit is needed for system recovery and a faulty one might be trying to
carry out the recovery. This situation is overcome by an ingenious device

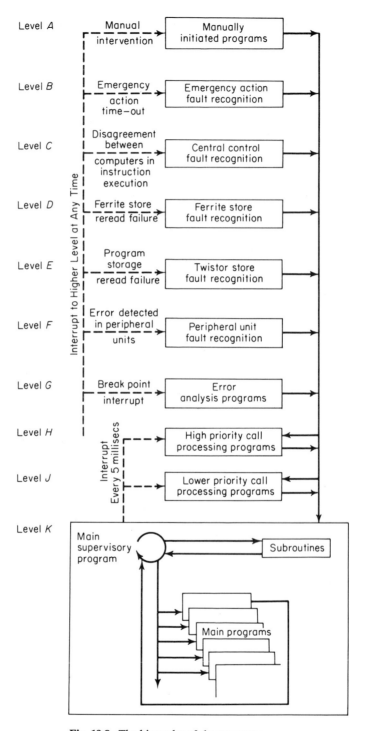

Fig. 19.8. The hierarchy of the programs.

called *the emergency action facility.* When an interrupt to a recovery program occurs, an *emergency action timer* is started. This timer counts down 40 milliseconds regardless of what else is happening. If a correct recovery occurs, it will be stopped. If not it starts an *emergency action circuit* which again operates regardless of processing unit.

The emergency action circuit will connect together various possible system configurations. It will do this without using programming. When it has established a configuration, it will attempt to transfer control to the programs of interrupt level B (Fig. 19.8.) The purpose of these programs is to discover whether that configuration is working or not. When the transfer is made a clock called *the sanity timer* is started. The level B programs continually reset this if they are working correctly. If not, after 128 machine cycles of not being reset, the sanity timer instructs the emergency action circuit to try a new configuration. This process continues, the system "searching" for a configuration which works. The emergency action devices and sanity timer are completely independent of the health of the rest of the system. When a working configuration is found, the level B program then re-establishes the call-processing ability of the system.

As with any real-time program of this size its preparation was a major task. Many support programs were needed to accomplish it. These were mostly run on an IBM 7094 computer. A compiler known as PROCESS III (*PRO*gram for *C*ompiling *ESS*) was produced to run on the 7094.[9] The compiler produces a binary tape which serves as input to a card preparation program. This is also run on the 7094 and produces another tape which controls the card writing machine. The compiler also produces another binary tape which serves as input to a simulation program. Much of the program testing takes place in a simulated mode on the 7094 before the programs are tested in the ESS computers. The 7094 simulates a stream of input calls and lists how the programs handle them, along with the times that would be taken.

THE PROCESSING
OF A TYPICAL CALL

Let us conclude this description by describing the processing of a typical call on ESS No. 1, in a manner similar to that in the last chapter.

1. When a subscriber picks up his telephone, the electronic exchange must detect that service is needed. Every 100 milliseconds the line in question will be inspected by the scanner using ferrod sensor. When the customer lifts his telephone, this will detect the flow of current.

    The computer, comparing the 24-bit word it receives from the scanner with that it received 100 milliseconds ago and stored in the ferrite store, will

[9] Martellotto, N. A., H. Ochring, and M. C. Paull, "PROCESS III—A Compiler-Assembler for No. 1 ESS," *Bell System Tech J.* (September 1964).

detect a change. The computer will then examine the change more closely and will see that one bit has changed, relating to the line in question.

2. The computer then connects this line to a digit receiver by instructing the switching controls to set up interconnection path. The ferrod sensor is disconnected from the line until the completion of the call, and a dial tone is connected to the line.

3. On hearing the dial tone, the customer will dial. If he has a Touch-Tone telephone, this type of digit receiver will be used, otherwise a rotary dial pulse receiver will be used. The computer will read the digit receiver for the line every 10 milliseconds, the clock interrupts every 5 milliseconds ensuring that none of these readings are missed.

4. If the telephone number dialed is to a telephone connected to this central office, the computer will look at the condition of that line, as recorded on the last scan. If it is busy, the computer will connect a "busy" tone to the calling line. If not, it will switch a ringing tone to the called line, again by instructing the switching controls to make an interconnection to a ringing circuit.

5. At this time both the calling and the called line must be supervised. If the caller hangs up, this must be detected and the call abandoned. Such detection is not now done by the ferrods and scanner but by other circuits associated with the digit receiver and ringing tone circuit. Signals, as described in Chapter 17, must be supervised on the trunk to detect successful connection, or a busy condition.

6. When the called party answers, the ringing tone is removed from the line and the computer instructs the switching controls to complete the necessary interconnection.

7. While the parties talk, the calling and called lines are supervised so that the termination of the call can be detected. On a trunk call this would be done by the ferrods on the trunk circuit.

8. When the call is terminated the computer disconnects the circuit and restores the lines to their former status. The 100-millisecond scanning takes place as initially.

9. The computer then completes a record for accounting purposes. To do so it will have timed the trunk call.

In all cases throughout this operation signals on the lines and changes in line state do not of themselves cause system actions to take place, as was the case on electromechanical exchanges. Such conditions are detected by the computer, by scanning, and the computer decides what to do. In this mode of operating lies the potential for building a more "intelligent" communication network in the future, capable of many operations not possible with today's telephone exchanges.

NO. 101 ESS   Stored-program-controlled exchanges of this type are only economical today in large sizes— about the size-range indicated for No. 1 ESS. Therefore, to produce an electronic private branch exchange which might handle, say, 200 extensions or less, presented a problem. This was overcome by designing a computer system in which one pair of computers at the local central office would control many remote private branch exchanges. No. 101 ESS can control up to 32 private branch exchanges (PBX) in different locations giving at present a total of up to 3200 extensions. The locations could in theory be any distance from the computer.

The switching unit at each location is under the control of the remote computer, and itself is relatively inexpensive. Figure 19.9 shows a 200-line switch unit and attendant's console. This way, several customers share the distant computer and can all have the new features brought by stored program flexibility. It is interesting to reflect on the future possibilities of such techniques.

Fig. 19.9. A switch unit and console on the Bell System ESS No. 101. This is an electronic private branch exchange. The switching operation is carried out remotely by a computer at the local central office, which controls many such exchanges, and thus replaces switch-gear of the user's premises.

REFERENCES

1. Bell System Technical Journal, Sept. 1964, Part I and Part II. Two issues devoted to ESS No. 1.

2. A. H. Bobeck, "A New Storage Memory Suitable for Larger-Sized Memory Arrays—The Twister." *Bell Systems Tech. J.*, Nov. 1957.

3. "Digital Applications of Magnetic Devices," ed. A. J. Meyerhoff, *et al.* John Wiley and Sons, New York, 1960, pp. 372–390.

4. E. W. Downing, J. S. Novak, and L. S. Tuomenoksa, "No. 1 ESS Maintenance Plan." *Bell System Tech. J.*, Sept. 1964.

5. "Electronic Switching Systems, 1. TXE 2. Electronic Exchanges," booklet published by the GPO, London, England.

6. J. A. Harr, F. F. Taylor, and W. Ulrich, "Organization of No. 1 ESS Central Processor." *Bell System Tech. J.*, Sept. 1964.

7. W. H. C. Higgins, "A Survey of Bell System Progress in Electronic Switching," *Bell System Tech J.*, July–Aug. 1965.

8. W. Keister, R. W. Ketchledge, and H. E. Vaughan, "No. 1 ESS: System Organization and Objectives," *Bell System Tech. J.*, Sept. 1964.

9. N. A. Martellotto, H. Ochring and M. C, Paull, "PROCESS III— A Compiler—Assembler for No. 1 ESS." *Bell System Tech. J.* Sept. 1964.

10. "Stored Program Controlled Switching System AKE," manufacturer's booklet from L. M. Ericsson Telephone Company, Stockholm 32, Sweden.

20 COMMUNICATION SATELLITES

On April 6, 1965, the world's first commercial satellite, Early Bird, rocketed into the evening sky at Cape Kennedy. The success of the transmission experiments that followed this was spectacular. Before long earth stations were being built around the world, and new and more powerful satellites were on the drawing boards.

Originally, the satellites were intended primarily to span the oceans. As has been discussed earlier, the laying of subocean telephone cables is expensive and these cables have a bandwidth too low to carry live television. Early Bird alone increased transatlantic telephone capacity by more than one third. The television pictures were excellent. Pope Paul VI was soon seen live from the Vatican in the United States and President Johnson was seen all over Europe. A Pacific satellite followed in January 1967, and President Johnson was seen "live" in Asia.

The satellites were soon used with computer systems. Pan American successfully hooked up their real-time Panamac system to Early Bird, so that reservation agents in Rome or London could smile at their customers while conversing with a computer in New York via satellite. IBM linked its laboratories on opposite sides of the Atlantic, and was soon talking about a far-flung information system using satellite-transmitted data responses to oil the wheels of its World Trade operations.

Early Bird is demonstrating a lifetime in orbit far beyond its original design estimates. The INTELSAT II satellites, which might be regarded as the second generation of synchronous satellites, were found in practice to be capable of handling considerably more traffic than their design capacity. These are the two main factors which determine the economics of a satellite once it is launched. New generations of satellites are now being planned with much greater capacity and probably much longer life than the early ones. Because of this, satellites appear a good contender for the American *domestic* market for long distance transmission, as well as the international market. It will almost certainly become cheaper to transmit from New York to Los Angeles via satellite than via coaxial cables or microwave links.

This has interesting implications for international links. If we transmit from New York to Chicago by satellite, the cost of doing this is about the same as the cost of transmitting from New York to Australia by satellite. If a firm has a tie-line from New York to Chicago it could have one to Sydney as cheaply if the tariffs reflected the system cost. If you see a relative in Chicago by calling on a Picturephone set in New York, you could presumably afford to call friends in Tokyo or Tel Aviv on a Picturephone too. The links between nations will indeed have shrunk.

In data-processing systems, too, a firm that can today contemplate an on-line network for its domestic organization, may before long be able to hook up its international organization for the same order of cost.

SATELLITE ORBITS   The Early Bird and INTELSTAT satellites have orbits very different to their experimental predecessors such as AT&T's Telstar satellites and RCA's Relay satellites. These traveled rapidly around the Earth at a relatively low height. The Telstar satellites had highly elliptical orbits; Telstar I from about 600 to 3800 miles and Telstar II from 600 to 6200 miles. The apogee of the ellipse was positioned so that the satellite was within line-of-sight of certain stations for as long as possible. As with early manned orbital flights and most other satellites launched in the first decade of space flight, they travel around the earth in a few hours; Telstar I: 2 hours 38 minutes, and Telstar II: 3 hours 45 minutes. Herein lies their disadvantage for telecommunications: they are within line of sight of the tracking station for only a brief period of time, often less than half an hour.

A higher orbit than this seems desirable, otherwise a large number of satellites are needed. The antennas are constantly leaving one satellite as it disappears over the horizon, and searching for the next. If the orbit is raised to a mean height of 6000 miles, the satellite then takes between five and six hours to travel around the Earth, and thus it is likely to be in contact with the Earth station for two hours or more. A lower number of satellites are needed for a continuous link, or for a partially continuous global coverage.

Better still, and this is the idea behind Early Bird, the satellite can be launched into an orbit 22,300 miles above the Earth, and it can then be made to travel around the earth in exactly 24 hours, the earth's rotation time. If its orbit is over the Equator, and it travels in the same direction as the Earth's surface, then it appears to hang stationary over one point of the earth.

This apparently stationary satellite is referred to as a *synchronous satellite*. Figure 20.1 plots the time a satellite takes to travel around the Earth, against its height.

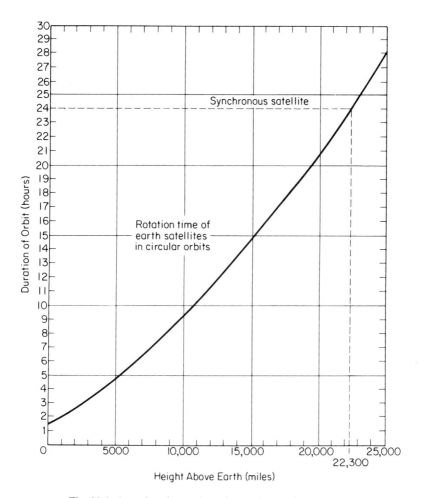

Fig. 20.1. Rotation times of Earth satellites in circular orbits.

Early Bird hangs in the sky stationary over the Atlantic, between Brazil and Africa, actually traveling at 6900 miles per hour but remaining over the same point on the Earth's Equator. The first successfully launched INTELSAT II satellite was similarly placed over the Equator in mid-Pacific near the International Date Line. Microwave signals are beamed to the satellite with a large steerable antenna. The satellite amplifies and relays them back to Earth, where other steerable antennas pick them up, very weak now, but relatively free from interference.

Instead of building a microwave tower on a hill top with its range limited to 30 miles or so, we now, in effect, have it in the sky 22,300 miles up. Three such satellites enable us to relay a signal to any point on earth, with the exception of the region close to the Poles. Comsat achieved this global coverage with its INTELSAT III series of satellites in 1968 and 1969. Figure 20.2 illustrates the main types of satellite orbits.

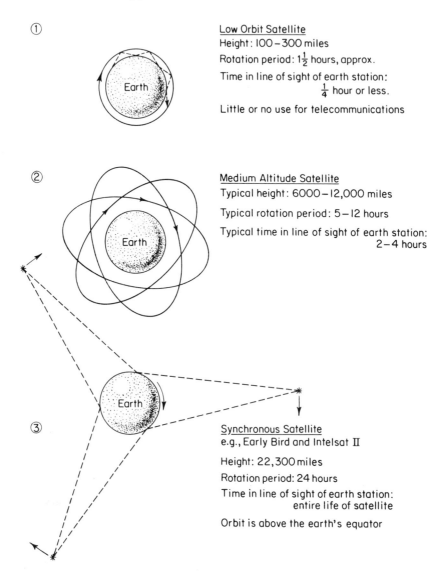

①

Low Orbit Satellite
Height: 100–300 miles
Rotation period: $1\frac{1}{2}$ hours, approx.
Time in line of sight of earth station:
$\frac{1}{4}$ hour or less.
Little or no use for telecommunications

②

Medium Altitude Satellite
Typical height: 6000–12,000 miles
Typical rotation period: 5–12 hours
Typical time in line of sight of earth station:
2–4 hours

③

Synchronous Satellite
e.g., Early Bird and Intelsat II
Height: 22,300 miles
Rotation period: 24 hours
Time in line of sight of earth station:
entire life of satellite
Orbit is above the earth's equator

Fig. 20.2. Satellite orbits.

With a satellite as high as 22,300 miles, the Earth stations which use it can be almost on opposite sides of the Earth. Figure 20.3 shows the Earth station distance possible with different satellite altitudes. This assumes that 5° is the minimum angle of elevation of the ground station antennas. To transmit over a greater distance than these a double-hop link would be needed, in which case the distance would be somewhat less than twice these, depending upon the degree of overlap of the areas covered by the two satellites.

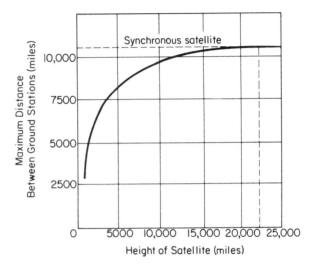

Fig. 20.3. Maximum separation of Earth satellite stations.

To place a satellite in a synchronous orbit needs very high precision spacemanship. The launch vehicle first places it into a lengthy elliptical orbit with the highest part of the ellipse about 22,300 miles from Earth. This orbit is then measured as exactly as possible and the satellite orientation adjusted so that it will be in precisely the right attitude for the next step. When the satellite is at the farthest end of its ellipse, traveling approximately at right angles to the earth's radius, a motor is fired at precisely the right instant to put the satellite in a circular orbit around the Earth. The satellite's velocity is then adjusted to synchronize with the Earth's rotation, and its attitude is swung so that its antenna points in the right direction.

During the launching of the first INTELSAT II satellite, the "apogee" motor, which should change the elliptical orbit into the circular one, terminated its 16-second thrust prematurely and left the satellite plunging through space on a large elliptical nonsynchronous orbit. Comsat, however, managed to use it. Following its unplanned journey through space with their big antennas they succeeded in transmitting the first live color TV between Hawaii and the American mainland. It was also used for commercial telephone circuits during those periods when its wanderings brought it within line-of-sight of suitable Earth stations.

Once a synchronous orbit is achieved the satellite will need periodic adjustment to keep it where it is needed. Unless its velocity is *exactly* in synchronization with the Earth it will drift along the Equator over a period of months. Similarly, its attitude will drift slightly, and after a long period, its antennas may not point correctly towards earth. To compensate for this, the satellite is equipped with small gas jets which can be fired from earth to make minor adjustments to its velocity and attitude. A typical communications satellite has four such jets powered by hydrogen peroxide. These can be operated in short squirts by signals from an Earth station, to nudge the satellite into the required position and to keep its orbit "stationary." Early Bird was so accurately placed in orbit in 1965 that the jets need only be triggered once a year or so. In its first ten days after launch, however, 25 such maneuvers were carried out.

EARTH STATIONS

The satellites in use and planned, for commercial telecommunications, at the time of writing, are built by Comsat and owned jointly by the members of the INTELSAT consortium (see Chapter 5). The Earth stations for transmitting and receiving the signal, however, can be set up anywhere in the large number of countries that participate. They are owned by the country or designated company in that country. A wide variety of Earth station designs is possible, and the building of these is open to normal commercial competition. The world map is becoming covered with sites for satellite Earth stations. At the time of writing, 47 are in existence or being built in the noncommunist countries, and this number is likely to increase rapidly. They are scattered fairly evenly across the globe in both the northern and southern hemispheres. The countries under Russian influence are also planning Earth stations for their equivalent of the INTELSAT system. In addition to this, there are military satellite communication networks. The United States military has far more synchronous satellites in orbit than Comsat as part of their international AUTOVON and AUTODIN networks.

The Earth station consists, in essence, of a large dish or horn which points at the satellite, in basically the same way as an Earthbound microwave relay dish points at the next tower in the chain. The Earth station antenna, however, is much larger, giving a much narrower beam angle. A typical antenna width is 85 feet. It is steerable so that it can follow the satellite when it drifts slightly in its location. Many Earth stations are designed not only to track an almost stationary synchronous satellite but also medium-altitude satellites which may move across the sky in two to five hours. Some tracking sys-

(A)

Early Bird, the world's first communications satellite was launched from Cape Kennedy in April 1965.

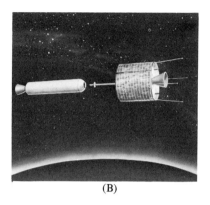

(B)

When the third stage of the Delta launch vehicle burned out the satellite was in an elliptical orbit. After careful measurement and computation, the apogee 22,300 miles from Earth was determined and the small satellite motor was fired by a command from the station at Andover, Maine (Fig. 8.9) to put the satellite into a circular equatorial orbit.

(C)

COMSAT's Operations Center at Washington D. C. directs the complex sequence of maneuvers required to place and maintain the satellites in synchronous orbit.

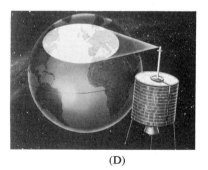

(D)

The satellite linked North America and Europe with 240 voice channels and made transatlantic live television possible for the first time. The voice circuits were soon to be used for data transmission.

Fig. 20.4. *Photographs from the Communications Satellite Corporation.*

tems operate from a signal picked up from the satellite itself (auto-track mode); others on a basis of orbit information, fed externally to the tracking mechanism (program-track mode). In climates where much snow is expected, the antenna is underneath a geodesic dome covered in a material such as dacron which is transparent to the radio signals. This "radome" is sometimes heated from inside; while many tracking stations are permanently situated, others are transportable. These, sometimes employing an antenna of 40 feet, are expected to be of value in less developed countries. At the other end of the scale, the first United States tracking station at Andover, Maine, originally built to work with Telstar but now used with Early Bird and its successors, has a radome 18 stories high and a huge horn-shaped antenna weighing 380 tons. Figures 20.5 and 8.9 show some typical earth stations.

While most of the earth stations simply transmit and receive the telecommunication signal, at least one must carry out the additional function of *controlling* the satellite. Early Bird carries a VHF (*Very High Frequency* radio) system, as well as the microwave system used for telecommunications. The VHF system transmits signals for tracking the satellite during its original orbital placement, and for telemetry about the performance of the satellite. It radios back details such as battery voltages, temperature in the satellite, pressure in the propulsion system, and so on. One of the Earth stations monitors the satellite's position and performance, and sends the signals which make minor adjustments to its orbit.

FUTURE GENERATIONS OF SATELLITE SYSTEMS

The power of telecommunication satellites is expected to increase considerably in the years to come. Early Bird was able to handle 240 two-way telephone channels or two-way television. INTELSAT II improved upon this giving 1200 two-way voice channels. In 1968, Comsat launched INTELSAT III satellites with still greater power, and giving a global coverage. Comsat has projected three more generations of satellites to be launched in 1970, 1973, and 1978, and Earth stations for American domestic service. The 1970 system would have four satellites with a combined capacity for handling 48 full-time color TV channels, or up to 84,000 telephone channels or equivalent. The 1973 satellites would have twice the capacity of the 1970 ones, and those in 1978 are envisioned as having a total capacity of at least five times 1970, or 420,000 telephone channels.

Comsat's legal right to use its satellites for domestic operations is in dispute. If Comsat did use them, as it intends to, the profits of distributing American television and telecommunications would be shared by other countries holding shares in Comsat. However, the legal difficulties in the United States will no doubt be overcome somehow. Russia is already establishing

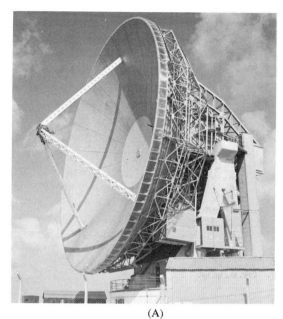

A typical earth satellite station at Goonhilly Downs, England. The steerable 85-foot-diameter antenna is connected to the General Post Office links for voice, data, and television transmission. Smaller transportable antennas are now in use also.

(A)

The antenna steering control console.

(B)

Fig. 20.5. *Photographs courtesy GPO England.*

a domestic television service by satellite. At the time of writing, Russia's communication satellites are substantially more powerful than those of the United States. Ground stations in Eastern Europe, France, and Cuba communicate via the Russian *Molniya* satellites.

The battle for satellite rights will become more interesting when synchronous satellites are launched sufficiently powerful to broadcast television directly to home. In other words, with a disk-shaped antenna on the roof you pick up television programs from the satellites, perhaps relayed from the other side of the earth. Russia has announced her intention to do this.

It is possible that a global system will contain phased medium-altitude satellites, as well as synchronous ones. The medium-altitude satellite needs more expensive Earth stations than the synchronous one because of its continuous motion through the sky. In addition, more satellites would be needed in a medium-altitude system. Twelve would be needed for global coverage, as opposed to three synchronous. The medium-altitude satellite, however, is able to cover the polar regions, and being closer to the Earth gives less echo problems than the synchronous satellite. The radio signal takes approximately 0.26 second to travel to the synchronous satellite and back. With echo suppressors this is found to be acceptable to subscribers. However, on a call to the far side of the world the signal may be relayed twice by satellite with a delay of 0.52 second. This is thought to be too long for telephone circuits, though of no problem on television or telegraphy. It would add one second to the time a person appears to take to reply in a conversation. A medium altitude satellite with a rotation time of 10 hours has an echo delay of about 0.14 second and so a double hop can be tolerated. Figure 20.6 plots the time delay in transmission in one direction against the satellite altitude.

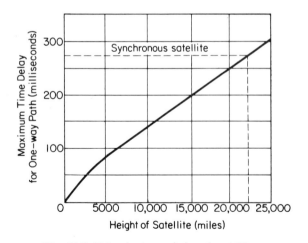

Fig. 20.6. Delay in transmission via satellite.

USE OF SATELLITES IN COMPUTER SYSTEMS The quality of the transmission link provided by satellites is good, and without severe noise problems. Such a link is unlikely to have much impulse noise of the type that plagues earth-bound transmission links though these might still arise from the ground links to the antennas.

The main problem in the use of such a link for data transmission lies in the increased propagation time. Many existing data terminals with retransmission error control would be severely reduced in efficiency by the delay in receiving the return signal. New terminals can be designed which do give high-transmission efficiency, changing the logic of error control. The response to the transmitting machine saying whether or not the data message or block was received correctly will not arrive until half a second or slightly more after the block was sent. Several blocks may be sent in this half second, even if only a voice channel is being used. The transmitting machine must therefore have sufficient storage to retain the blocks until their response is received, so that it can transmit them again if necessary. There must be some means of associating the message acknowledgement with the correct message. This may need an identifying code on the response.

A real-time system requiring a fast response might be slowed down by the satellite link, especially when the communication line has many devices on it as is likely to be the case with such a lengthy path. A new means of line control might be needed to give efficiency. If the computer "polls" the devices at the other side of the satellite link in the manner used on conventional lines, asking them one by one if they have anything to transmit, the delay now introduced could degrade the response time prohibitively. Such a system would need to have a separate polling device on the other side of the satellite link. Such concentrators with their own polling capability are in use on other long lines today. Alternatively, "hub" polling could replace the above "roll-call" polling.[1] With this, a negative answer from a terminal having nothing to send is not sent back to the computer, but the polling message is passed by one terminal location to the next until a machine is found that does have something to send. This is then immediately sent. A negative poll response is only returned to the computer if none of the locations which the line connects have any traffic.

---

[1] *Teleprocessing Network Organization* by James Martin, Prentice-Hall, Englewood Cliffs, N.J., in press.

21 DATA ERRORS

Because of the noise on communication lines, especially impulse noise, there will be a number of errors in data transmitted. We cannot prevent all of the errors occurring; all we can hope to do is to detect them and somehow correct them. The next chapter discusses the various ways of dealing with errors. This chapter summarizes the quantity and nature of errors that can be expected.

Many measurements of transmission errors have been made on communication lines. Telecommunication companies throughout the world have statistics about the error rates and patterns that can be expected on different types of lines. In studying this mass of documentation a pattern emerges. There is generally a similarity between a line in one location and a similar type of line elsewhere. This is not surprising as there has been much international standardization of the design parameters. However, some networks do deviate from this pattern, and, as will be seen in the figures to follow, the error rates differ somewhat from one time to another depending upon such factors as the load on the switching centers, the maintenance activity, and whether the line termination equipment is correctly adjusted.

The systems designer or analyst needs to have some knowledge of the error rates and patterns his system will encounter. On some systems this is obtained by taking measurements on the network that will be used. Typically, a paper tape or magnetic tape of data is transmitted many times over the lines in question. The data received are then compared with the original and a computer program produces statistics about the errors that occurred. This is how most of the figures in this chapter were obtained.

Often, however, such machines are not available or it is not practical for the user to test in this way the lines he wants to use. He may be able to obtain figures from the telephone company in question. In practice, systems analysts working in this area constantly complain that they do not know what error rates to expect and cannot obtain any figures for this. To persons in this position it is suggested that they should use the figures in this chapter as being typical. They should at the same time realize that there is no substitute for actual measurements from the lines they intend to use. Their particular lines may happen to give different error rates than those quoted below.

Let us then examine these typical error rates for different line types:

1. TELEGRAPH AND TELEX CIRCUITS

ERROR
RATES
The CCITT Study Group on Data Transmission has made and analyzed tests on the world's 50-baud leased telegraph channels and on the International Telex circuits of many countries.[1] The results are as follows:

Most Probable Error Rate:
  a. *In point-to-point service:*
      on elements: one- to two-bit errors in 100,000 transmitted
      on characters: one- to eight-character errors in 100,000 transmitted
  b. *On switched Telex circuits:*
      on elements: one- to two-bit errors in 100,000 transmitted
      on characters: four- to five-character errors in 100,000 transmitted

The character error rate of one in 100,000 corresponds to one error in approximately four hours, and eight in 100,000 to one error in approximately half an hour. The most probable time interval without error was found to be one hour approximately.

BURSTS
As was expected, a considerable proportion of the errors were found to come in *bursts*. A *burst of errors* was defined here as elements in error separated by less than ten nonerroneous elements. The proportions of bursts were then found to be as follows:

Isolated errors on elements:	50–60%
Bursts with two errors:	10–20%
Bursts with three errors:	3–10%
Bursts with four errors:	2– 6%

[1] CCITT Special Study Group A (Data Transmission) Contribution 92, Annex XIII, p. 131 (October 18, 1963).

These figures are important for predicting the effectiveness of different error-detecting codes.

Time periods in which the "start" condition remains on the line for more than 300 milliseconds are referred to as "drop outs," the line being regarded as temporarily out of service. These are not included in the preceding figures.

CCITT recommends that the above performance be taken as that of *standard* 50-baud telegraph and telex circuits.

VARIATION WITH NUMBER OF LINE SECTIONS The number of line segments that comprise the telegraph or telex connection has an effect on the error rate. The curves in Fig. 21.1 are taken from a study of the telex network in Germany which reveals this clearly.[2]

In this study, test messages were transmitted from 300 different subscriber sets throughout Germany to an evaluation center. The messages were sent from plastic tapes containing 1000 characters repeated several times. The

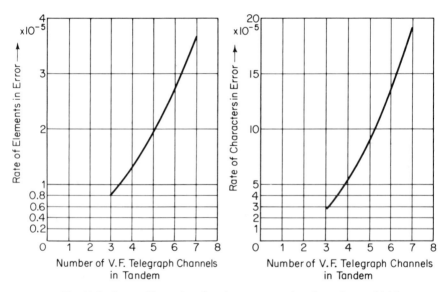

Fig. 21.1. Curves illustrating that the error rates in telegraphy are highly dependent upon the number of tandem links over which the data passes. *From "Tests Conducted in the German Tele-Network with 50-Baud Start-Stop Transmission," CCITT Blue Book. Supplement No. 4, published by the International Telecommunication Union, Geneva, November 1964.*

---

[2] *Tests Conducted on the German Telex Network with 50-Band Start-Stop Transmission.* CCITT *Blue Book*, Supplement No. 4. Published by the International Telecommunication Union, Geneva (November 1964).

connections used were subdivided into categories depending on the number of voice-frequency telegraph sections they comprised. They were selected in such a way that the ratio of these connection types is equivalent to the distribution of actual connections in Germany (for example, see Table A).

Table A

Category	Number and Kind of V.F. Telegraph Systems		Number of Connections
A (3 sections)	3 AM		1355
B (4 sections)	3 AM	1 FM	804
C (5 sections)	5 AM		745
D (7 sections)	5 AM	2 FM	103

Category A: Local exchange—central exchange—central exchange—local exchange.

Category B: Subexchange—local exchange—central exchange—central exchange—local exchange.

Category C: Subexchange—local exchange—central exchange—central exchange—local exchange—subexchange.

Category D: Subscriber for toll service only—subexchange—local exchange—central exchange—central exchange—local exchange—subexchange—subscriber for toll service only.

The results of the tests are shown in more detail in Table 21.1. It will be seen that the error rate is strongly dependent upon the number of line sections, and that lines of six or more sections are worse than the CCITT performance figures quoted in Table A. Only a small number of connections in Germany exceed six sections, however.

BLOCK ERROR RATE   Where data are to be sent in blocks, it is desirable to know how the error rate varies with the block length so that different block-checking schemes can be evaluated, and an estimate can be made of the number of blocks that have to be retransmitted. Figure 21.2, taken from the same German telex study, plots the probability of a block error against the block lengths. Again the variation in error rate with number of line sections is clear. These results can be regarded as typical of 50-baud telex networks.

2. 200-BAUD CIRCUITS

The character error rate over 200-baud circuits is generally somewhat better than over slower circuits. Here the voice channel is typically divided

Table 21.1 RESULTS OF MEASUREMENTS OF ERRORS IN DATA TRANSMITTED ON THE GERMAN

Number of Sections of V.F.T.	Number of Connections	Number of Characters Transmitted	Number of Faulty Characters	Average Error Rate of Telegraph Communication	Number of Elements Transmitted (7 × Column 3)	Number of Elements in Error	Number of Errors with x Elements in Sequence Changed to Z or A (Z ≡ Space ≡ 0 Condition, A ≡ Mark ≡ 1)					
							$x = 1$		$x = 2$		$x = 3$	
							Z	A	Z	A	Z	A
1	2	3	4	5	6	7	8		9		10	
3	1355	1,355,000	38	2.804×10^{-5}	9.48×10^6	54	14	12	12	10	4	2
4	804	804,000	44	5.47×10^{-5}	5.63×10^6	71	22	24	9	13	—	3
5	745	745,000	50	6.71×10^{-5}	5.22×10^6	81	22	17	10	12	5	7
7	103	103,000	20	19.4×10^{-5}	0.721×10^6	23	3	14	5	1	—	—
5	108	1,003,694	—	—	7.03×10^6	92	54	11	7	11	5	4
5	108	1,045,518	—	—	7.32×10^6	219	55	54	36	30	17	19
6	65	628,883	89	14.1×10^{-5}	4.40×10^6	160	49	27	22	18	8	13
8	12	203,715	28	13.7×10^{-5}	1.426×10^6	42	8	5	5	7	5	7

*Reproduced from CCITT *Blue Book*, Supplement No 4, The International Telecommunication Union,

into 480-hertz spacing (360 hertz in some countries), as opposed to 120 hertz for 50-baud transmission. The slightly better performance is attributed to the fact that the error-free intervals are about the same and that more characters are transmitted during these periods.

Table 21.2 shows the results of transmitting data over 200-baud connections in Germany.

3. VOICE-GRADE LINES

Yet a further improvement is found in going from 200-baud lines to voice-grade lines. In general, as one progresses from a lower to a higher

Table 21.2 RESULTS OF MEASUREMENTS OF ERRORS IN DATA TRANSMITTED ON THE GERMAN

Number of V. F. Telegraph Sections	Number of Transmitted Characters	Number of Erroneous Characters	Average Error Rate	Number of Error Sequences Following Each					
				$x = 1$	$x = 2$	$x = 3$	$x = 4$	$x = 5$	$x = 6$
1	2	3	4	5	6	7	8	9	10
2	8,046,367	201	2.50×10^{-5}	144	2	1	1	2	—
3	3,936,849	115	2.925×10^{-5}	61	2	2	1	3	—

*Reproduced from CCITT *Blue Book*, Supplement No. 6, The International Telecommunication Union,

50-BAUD TELEX NETWORK.*

Number of Errors with x Elements in Sequence Changed to Z or A ($Z \equiv$ Space $\equiv 0$ Condition, $A \equiv$ Mark $\equiv 1$)			Number of Disconnections Which Caused No Printing of Characters			Sum of Elements Changed of Position		Number of Elements in Error (Column 7 + Column 14×3.5 + Column 15×7)	Number of Transpositions	Average Error Rate of Elements	Number of Error Bursts	Number of Faulty Elements in Error Bursts (%)
$x = 4$ Z A	$x = 5$ Z A	$x > 5$	< 150 ms	< 300 ms	More than 300 ms	Z	A			$\left(\dfrac{\text{Column 19}}{\text{Column 4}}\right)$		
11	12	13	14	15	16	17	18	19	20	21	22	23
— —	— —	0	5	1	—	30	24	78	10	8.28×10^{-6}	13	37 = 68
— —	— —	0	1	—	—	31	40	74	9	13.2×10^{-6}	9	50 = 70
2 6	— —	0	6	—	—	39	42	102	14	19.5×10^{-6}	14	65 = 80
— —	— —	0	1	—	—	8	15	26	1	36.8×10^{-6}	2	6 = 26
— —	— —	0	4	1	1	66	26	113	13	16.1×10^{-6}	13	37 = 40
3 5	— —	0	7	1	1	111	108	250	36	34.3×10^{-6}	21	112 = 51
4 4	11 4	0	1	1	2	94	66	170	28	27.1×10^{-6}	25	124 = 77
— —	3 2	0	3	—	1	21	21	52	8	37.0×10^{-6}	9	37 = 88

Geneva (November 1964).

bandwidth with a proportionately higher transmission speed, the error rate decreases. Table B on p. 366, for example, shows typical error rates.

On the other hand, given a specific channel, it is possible to transmit over it at different speeds using different modems. In this case, as might be expected, the faster the transmission rate the greater the number of errors. For example, where a voice line is used, a typical error rate for 600 bits/second transmission is one bit wrong in 500,000. For transmission at 1200 bits/second, however, it would be more reasonable to expect one bit wrong in 200,000. For transmission at 2000 bits/second error rates of one bit wrong in 100,000 are typical. At higher speeds than this the error rate may increase rapidly and one is beginning to pay heavily for extracting the maximum line efficiency. The high-speed figures will probably become better, though, as modem design improves.

200-BAUD TELEGRAPH NETWORK*

With x Erroneous Characters Other Immediately						Number of Disconnections Resulting in the Nonprinting of Characters			Number of False Clearings
$x = 7$	$x = 8$	$x = 9$	$x = 10$	$x = 11$	$x = 12$	< 40 ms	< 80 ms	< 120 ms	
11	12	13	14	15	16	17	18	19	20
—	1	1	1	—	—	1	1	2	6
—	—	—	1	—	1	—	—	1	6

Geneva (November 1964).

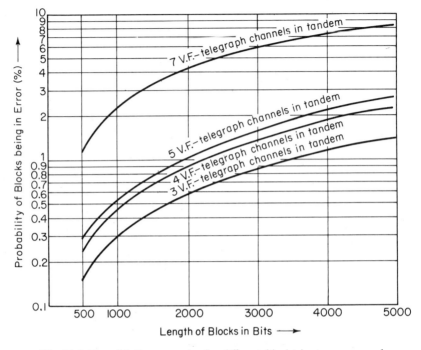

Fig. 21.2. Data block error rates for different block sizes, as measured on the German 50-baud Telex network. *From op. cit. Fig. 21.1.*

Table B

Type of Channel	(Hertz)		Transmission Rate (bits/second)	Bit Error Rate
50-baud Telex	Channel spacing:	120	50	1 in 50,000
200-baud telegraph	Channel spacing:	480	200	1 in 100,000
Public voice line	Usable bandwidth:	1700	600	1 in 500,000

Figure 21.3 and some of the following figures relate to tests made on the switched telephone network in the American Telephone and Telegraph Company.[3] These tests give results fairly similar to some tests made on the

---

[3] American Telephone & Telegraph Company, "Data Transmission Possibilities of the Telephone Network with Switching." CCITT *Red Book*, Vol. VII, The International Telecommunications Union, Geneva (March 1961).

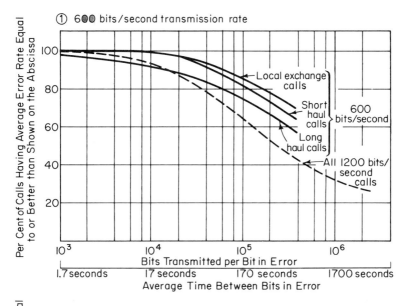

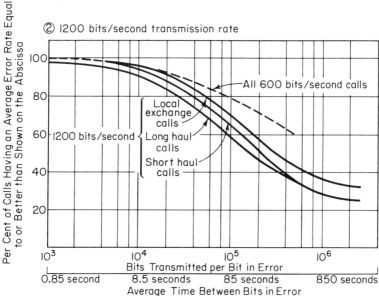

Fig. 21.3. Error rates measured when transmitting data over AT&T's switched public telephone network (U.S.A.). The probabilities of different error rates are shown for three types of connection. Transmission at 600 bits/sec and 1200 bits/sec are compared. *Redrawn from CCITT Red Book, Vol. VII, published by the International Telecommunication Union, Geneva, March 1961.*

telephone network in other countries. The telephone calls from which these statistics were compiled were made using three types of connection. About 25% of the calls were local calls using the local central office, and no long-distance offices. A further 25% were short-haul long-distance calls with air-mile distances up to 500 miles. The remaining 50% were long-haul calls, from 400 to 3000 miles long. On all of these calls, the data were transmitted with binary FM modulation.

As might have been guessed, and as is shown clearly in Figs. 21.3 and 21.5, the long-haul calls have more errors than the short-haul calls, and the short-haul calls have more than the local exchange calls. Figure 21.3 gives the probabilities of having different error rates, and compares 600 bit-per-second transmission with 1200 bit-per-second. It will be seen that when a local number is dialed, and data transmitted at 600 bits per second, there is a probability of about 85% of obtaining a line with an error-rate equal to or better

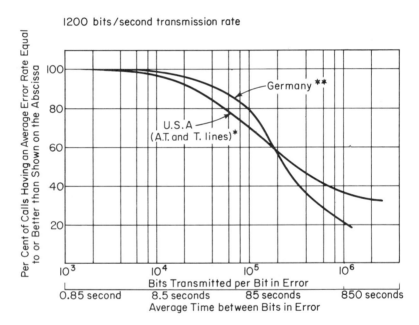

Fig. 21.4. A comparison of error measurements made in America and Germany. Both curves are for 1200 bit/sec transmission over the switched public telephone network using local exchange calls. *This curve is from CCITT Red Book, Vol. VII, published by the International Telecommunication Union, Geneva, March 1961. **This curve is redrawn from CCITT Blue Book, Vol. VIII. Supplement No. 29. "Report on Data Transmission Tests on the German Telephone Newtowrk," published by the International Telecommunication Union, Geneva, November 1964.

than one error bit in 100,000 bits transmitted. The probability of obtaining a line with an error rate better than one in 10,000 is about 99 %. With transmission at 1200 bits per second these probabilities drop to about 70% and 96%, respectively. With a long-distance 600 bit-per-second connection they drop to about 86 % and 91 %, respectively. It will be seen that the probability of obtaining a very poor local circuit was too small to show on these curves, but that of obtaining a very poor long-haul circuit is not negligible.

Measurements made on the German telephone system, are compared with the AT&T results in Fig. 21.4. Both of these curves are for local exchange calls only, at a 1200 bit per second transmission rate. The results are remarkably similar. On some networks, however, one occasionally has "bad" connections which give an unusually high amount of noise. In England, tests indicated that with a transmission rate of 600 or 750 bits per second, an error rate less than 1 bit in 100,000 should always be obtained "under normal conditions over any private line circuit." It should be obtained also over a "switched line connected through busy automatic telephone exchanges" provided that the signal level at any of the switches does not fall too low. The circuits were monitored with earphones during these trials and it was found that when, as occasionally occurred (and as was made to happen artificially by lowering the transmitting signal level), the error rate fell below one in 100,000, then the audible level of noise was "high enough to have constituted a real nuisance in the reception of speech."

ERROR-FREE
INTERVALS
BETWEEN
ERROR BITS

Figure 21.5 shows the numbers of error-free bits between errors.[4] The probabilities of having succeeding errors closely following the first error are important in designing error detection and correction codes.

Suppose, for example, that a single *parity check* is used for error detection on an eight-bit character. The character contains seven data bits plus a parity bit selected to always give an odd number of 1 bits in the character. If now during transmission a single-bit error occurs in that character, there will no longer be an odd number of 1's and so the parity check will reveal that the error has occurred. If, however, *two* of the eight bits are changed erroneously then the parity will still be correct, and the check will have failed to detect the error. If the character is in error, the probability that the first erroneous bit is the first bit of the character is approximately $\frac{1}{8}$. The parity check will then operate correctly if the next *seven* bits are error-free. From

---

[4] "Automatic Telephone and Electric Co., "Contribution on Data Transmission," CCITT *Red Book* ,Vol. VII, The International Telecommunication Union, Geneva, 1961.

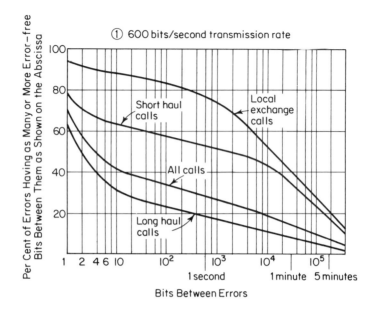

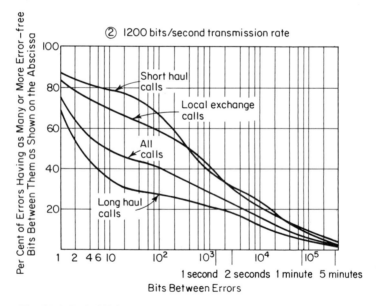

Fig. 21.5. Probabilities of obtaining error-free transmission of different numbers of bits between successive error bits. *Taken from measurements on AT&T's switched public telephone network. Reproduced from CCITT Red Book, Vol. VII, published by the International Telecommunication Union, Geneva, March 1961.*

Fig. 21.5 we see that the probability of having an error-free interval of seven or more bits (taking the curve for all types of calls at 1200 bits per second) is approximately 0.51. In other words, 49% of the error bits will have another error following within seven bits. The probability that the first erroneous bit of the error character is in the second bit is also approximately $\frac{1}{8}$, and then six error-free bits must follow if the parity check is to work (ignoring as yet the probability of having 3, 5, or 7 bits in error). The probability of this, from Fig. 21.5, is about 0.52. The probability that the parity check will not work is 0.48. Adding together all of the possible two-bit errors in an eight-bit character, from Fig. 21.5, we find that the probability of the parity check not working is: $\frac{1}{8} \times 0.49 + \frac{1}{8} \times 0.48 + \frac{1}{8} \times 0.47 + \frac{1}{8} \times 0.45 + \frac{1}{8} \times 0.41 + \frac{1}{8} \times 0.37 + \frac{1}{8} \times 0.27 = 0.37$. From this we must subtract the probability of 3, 5, or 7 bits in error, and we conclude that approximately 30% of the time the simple parity check will fail to detect the errors. This is an interesting conclusion, as many transmission schemes employ parity checks. (They usually but not always include block or "longitudinal" checks in addition to parity checks on characters.)

BURSTS OF ERRORS

What Fig. 21.5 is saying, in effect, is that the bit errors are not evenly distributed. If they were, and we had an error rate of one bit in 300,000, then it would be an extremely rare event for two bits to occur in the same character, and a simple parity check would be very effective. But such is not the case. When trouble comes, it comes fast and furious. Bursts of errors are the rule rather than the exception, and sometimes they go on for hundreds of bits.

Figure 21.6 shows measurements of burst length made on a long-distance leased line in Europe. In these measurements the transmission rate was 2000 bits per second using binary phase modulation, and the data were sent in blocks of 792 bits. Of these blocks, 36% of those in error had only one bit in error, 81% had less than 10 bits, but 15% had large numbers of errors. The upper curve in Fig. 21.6 shows this distribution.

The lower curve in Fig. 21.6 shows the distribution of burst lengths. This is defined here as being the distance in bits between the first bit error and last bit error in the blocks. This curve states again that 36% of the error blocks have a burst length of only one bit. 34% of the bursts are from two to eight bits in length and 30% are longer than eight bits.

In evaluating error-detection and correction schemes it is interesting to know the error-free interval between bursts, as well as the interval between bits. This is shown in Fig. 21.7. In this illustration the burst size is defined as being 1, 2, 4, 6, 8, 10, or 20. For the curve relating to burst size 4, four bits are counted when an error is detected and then the error-free bits before

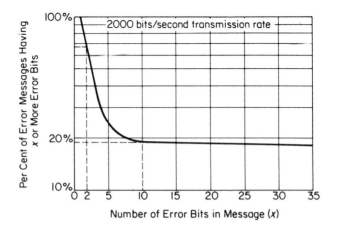

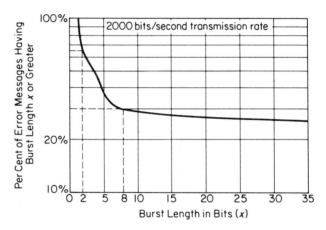

Fig. 21.6. Burst lengths and number of error bits per message encountered on data transmission tests, at a 2000-bit/sec transmission rate, on a multipoint leased voice line from London to Rome. Fixed message lengths of 792 bits were used. *Redrawn from "Data Transmission Test on a Multipoint Telephone Network in Europe," CCITT* Blue Book. *Supplement No. 37 published by the International Telecommunications Union, Geneva, November 1964.*

the next error are counted. Let us illustrate this by representing a stream of bits using "E" for error bits and "C" for correct bits:

CCCCCCECCCCCCCEECECCCCCCECCCEECCCCCCCCCCCECCECCEECCCCC

If we assess this in terms of the four-bit bursts, the bursts would be as follows, the figures being the number of correct bit between bursts:

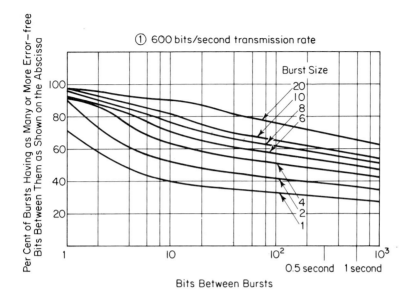

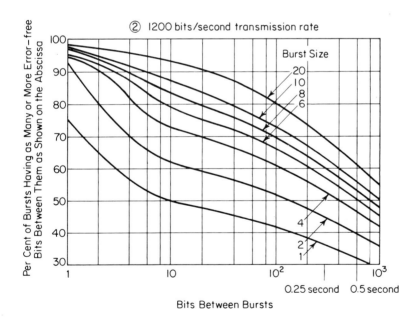

Fig. 21.7. Probabilities of obtaining error-free transmission of different numbers of bits between error bursts as taken from measurements on AT&T's switched public telephone network (curves relate to the mean of all type of calls). *Redrawn from CCITT Red Book, Vol, VII, published by the International Telecommunication Union, Geneva, March 1961.*

And if it is assessed in terms of six-bit bursts:

In Fig. 21.7 the curves for "burst size 1" give the same information as the curves for "all calls" in Fig. 21.5. The curves for the bigger burst sizes are substantially higher than these, indicating again that the errors are to a large extent clustered.

These curves can be used to gain an indication of the efficiency of different error detecting or correcting codes. Many codes can detect or correct errors within a given burst size as we have explained, provided that the gap between bursts is sufficiently great. A code might, for example, be able to detect *single errors* provided that there are eight bits or more between the errors. About 42% of the errors in the lower curve of Fig. 21.7 satisfy this criteria and so will be detected. Again, the code might be able to detect four-bit bursts but now requires 20 error-free bits between the bursts. The same set of curves indicate that now about 59% of the bursts satisfy this criteria, which is not a great improvement. A certain Hagelbarger code which is designed to correct bursts eight bits in duration requires an interval of 26 error-free bits between bursts. The curves show that about 69% of eight-bit bursts have the requisite 26 error-free bits between them.

A comprehensive evaluation of the many different error-detecting and error-correcting codes, using data such as that in Fig. 21.7 would be complex. The subject is beyond the scope of this book. Many mathematical papers have been written on this subject. Most of these, however, make assumptions that the distribution of errors is more uniform than is the case in these measurements. To evaluate the performance of various codes in the presence of these burst patterns, Monte Carlo methods seem warranted.

THE EFFECT OF CLUSTERING   The fact that the errors are clustered in bursts rather than evenly dispersed has both good and bad aspects. Its good aspect is that there are longer periods of error-free transmission than there would be if the errors were evenly spread out. A larger proportion of messages, then, have no errors occurring in them at all.

On the other hand, the clustering of errors makes it more difficult to produce efficient error-detecting or correcting codes. Codes which correct single bit errors, for example, would be highly effective if the one bit-errors in 300,000 or so were not clustered. With clustering such as that described, however, even quite complex codes will leave errors undetected.

Figure 21.8 compares transmission with no error correction, correction of single errors and a code capable of correcting bursts of up to eight errors. The latter code is the Hagelbarger code mentioned which requires 26 error-free bits between bursts. These curves relate to the same AT&T lines as those before, being the mean of all types of calls.

It will be seen that about 63% of the connections achieve an error rate below one in 400,000 with 600-bit-per-second transmission, and about 44% with 1200-bit-per-second transmission. With single-error correction about 74% achieve this error rate on 600-bit-per-second lines and about 57% on 1200-bit-per-second lines. With the burst correction these figures become about 87% and 75%.

Systems analysts sometimes have the belief that an error detection code as elaborate as this gives a very high degree of protection. Such would be the case if the errors were not clustered, but in Fig. 21.8 we see that, while the curves have been pushed upwards significantly, they are still some distance away from the 100% line.

It is possible to devise transmission schemes which give much higher protection than this, but in order to do so they give very low transmission efficiency. The efficiency of the Hagelbarger code is only 50%. In other words, only half of the bits transmitted are data bits. We ought really to be comparing the curve with burst correction at 600 bits per second with that without burst correction at 1200 bits per second. The improvement given by the code does not then look too good. The code referred to here is an error-*correcting* code. As will be discussed in the next chapter, it is generally better to use an error-*detecting* code with retransmission of error messages.

ERRORS AS A
FUNCTION OF
MESSAGE LENGTH

Where error-detecting codes are used with retransmission, it is desirable to know how many blocks or messages will have to be retransmitted. This will vary with the message length. If very short message lengths are used, retransmission will not be necessary for most of them, but if the messages are long, a high proportion may have an error and have to be re-sent. Fortunately, the clustering of error bits increases the proportion of error-free messages.

Figure 21.9 shows the probabilities of having no errors in blocks of different lengths or, in other words, the fraction of messages that do not have to be retransmitted. The curves relate the same AT&T switched public lines as

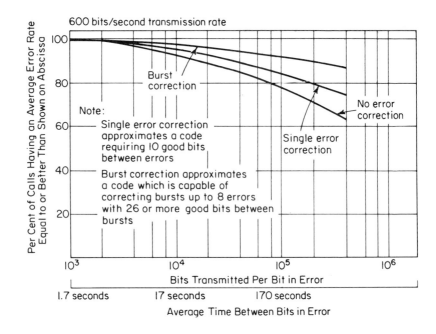

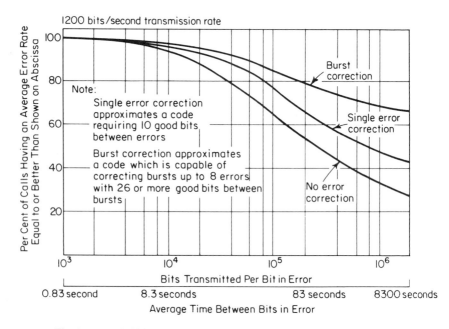

Fig. 21.8. Probabilities of different error rates on AT&T public switched voice lines. (a) with no error correction, (b) with single error correction, and (c) with error burst correction. *Redrawn from CCITT Red Book, Vol. VII, published by the International Telecommunication Union, Geneva, March 1961.*

before. The curves are drawn using two different scales because we are interested in a wide range of different block lengths.

Suppose that we transmit messages of 100 bits. The curve for no error correction shows us that with transmission at 600 bits per second, we can expect 0.999 of the messages to be error-free (using the dotted curve). At 1200 bits per second this drops to about 0.998. If we can detect the messages in error and retransmit them, this means that approximately one message in a thousand will be retransmitted with the 600-bits-per-second line, and two in a thousand with the 1200-bits-per-second line.

With messages or blocks of data of 100,000 bits, on the other hand, about 0.76 will be correct on the 600-bits-per-second line, and 0.69 on the 1200-bits-per-second line. About 240 and 310 blocks in a thousand, respectively, will have to be retransmitted and, of course, some of these will be wrong the second time. If the blocks are a million bits long, about 70% of them will be retransmitted, so this is clearly too great a block size.

There is generally a timing advantage to be gained in retransmission systems by sending large blocks. The equipment on the line such as modems and echo suppressors takes some time to turn around at the end of a block before transmitting the control signal in the opposite direction. The data handling machines also may require some time interval between one block and the next. There is therefore an *optimum block size* for achieving the maximum speed. If the block size is too short, too much time will be lost between blocks. However, if it is too long, too many blocks will have to be retransmitted because of errors. The optimum will, then, depend upon the line error rate and the time interval needed between blocks.

The upper curves show the proportion of messages in error when error correcting codes are used, both for single-error correction and burst correction. The burst correction does not seem to give enough improvement over single error correction to warrant its high degradation in transmission efficiency.

HOUR-BY-HOUR VARIATION IN ERROR RATES   When transmitting data over the switched public telephone network considerable variation in the error rate is found from one period of time to another. A typical illustration of this is shown in Fig. 21.10. This shows the result of transmitting blocks of data over the local public network of Stuttgart, Germany. The blocks received in error were counted electronically. It will be seen that occasionally there are periods when the error rate is several times higher than the average. The error rate is generally higher during periods of high traffic intensity. Measurements on other telephone networks show similar results. The curves in Fig. 21.11 show the variation on 1000-baud transmission tests carried out on

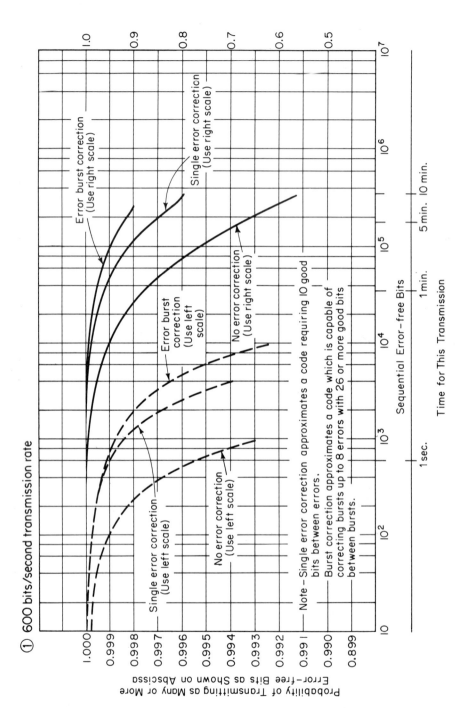

Fig. 21.9. Probabilities of obtaining error-free transmission on voice lines for messages of different lengths, taken from measurements made on AT&T's switched public network. *Redrawn from CCITT Red Book, Vol. VII, published by International Telecommunication Union, Genva, March 1961.*

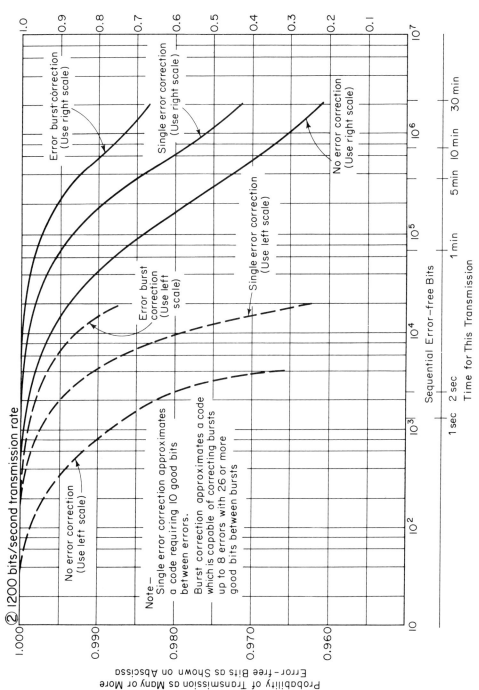

Fig. 21.9. (*Cont.*)

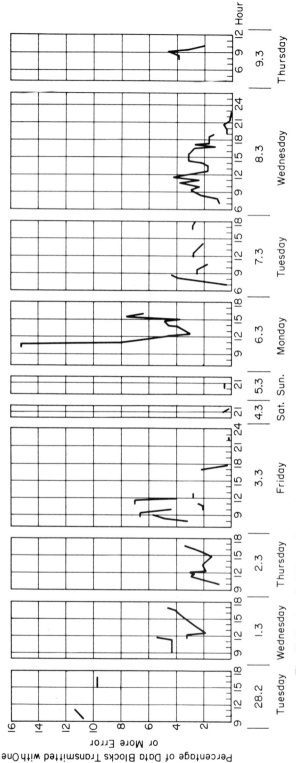

Fig. 21.10. A typical illustration of the hour-by-hour variation in error rate for data transmitted over a switched public network. These measurements were made on the Stuttgart Telephone Newtork.

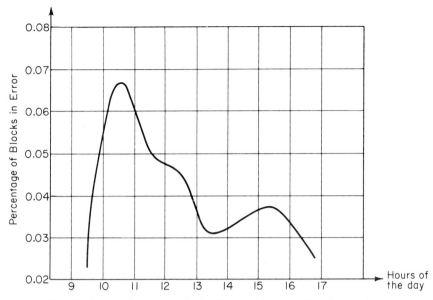

Distribution of Erroneous Blocks Transmitted over the Switched
Public Network of Chile[1] (Using 50 – bit Blocks)

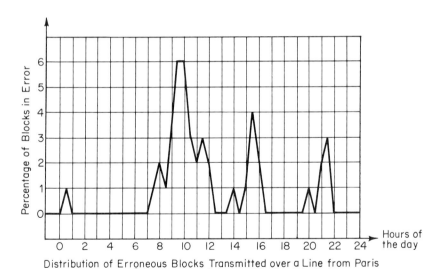

Distribution of Erroneous Blocks Transmitted over a Line from Paris
to Hilversum[2] (Netherlands) (using 85 – bit Blocks)

Fig. 21.11. Hour-by-hour variation of error rates encountered. Both
illustrations use transmission at 1000 bauds over voice grade lines. (1)
*Extract from CCITT contribution COM Sp. A/No. 7, July 1961, by the
Chile Telephone Company.* (2) *Extract from CCITT contribution Com Sp.
A/No. 16, September 1961, by N. V. Philips Telecommunicatie Industrie.*

telephone lines in Europe and Chile. The error rate rises during the morning and afternoon peaks in telephone traffic.

While traffic peaks cause a change in error rate which is somewhat predictable, *maintenance work on the lines or in the exchanges can cause sudden and unpredictable peaks.* These frequently cause a greater error rate for a period than the normal daily variations.

VARIATION IN ERROR RATE WITH TRANSMISSION VOLTAGE The numbers of errors have been found to vary widely with the voltage level at which the signal is transmitted. If the voltage is low, then the noise, which does not change its level, does more damage. Figure 21.12 illustrates how wide this variation is. Perhaps a more significant measure than the transmission voltage would be the lowest level of the signal when it passes through the exchanges, as it is here that much of the impulse noise originates.

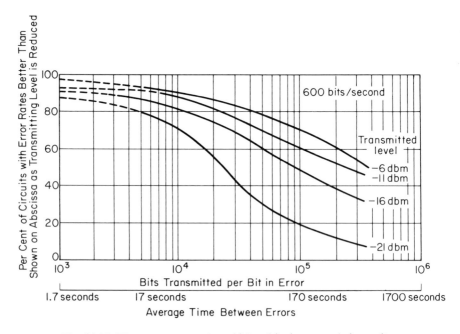

Fig. 21.12. The error rate varies widely with the transmission voltage used. Incorrectly adjusted terminal equipment can give rise to error rates higher than those shown in this chapter. These measurements were made on AT&T public switched line. *Curves reproduced from CCITT Red Book, Vol. VII, published by the International Telecommunication Union, Geneva, March 1961.*

The statistics in this chapter have all been collected on lines with the transmission voltage adjusted for near-optimum performance. In practice, if the line termination equipment is not correctly adjusted then the error rate can be expected to be worse than in these illustrations.

In my own experience with data transmission I have encountered error rates definitely greater than those here. Sometimes, too, operating a terminal and observing errors I have suspected that the performance is substandard. This is probably due to the incorrect adjustment of terminal equipment—though it is usually difficult at the time to be sure what is causing it. If the performance is consistently poorer than that shown in the above curves, an engineer should check that the modems are correctly adjusted. If performance is still poor on a leased line, this should be discussed with a common carrier, as some adjustment on their part might be needed.

It seems advisable to end this chapter with the caution with which it began. There is no substitute for actual measurements on the lines intended for us. While the figures given can be used by systems analysts in the absence of anything better, to do their design calculations, it must be noted that specific lines may differ from them considerably in their error rates.

22　THE TREATMENT
　　OF ERRORS

On many data-transmission systems the control of errors is of vital importance. On some, however, it is not of great significance. A variety of error
correction procedures are in use, but, as would be expected from the figures
in the previous chapter, most of those in common use still leave a number of
undetected errors which is greater than the number that would be expected on
other components of a computer system. Tape and file channels on a computer, for example, have an error rate much lower than the telecommunication links in conventional use today.

In addition to transmission errors, the errors made by operators constitute
a significant problem in the design of on-line systems. The number of errors
made by the operators of the input/output devices on a large system will
usually far exceed the number of errors caused by noise or distortion on the
transmission lines. It is usually important that accuracy controls are devised
for the human input. Also on many systems, a tight network of controls is
necessary to stop abuse or embezzlement. It is also important to insure that
nothing is lost or double-entered when hardware failures occur on the system
or when switchover takes place. These systems design considerations are
beyond the scope of this book, and in this chapter we will discuss the treatment of errors arising from noise and distortion on the communication lines.

There are a variety of approaches that a computer system designer can
take to the dealing with errors on transmission lines. All of the approaches
we will discuss next are found on data-transmission systems in use today.

The first, and easiest approach, is to ignore the errors, and this is often
done. The majority of telegraph links in operation today, for example, have
no error checking facilities at all. Part of the reason for this is that they normally transmit English language text that will be read by human beings.

Errors in English language caused by the changing of a bit or of a small group of bits are usually obvious to the human eye, and we correct these in the mind as we read the material. Telegrams which have figures as well as text in them commonly repeat the figures. This inexpensive approach is also taken on computer systems where the transmission handles verbal text. For example, on administrative message switching systems, it is usually acceptable to have transmission to and from unchecked telegraph machines. If the text turns out to be unintelligible, the user can always ask for a retransmission.

An error rate of one bit in 10^5 is possibly not quite so bad as it sounds. Suppose that we considered transmitting the text of this book, for example, and coded it in five-bit Baudot code. If one bit in 10^5 was in error, that would mean that in the entire book there would be about 40 letters that were wrong. The book would certainly still be readable, and the majority of its readers would not notice most of these errors. The human eye has a habit of passing unperturbed over minor errors in text. This book was first set in galley proofs by the publishers. The text was then scrutinized and checked by a team of professional editors. It was then divided into pages and page proofs were produced. By now, most of the errors should have been removed from the text, but, in fact, those remaining corresponded to an error rate of one bit in 10^4, an error level higher than that which would be found on unchecked telegraph transmission.

In any case, on most data-processing systems *some* of the errors are ignored. An error detection procedure which catches all of them is too expensive. Many systems in current use might improve the level of undetected errors from one bit in 10^5 to one bit in 10^7. It is possible to devise a coding scheme which gives *much* better protection than this. In fact, one that is on the market gives an undetected error rate of one bit in 10^{14}, but this is expensive. Line throughput decreases as the error control is improved.

In designing a computer system it is important to know what error rate is expected and to estimate the effect of this error rate on the system *as a whole*. On some systems, the effect of infrequently occurring errors is cumulative. For example, if messages cause the updating of files, it is possible on some systems that as the months pass by, the file will accumulate an increasing number of inaccuracies. In such a case well-thought-out means are needed to detect errors and keep the files "clean."

DETECTION
OF ERRORS
To detect communications errors, redundancy is built into the messages transmitted. In other words, more bits are sent than need be sent for the coding of the data alone. One simple method is to use a parity check. With this, one extra bit is added to each character and this is coded so that the total number of ones in a character is always an odd number (on

some systems an even number). However, as was discussed in the last chapter, often two bits are changed, and the simple parity check does not work. Unfortunately, this is often the case because many noise pulses are of sufficient duration to wipe out two adjacent bits. Figure 21.8 indicates that an undetected error rate of about one bit in 10^6 can be expected on a typical leased voice line operating at 1200 bits per second, even with parity error detection. A four-out-of-eight code, on the other hand (requiring exactly four "1" bits in a character, no more, no less), would detect errors in small numbers of adjacent bits, and its error detecting capability is much better than the simple parity check. A wide variety of character coding schemes which detect errors are possible.

In addition to applying an error-detecting code to each character, one is often applied to a *block* of characters, or to a complete message. One or more error detection characters, or a pattern of bits, are transmitted with the message. This redundancy check is derived from the bits in the message by the transmitting terminal. When the message is received, the same process is applied to the message by the receiving terminal, and if this does not generate the same pattern, then the receiving terminal knows that an error has occurred somewhere in the message. The message will not be processed.

Here again there is a very wide variety of error-detection schemes. They differ considerably in their power and in the degree of redundancy that is needed. A comparative study of these is beyond the scope of this book. By building a *sufficient* amount of redundancy into a message, the probability of a transmission error remaining undetected can be made extremely low indeed.

DEALING WITH ERRORS

Having detected the errors the question arises, what should the system do about them? It is generally desirable that it should take some automatic action to correct the fault. Some data-transmission systems, however, do not do this and leave the fault to be corrected by human means at a later time. For example, one system which transmits data to be punched into cards causes a card to be offset in its position in the stacker when an error is detected. The offset cards are later picked out by the operator who then arranges for retransmission. In general, it is much better to have some means of automatic retransmission rather than a manual procedure, and this is usually less expensive than employing an operator for this.

ERROR CORRECTING CODES

Automatic correction can take a number of forms. First, sufficient redundancy can be built into the transmission code so that the code itself permits automatic error correction, as well as detection. To do this effectively can require a number of redundant bits almost as great as the data bits in the message itself. Codes which give automatic error correction are therefore inefficient in their use of communication line capacity. If the communication line permitted the transfer of information in one direction only, then they would be extremely valuable. However, it is far more common today to use half duplex or full duplex communication links.

In general, error-*correcting* codes used on a half duplex or full duplex lines do not give as good value for money, or value for bandwidth, as error-*detecting* codes coupled with the ability to retransmit automatically data that is found to contain an error.

LOOP
CHECK

One method of detecting errors does not use a code at all. Instead, all of the bits received are retransmitted back to their sender, and the sending machine checks that they are still intact. If not, then the item in error is retransmitted. This is sometimes referred to as a "loop" or "echo" check. This scheme is normally used on a full duplex line. Again it uses the channel capacity less efficiently than would be possible with an error-detection code, although often the return path of a full-duplex line is underutilized in a system because the system does not produce enough data to keep the channel loaded with data in both directions. A loop check is most commonly found on short lines and in-plant lines where the waste of channel capacity is less costly. It gives a degree of protection which is more certain than most other methods.

RETRANSMISSION
OF DATA IN
ERROR

A variety of different forms of error detection and retransmission are built into data-handling equipment. In a typical high-speed paper-tape transmission system a "vertical" parity check, that is a parity check on each character, is used along with a "horizontal" checking character at the end of a block of characters. At the end of each block the receiving station sends a signal to the transmitting station saying whether the block has been received correctly or whether an error has been detected. If any error is found, both the transmitting tape reader and the receiving tape punch go into reverse and run backwards to the beginning of that block. The punch then erases the incorrect data by punching a *delete* code. The block is then retransmitted. If transmission of the same block is attempted several times (four times on much equipment) and is still incorrect, then the equipment will stop and notify its operator by means of a warning light and bell or buzzer. Other automatic facilities are usually used to detect broken or jammed paper tape; and to warn when the punch is running short of tape.

Where data are being transmitted to a computer, automatic retransmission is sometimes handled under control of the program, and sometimes by circuitry external to the main computer.

ERROR CONTROL
ON RADIO CIRCUITS

When high-frequency radio is used for telegraphy the mutilation of bits is normally much worse than with land-based telegraph circuits. It is subject to severe fading and distortion, especially in times of high sunspot activity. Because of its high error rate and general unreliability its use is avoided as far as possible for transmission of computer data. However, it is still used in some more isolated areas and in ship-to-shore links. A scheme of error detection and retransmission known as ARQ is used.

The system most commonly in use for radio telegraphy is the van Duuren ARQ system. This transmits full duplex, synchronously, the characters being sent in blocks or "words," using a three-out-of-seven code (which permits 35 different combinations as opposed to 32 with the five bits of normal telegraphy). The start and stop bits of the Baudot code are stripped off and the remaining five recoded into three-out-of-seven code and transmitted.

If the receiving equipment detects more, or less, than three bits in any character, transmission of data in the opposite direction is interrupted. An error signal is sent back to the transmitter of the data now in error. This transmitter then interrupts its sending, returns to the invalid word and retransmits it. On a long radio link, one or more words may have been sent after the message that had the error, depending upon the duration of the transmission path. These are discarded by the receiver. When the transmitter receives the error indication, it stops what it is transmitting, backtracks to the word in error and retransmits that and all following words.

High-frequency radio links can be expected to have an error rate before correction of one character in 1000, and sometimes much worse than this. Most of these errors will be detected with the three-out-of-seven code, but there is a certain probability of a double mutilation which makes a character incorrect while still leaving it with three "1" bits. The number of *undetected* errors in this case is one character error in 10,000,000, approximately. This mutilation rate can rise as high as one character in 40 or even as high as one character in four on bad links, and at certain bad periods of time. If the mutilation rate is one character in 40, the undetected error rate rises to one character in 16,000, and the effective speed of the link would drop to a speed of perhaps 90% of the nominal speed, depending upon the word size and link retransmission time. If the mutilation rate rises to one character in four, the rate after error detection and retransmission is about one character in 160, and the effective speed is likely to have dropped to about half the nominal speed. This is still usable for human language messages because we can apply our error correction thinking.

HOW MUCH IS
RETRANSMITTED ?
Systems differ in how much they require to be retransmitted when an error is detected. Some retransmit only one character when a character error is found. Others retransmit many characters or even many messages.

There are two possible advantages in retransmitting a small quantity of data. First, it saves time. It is quicker to retransmit five characters than 500 when an error is found. Though if the error rate is one character error in 20,000 (a typical figure for TELEX and telegraph lines) the percentage loss in speed does not differ greatly between these two cases. It would be significant if a block of 5000 had to be retransmitted.

Second, when a large block is retransmitted, it has to be stored somewhere until the receiving machine has confirmed that the transmission was correct. This is often no problem. In transmitting from paper tape, for example, the tape reader merely reverses to the beginning of that block. The paper tape is its own message storage. The same is true with transmission from magnetic tape or disk. With transmission from a keyboard, however, an auxiliary storage or *buffer* is needed if there is chance that the message may have to be retransmitted automatically. On some input devices, a small core storage unit constitutes the buffer. On others, the keys themselves are the storage. They remain locked down until successful transmission is acknowledged. Again, several input devices may share a common control unit and this contains the buffer storage. Buffer storage in quantity can be fairly expensive and so it may be better to check and retransmit only a small number of characters at a time. Again, when data on punched cards are transmitted, a buffer is needed for retransmission unless the machine is designed in an ingenious manner so that the card can be reread if required.

The disadvantages of using small blocks for retransmission are first that the error detection codes can be more efficient on a large block of data. In other words, the ratio of the number of bits needed *with* the error detection code to the number if the data were sent *without* protection is smaller for a given degree of protection, if the quantity of data is large. Second, where blocks of data are sent synchronously, a period of time is taken up between blocks, with control characters and line turnaround procedures. The longer the block, the less significant this wasted time.

TRANSMISSION ERROR
CONTROL CHARACTERS
In order to govern the automatic retransmission of information in which an error has been detected, a number of special characters are used—sometimes sequences of characters.

In one typical system characters labeled ACK, NAK, CAN, and DEL are used. The ACK code is used by the receiver to signal the transmitter that a block of code had been received correctly. Similarly, the NAK code is sent by the receiving terminal to tell the transmitter that a block of code received had an error in it. When the transmitter sends a block of code on most systems, it will wait before it sends the next one until the ACK or NAK control character is received from the transmitter. If ACK is received, it will proceed normally; if NAK, it will resend the block in error.

The transmitter itself will commonly do some error checking on what it sends. It is possible that the circuits doing this will detect an error in a message on which transmission has already begun. The transmitter must then cancel the message, and so it sends a CAN character. The DEL character is normally a character which should be totally ignored. It is used to delete characters already punched in paper tape, by punching a hole in every position.

The transmitting and receiving machines have circuits designed to detect these special characters.

ODD–EVEN
RECORD COUNT

It is possible that the control characters themselves, or end-of-transmission characters, could be invalidated by a noise error. If this happens then there is a danger that a complete message might be lost, or two messages inadvertently joined together. It is possible that during the automatic retransmission process a message could be erroneously sent twice. To prevent these errors, an odd–even count may be kept of the records transmitted.

Sometimes at the start of a block a control character is sent to indicate whether this is an odd-numbered or even-numbered block. On some systems two alternative start-of-transmission characters are used. With other schemes, it is the ACK characters which contain this odd–even check. Two different ACK-type signals may be sent: ACK 0 and ACK 1. In the ASCII (American Standard Code for Information Interchange) code, there is only one ACK character and so if this is used a two-character sequence may be employed.

If an odd-numbered block does not follow an even-numbered block, then the block following the last correct block will be retransmitted. It is very improbable indeed that two blocks could be lost together, or two blocks transmitted twice in such a manner that the odd–even count would not detect the error. However, some systems use a serial number to check that this has not happened, instead of the odd–even count. The serial number may be examined by hardware, but often it is a check that is applied by a computer program and one of its main values is to bridge the continuity gap when a terminal computer or other hardware failure occurs. During the period of recovery from such a failure there is a danger of losing or double-processing a transaction.

23 LINE TERMINATION EQUIPMENT FOR DATA TRANSMISSION[1]

We have now seen that the signal we send down a communication line can travel to its destination by a wide variety of possible means. When it disappears into our wall plaster on its telephone or telegraph wires we are not necessarily sure how it is going to travel. It may go by itself on a wire circuit, or it may be huddled with hundreds of other signals on coaxial cable or microwave. It may even race 22,300 miles into space to be beamed back by a satellite. When my time-sharing terminal chatters back to me after a pause of a second or so I do not know how the data have been transmitted.

Whatever way the signal has traveled, though, for a telephone channel the curve of attenuation against frequency is likely to look more or less like that in Fig. 23.1. Telephone channels are engineered to this specification whether they are satellite channels or open-wire pairs singing into the wind between wooden poles. It is therefore into this frequency range that we must fit our signal.

MODEMS AND DATA SETS   Data put out by computer circuits are usually in the form of rectangular pulses, something like those in Fig. 23.2. We may want to send just one set of such pulses down the telephone line, or possibly more than one at the same time with systems using slow machines. We may be content to transmit in one direction only, or we may wish to transmit in both directions at the same time. Line termination equipment is needed to enable signals such as those in Fig. 23.2 to travel down lines having charac-

---

[1] For details of data devices attached to the lines, and line organization, see *Teleprocessing Network Organization* by James Martin, Prentice-Hall, Englewood Cliffs, N.J., in press.

teristics such as that in Fig. 23.1, in the optimum manner. Often the line termination equipment is simply a modem (data set) as discussed in Chapters 10 and 13.

The lowest frequencies in Fig. 23.1 are attenuated severely. In fact, the line will not pass DC current. As the computer output in Fig. 23.2 consists of a series of DC pulses, it would not be sent over the line without modification. In any case, as was indicated in Chapter 13, it would be inefficient to send this waveform as it stands even if the channel did transmit DC current, as a noncarrier circuit might. The modulation process enables the maximum amount of data to be packed into the space of Fig. 23.1, and it gives it as much protection as possible from the noise and distortion on the line—there being a tradeoff between noise protection and speed.

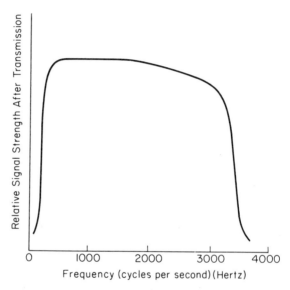

Figure 23.1

As stated in Chapter 10, there are two quite distinct and physically separate places at which modulation occurs. The reader should distinguish clearly between these to avoid confusion. First, they are used by the common carriers in their plant to multiplex many signals together for transmission over a medium with a bandwidth sufficiently wide to carry several or many channels. This was illustrated in Figs. 10.5 and 15.3. The computer system designer has no say in this area. He merely has to use the channels in the form provided. Second, a modem or data set is used, as was shown in Fig. 10.6, to convert a signal like the one we have described so that it can be sent over a given channel efficiently.

There are a variety of different modulation schemes in use. These differ in their cost, speed, reliability, and tolerance to noise and distortion. One of the design decisions that may be necessary in planning a computer system is the selection of appropriate modems or data sets for that application. The choice depends partly on the characteristics of the communications links themselves, and partly on computer systems considerations such as whether speed is more important than error-free operation, the significance of cost, breakdown-free operation and the facilities for maintenance.

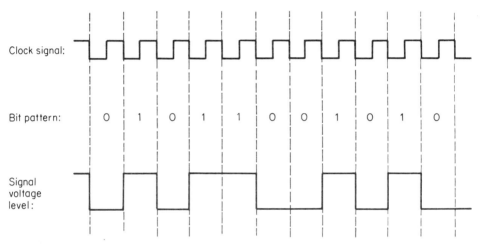

Figure 23.2

In its most elementary form, modulation of the pulse train in Fig. 23.2 can simply replace the "zero" condition on the line by one amplitude, frequency, or phase of a carrier and the "one" condition by another. CCITT established a recommended set of equivalent binary conditions, as shown in Table 23.1.

The properties of the communication links provided by different common carriers or on different tariffs vary considerably. A private line differs from public lines. Different grades of private lines can be provided. Voice lines have different grades of conditioning. Public lines vary between one country and another, and this can be a problem in designing data transmission networks that, for example, span Europe or link into the transatlantic cable. A modem that gives an optimum performance on one type of telephone line may be unworkable, or far from optimum, on another.

The differences are partially due to the frequencies available for transmitting, the bandwidth and the signaling frequencies. As was illustrated in Figs. 17.2 and 17.3, the signaling frequencies of public telephone lines provided by the GPO in England, and the Bell System in the United States differ considerably, and thus the modem characteristics differ. A good private

Table 23.1. CCITT SUMMARY TABLE OF EQUIVALENCE IN TWO-CONDITION CODES.*

	Digit 0 "Start" signal in start–stop code. Line available condition in telex switching. "Space" element of start–stop code. Condition A	Digit 1 "Stop" signal in start–stop code. Line idle condition in telex switching. "Mark" element of start–stop code. Condition Z
Telegraph-like single current signaling (as in Fig. 6.1)	No current	Positive current
Telegraph-like double current signaling (Fig. 6.1)	Negative current	Positive current
Amplitude modulation (Fig. 13.1)	Tone-off	Tone-on
Frequency modulation (Fig. 13.1)	High frequency	Low frequency
Phase modulation with reference phase (Chapter 13)	Opposite phase to the reference phase	Reference phase
Differential phase modulation (Chapter 13)	Inversion of the phase	No-phase inversion
Perforation in tape	No perforation	Perforation

Note. The standardization described in this recommendation is general and applies to any two-condition transmission, whether over telegraph-type circuits or over circuits of the telephone type, making use of electromechanical or electronic devices.

*CCITT data transmission recommendation V.I., 1961 and 1964.

speech line may have a wider bandwidth than either of these, and a line provided specially for data transmission may be wider still. The type and quantity of noise encountered creates a further difference. Lines passing through public switching centers, especially where an old plant is in use, pick up pulses of noise which may add or delete bits. Here, phase modulation may give better protection from impulse noise. Long lines will suffer more envelope delay distortion than short lines and thus may have more affect on phase modulation systems.

A variety of modulation systems have been developed in recent years both for public and private lines, and also for other types of communication link such as radio and microwave, where modulation was used long before it was needed on telephone lines. Various methods have their devotees and it is interesting to consider the arguments submitted in support of different methods. The speed at which data can be sent over a given voice line has been steadily increasing over the last few years, and this increase is largely a result of improved modem design. It is an area which is still developing fast. The art of modem design involves considerable ingenuity and it seems likely that their development will continue to progress in the 1970's.

On some lines it is not important to achieve the maximum speed of which the line is capable. Often the data processing devices themselves set the maximum. IBM's 1050 series of terminals (Fig. 2.3), for example, are frequently installed on voice lines, often because of the convenience of using telephone dialing on the public network or of using a company's telephone tie line. The 1050 series transmits at 14.8 characters per second—a speed geared to the technology of electric typewriters—yet the public phone lines are capable of transmitting 120 such characters, or more with good modems. Speed, then, is certainly not a consideration in the design of a modem for using the 1050 on a telephone line. Low cost and error-free operation would dominate the design instead.

TRANSMISSION
WITHOUT MODEMS
Modems are not necessarily used on noncarrier lines, though here, still, they can increase greatly the speed of transmission. Telegraph links used to be simple electrical paths with no multiplexing, and so a rectangular pulse train from the teleprinter is sent directly down the circuit. Today many telegraph links are multiplexed, and when this is so the common carrier does the modulation necessary, either at the teleprinter machine itself or at the central office or location where the multiplexing takes place.

Many computer users need to have data transmission lines within their own premises, and privately owned lines linking two buildings near to each other. The terms "in-plant" and "out-plant" system are used. The former means that common carrier lines are not used and usually the communication links are within one plant or localized area. "Out-plant" implies that common carrier lines are used. In-plant lines will normally not use frequency-division multiplexing in the way the common carriers do. (They may use a different form of multiplexing device for scanning instruments or terminals). They will normally be a straightforward copper path, possibly coaxial cable, connecting the points in question. Private links of this type are often installed by a firm's own engineers. Sometimes they are also provided by telecommunication companies, but external to any major telecommunication network.

Devices which use these lines usually operate by the simple making and breaking of relay contacts, or the sending of rectangular pulse trains such as those in Fig. 23.2. No modulation is needed. Over a wire pair a few miles in length, DC pulses can be sent at speeds up to about 300 bits per second. As we noted in Chapter 7, a system could have many terminals in a local area connected to a computer or a concentrator, each operating at typewriter speeds, and using DC signaling so as to avoid the cost of modems.

FULL DUPLEX VS.
HALF DUPLEX

Over a given physical line, the terminal equipment may be designed so that it can either transmit in both directions at once—*full-duplex* transmission—or else so that it can transmit in either direction but not both at the same time—*half duplex*. It is possible also to have simplex transmission which can take place in one direction only, but this is rarely used for data transmission as there is no easy way of controlling the flow of data. If the receiving machine breaks down or loses some of the data, this cannot be conveyed to the transmitting machine. All four-wire facilities are capable of full-duplex working though sometimes one finds them used in a half-duplex manner. Some two-wire facilities can only operate in a half-duplex mode, though over many two-wire links full-duplex operation is possible at a lower speed, given an appropriately designed data set at each end.

An input/output terminal or a computer line adapter will work somewhat differently depending upon which of these possibilities is used. Where full-duplex transmission is employed it may be used either to send data streams in both directions at the same time, or to send data in one direction and control signals in the other. The control signals would govern the flow of data and would be used for error control. Data at the transmitting end would be held until the receiving end indicated that it had been received correctly. If it was not received correctly, the control signal would indicate this and it would be retransmitted. Control signals would ensure that no two terminals transmit at once on a line with many terminals, and would organize the sequence of transmission.

Simultaneous transmission in two directions can be obtained on a two-wire line by using two separate frequency bands. One is used for transmission in one direction and the other for the opposite direction. By keeping the signals strictly separated in frequency, they can be prevented from interfering with each other.

The two bands may not be of the same bandwidth. A much larger channel capacity is needed for sending data than for sending the return signals which control the flow of data. If, therefore, data are to be sent in one direction only, the majority of the line bandwidth can be used for data. Figure 23.3 illustrates a possible division of line frequencies for this purpose. The band used for data is much wider than that used for control signals traveling in the opposite direction. On a line such as this, the data and control signal directions may reverse together when information is to be sent in the opposite direction. The bands used in Fig. 23.3 avoid the line's signaling frequency. A more efficient, but probably more expensive, scheme would use the whole bandwidth, randomizing the data transmitted so that they would not trigger the line's signal detection circuits (Chapter 17). One system (not available commercially at the time of writing) permits transmission of data at 3600 bits per second in one direction and provides a simultaneous return path for control signals at 150 bits per second.

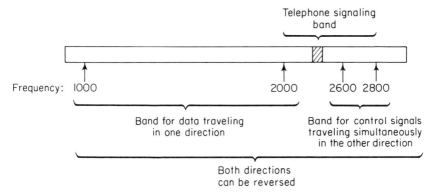

Fig. 23.3. The bandwidth of public telephone lines (Great Britain) split into a band for data traveling in one direction and a band for control signals in the others.

Many data processing situations are not able to take advantage of the facility to transmit streams of data in both directions at the same time. Consequently, where full-duplex transmission is used, it is often with data traveling in one direction only, and the other direction being used for control signals.

PARALLEL VS. Digital data can be sent over communication
SERIAL lines either in a serial mode or a parallel mode.
TRANSMISSION The stream of data is often divided into characters as with the characters printed by a teleprinter. The characters are composed of bits. This stream may be sent either serial-by-character, serial-by-bit; or serial-by-character, parallel-by-bit.

Let us suppose that the characters are composed of six bits each. The serial-by-character, parallel-by-bit system must then transmit six bits at once. This is done on some terminals by using six separate communication paths usually with a seventh for control purposes. It may, for example, require eight separate wires. This is not likely to be done on long-distance low-speed lines, as it would be more expensive than other means. A brief look at the line costs in the last chapter will indicate that several low-speed lines are more expensive than one higher speed line. This form of parallel transmission is occasionally used between machines some miles apart when it is not possible to obtain a broadband link such as an AT&T Series 8000 line (see Chapter 5).

Parallel wire transmission does, however, have the advantage that it can lower the terminal cost somewhat. No circuitry is needed in the terminals for deciding which bits are which in a character. Parallel wire transmission is therefore commonly used over short distances where the wires are laid down by the user. For data collection terminals in a factory, for example, which connect to a computer or other machine within that factory, bunches of wires are often installed to connect the machines in a parallel fashion. The economics of what line connections are employed changes when the lines are laid down by the user.

Some machines are designed for parallel-by-bit transmission, but separate parallel wires are not used to connect them. Instead, the bits travel simultaneously using different frequency bands on the same communication path. This can be regarded as a form of *frequency-division multiplexing*, as discussed in Chapter 15 and illustrated in Fig. 10.4. One physical channel is split up into several effective channels each operating on a different frequency band.

In similar manner, a data set is sometimes used to provide parallel channels *for different machines*, over a single telephone line or other communication path. IBM, for example, manufactures a "Shared-line Adapter" designed to derive four subchannels from a leased voice line. Over each subchannel, machines of the speed of an IBM 1050 can transmit at about 135 bits per second. The subchannels operate over approximately the following frequency ranges:

Subchannel 1:   735–1075 Hertz
Subchannel 2:   1145–1485 Hertz
Subchannel 3:   1555–1895 Hertz
Subchannel 4:   1965–2305 Hertz

It will be seen that these fit easily into the relatively flat portion of the attenuation-frequency curve of the telephone line, and avoid the United States signaling frequencies (Fig. 17.2). They would not, however, avoid the British signaling frequencies (Fig. 17.3) and so this machine would not be permitted in Britain's public lines without redesign.

Frequency shift keying is used in each subchannel, a "1" bit or stop signal being sent as a low frequency and a "0" bit or start signal being sent as a high frequency. Each subchannel is filtered to prevent stray frequencies interfering with the other channels. The filters and frequencies used are shown in Fig. 23.4. The reader should note the similarity between this figure and Fig. 15.5 which illustrates the common carriers' frequency-division multiplexing.

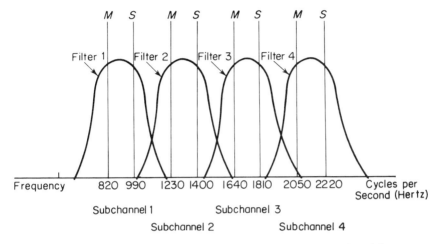

Fig. 23.4. Frequency allocations and filter ranges for IBM shared-line adapter. *Redrawn from IBM Manual No. 226–3003: Field Engineering Manual on IBM Line Adapters (Modems). IBM Systems Development Division, 1966.*

The Collins "Kineplex" TE-202 data set used four-phase modulation of 20 separate carriers, spaced 100 cycles per second apart, in the range from 700 to 2700 cycles, in a leased voice channel. In this way it could transmit 40 separate teletype signals over one conditioned voice line. Each carrier was modulated with two 75-bit-per-second signals. A synchronizing signal at 2900 cycles was also transmitted.

MULTITONE
TRANSMISSION
Another form of parallel transmission uses tones such as those generated by a push-button telephone. A Bell System touch-tone telephone keyboard can transmit eight possible audible frequencies: 697, 770, 852, 941, 1209, 1336, 1477, and 1633. The pressing of any one key produces a discordant combination of two of these frequencies one from the first four and one from the second. The Bell System 400 series data sets use the same eight frequencies plus others, and to these a data transmission device operating at 10 characters per second, or less, may be connected. This is illustrated in Fig. 23.5. The IBM 1001 shown in Fig. 23.6 operates in this manner. A code is used in which two frequencies out of the eight possible are trans-

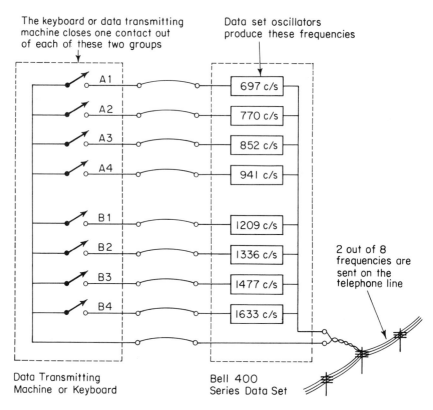

Fig. 23.5. Parallel transmission using the Bell 400 series data sets.

Fig. 23.6. The IBM 1001 terminal (left) transmits card and keyboard data using multifrequency tones as in Fig. 23.7.

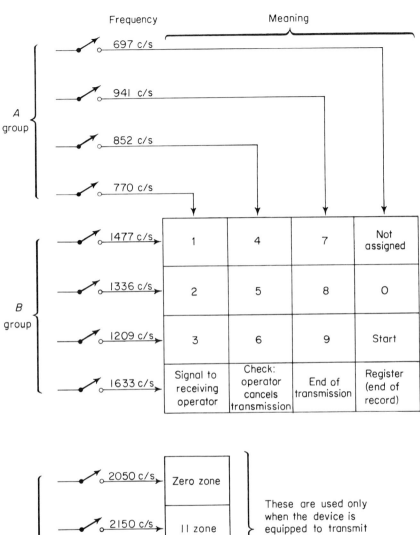

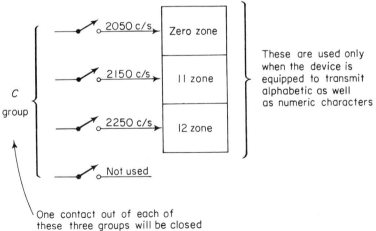

One contact out of each of
these three groups will be closed

Fig. 23.7. An example of coding using 3 out of 12 parallel multifrequency transmissions.

401

mitted at any one instant. This gives 16 possible combinations that can be transmitted. It gives some measure of transmission error detection, in that a fault causing only one, or more than two, frequencies to be received will be noted as an error but this is not comprehensive error detection as in a four-out-of-eight code. This code does not have enough combinations for alphabetic transmission. When cards with alphanumeric punches are to be transmitted on the IBM 1001, three more frequencies are needed, one for each alphabetic "zone" punch. The coding remains the same as we have discussed, but now an extra (third) frequency can be sent. A frequency from the third (C) group can also be transmitted by itself. The way the characters are coded is shown in Fig. 23.7. The C-group frequencies are used when an alphabetic character is to be sent. The 12 "zone" combined with a digit gives the letters A to I, as on the punched cards. The 11 "zone" gives J to R, and the zero "zone," S to Z, and a special character composed of an 0 and 1 punch.

It should be noted that the frequencies used here avoid the signaling frequencies used on the American public telephone network. Such machines can therefore be used on a dial-up line. However, again, the signaling frequencies of the British public network (Fig. 17.3) are not avoided, even with the machine which transmits numeric characters only. Therefore, such machines can only be used on private lines in England. This problem could easily be solved by rebuilding the data set to use different frequencies, however, at the time of writing no suitable data set is on the market. This same problem applies also to many other countries.

ACOUSTICAL COUPLING

Where audible tones are used, there is no need to have, as with the above machines, a direct wire connection to the communication line. Instead, acoustical coupling can be used, in which the signals are converted into sound of the frequencies illustrated in Fig. 23.1. These sounds are picked up by an ordinary telephone microphone and reproduced at the far end of the connection by a telephone earpiece. They are then converted back into data signals. Acoustical coupling is somewhat less efficient than direct coupling. At the time of writing, it is used for transmitting between relatively slow machines such as typewriter-like terminals.

In a typical acoustical-coupling device the telephone handpiece fits in a special cradle as shown in Fig. 23.8. An advantage of acoustical coupling is that the terminal can easily be made portable. A small terminal could be made to transmit to a computer from a public call box. Nondigital machines also use acoustical coupling. Documents can be copied at a distance with a Xerox machine in this way. Figure 2.1 shows an acoustically coupled tape reader.

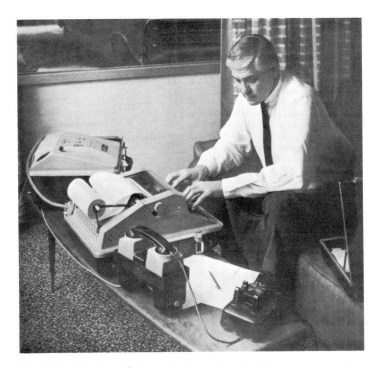

Fig. 23.8. A Dataport® terminal. *Reproduced with permission of the Vernitron Corporation, Farmingdale, New York.*

Although there is no electrical connection to the telephone lines, it is still possible for acoustically coupled machines to interfere with the public network's signaling, as with a directly coupled device. Also severe cross talk can be caused on a multiplexed link by the transmission of a continuous frequency, as with a repetitive data pattern. It is therefore desirable that the coupling device randomizes the signal before it is sent, though not all devices do so today.

SYNCHRONOUS VS. ASYNCHRONOUS TRANSMISSION

Data transmission can be either *synchronous* or *asynchronous*. With synchronous transmission, characters are sent in a continuous stream. A block of perhaps 100 characters or more may be sent at one time and for the duration of that block the receiving terminal must be exactly in phase with the transmitting terminal. With asynchronous transmission, sometimes referred to as "start–stop," one character is sent at a time. The character is initialized by a START signal, shown in Fig. 23.9 as a "0" condition on the line, and terminated by a STOP signal, here a "1" condition on the line. The pulses between these two give the bits of

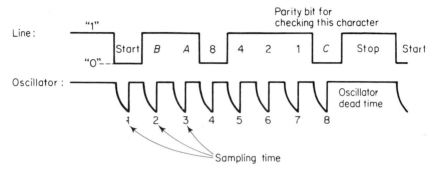

Fig. 23.9. Start-stop transmission.

which the character is composed. Between characters the line is in a "1" condition. As a START bit switches it to "0," the receiving machine starts sampling the bits.

An example of start–stop signaling was given in Chapter 6 where telegraph machines were discussed. All telegraph machines operate with start–stop transmission and a simplified example of such a mechanism was shown in Fig. 6.6. Many data transmission devices made by the computer manufacturers also use start–stop transmission sometimes working at considerably higher speeds than telegraph machines. On these machines the pulses received may be sampled electronically as indicated in Fig. 23.9. The sampling is done at regular intervals determined by an oscillator.

Start–stop transmission is usually used on keyboard services which do not have a buffer, and on which the operator sends characters along the line at more or less random intervals as she happens to press the keys. The START pulse initiates the sampling and thus there can be an indeterminate interval between the characters. Characters are transmitted when the operator's finger presses the keys. If the operator pauses for several seconds between one keystroke and the next, the line will remain in the "1" condition for this period of time.

Start–stop machines are generally less expensive to produce than synchronous machines, and for this reason many machines which transmit card-to-card or paper-tape-to-printer, card-to-computer, and so on, are also start–stop although the character stream does not have the pauses between characters a keyboard transmission has.

SYNCHRONOUS
TRANSMISSION
When machines transmit to each other continuously with regular timing, *synchronous* transmission can give the most efficient line utilization. Here the bits of one character are followed immediately by those

of the next. Between characters there are no START or STOP bits and no pauses. The stream of characters of this type is divided into blocks. Devices using synchronous transmission have a wide variety of block lengths. The block size may vary from a few characters to many hundreds of characters. Often it relates to the physical nature of the data medium. For example, in the transmission of punched cards it is convenient to use 80 characters as the maximum block length as there are that many characters per card. Similarly, the length of print lines, the size of buffers, the number of characters in records, or some such system consideration may determine the block size. Some time is taken up between the transmission of one block and the next and so the larger the block length, in general, the faster the overall transmission.

On many systems the synchronization of the transmitting and receiving machines is controlled by oscillators. Before a block is sent, the oscillator of the receiving machine must be brought exactly into phase with the oscillator of the transmitting machine. This is done by sending a synchronization pattern at the start of the block. If this were not done the receiving device would not be able to tell which bit received was the first bit in a character, which the second, and so on. Once the oscillators at each end are synchronized, they will remain so until the end of the block. Oscillators do, however, drift apart very slightly in frequency. This drift is very low if highly stable oscillators are used, but with those low enough in price to be used in quantity in input–output units it will be significant. Oscillators in common use in these machines are likely to be accurate to about one part in 100,000. If they are sampling the transmission 2500 times per second, say, then they are likely to stay in synchronization for a time of the order of 20 seconds. Most data processing machines resynchronize their oscillators every one or two seconds for safety. Synchronization can also be maintained by "framing" blocks and carrying timing information in the frames as in time-division multiplexing (Fig. 15.9).

In addition to giving faster transmission because no START and STOP bits are needed between characters, synchronous transmission permits higher speed modulation techniques to be used. Multilevel signaling can be used (Fig. 13.8) whereas this is not normally used in start-stop transmission. The signal can be randomized to prevent repetitive codes causing harmful interference with other telephone users, and hence a higher transmission level can be tolerated, giving a better signal-to-noise ratio. (Many synchronous data sets do not do this as yet.) On high-speed circuits, synchronous transmission can tolerate a higher degree of jitter and distortion than start–stop transmission, and for this reason it is usually used.

Synchronous transmission can give better protection from errors. At the end of each block an error-checking pattern will be transmitted. The coding of this is selected to give the maximum protection from noise errors on the line. As well as the error-code at the end of the block, each character may also have parity bit for checking as does the character in Fig. 23.9. This, however, is often not done, and an end-of-block check is used alone. A parity bit is not too useful as a protection against communication line errors. It is an extremely useful protection against loss of bits in the core of a computer because there it is likely that only one bit will be lost at a time. On a communication line however, several bits are often lost at once because of a noise impulse or dropout (Fig. 21.6). Where two, four, or six bits are changed in a character, a parity check will not detect this. Some form of block is therefore desirable which can detect the loss of several consecutive bits. The faster the transmission, the more likely is the loss of more than one adjacent bit, and thus the block check becomes more important with faster transmission. Start–stop transmission may also have a block check.

HIGH-SPEED LINE TERMINATION   Data sets are available for transmitting over wideband lines. The Bell System Data Set 301B, for example, is designed for transmission at 40,800 bits per second over a Series 8000 line. Transmission in both directions simultaneously is possible. The frequency range 10.2 to 51 kilohertz is used with four-phase modulation of a 30.6-kilohertz carrier. This can be on the multiplex carrier facilities discussed in earlier chapters or it can be over non-loaded cable pairs with wideband amplifiers. Four local loops have been used to carry the signal to the subscribers' premises. Included with these facilities is a voice channel for coordination purposes.

With high-speed data transmission, maintaining synchronization becomes a bigger problem than at low speeds. The Bell 301 B data set can do this either with its own internal oscillators or by means of the data machine providing a bit synchronization signal which consists in essence of a 40.8-kilohertz $\pm$ 0.01 % square wave.

Parallel transmission is employed by the Collins TE-217A Adaptive Kineplex Communication Modem. In this, eight carrier frequencies are used in a 48-kilohertz bandwidth channel. Each of these frequencies is four-phase modulated by two binary channels, and simultaneously a third binary channel is obtained by amplitude modulation of the carrier. This gives 24 channels. The nominal data rate of each channel is 3850 bits per second, giving a total data rate of 92,400 bits per second. The transmission rate can, however, be varied on this modem to compensate for variations in the characteristics of the line such as noise and amplitude, frequency and phase stability.

24 CONVERSATIONS WITH COMPUTERS[1]

While in many applications of communication lines data is sent in *batches,* there are a rapidly growing number of real-time systems in which a man carries on some form of "conversation" with a distant machine. To end this book, let us examine some of these conversations and their line requirements. Because of the state of the art in today's computer programming, very precise language has to be used in communicating with a computer. The reader may ask, "What exactly do you say to the computer and what does it say back and what communications facilities are needed for this?"

When studying these examples, the reader should relate the amount of data that is passing to the speed and cost of the communication line. For illustration, some typical figures for the cost of a leased 100-mile communication line with its terminations (without including the machines that use it) are shown in Table 24.1.

If the computer responds with a reply of 300 characters (perhaps including spaces on the line), this, typically, would take 50 seconds over a 50-baud line, 30 seconds over a 75-baud line and 20 seconds on the fastest subvoice grade line. These are sufficiently slow to inhibit many types of real-time conversation. Over a voice line (a conventional telephone line), the reply would only take two seconds, however, providing the output machine was fast enough to handle this. Over a conditioned voice line it would take one second. A voice line, possibly conditioned, possibly not, is likely to be used in this situation. On the other hand, if the replies have an average length of 30 characters, a teletype line would suffice.

---

[1] Some of the examples in this chapter are taken from the author's previous book *Design of Real-Time Computer Systems.* Englewood Cliffs, New Jersey, Prentice-Hall, 1967. The reader is referred to this work for more detail.

Table 24.1*

	Speed in bits per second	Typical line speed in characters per second	Typical cost per month of half-duplex 100-mile line ($)		
			USA	England	Germany
Sub-voice grade lines	50	6		132	270
	75	10	163		
	100	12		166	480
	180	15	186		585
Voice grade lines	1200	150	252	329	745
"Conditioned" voice grade lines	2400	300	280		
Wideband channel	(48 kilohertz)	5000	2000	2100	

*Note these figures are very approximate as several factors not listed in this simplified table could cause them to vary, and the prices quoted are likely to change considerably. The prices are for monthly leasing charges and do not include installation charge.

The wideband channel listed would not normally be considered for transmitting characters in a man-machine conversation. The eye cannot read at speeds near to 5000 characters per second, though it might scan a page such as that in a telephone directory at this speed. However, if the reply were in the form of a picture such as those commonly used on devices using a screen and light pen, it might require a large number of bits, perhaps 20,000 or more to compose the picture. In this case, conversation may be too slow with a voice channel and a wideband channel would be needed. Because of the expense of wideband channels, and in some cases the difficulty in obtaining them, the screens attached to distant computers are often of the type that display characters only, not pictures. In those spectacular man-machine conversations where computer-generated pictures are involved, the screen unit is usually close to a computer. It may, however, be a small peripheral computer which is, itself, remotely connected to a larger machine.

For clarification of the illustrations below, the data the operator keys in are in **heavy print,** and the computer responses are in *italics*.

INVOICE PREPARATION   First, a simple example, an invoice is prepared on a typewriter-like terminal. The operator keys in only the customer number and the part numbers and quantities, as shown in Fig. 24.1. The computer prints the rest in front of her on preprinted invoice stationary. The computer extends the invoice, records the data in its customer files, makes adjustments to the stock records noting whether any reordering is needed, and deals with any exceptional conditions such as credit limit exceeded. Most operator errors

BONNINGTON COSMETICS
287–9 Castle St., London, S.W.17.

0023108

Sold to
THE DRUGGIST
BENTYRE ROAD,
BUDE, CORNWALL

Deliver to
THE DRUGGIST
BENTYRE ROAD,
BUDE, CORNWALL

Invoice

Territory	Invoice date	Invoice No	Order No	Despatch method	Despatch date	P. Tax Reg. No.
09	30.04.65	20048	587691	VAN	17.01.64	

Quantity	Item No.	Item description	Retail price incl. tax	Net price per doz	Purchase tax	Goods value
120	211	PERFUME COLUMBINARY W9	4 6	26 0	6 19 5	13 0 0
24	615	NAIL ENAMEL STRIPPER	3 11	21 6	1 3 1	2 3 0
8	513	NAIL ENAMEL RACING RED	4 9	26 0	9 4	17 4
12	223	HAND CARE MY SKIN	5 9	32 6	17 5	1 12 6
		DISCOUNT				17 8

56	Total quantity		Total purchase tax	Total goods value
			9 9 3	16 15 2

Total due for payment: 26 4 5

Figure 24.1

can be controlled as they occur. Self-checking numbers may be used for customer numbers and part numbers. The operator can enter special rates or comments if necessary. In this example, teletype speeds are quite acceptable.

AIRLINE RESERVATIONS The early airline-reservation systems which handled passenger names and details on-line used terminals which operated at typewriter speeds. This was true also of hotel-booking systems and other systems which enquire about and update a specific file of data. Use of these speeds limited the length and hence the complexity of the response that was permissible from the computer. Because of this, considerable complexity had to be built into the terminals. Airline terminals, and those for other applications, before 1966 had elaborate and expensive devices for working with matrix cards (Fig. 24.4). The set of matrix cards at each terminal gave much of the information that was in the airline timetable. Airline systems installed in 1968 and after used a less expensive terminal with a display tube. The matrix cards disappeared and the data they gave were stored in the computer files instead, and were (more conveniently) updated at the computer center. Somewhat lengthier messages had to be sent from the computer to the display screen, and the communication costs were somewhat higher, terminals as these are faster and in many cases cheaper than typewriters. The following example is taken from Pan American Airways' PANAMAC system. An agent in Picadilly, London, England, shown in Fig. 24.2, is conversing with an IBM 7080 computer in New York at the same time as handling a customer. The responses from across the Atlantic are typed after a pause of about a second.

The agent selects a matrix card relating to the journey the passenger wishes to make and fits it into place in the terminal shown in Fig. 24.4. She presses keys above the card to indicate to the computer the departure point of the flight. She also keys in the date on which the customer wants to fly

Fig. 24.2. Transatlantic conversation. Many terminals, such as these in London, are attached to the transatlantic cable and a response is obtained in less than three seconds from Pan American's reservation computers in New York.

and the number of seats required and presses a key indicating that she wants to know the *availability* of such seats. The computer checks the validity of this date. Lights at the side of the card light up to indicate those flights which meet the requirements.

The agent passes this information on to the customer. The customer selects a flight he would like to travel on, and the agent presses a button adjacent to one of the lights which came on. She presses a key indicating that she wishes to sell these seats, and the computer decreases the record of seat availability by the appropriate number. The computer now prints out details of the sale on the terminal typewriter as shown in Fig. 24.3.

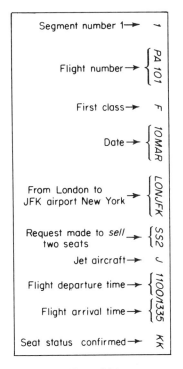

Figure 24.3

If the customer had wanted to make a longer journey of several segments, the print-out might look as shown in Fig. 24.5.

The agent will compare these print-outs with the customer's requests to ensure that the correct itinerary has been booked. She must then enter his name and other relevant details. The keyboard for doing this is basically a typewriter keyboard, but the top row of keys also has labels, NAME, PHONE, REVD, RMKS, and so on, for entering passenger details.

The conversation with the machine might go as shown in Fig. 24.6, in which General and Mrs. H.F. Owen-Evans are booking a return trip to New York.

Certain entries are obligatory. If, for example, the agent left out the telephone entry, the computer would reply:

TELEPHONE ENTRY OMITTED

If the passenger has no telephone, the agent must type in: 4 **NIL**.

When the entry is correct the machine will file it away, typing out the message *OK*, and, if General or Mrs. H.F. Owen-Evans comes into a Pan American office or phones up about the trip, the first action of the agent will be to display their "passenger name record" as shown in Fig. 24.7.

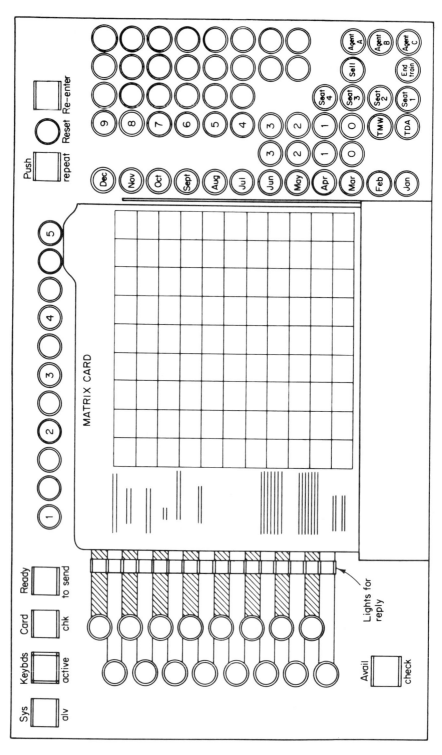

Figure 24.4

412

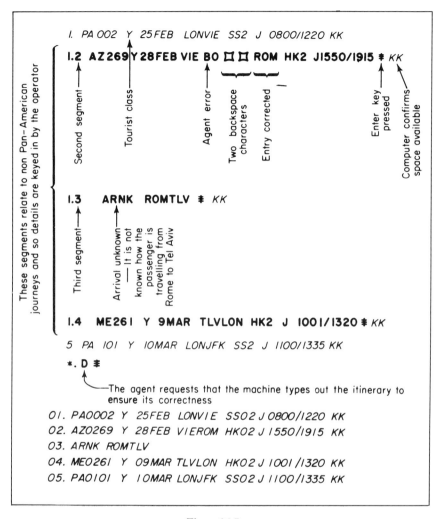

I. PA 002   Y   25 FEB   LONVIE   SS2   J   0800/1220 KK

I.2 AZ 269 Y 28FEB VIE BO ⌑ ⌑ ROM HK2 J1550/1915 ✳ KK

These segments relate to non Pan-American journeys and so details are keyed in by the operator

Second segment

Tourist class

Agent error

Two backspace characters

Entry corrected

Enter key pressed

Computer confirms space available

I.3   ARNK   ROMTLV ✳ KK

Third segment

Arrival unknown — It is not known how the passenger is travelling from Rome to Tel Aviv

I.4   ME261   Y 9MAR   TLVLON HK2   J   1001/1320 ✳ KK

5   PA 101   Y   10MAR   LONJFK   SS2   J   1100/1335 KK

✳. D ✳

—The agent requests that the machine types out the itinerary to ensure its correctness

01. PA0002 Y 25FEB LONVIE SS02 J 0800/1220 KK
02. AZ0269 Y 28FEB VIEROM HK02 J 1550/1915 KK
03. ARNK ROMTLV
04. ME0261 Y 09MAR TLVLON HK02 J 1001 /1320 KK
05. PA0101 Y 10MAR LONJFK SS02 J 1100/1335 KK

Figure 24.5

One of the main advantages of using a cathode-ray tube display for man–machine conversation is that the response can come back very rapidly. The typewriter, operating, as it does, at speeds of about fifteen characters per second or less, produces information at a much slower rate than that at which a human being can digest it. The telephone lines used for data transmission can pour out written information at speeds roughly equivalent to human scanning and speaking rates. A display tube on a telephone line is therefore a better facility for conversing with a machine, particularly when the subject is one about which the machine has a lot to say.

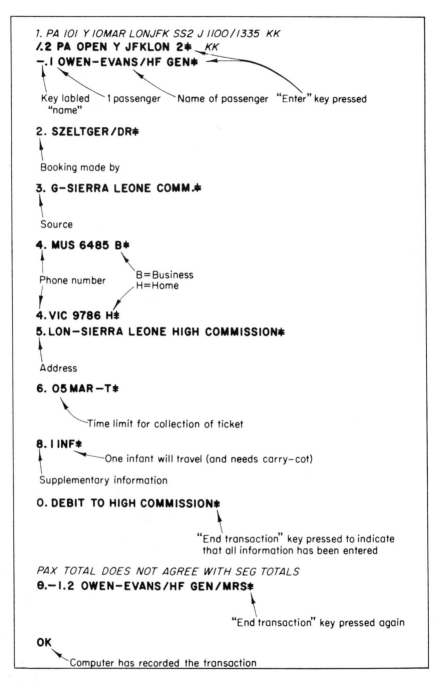

Figure 24.6

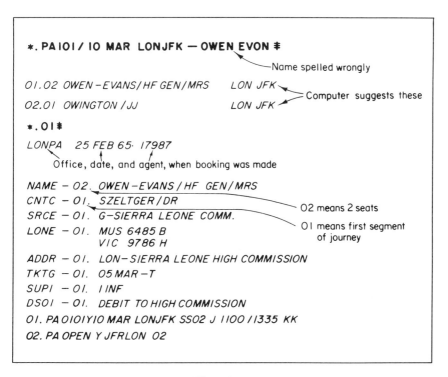

Figure 24.7

The conversation between man and machine in making a booking with a display tube might look something like that shown in Fig. 24.8. The agent selects the flight she wants (Fig. 24.9), and the computer condenses the contents of the screen to one line, eliminating all the unwanted data (Fig. 24.10). If the desired flight had not been among the four shown, the girl would have asked for further possible flights to be displayed.

The agent can now enter passenger details as before. The computer acknowledges receipt of each detail line by displaying an asterisk. When an agent makes a mistake which is picked up by the computer, she modifies it and the screen is cleaned up appropriately.

When an agent displays an itinerary booked previously in order to make a change in it, the computer will give her as much help as possible. She may wish to change segment 3, so she types in: **X3.**

The computer then flashes the message on the screen:

NEXT SEGMENT ENTRY REPLACES 3

She then types in the change, and, as always, the computer checks it. When the agent and the passenger are satisfied with the change, she displays

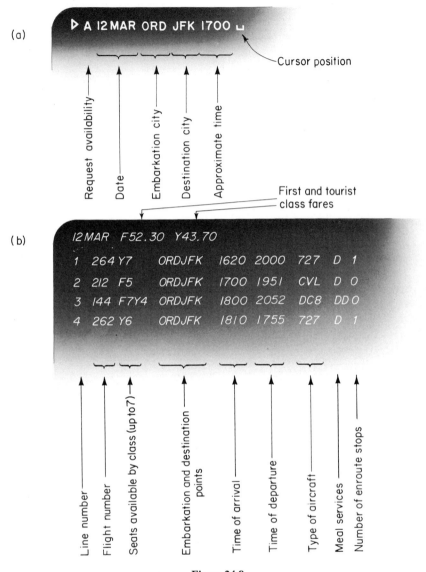

Figure 24.8

the amended passenger record, and so condenses and cleans up the information on the screen.

In attempting to display or modify the record of a passenger who telephones or calls in the airline office, the girl operating the terminal may spell the name incorrectly, or differently to have it as originally input. The computer will then automatically display similar names on that flight, as in

Fig. 24.11. If the computer does not find the correct name at the first attempt, the operator will tell it to search further.

Many codes other than those illustrated are used on an airline reservation system. The array of codes is complicated for the agent to learn and so must be made as similar as possible to codes she already knows and understands. A standard set of teletype codes is in use in the airlines, and the new on-line language is constructed so as to resemble this. It is a general principle when designing any such language that it should be *as natural as possible* for the operator to use. As much familiarity as possible must be built into the codes.

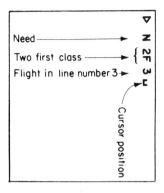

Figure 24.9

Figure 24.10

CALCULATIONS Time-sharing systems are enabling engineers and other personnel to do calculations and obtain quick answers. Sometimes a knowledge of programming is needed for this. Some systems, on the other hand, can be operated without detailed programming knowledge.

IBM's QUIKTRAN system used a language with a format like the already familiar FORTRAN, thus:

$$y = A(x + ut) \quad \text{would be written} \quad Y = A * (X + U * T)$$
$$E = mC^2 \quad \text{would be written}^2 \quad E = EM * C * * 2$$

---

[2] EM is written instead of M to make the variable floating point.

—Code for display record

*. PA 101/22 MAR LONJFK–MCIERNAN ⧻

01. 02 MCMAHAN/C   LONJFK

02. 02 MCCALL/AM   LONJFK

03. 01 MACKIERNAN/GEN/JS   LONJFK

*.3 ⧻

LONPA   18 MAR 65   17930

NAME – 01. 01 MACKIERNAN/GEN/JS

CNTC – 01. REF AM

SRCE – 01. A–JD HOWARD

FONE – 01. WH 1 3535 B AM

ADDR – 01. LON –

TKTG – 01. TKD –AGT

SUPI – 01. VIP

01.   PA 101Y 22 MAR   LONJFK 5501   J   1200/1335 KK

02.   PA OPEN Y   JFKLON 01

Figure 24.11

$$E = EM * C ** 2 * (1./SQRT(1. - U ** 2/C ** 2) - 1.)$$

$$P = \frac{A + 2T(U - \sin^2 x)}{N} \quad \text{would be written}$$

$$P = (A + 2. * T * (U - (SIN (X)) ** 2))/N$$

Floating point numbers can also be expressed. Thus,

1.458×10^9 would be written   1.458E9

2.6×10^{-18} would be written   2.6E–18

The terminal operator wishing to evaluate an expression in this mode might type in

BASE = 2.E − 9 ⋆ 50. ⋆ (ALOG(2. ⋆ 50./10.) − 1. + 10./50.)

and the terminal would reply

BASE = 0.15025850E − 06.

As far as possible the machine would pick up errors in input; thus,

Q = (2./(3.1416 ∗ 10.) ∗ 0.5 ∗ SIN (10.)

would receive the reply

ERROR PARENTHESES NOT IN BALANCE

The operator would then type

Q = (2./(3.1416 ∗ 10.)) ∗ ∗ 0.5 ∗ SIN (10.)

and receive the reply he sought

Q = 0.13726357E − 00

On the QUIKTRAN system errors are pointed out where possible at the time each statement is typed in. This can speed up the writing of a bug-free program and shorten the time taken to obtain results.

As on the other time-sharing systems, the user may either type in simple calculations rather like using a calculating machine or may type in a complete program. Programs may in this way be composed and edited on real-time terminals of time-sharing systems.

Figure 24.12 illustrates a simple program being produced using the BASIC language marketed by General Electric and IBM. A teleprinter such as that in Figure 6.8 was used, and was connected by a teletype line to a distant GE 635 computer. The results were obtained within about 20 minutes of going to the teleprinter—much quicker than with a conventional data center, or with a calculating machine.

The calculations above can all use subvoice grade lines. Occasionally, the slow typewriter-speed printing is frustrating, especially in programs involving a long print-out, and there is something to be said for a faster stick-printer on a voice line, or possibly a display screen terminal. The display screen is not very satisfactory for program preparation because the user almost always needs a print-out. Some screen units have a printer available on a control unit they share with other screens. Some programmers use a Polaroid camera.

Often the teletype-speed terminals are nevertheless used on a voice line because of the convenience of being able to *dial* the computer or a variety of computers. In this case, if a faster terminal could be used to advantage, it seems unfortunate that the line speed is largely wasted.

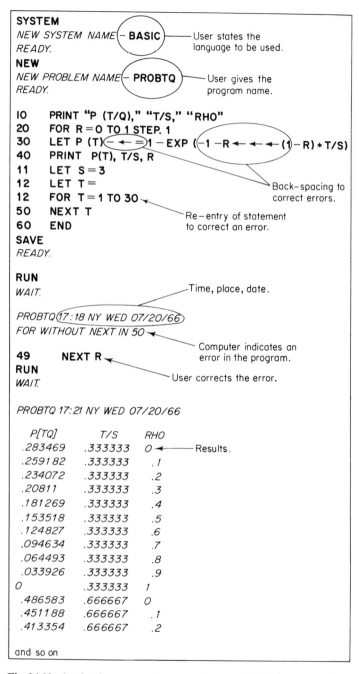

Fig. 24.12. A teleprinter connected remotely to a GE 635 computer here uses the BASIC language.

**VOICE
ANSWERBACK**

The least expensive form of terminal is the telephone itself, and many systems have been designed to respond by voice answerback. One of the first of these was the New York Stock Exchange system, which gives up-to-the-minute quotations of stock prices. Figure 24.13 shows a New York City high school student doing her homework with the help of an IBM computer 50 miles away. The device she is using is like a normal Touch-Tone

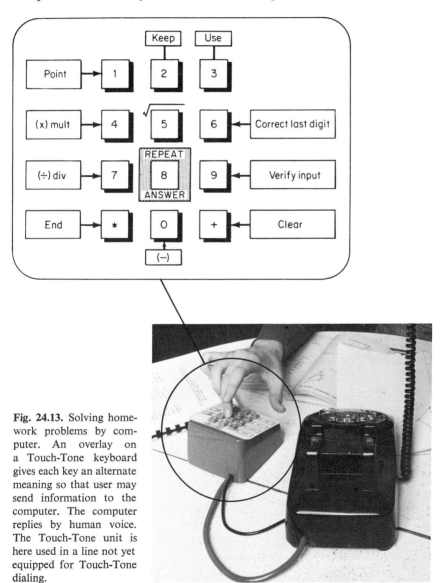

Fig. 24.13. Solving homework problems by computer. An overlay on a Touch-Tone keyboard gives each key an alternate meaning so that user may send information to the computer. The computer replies by human voice. The Touch-Tone unit is here used in a line not yet equipped for Touch-Tone dialing.

telephone keyboard. It has twelve keys instead of the ten that are conventional on a telephone. They are labelled as shown. (Note that each key has two possible meanings. The key "8" can be used to tell the computer to repeat its answer.) Now that the conventional Touch-Tone telephone is being marketed with twelve keys, this could be an ordinary telephone keyboard as in Fig. 2.9 with a plastic labeled overlay on it. The girl keys in details of the calculation she wants to perform and the computer replies by voice.

She keys in the digits and operators of the calculation. Each operator keyed in (except +) must be followed by an *, in order that the computer can tell that it is an operator. She ends each operation by signaling **. Thus if she wishes to divide 3 by 14, she keys in:

3 7* 14 **   ("7 *" means divide)

and the computer speaks back over the telephone with a distinct human voice:

Your answer: Two. One. Four. Two. Eight. Five. Seven. One. Four. Two . . .

and so on for fourteen digits.

She keys 1 * to mean "decimal point", thus to subtract 3.8692 from 14.908 she would key:

14 1* 908 0* 3 1* 8692 **

The machine replies:

Your answer: One. One. Point. Zero. Three. Eight. Eight.

If she failed to write this all down and wants it repeated, she presses 8 * * *, and the machine repeats it.

The machine is equipped with temporary and permanent storage locations into which results may be placed with keys 2 and 3. The storage may be cleared with the "+" key. Using these storages, lengthy calculations may be performed. Thus if she presses 2 * 0 this means "Place a number into temporary storage 0 for use in the next problem." If she presses 2 * 7, this means "Place a number in permanent storage 7 for future use".

To calculate $\pi \times 3.78^2$, the sequence would be as follows:

3 1* 78 4* 3 1* 78 2 * 0 * *

Your answer: Holds One. Four. Point. Two. Eight. Eight. Four. Key your function.

4 * 3 1* 1417 * *

Your answer: Four. Four. Point. Eight. Eight. Nine. Eight. Six. Six. Two. Eight.

Similarly, she may use the contents of, for example, permanent storage 9, by keying 3 ∗ 9.

If she makes mistakes which the computer can detect, it will inform her, as with other terminal systems, thus:

3 1∗ 78 4 ∗ 3 1∗ 78 2 ∗ ∗ ∗

A storage location has not been indicated. Please re-enter your problem and specify a storage location after the Use function.

3 1∗ 78 4∗ 3 1∗ 78 2∗ 97 ∗ ∗

You have specified a storage location which does not exist. Please re-enter your problem.

723 7∗ 3∗9 ∗ ∗

You have indicated a division by zero. Change your division and re-enter the problem.

723 7∗ 379 ∗ ∗

Your answer: One. Nine. Zero. Seven. Six. Five. One. Seven. One. Five. Three.

Nine. Five. Seven. Your message has not been followed by the End function. Verify your entry.

9∗ ∗∗

Your entry: Seven. Two. Three. Divided by. Three. Seven. Nine.

Voice answerback has been used in a variety of commercial applications in a somewhat similar manner. It has been used, for example, with a terminal for checking a customer's credit rating in a department store, and in a system which can be dialed to check a stock situation. In some systems, the computer dials to initiate the call and speaks to whoever picks up the telephone, perhaps to indicate that some exceptional condition has arisen. It will require a reply to confirm that the message has been correctly received.

PROBLEM-ORIENTED LANGUAGE   Some languages are designed for one specific type of calculation, or one type of problem. In this way a problem can be made much easier to tackle than by using a general language such as FORTRAN or ALGOL. Various categories of engineering problems, for instance, can be given a *problem-oriented* language which enable that particular problem to be

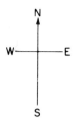

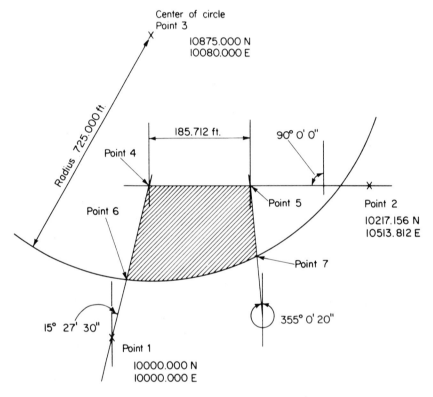

Fig. 24.14. A problem in civil engineering geometry; find details of the shaded area (see Fig. 24.15).

tackled quickly and easily. A remote computing system may have in its files many such languages for different users, which can be called into operation from the terminal. This approach holds great promise of widening the range of scientists who use computers in their daily work.

A simple example of such a language is IBM's COGO. This is designed as a very quick means of solving civil engineering coordinate geometry

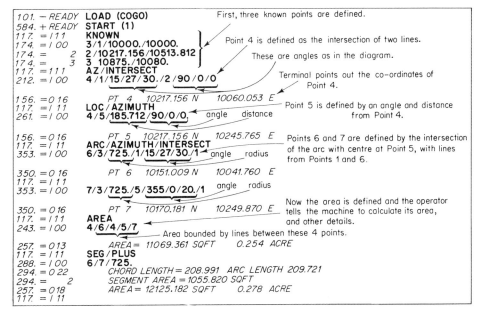

```
101. — READY  LOAD (COGO)              First, three known points are defined.
584. + READY  START (1)
117. = / 1 1  KNOWN
174. = / 0 0  3/1/10000./10000.      ⎫
174. =      2  2/10217.156/10513.812  ⎬   Point 4 is defined as the intersection of two lines.
174. =      3  3 10875./10080.        ⎭   These are angles as in the diagram.
117. = / 1 1  AZ/INTERSECT
212. = / 0 0  4/1/15/27/30./2/90/0/0       Terminal points out the co-ordinates of
                                                    Point 4.
156. = 0 16         PT  4   10217.156 N   10060.053 E
117. = / 1 1  LOC/AZIMUTH                              Point 5 is defined by an angle and distance
261. = / 0 0  4/5/185.712/90/0/0,  angle   distance                from Point 4.

156. = 0 16         PT  5   10217.156 N   10245.765 E   Points 6 and 7 are defined by the intersection
117. = / 1 1  ARC/AZIMUTH/INTERSECT                     of the arc with centre at Point 5, with lines
353. = / 0 0  6/3/725./1/15/27/30./1  angle   radius    from Points 1 and 6.

350. = 0 16         PT  6   10151.009 N   10041.760 E
117. = / 1 1
353. = / 0 0  7/3/725./5/355/0/20./1  angle   radius
                                                       Now the area is defined and the operator
350. = 0 16         PT  7   10170.181 N   10249.870 E   tells the machine to calculate its area,
117. = / 1 1  AREA                                       and other details.
243. = / 0 0  4/6/4/5/7
                          Area bounded by lines between these 4 points.
257. = 0 13        AREA= 11069.361 SQFT     0.254 ACRE
117. = / 1 1  SEG/PLUS
288. = / 0 0  6/7/725.
294. = 0 22        CHORD LENGTH = 208.991  ARC LENGTH 209.721
294. =      2      SEGMENT AREA = 1055.820 SQFT
257. = 0 18        AREA = 12125.182 SQFT     0.278 ACRE
117. = / 1 1
```

Fig. 24.15. Use of COGO on the problem in Fig. 24.14.

problems. Figure 24.15 is an example of using COGO at a QUIKTRAN terminal. This version of COGO has, in fact, been written in the QUIKTRAN language.[3]

Figure 24.15 is the work of a terminal user tackling the problem sketched in Fig. 24.14. It is desired to find the area of the shaded portion of this diagram, and other details of that area. First, the operator calls in the COGO program by typing **LOAD (COGO)**. He then starts the COGO program by typing **START (1)** and this enables him to type in the known details of the map in question as shown.

Conversation between man and machine can well be a somewhat one-sided affair as the two have rather different talents. The computer can be a prolific "talker." It can display masses of facts in natural language very quickly, if so desired. It does not, however, have an equal flair for under-standing what its human operators say. Usually they have to use messages which are simple, perfectly accurate, and completely preplanned. Any deviation from this and the machine will abruptly ask its user to rephrase his statement.

In many commercial applications it is, indeed, desirable to design the conversation language so that the operator keys in as little as possible, and the computer helps her with its high speed displays.

---

[3] IBM manual on QUIKTRAN/COGO, Form H20-0204-0. International Business Machines Corp., 1965.

UNTRAINED
OPERATORS

For most of the conversations discussed, above, the operator needs special training in the language he must use to converse with the machine. Certainly with QUIKTRAN and the airline reservation systems we have discussed, the operator needs careful tuition and some practice. Training is an important consideration in the implementation of a commercial real-time system.

It is also desirable, however, to devise "languages" in some applications for which the operator will need little or no training. He will need to be trained to use the terminal hardware, but once he knows this, what he keys into the machine becomes largely self-evident. We might, in fact, categorize our terminal operators into three groups.

(1) Programmers, such as those using BASIC, QUIKTRAN, etc.

(2) Operators trained in a special language, who use the terminal uniquely for one particular application—e.g., airline reservations, etc.

(3) Operators who know how to work the terminal but who have had no special training in any "language" for conversing with the computer.

A major part of the computer manufacturer's revenue in the years to come is likely to be through terminal applications which "bring the computer to the masses." How fast this comes about will depend to a large extent on our success in devising simple means for the man in the street to communicate with a computer via a terminal—means which do not frighten away people who are not in the high I.Q. brackets, and people too busy to learn elaborate terminal "languages."

In industry, a terminal for administrative purposes or a terminal for providing management with information, will operate, not on one application, like the airline reservation terminals, but on a whole range of different applications. An office clerk may at one moment want to enquire about the status of a given order, and at another time enter details about payments received. He needs a simple means of doing a wide variety of different operations.

In order to make the terminal language easy for the user we almost invariably have to increase considerably the length of reply from the computer. Sometimes the reply is many times longer than could be the case with a tightly coded conversation. We thus have a compromise between ease of use of terminal and telecommunication costs.

Consider the following conversation in which a company has details of its customers and their orders stored in the computer files. A customer

Fig. 24.16. An RCA Video Data Terminal connected by telephone line to an RCA 3301 computer in Detroit. In regional sales offices of the Chrysler Corporation, personnel have access to a file of warranty information on more than eight million vehicles. Here a supervisor in Philadelphia is keying in a repair order to update the master file in Detroit. Many such terminals may be connected via control units to one telephone line. *Courtesy RCA.*

telephones, wishing to bring forward the delivery date of an order. The clerk sits at a terminal and the computer tells him to enter the customer number if known. However, the clerk does not have it immediately available. The conversation is shown in Fig. 24.17.

The order records are tied into a factory schedule which indicates that the requested delivery date cannot quite be achieved unless the priority is changed.

It is necessary for the terminal operator, as in other applications, to identify himself, and to have some means of indicating to the computer that he has the authority to make the change to the records. This may be done by keying in a code number whenever he uses the terminal, or by using a hardware device which enables him to insert a unique card, or key, or badge.

Notice that the conversation above does not require knowledge of special codes or mnemonics on the part of the operator. The terminal always tells him precisely what to do. He need not learn any terminal "language." This differs considerably from the airline reservation examples given earlier. For the latter, it is common that the operators have a two-week training course. The operator of the administrative terminal in Fig. 24.17 may have to do such a wide variety of operations that the preceding means of conversing is desirable. It is, however, used at the expense of a considerable increase in the number of characters that must be sent on the transmission lines from the computer. Such squandering of transmission line capacity could be prohibitively expensive for a far-flung airline reservation system.

TEACHING   A further step to help the operator can be the inclusion of what is virtually a *teaching program* on-line. This can be useful with any of the three categories of operators listed. When the operator fumbles or makes mistakes in his use of the terminal or its language, the computer can give him a few lessons on the spot. He can ask for assistance whenever there is something he would like explained.

A user of System Development Corporation's TINT language for on-line programming can ask the computer to explain any part of the language he has forgotten or is not familiar with. Thus,

? EXPLAIN RENUMBER

* TO MAKE TINT RENUMBER YOUR PROGRAM LINES, TYPE : ? RENUMBER

YOUR PROGRAM LINES WILL BE RESEQUENCED STARTING AT 1.00.
THE SECOND LINE WILL BE 2.00, ETC.

However, if he asks it to explain something not in its vocabulary or if he spells the item incorrectly, it asks for clarification thus,

? EXPLAIN HOLLERITH VALUES

*EXPLAIN WHAT ?

? EXPLAIN HOLLERITH

*EXPLAIN WHAT ?

The Rand Corporation's JOSS system is briefer in demanding an explanation of input it does not understand and simply says,

Eh ?

In the years to come, *teaching* is probably going to become a major application of time-shared computers. The indications to date are that it can be very efficient and quite fascinating for the pupil. Writing a good teaching program, however, that deals with all types of student reaction is lengthy and skilled work.

TERMINALS WITH GRAPHICS   An increasing number of computer applications display *pictures* at a terminal. This is likely to be a common way of working with computers in the future—not only with highly complex applications like engineering design, but also in communication with, say, the foreman on the shop floor of a factory. The pictorial interface can clarify the conversation, present facts more concisely, and increase the probability that the computer obtains the right information from the terminal users. In teaching, too, pictures on the screen are invaluable.

Some very intricate uses of computer graphics have been developed in which the user can modify a design he is working on with a light pen, the computer carrying out design calculations and displaying the results on the screen. Examples have been carried out in such areas as bridge design and the design of electronic circuits. In one case, this technique was used to lessen noise at the rear of a civil jet airliner. The tail and engine cross-section was shown with the vibrations slowed down and magnified thousands of times so that it moved on the screen like an amoeba. Adjustments in the plane structure were then made and the effect they had on the vibrations was observed. Eventually, by means of small swinging weights the oscillations and hence the noise were reduced to low proportions. General Motors has,

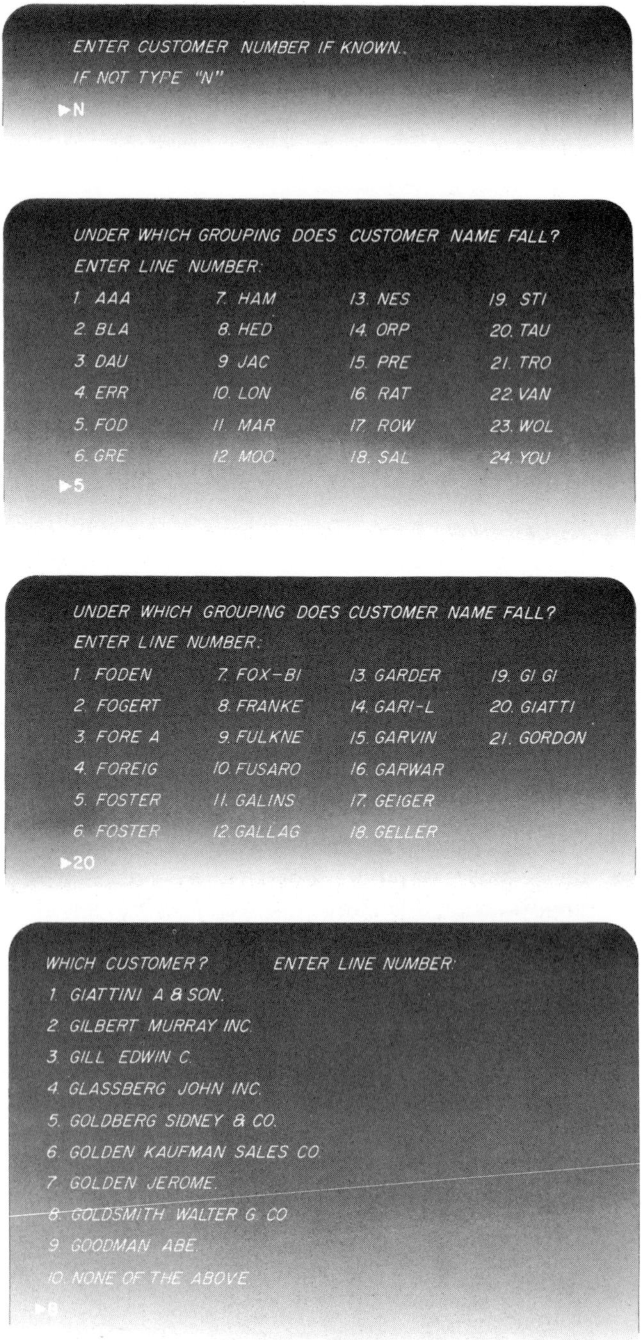

```
ENTER CUSTOMER NUMBER IF KNOWN.
IF NOT TYPE "N"
▶N
```

```
UNDER WHICH GROUPING DOES CUSTOMER NAME FALL?
ENTER LINE NUMBER:
  1. AAA       7. HAM      13. NES      19. STI
  2. BLA       8. HED      14. ORP      20. TAU
  3. DAU       9. JAC      15. PRE      21. TRO
  4. ERR      10. LON      16. RAT      22. VAN
  5. FOD      11. MAR      17. ROW      23. WOL
  6. GRE      12. MOO      18. SAL      24. YOU
▶5
```

```
UNDER WHICH GROUPING DOES CUSTOMER NAME FALL?
ENTER LINE NUMBER:
  1. FODEN      7. FOX-BI    13. GARDER    19. GI GI
  2. FOGERT     8. FRANKE    14. GARI-L    20. GIATTI
  3. FORE A     9. FULKNE    15. GARVIN    21. GORDON
  4. FOREIG    10. FUSARO    16. GARWAR
  5. FOSTER    11. GALINS    17. GEIGER
  6. FOSTER    12. GALLAG    18. GELLER
▶20
```

```
WHICH CUSTOMER?        ENTER LINE NUMBER:
  1. GIATTINI A & SON.
  2. GILBERT MURRAY INC.
  3. GILL EDWIN C.
  4. GLASSBERG JOHN INC.
  5. GOLDBERG SIDNEY & CO.
  6. GOLDEN KAUFMAN SALES CO.
  7. GOLDEN JEROME.
  8. GOLDSMITH WALTER G CO
  9. GOODMAN ABE.
 10. NONE OF THE ABOVE
▶8
```

Figure 24.17

```
CUSTOMER NUMBER:     17-8341
GOLDSMITH WALTER G. CO.
745, OLD STONE HIGHWAY, SPRINGS,
EAST HAMPTON, NY., 11937
REPRESENTATIVE K.B. JENKINS  #45731

PRESS ENTER IF CORRECT
```

The clerk presses the ENTER key

```
WHICH INFORMATION IS TO BE CHANGED?
ENTER LINE NUMBER:
1. NEW ORDER              9. INVOICE TO ADDRESS
2. CANCEL ORDER          10. SHIP TO ADDRESS
3. ORDER QUANTITY        11. CUSTOMER ADDRESS
4. DELIVERY DATE         12. CUSTOMER NAME
5. PRIORITY CODE         13. MISC INSTRUCTIONS
6. ORDER DETAILS         14. REPRESENTATIVE DETAILS
7. DISCOUNT              15. BRANCH OFFICE
8. TAX DETAILS           16. OTHER
►4
```

```
WHICH ORDER IS TO BE CHANGED?
ENTER LINE NUMBER:
  ORDER #   ITEM #S                     ORDER DATE  DEL DATE
1. 573824   87289   00241   00029        4/1/66     4/1/67
            00310   77139   04126
            00900
2. 575931   00391   00700   00421       10/1/66     4/1/68
3. 575828   00750   00900               12/1/66    12/1/67
4. 579003   02107                        6/1/66     8/1/67
►2
```

```
ORDER NUMBER 575931
ITEM #S    DESCRIPTION                          QTY
00391      MAGNETIC D EXTRACTOR 7 BR              5
00700      LINK ADAPTOR ADDL                      5
00421      CTC DIRECT CONTROL                     5
ORDER DATE   10/1/66          DELIV DATE    4/1/68

ENTER NEW REQUIRED DELIV DATE   (XX/XX/XX)
►10/01/66
```

```
EARLIEST DELIVERY DATE POSSIBLE AT PRIORITY 3 IS
2/1/66
IF THIS IS REQUESTED ENTER "Y"
►Y
```

for some time, experimented with graphic consoles in car design. Some of this work is illustrated in Figs 24.18 and 24.19. The drawings of the car parts can be enlarged, modified, and rotated on the screen. A designer can make a revision to the design and instruct the computer to rotate it so that he can view it from many angles. The interaction of a change in one part of the design, on other parts, can be quickly computed in some cases.

As we commented at the start of the chapter, terminals permitting an elaborate graphical man–machine interaction need (at least with machines available at the time of writing) a channel with higher capacity than a voice channel for their more complex applications. Since wideband channels are expensive, these terminals are normally in the same building as the computer.

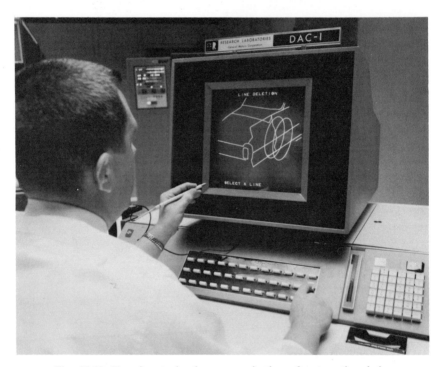

Fig. 24.18. Experiments in the communication of automotive design information between man and computer are being conducted at the General Motors Research Laboratories using the GM DAC-I system (Design Augmented by Computers) shown here. At the console of DAC-I, a research engineer checks out a computer program that allows him to modify a design "drawing." A touch of the light pen to the tube face signals the computer to begin an assigned task, in this case, "line deletion," where indicated. The man may also instruct the computer using the keyboard at the right, the card reader below the keyboard, or the program control buttons below the screen. Hundreds of special computer programs, written by GM computer research programmers, are needed to carry out these studies in man-machine communications. *Courtesy General Motors.*

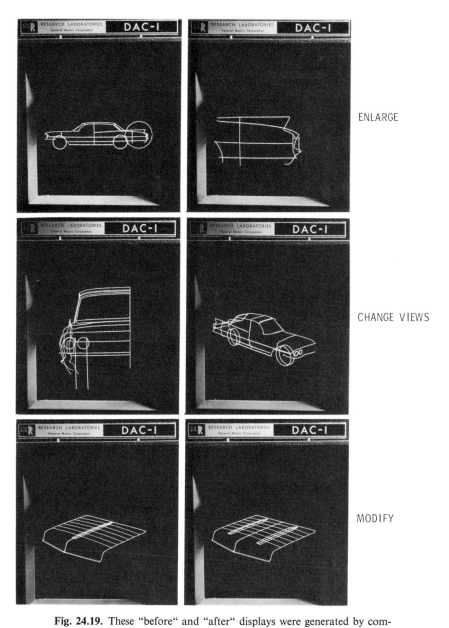

ENLARGE

CHANGE VIEWS

MODIFY

Fig. 24.19. These "before" and "after" displays were generated by computer under instructions from a General Motors designer. They illustrate three of the capabilities of DAC-I. The drawings appear on the viewing screen of the designer's console and come from a mathematical representation of the design stored in the computer's memory. In the bottom example, MODIFY, the DAC-I system has enabled the designer, while working at his console, to make a revision in the deck lid of a car, and to see immediately the results of his changes. *Courtesy General Motors.*

It is, however, possible to attach certain screen units to a small and relatively inexpensive local computer which can carry out such functions as rotating, enlarging, or modifying the displays. This computer would be linked to a larger, distant machine, which would have access to large files of data and would have the power to do fast and complex numerical operations. It would then be possible to connect these machines with a link of voice-line speed for most applications.

The quantity of data that needs to be transmitted to the screen can be lessened by means of elaborate logic circuitry in the terminal unit. The computer should not transmit the entire screen-full each time a change is made, but should only show the details of the change. The screen is not scanned like a television screen, but lines are drawn from their starting

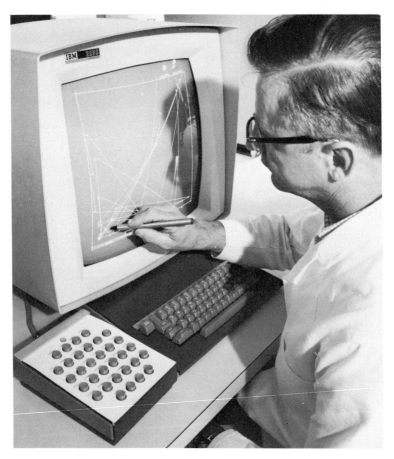

Fig. 24.20. An IBM 2250 graphic display, and light pen, here used by the Upjohn Company in investigating the body's response to new drugs.

coordinates, angle and length, and ending coordinates. Alternatively, instructions may be transmitted for incremental movements of a point, and the point would trace out the requisite picture like a plotting machine. The voice-line transmission of such information, however, would be too slow for some applications, for example, those showing movement, like the vibrating tail section of the jet plane. However, for the majority of uses it would be satisfactory. Figure 24.20, for example, shows a screen which is not usually attached directly to a telecommunication line, but it also shows an application which could be easily carried on over a voice line providing the system is designed with efficient encoding of the graphic data to permit this.

Figure 2.10 showed a terminal which *is* normally connected to a telephone line. The small screens are used side by side. The screen on the left is designed

Fig. 24.21. An IBM 1500 terminal in use for computer assisted instruction at Brentwood School, East Palo Alto, California. The picture on the left-hand screen is selected from a reel of 16-mm color film in the terminal, thereby avoiding the necessity of sending such a picture over the data channel. On the right-hand screen, data from the computer are displayed —alphanumeric or simple graphic data. The pupil communicates with the system by means of a keyboard and light pen operating on the right-hand screen. Headphones give audio data from the computer which is linked to the visual displays. In years to come, many schools will use such systems —probably linkable by telephone line to different teaching computers.

so that the stock performance, and other, charts can be transmitted in a quantity of bits small enough to send over a voice line.

Another way to produce pictures at a terminal is to store them inside the terminal on a reel of film or slides and thus avoid the need to transmit them. This is the approach taken on the teaching terminal in Fig. 24.21. Pictures are extremely valuable in certain teaching programs. This is true both with small children and with advanced teaching—an example of the latter is a medical school in which the machine displays relavent pictures of the organs it is discussing. Suitable frames from a reel of color film inside the terminal are selected by the computer. In some such terminals, the user may respond with a light pen, touching the appropriate parts of the picture. The position of the pen response is detected and sent back to the computer.

PICTUREPHONE LINES   Our thinking today about the faster types of man–machine telecommunications is generally restricted to voice-line data rates. This situation is likely to improve in the years ahead. First, voice-line data rates will become somewhat higher than those in use at the time of writing because of better modem design. Second, it seems likely that the Picturephone service will be sold widely in industry, at least in North America. It is possible that before many years have passed, few office buildings will be complete without a Picturephone conference room. If this is so, a generation of terminals will probably arise that is geared to Picturephone line speeds. The Picturephone channel in Fig. 16.4 is equivalent to 96 voice channels. Such a facility will open the way to intricate graphic applications, and other major changes in the organization of data processing.

GLOSSARY

There is little point in redefining the wheel, and where useful the definitions in this glossary have been taken from other recognized glossaries.

A suffix "2" after a definition below indicates that it is the CCITT definition, published in *List of Definitions of Essential Telecommunication Terms*, International Telecommunication Union, Geneva.

A suffix "1" after a definition below indicates that the definition is taken from the *Data Communications Glossary*, International Business Machines Corporation, Poughkeepsie, 1967 (Manual number C20-1666).

Address. A coded representation of the destination of data, or of their originating terminal. Multiple terminals on one communication line, for example, must have unique addresses. Telegraph messages reaching a switching center carry an address before their text to indicate the destination of the message.

Alphabet (telegraph or data). A table of correspondence between an agreed set of characters and the signals which represent them. (2).

Alternate routing. An alternative communications path used if the normal one is not available. There may be one or more possible alternative paths.

Amplitude modulation. One of three ways of modifying a sine wave signal in order to make it "carry" information. The sine wave, or "carrier," has its amplitude modified in accordance with the information to be transmitted.

Analog data. Data in the form of *continuously variable* physical quantities. (Compare with **Digital data.**) (1).

Analog transmission. Transmission of a continuously variable signal as opposed to a discretely variable signal. Physical quantities such as temperature are continuously variable and so are described as "analog." Data characters, on the other hand, are coded in discrete separate pulses or signal levels, and are referred to as "digital." The normal way of transmitting a telephone, or voice, signal has been analog; but now digital encoding (using **PCM**) is coming into use over trunks.

ogram. The working programs in a system may be classed as *ap-rograms* and *supervisory programs.* The application programs are ta-processing programs. They contain no input-output coding except n of macroinstructions that transfer control to the supervisory programs. They are usually unique to one type of application, whereas the supervisory programs could be used for a variety of different application types. A number of different terms are used for these two classes of program.

ARQ (Automatic Request for Repetition). A system employing an error-detecting code and so conceived that any false signal initiates a repetition of the transmission of the character incorrectly received. (2).

ASCII (American Standard Code for Information Interchange). Usually pronounced "ask'-ee." An eight-level code for data transfer adopted by the American Standards Association to achieve compatibility between data devices. (1).

Asynchronous transmission. Transmission in which each information character, or sometimes each word or small block, is individually synchronized, usually by the use of start and stop elements. The gap between each character (or word) is not of a necessarily fixed length. (Compare with **Synchronous transmission.**) Asynchronous transmission is also called *start-stop transmission.*

Attended operation. In data set applications, individuals are required at both stations to establish the connection and transfer the data sets from talk (voice) mode to data mode. (Compare **Unattended operation.**) (1).

Attenuation. Decrease in magnitude of current, voltage, or power of a signal in transmission between points. May be expressed in decibels. (1).

Atenuation equalizer. (*See* **Equalizer.**)

Audio frequencies. Frequencies that can be heard by the human ear (usually 30 to 20,000 cycles per second). (1).

Automatic calling unit (ACU). A dialing device supplied by the communications common carrier, which permits a business machine to automatically dial calls over the communication networks. (1).

Automatic dialing unit (ADU). A device capable of automatically generating dialing digits. (Compare with **Automatic calling unit.**) (1).

Bandwidth. The range of frequencies available for signaling. The difference expressed in cycles per second (hertz) between the highest and lowest frequencies of a band.

Baseband signaling. Transmission of a signal at its original frequencies, i.e., a signal not changed by modulation.

Baud. Unit of signaling speed. The speed in bauds is the number of discrete conditions or signal events per second. (This is applied only to the actual signals on a communication line.) If each signal event represents only one bit condition, baud is the same as bits per second. When each signal event represents other than one bit (e.g., see **Dibit**), baud does not equal bits per second. (1).

Baudot code. A code for the transmission of data in which five equal-length bits represent one character. This code is used in most DC teletypewriter machines where 1 start element and 1.42 stop elements are added. (See page 109.) (1).

Bel. Ten decibels, q.v.

BEX. Broadband exchange, q.v.

Bias distortion. In teletypewriter applications, the uniform shifting of the beginning of all marking pulses from their proper positions in relation to the beginning of the start pulse. (1).

Bias distortion, asymmetrical distortion. Distortion affecting a two-condition (or binary) modulation (or restitution) in which all the significant conditions have longer or shorter durations than the corresponding theoretical durations. (2).

Bit. Contraction of "binary digit," the smallest unit of information in a binary system. A bit represents the choice between a mark or space (one or zero) condition.

Bit rate. The speed at which bits are transmitted, usually expressed in bits per second. (Compare with **Baud.**)

Broadband. Communication channel having a bandwidth greater than a voice-grade channel, and therefore capable of higher-speed data transmission. (1).

Broadband exchange (BEX). Public switched communication system of Western Union, featuring various bandwidth FDX connections. (1).

Buffer. A storage device used to compensate for a difference in rate of data flow, or time of occurrence of events, when transmitting data from one device to another. (1).

Cable. Assembly of one or more conductors within an enveloping protective sheath, so constructed as to permit the use of conductors separately or in groups. (1).

Carrier. A continuous frequency capable of being modulated, or impressed with a second (information carrying) signal. (1).

Carrier, communications common. A company which furnishes communications services to the general public, and which is regulated by appropriate local, state, or federal agencies. The term strictly includes truckers and movers, bus lines, and airlines, but is usually used to refer to telecommunication companies.

Carrier system. A means of obtaining a number of channels over a single path by modulating each channel on a different carrier frequency and demodulating at the receiving point to restore the signals to their original form.

Carrier telegraphy, carrier current telegraphy. A method of transmission in which the signals from a telegraph transmitter modulate an alternating current. (2).

Central office. The place where communications common carriers terminate customer lines and locate the switching equipment which interconnects those lines. (Also referred to as an *exchange, end office*, and *local central office*.)

Chad. The material removed when forming a hole or notch in a storage medium such as punched tape or punched cards.

Chadless tape. Perforated tape with the chad partially attached, to facilitate interpretive printing on the tape.

Channel. 1. (CCITT and ASA standard) A means of one-way transmission. (Compare with **Circuit.**)
2. (Tariff and common usage) As used in the tariffs, a path for electrical transmission between two or more points without common-carrier-provided terminal equipment. Also called *circuit, line, link, path,* or *facility.* (1).

Channel, analog. A channel on which the information transmitted can take any value between the limits defined by the channel. Most voice channels are analog channels.

Channel, voice-grade. A channel suitable for transmission of speech, digital or analog data, or facsimile, generally with a frequency range of about 300 to 3400 cycles per second.

12-channel group (of carrier current system). The assembly of 12 telephone channels, in a carrier system, occupying adjacent bands in the spectrum, for the purpose of simultaneous modulation or demodulation. (2).

Character. Letter, figure, number, punctuation or other sign contained in a message. Besides such characters, there may be characters for special symbols and some control functions. (1).

Characteristic distortion. Distortion caused by transients which, as a result of the modulation, are present in the transmission channel and depend on its transmission qualities.

Circuit. A means of both-way communication between two points, comprising associated "go" and "return" channels. (1).

Circuit, four-wire. A communication path in which four wires (two for each direction of transmission) are presented to the station equipment. (1).

Circuit, two-wire. A metallic circuit formed by two conductors insulated from each other. It is possible to use the two conductors as either a one-way transmission path, a half-duplex path, or a duplex path. (1).

Common carrier. (*See* **Carrier, communications common.**)

Compandor. A compandor is a combination of a compressor at one point in a communication path for reducing the volume *range* of signals, followed by an expandor at another point for restoring the original volume range. Usually its purpose is to improve the ratio of the signal to the interference entering in the path between the compressor and expandor. (2).

Compressor. Electronic device which compresses the volume range of a signal, used in a compandor (q.v.). An "expandor" restores the original volume range after transmission.

Conditioning. The addition of equipment to a leased voice-grade channel to provide minimum values of line characteristics required for data transmission. (1).

Contention. This is a method of line control in which the terminals request to transmit. If the channel in question is free, transmission goes ahead; if it is not free, the terminal will have to wait until it becomes free. The queue of contention requests may be built up by the computer, and this can either be in a prearranged sequence or in the sequence in which the requests are made.

Control character. A character whose occurrence in a particular context initiates, modifies, or stops a control operation—e.g., a character to control carriage return. (1).

Control mode. The state that all terminals on a line must be in to allow line control actions, or terminal selection to occur. When all terminals on a line are in the control mode, characters on the line are viewed as control characters performing line discipline, that is, polling or addressing. (1).

Cross-bar switch. A switch having a plurality of vertical paths, a plurality of horizontal paths, and electromagnetically operated mechanical means for interconnecting any one of the vertical paths with any of the horizontal paths. See page 326. (2).

Cross-bar system. A type of line-switching system which uses cross-bar switches.

Cross talk. The unwanted transfer of energy from one circuit, called the *disturbing* circuit, to another circuit, called the *disturbed* circuit. (2).

Cross talk, far-end. Cross talk which travels along the disturbed circuit in the same direction as the signals in that circuit. To determine the far-end cross talk between two pairs, 1 and 2, signals are transmitted on pair 1 at station A, and the level of cross talk is measured on pair 2 at station B. (1).

Cross talk, near-end. Cross talk which is propagated in a disturbed channel in the direction opposite to the direction of propagation of the current in the distrubing channel. Ordinarily, the terminal of the disturbed channel at which the near-end cross talk is present is near or coincides with the energized terminal of the disturbing channel. (1).

Dataphone. Both a service mark and a trademark of AT & T and the Bell System. As a service mark it indicates the transmission of data over the telephone network. As a trademark it identifies the communications equipment furnished by the Bell System for data communications services. (1).

Data set. A device which performs the modulation/demodulation and control functions necessary to provide compatibility between business machines and communications facilities. (*See also* **Line adapter, Modem,** *and* **Subset.**) (1).

Data-signaling rate. It is given by $\sum_{i=1}^{m} \frac{1}{T_i} \log_2 n_i$, where m is the number of parallel channels, T is the minimum interval for the ith channel, expressed in seconds, n is the number of significant conditions of the modulation in the ith channel. Data-signaling rate is expressed in bits per second. (2).

Dataspeed. An AT&T marketing term for a family of medium-speed paper tape transmitting and receiving units. Similar equipment is also marketed by Western Union. (1).

DDD. (*See* **Direct distance dialing,** q.v.)

Decibel (db). A tenth of a bel. A unit for measuring relative strength of a signal parameter such as power, voltage, etc. The number of decibels is ten times the logarithm (base 10) of the ratio of the measured quantity to the reference level. The reference level must always be indicated, such as 1 milliwatt for power ratio. (1). See Fig. 9.5.

Delay distortion. Distortion occurring when the envelope delay of a circuit or system is not constant over the frequency range required for transmission.

Delay equalizer. A corrective network which is designed to make the phase delay or envelope delay of a circuit or system substantially constant over a desired frequency range. (*See* **Equalizer.**) (1).

Demodulation. The process of retrieving intelligence (data) from a modulated carrier wave; the reverse of modulation. (1).

Diagnostic programs. These are used to check equipment malfunctions and to pinpoint faulty components. They may be used by the computer engineer or may be called in by the supervisory programs automatically.

Diagnostics, system. Rather than checking one individual component, system diagnostics utilize the whole system in a manner similar to its operational running. Programs resembling the operational programs will be used rather than systematic programs that run logical patterns. These will normally detect overall system malfunctions but will not isolate faulty components.

Diagnostics, unit. These are used on a conventional computer to detect faults in the various units. Separate unit diagnostics will check such items as arithmetic circuitry, transfer instructions, each input-output unit, and so on.

Dial pulse. A current interruption in the DC loop of a calling telephone. It is produced by the breaking and making of the dial pulse contacts of a calling telephone when a digit is dialed. The loop current is interrupted once for each unit of value of the digit. (1).

Dial-up. The use of a dial or pushbutton telephone to initiate a station-to-station telephone call.

Dibit. A group of two bits. In four-phase modulation, each possible dibit is encoded as one of four unique carrier phase shifts. The four possible states for a dibit are 00, 01, 10, 11.

Differential modulations. A type of modulation in which the choice of the significant condition for any signal element is dependent on the choice for the previous signal element. (2).

Digital data. Information represented by a code consisting of a sequence of discrete elements. (Compare with **Analog data.**) (1).

Digital signal. A discrete or discontinuous signal; one whose various states are discrete intervals apart. (Compare with **Analog transmission.**) (1).

Direct distance dialing (DDD). A telephone exchange service which enables the telephone user to call other subscribers outside his local area without operator assistance. In the United Kingdom and some other countries, this is called *Subscriber Trunk Dialing* (STD).

Disconnect signal. A signal transmitted from one end of a subscriber line or trunk to indicate at the other end that the established connection should be disconnected. (1).

Distortion. The unwanted change in waveform that occurs between two points in a transmission system. (1).

Distributing frame. A structure for terminating permanent wires of a telephone central office, private branch exchange, or private exchange, and for permitting the easy change of connections between them by means of cross-connecting wires. (1).

Double-current transmission, polar direct-current system. A form of binary telegraph transmission in which positive and negative direct currents denote the significant conditions. (2).

Drop, subscriber's. The line from a telephone cable to a subscriber's building. (1).

Duplex transmission. Simultaneous two-way independent transmission in both directions. (Compare with **Half-duplex transmission**. Also called *full-duplex transmission*.) (1).

Duplexing. The use of duplicate computers, files or circuitry, so that in the event of one component failing an alternative one can enable the system to carry on its work.

Echo. An echo is a wave which has been reflected or otherwise returned with sufficient magnitude and delay for it to be perceptible in some manner as a wave distinct from that directly transmitted.

Echo check. A method of checking data transmission accuracy whereby the received data are returned to the sending end for comparison with the original data.

Echo suppressor. A line device used to prevent energy from being reflected back (echoed) to the transmitter. It attenuates the transmission path in one direction while signals are being passed in the other direction. (1).

End distortion. End distortion of start-stop teletypewriter signals is the shifting of the end of all marking pulses from their proper positions in relation to the beginning of the start pulse.

End office. (*See* **Central office.**)

Equalization. Compensation for the attenuation (signal loss) increase with frequency. Its purpose is to produce a flat frequency response while the temperature remains constant. (1).

Equalizer. Any combination (usually adjustable) of coils, capacitors, and/or resistors inserted in transmission line or amplifier circuit to improve its frequency response. (1).

Equivalent four-wire system. A transmission system using frequency division to obtain full-duplex operation over only one pair of wires. (1).

Error-correcting telegraph code. An error-detecting code incorporating sufficient additional signaling elements to enable the nature of some or all of the errors to be indicated and corrected entirely at the receiving end.

Error-detecting and feedback system, decision feedback system, request repeat system, ARQ system. A system employing an error-detecting code and so arranged that a signal detected as being in error automatically initiates a request for retransmission of the signal detected as being in error. (2).

Error-detecting telegraph code. A telegraph code in which each telegraph signal conforms to specific rules of construction, so that departures from this construction in the received signals can be automatically detected. Such codes necessarily require more signaling elements than are required to convey the basic information.

ESS. (Electronic Switching System). Bell System term for computerized telephone exchange. ESS 1 is a central office. ESS 101 gives private branch exchange (PBX) switching controlled from the local central office. (*See* Chapter 19.)

Even parity check (odd parity check). This is a check which tests whether the number of digits in a group of binary digits is even (even parity check) or odd (odd parity check). (2).

Exchange. A unit established by a communications common carrier for the administration of communication service in a specified area which usually embraces a city, town, or village and its environs. It consists of one or more central offices together with the associated equipment used in furnishing communication service. (This term is often used as a synonym for "central office," q.v.)

Exchange, classes of. Class 1 (*see* **Regional center**); class 2 (*see* **Sectional center**); class 3 (*see* **Primary center**); class 4 (*see* **Toll center**); class 5 (*see* **End office**).

Exchange, private automatic (PAX). A dial telephone exchange that provides private telephone service to an organization and that does *not* allow calls to be transmitted to or from the public telephone network.

Exchange, private automatic branch (PABX). A private automatic telephone exchange that provides for the transmission of calls to and from the public telephone network.

Exchange, private branch (PBX). A manual exchange connected to the public telephone network on the user's premises and operated by an attendant supplied by the user. PBX is today commonly used to refer also to an automatic exchange.

Exchange, trunk. An exchange devoted primarily to interconnecting trunks.

Exchange service. A service permitting interconnection of any two customers' stations through the use of the exchange system.

Expandor. A transducer which for a given amplitude range or input voltages produces a larger range of output voltages. One important type of expandor employs the information from the envelope of speech signals to expand their volume range. (Compare **Compandor.**) (1).

Facsimile (FAX). A system for the transmission of images. The image is scanned at the transmitter, reconstructed at the receiving station, and duplicated on some form of paper. (1).

Fail softly. When a piece of equipment fails, the programs let the system fall back to a degraded mode of operation rather than let it fail catastrophically and give no response to its users.

Fall-back, double. Fall-back in which two separate equipment failures have to be contended with.

Fall-back procedures. When the equipment develops a fault the programs operate in such a way as to circumvent this fault. This may or may not give a degraded service. Procedures necessary for fall-back may include those to switch over to an alternative computer or file, to change file addresses, to send output to a typewriter instead of a printer, to use different communication lines or bypass a faulty terminal, etc.

FCC. Federal Communications Commission, q.v.

FD or **FDX.** Full duplex. (*See* **Duplex.**)

FDM. Frequency-division multiplex, q.v.

Federal Communications Commission (FCC). A board of seven commissioners appointed by the President under the Communication Act of 1934, having the power to regulate all interstate and foreign electrical communication systems originating in the United States. (1).

Figures shift. A physical shift in a teletypewriter which enables the printing of numbers, symbols, upper-case characters, etc. (Compare with **Letters shift.**) (1).

Filter. A network designed to transmit currents of frequencies within one or more frequency bands and to attenuate currents of other frequencies. (2).

Foreign exchange service. A service which connects a customer's telephone to a telephone company central office normally not serving the customer's location. (Also applies to TWX service.) (1).

Fortuitous distortion. Distortion resulting from causes generally subject to random laws (accidental irregularities in the operation of the apparatus and of the moving parts, disturbances affecting the transmission channel, etc.). (2).

Four-wire circuit. A circuit using two pairs of conductors, one pair for the "go" channel and the other pair for the "return" channel. (2).

Four-wire equivalent circuit. A circuit using the same pair of conductors to give "go" and "return" channels by means of different carrier frequencies for the two channels. (2).

Four-wire terminating set. Hybrid arrangement by which four-wire circuits are terminated on a two-wire basis for interconnection with two-wire circuits.

Frequency-derived channel. Any of the channels obtained from multiplexing a channel by frequency division. (2).

Frequency-division multiplex. A multiplex system in which the available transmission frequency range is divided into narrower bands, each used for a separate channel. (2).

Frequency modulation. One of three ways of modifying a sine wave signal to make it "carry" information. The sine wave or "carrier" has its frequency modified in accordance with the information to be transmitted. The frequency function of the modulated wave may be continuous or discontinuous. In the latter case, two or more particular frequencies may correspond each to one significant condition.

Frequency-shift signaling, frequency-shift keying (FSK). Frequency modulation method in which the frequency is made to vary at the significant instants. 1. By smooth transitions: the modulated wave and the change in frequency are continuous at the significant instants. 2. By abrupt transitions: the modulated wave is continuous but the frequency is discontinuous at the significant instants. (2).

FSK. Frequency-shift keying, q.v.

FTS. Federal Telecommunications System.

Full-duplex (FD or FDX) **transmission.** (*See* **Duplex transmission.**)

Half-duplex (HD or HDX) **circuit.**
1. CCITT definition: A circuit designed for duplex operation, but which, on account of the nature of the terminal equipments, can be operated alternately only.
2. Definition in common usage (the normal meaning in computer literature): A circuit designed for transmission in either direction but not both directions simultaneously.

Handshaking. Exchange of predetermined signals for purposes of control when a connection is established between two data sets.

Harmonic distortion. The resultant presence of harmonic frequencies (due to non-linear characteristics of a transmission line) in the response when a sinusoidal stimulus is applied. (1)

HD or HDX. Half duplex. (*See* **Half-duplex circuit.**)

Hertz (Hz). A measure of frequency or bandwidth. The same as cycles per second.

Home loop. An operation involving only those input and output units associated with the local terminal. (1).

In-house. *See* **In-plant system.**

In-plant system. A system whose parts, including remote terminals, are all situated in one building or localized area. The term is also used for communication systems spanning several buildings and sometimes covering a large distance, but in which no common carrier facilities are used.

International Telecommunication Union (ITU). The telecommunications agency of the United Nations, established to provide standardized communications procedures and practices including frequency allocation and radio regulations on a world-wide basis.

Interoffice trunk. A direct trunk between local central offices.

Intertoll trunk. A trunk between toll offices in different telephone exchanges. (1).

ITU. International Telecommunication Union, q.v.

Keyboard perforator. A perforator provided with a bank of keys, the manual depression of any one of which will cause the code of the corresponding character or function to be punched in a tape. (2).

Keyboard send/receive. A combination teletypewriter transmitter and receiver with transmission capability from keyboard only.

KSR. Keyboard send/receive, q.v.

Leased facility. A facility reserved for sole use of a single leasing customer. (*See also* **private line.**) (1).

Letters shift. A physical shift in a teletypewriter which enables the printing of alphabetic characters. Also, the name of the character which causes this shift. (*Compare* with **Figures shift.**) (1).

Line switching. Switching in which a circuit path is set up between the incoming and outgoing lines. Contrast with message switching (q.v.) in which no such physical path is established.

Link communication. The physical means of connecting one location to another for the purpose of transmitting and receiving information. (1).

Loading. Adding inductance (load coils) to a transmission line to minimize amplitude distortion. (1).

Local exchange, local central office. An exchange in which subscribers' lines terminate. (Also referred to as *end office.*)

Local line, local loop. A channel connecting the subscriber's equipment to the line terminating equipment in the central office exchange. Usually metallic circuit (either two-wire or four-wire). (1).

Longitudinal redundancy check (LRC). A system of error control based on the formation of a block check following preset rules. The check formation rule is applied in the same manner to each character. In a simple case, the LRC is created by forming a parity check on each bit position of all the characters in the block (e.g., the first bit of the LRC character creates odd parity among the one-bit positions of the characters in the block).

Loop checking, message feedback, information feedback. A method of checking the accuracy of transmission of data in which the received data are returned to the sending end for comparison with the original data, which are stored there for this purpose. (2).

LRC. Longitudinal redundancy check.

LTRS. Letters shift, q.v. (*See* **Letters shift.**)

Mark. Presence of signal. In telegraph communications a mark represents the closed condition or current flowing. A mark impulse is equivalent to a binary 1. (*See* page 394.)

Mark-hold. The normal no-traffic line condition whereby a steady mark is transmitted.

Mark-to-space transition. The transition, or switching from a marking impulse to a spacing impulse.

Mark-hold. The normal no-traffic line condition whereby a steady mark is transmitted. This may be a customer-selectable option. (Compare with **Space-hold.**) (1).

Master station. A unit having control of all other terminals on a multipoint circuit for purposes of polling and/or selection. (1).

Mean time to failure. The average length of time for which the system, or a component of the system, works without fault.

Mean time to repair. When the system, or a component of the system, develops a fault, this is the average time taken to correct the fault.

Message reference block. When more than one message in the system is being processed in parallel, an area of storage is allocated to each message and remains uniquely associated with that message for the duration of its stay in the computer. This is called the *message reference block* in this book. It will normally contain the message and data associated with it that are required for its processing. In most systems, it contains an area of working storage uniquely reserved for that message.

Message switching. The technique of receiving a message, storing it until the proper outgoing line is available, and then retransmitting. No direct connection between the incoming and outgoing lines is set up as in line switching (q.v.).

Microwave. Any electromagnetic wave in the radio-frequency spectrum above 890 megacycles per second. (1).

Modem. A contraction of "modulator-demodulator." The term may be used when the modulator and the demodulator are associated in the same signal-conversion equipment. (*See* **Modulation** *and* **Data set.**) (1).

Modulation. The process by which some characteristic of one wave is varied in accordance with another wave or signal. This technique is used in data sets and modems to make business machine signals compatible with communications facilities. (1).

Modulation with a fixed reference. A type of modulation in which the choice of the significant condition for any signal element is based on a fixed reference. (2).

Multidrop line. Line or circuit interconnecting several stations. (Also called *multipoint line.*) (1).

Multiplex, multichannel. Use of a common channel in order to make two or more channels, either by splitting of the frequency band transmitted by the common channel into narrower bands, each of which is used to constitute a distinct channel (frequency-division multiplex), or by allotting this common channel in turn, to constitute different intermittent channels (time-division multiplex). (2).

Multiplexing. The division of a transmission facility into two or more channels either by splitting the frequency band transmitted by the channel into narrower bands, each of which is used to constitute a distinct channel (frequency-division multiplex), or by allotting this common channel to several different information channels, one at a time (time-division multiplexing). (2).

Multiplexor. A device which uses several communication channels at the same time, and transmits and receives messages and controls the communication lines. This device itself may or may not be a stored-program computer.

Multipoint line. (*See* **Multidrop line.**)

Neutral transmission. Method of transmitting teletypewriter signals, whereby a mark is represented by current on the line and a space is represented by the absence of current. By extension to tone signaling, neutral transmission is a method of signaling employing two signaling states, one of the states representing both a space condition and also the absence of any signaling. (Also called *unipolar*. Compare with **Polar transmission**.) (1).

Noise. Random electrical signals, introduced by circuit components or natural disturbances, which tend to degrade the performance of a communications channel. (1).

Off hook. Activated (in regard to a telephone set). By extension, a data set automatically answering on a public switched system is said to go "off hook." (Compare with **On hook.**) (1).

Off line. Not in the line loop. In telegraph usage, paper tapes frequently are punched "off line" and then transmitted using a paper tape transmitter.

On hook. Deactivated (in regard to a telephone set). A telephone not in use is "on hook." (1).

On line. Directly in the line loop. In telegraph usage, transmitting directly onto the line rather than, for example, perforating a tape for later transmission. (*See also* **On-line computer system.**)

On-line computer system. An on-line system may be defined as one in which the input data enter the computer directly from their point of origin and/or output data are transmitted directly to where they are used. The intermediate stages such as punching data into cards or paper tape, writing magnetic tape, or off-line printing, are largely avoided.

Open wire. A conductor separately supported above the surface of the ground— i.e., supported on insulators.

Open-wire line. A pole line whose conductors are principally in the form of open wire.

PABX. Private automatic branch exchange. (*See* **Exchange, private automatic branch.**)

Parallel transmission. Simultaneous transmission of the bits making up a character or byte, either over separate channels or on different carrier frequencies on the channel. (1). The simultaneous transmission of a certain number of signal elements constituting the same telegraph or data signal. For example, use of a code according to which each signal is characterized by a combination of 3 out of 12 frequencies simultaneously transmitted over the channel. (2).

Parity check. Addition of noninformation bits to data, making the number of ones in a grouping of bits either always even or always odd. This permits detection of bit groupings that contain single errors. It may be applied to characters, blocks, or any convenient bit grouping. (1).

Parity check, horizontal. A parity check applied to the group of certain bits from every character in a block. (*See also* **Longitudinal redundancy check.**)

Parity check, vertical. A parity check applied to the group which is all bits in one character. (Also called *vertical redundancy check.*) (1).

PAX. Private automatic exchange. (*See* **Exchange, private automatic.**)

PBX. Private branch exchange. (*See* **Exchange, private branch.**)

PCM. (*See* **Pulse code modulation.**)

PDM. (*See* **Pulse duration modulation.**)

Perforator. An instrument for the manual preparation of a perforated tape, in which telegraph signals are represented by holes punched in accordance with a predetermined code. Paper tape is prepared off line with this. (Compare with **Reperforator.**) (2).

Phantom telegraph circuit. Telegraph circuit superimposed on two physical circuits reserved for telephony. (2).

Phase distortion. (*See* **Distortion, delay.**)

Phase equalizer, delay equalizer. A delay equalizer is a corrective network which is designed to make the phase delay or envelope delay of a circuit or system substantially constant over a desired frequency range. (2).

Phase-inversion modulation. A method of phase modulation in which the two significant conditions differ in phase by π radians. (2).

Phase modulation. One of three ways of modifying a sine wave signal to make it "carry" information. The sine wave or "carrier," has its phase changed in accordance with the information to be transmitted.

Pilot model. This is a model of the system used for program testing purposes which is less complex than the complete model, e.g., the files used on a pilot model may contain a much smaller number of records than the operational files; there may be few lines and fewer terminals per line.

Polar transmission. A method for transmitting teletypewriter signals, whereby the marking signal is represented by direct current flowing in one direction and the spacing signal is represented by an equal current flowing in the opposite direction. By extension to tone signaling, polar transmission is a method of transmission employing three distinct states, two to represent a mark and a space and one to represent the absence of a signal. (Also called *bipolar.* Compare with **Neutral transmission.**)

Polling. This is a means of controlling communication lines. The communication control device will send signals to a terminal saying, "Terminal A. Have you anything to send?" if not, "Terminal B. Have you anything to send?" and so on. Polling is an alternative to contention. It makes sure that no terminal is kept waiting for a long time.

Polling list. The polling signal will usually be sent under program control. The program will have in core a list for each channel which tells the sequence in which the terminals are to be polled.

PPM. (*See* **Pulse position modulation.**)

Primary center. A control center connecting toll centers; a class 3 office. It can also serve as a toll center for its local end offices.

Private automatic branch exchange. (*See* **Exchange, private automatic branch.**)

Private automatic exchange. (*See* **Exchange, private automatic.**)

Private branch exchange (PBX). A telephone exchange serving an individual organization and having connections to a public telephone exchange. (2).

Private line. Denotes the channel and channel equipment furnished to a customer as a unit for his exclusive use, without interexchange switching arrangements. (1).

Processing, batch. A method of computer operation in which a number of similar input items are accumulated and grouped for processing.

Processing, in line. The processing of transactions as they occur, with no preliminary editing or sorting of them before they enter the system. (1).

Propagation delay. The time necessary for a signal to travel from one point on a circuit to another.

Public. Provided by a common carrier for use by many customers.

Public switched network. Any switching system that provides circuit switching to many customers. In the U.S.A. there are four such networks: Telex, TWX, telephone, and Broadband Exchange. (1).

Pulse-code modulation (PCM). Modulation of a pulse train in accordance with a code. (2).

Pulse-duration modulation (PDM) (**pulse-width modulation**) (**pulse-length modulation**). A form of pulse modulation in which the durations of pulses are varied. (2).

Pulse modulation. Transmission of information by modulation of a pulsed. or intermittent, carrier. Pulse width, count, position, phase, and/or amplitude may be the varied characteristic.

Pulse-position modulation (PPM). A form of pulse modulation in which the positions in time of pulses are varied, without modifying their duration. (2).

Pushbutton dialing. The use of keys or pushbuttons instead of a rotary dial to generate a sequence of digits to establish a circuit connection. The signal form is usually multiple tones. (Also called *tone dialing, Touch-call, Touch-Tone.*) (1).

Real time. A real-time computer system may be defined as one that controls an environment by receiving data, processing them, and returning the results sufficiently quickly to affect the functioning of the environment at that time.

Reasonableness checks. Tests made on information reaching a real-time system or being transmitted from it to ensure that the data in question lie within a given range. It is one of the means of protecting a system from data transmission errors.

Recovery from fall-back. When the system has switched to a fall-back mode of operation and the cause of the fall-back has been removed, the system must be restored to its former condition. This is referred to as *recovery from fall-back*. The recovery process may involve updating information in the files to produce two duplicate copies of the file.

Redundancy check. An automatic or programmed check based on the systematic insertion of components or characters used especially for checking purposes. (1).

Redundant code. A code using more signal elements than necessary to represent the intrinsic information. For example, five-unit code using all the characters of International Telegraph Alphabet No. 2 is not redundant; five-unit code using only the figures in International Telegraph Alphabet No. 2 is redundant; seven-unit code using only signals made of four "space" and three "mark" elements is redundant. (2).

Reference pilot. A reference pilot is a different wave from those which transmit the telecommunication signals (telegraphy, telephony). It is used in carrier systems to facilitate the maintenance and adjustment of the carrier transmission system. (For example, automatic level regualtion, synchronization of oscillators, etc.) (2).

Regenerative repeater. (*See* **Repeater, regenerative.**)

Regional center. A control center (class 1 office) connecting sectional centers of the telephone system together. Every pair of regional centers in the United States has a direct circuit group running from one center to the other. (1).

Repeater.
1. A device whereby currents received over one circuit are automatically repeated in another circuit or circuits, generally in an amplified and/or reshaped form.
2. A device used to restore signals, which have been distorted because of attenuation, to their original shape and transmission level.

Repeater, regenerative. Normally, a repeater utilized in telegraph applications. Its function is to retime and retransmit the received signal impulses restored to their original strength. These repeaters are speed- and code-sensitive and are intended for use with standard telegraph speeds and codes. (Also called *regen.*) (1).

Repeater, telegraph. A device which receives telegraph signals and automatically retransmits corresponding signals. (2).

Reperforator (receiving perforator). A telegraph instrument in which the received signals cause the code of the corresponding characters or functions to be punched in a tape. (1).

Reperforator/transmitter (RT). A teletypewriter unit consisting of a reperforator and a tape transmitter, each independent of the other. It is used as a relaying device and is especially suitable for transforming the incoming speed to a different outgoing speed, and for temporary queuing.

Residual error rate, undetected error rate. The ratio of the number of bits, unit elements, characters or blocks incorrectly received but undetected or uncorrected by the error-control equipment, to the total number of bits, unit elements, characters or blocks sent. (2).

Response time. This is the time the system takes to react to a given input. If a message is keyed into a terminal by an operator and the reply from the computer, when it comes, is typed at the same terminal, response time may be defined as the time interval between the operator pressing the last key and the terminal typing the first letter of the reply. For different types of terminal, response time may be defined similarly. It is the interval between an event and the system's response to the event.

Ringdown. A method of signaling subscribers and operators using either a 20-cycle AC signal, a 135-cycle AC signal, or a 1000-cycle signal interrupted 20 times per second. (1).

Routing. The assignment of the communications path by which a message or telephone call will reach its destination. (1).

Routing, alternate. Assignment of a secondary communications path to a destination when the primary path is unavailable. (1).

Routing indicator. An address, or group of characters, in the heading of a message defining the final circuit or terminal to which the message has to be delivered. (1).

RT. Reperforator/transmitter, q.v.

Saturation testing. Program testing with a large bulk of messages intended to bring to light those errors which will only occur very infrequently and which may be triggered by rare coincidences such as two different messages arriving at the same time.

Sectional center. A control center connecting primary centers; a class 2 office. (1).

Seek. A mechanical movement involved in locating a record in a random-access file. This may, for example, be the movement of an arm and head mechanism that is necessary before a read instruction can be given to read data in a certain location on the file.

Selection. Addressing a terminal and/or a component on a selective calling circuit. (1).

Selective calling. The ability of the transmitting station to specify which of several stations on the same line is to receive a message. (1).

Self-checking numbers. Numbers which contain redundant information so that an error in them, caused, for example, by noise on a transmission line, may be detected.

Serial transmission. Used to identify a system wherein the bits of a character occur serially in time. Implies only a single transmission channel. (Also called *serial-by-bit*.) (1). Transmission at successive intervals of signal elements constituting the same telegraph or data signal. For example, transmission of signal elements by a standard teleprinter, in accordance with International Telegraph Alphabet No. 2; telegraph transmission by a time-divided channel. (2).

Sideband. The frequency band on either the upper or lower side of the carrier frequency within which fall the frequencies produced by the process of modulation. (2).

Signal-to-noise ratio (S/N). Relative power of the signal to the noise in a channel. (1).

Simplex circuit.

1. CCITT definition: A circuit permitting the transmission of signals in either direction, but not in both simultaneously.

2. Definition in common usage (the normal meaning in computer literature): A circuit permitting transmission in one specific direction only.

Simplex mode. Operation of a communication channel in one direction only, with no capability for reversing. (1).

Simulation. This is a word which is sometimes confusing as it has three entirely different meanings, namely:

Simulation for design and monitoring. This is a technique whereby a model of the working system can be built in the form of a computer program. Special computer languages are available for producing this model. A complete system may be described by a succession of different models. These models can then be adjusted easily and endlessly, and the system that is being designed or monitored can be experimented with to test the effect of any proposed changes. The simulation model is a program that is run on a computer separate from the system that is being designed.

Simulation of input devices. This is a program testing aid. For various reasons it is undesirable to use actual lines and terminals for some of the program testing. Therefore, magnetic tape or other media may be used and read in by a special program which makes the data appear as if they came from actual lines and terminals. Simulation in this sense is the replacement of one set of equipment by another set of equipment and programs, so that the behavior is similar.

Simulation of superivsory programs. This is used for program testing purposes when the actual supervisory programs are not yet available. A comparatively simple program to bridge the gap is used instead. This type of simulation is the replacement of one set of programs by another set which imitates it.

Single-current transmission, (inverse) **neutral direct-current system.** A form of telegraph transmission effected by means of unidirectional currents. (2).

Space. 1. An impulse which, in a neutral circuit, causes the loop to open or causes absence of signal, while in a polar circuit it causes the loop current to flow in a direction opposite to that for a mark impulse. A space impulse is equivalent to a binary 0. 2. In some codes, a character which causes a printer to leave a character width with no printed symbol. (1).

Space-hold. The normal no-traffic line condition whereby a steady space is transmitted. (Compare with **Mark-hold.**) (1).

Space-to-mark transition. The transition, or switching, from a spacing impulse to a marking impulse. (1).

Spacing bias. *See* **Distortion, bias.**

Spectrum. 1. A continuous range of frequencies, usually wide in extent, within which waves have some specific common characteristic. 2. A graphical representation of the distribution of the amplitude (and sometimes phase) of the components of a wave as a function of frequency. A spectrum may be continuous or, on the contrary, contain only points corresponding to certain discrete values. (2).

Start element. The first element of a character in certain serial transmissions, used to permit synchronization, In Baudot teletypewriter operation, it is one space bit. (1).

Start-stop system. A system in which each group of code elements corresponding to an alphabetical signal is preceded by a start signal which serves to prepare the receiving mechanism for the reception and registration of a character, and is followed by a stop signal which serves to bring the receiving mechanism to rest in preparation for the reception of the next character. (Contrast with **Synchronous system.**) (Start-stop transmission is also referred to as *asynchronous transmission*, q.v.)

Station. One of the input or output points of a communications system—e.g., the telephone set in the telephone system or the point where the business machine interfaces the channel on a leased private line. (1).

Status maps. Tables which give the status of various programs, devices, input-output operations, or the status of the communication lines.

Step-by-step switch. A switch that moves in synchronism with a pulse device such as a rotary telephone dial. Each digit dialed causes the movement of successive selector switches to carry the connection forward until the desired line is reached. (Also called *stepper switch.* Compare with **Line switching** and **Cross-bar system.**) (1).

Step-by-step system. A type of line-switching system which uses step-by-step switches. (1).

Stop bit. (*See* **Stop element.**)

Stop element. The last element of a character in asychronous serial transmissions, used to ensure recognition of the next start element. In Baudot teletypewriter operation it is 1.42 mark bits. (*See also* **Start-stop transmission.**) (1.)

Store and forward. The interruption of data flow from the originating terminal to the designated receiver by storing the information enroute and forwarding it at a later time. (*See* **Message switching.**)

Stunt box. A device to 1. control the nonprinting functions of a teletypewriter terminal, such as carriage return and line feed; and 2. a device to recognize line control characters (e.g., DCC, TSC, etc.). (1).

Subscriber trunk dialing. (*See* **direct distance dialing.**)

Subscriber's line. The telephone line connecting the exchange to the subscriber's station. (2).

Subscriber's loop. (*See* **Local loop.**)

Subset. A subscriber set of equipment, such as a telephone. A modulation and demodulation device. (Also called *data set*, which is a more precise term.) (1).

Subscriber's loop. (*See* **Local loop.**)

Subvoice-grade channel. A channel of bandwidth narrower than that of voice-grade channels. Such channels are usually subchannels of a voice-grade line. (1).

Supergroup. The assembly of five 12-channel groups, occupying adjacent bands in the spectrum, for the purpose of simultaneous modulation or demodulation. (2).

Supervisory programs. Those computer programs designed to coordinate service and augment the machine components of the system, and coordinate and service application programs. They handle work scheduling, input-output operations, error actions, and other functions.

Supervisory signals. Signals used to indicate the various operating states of circuit combinations. (1).

Supervisory system. The complete set of supervisory programs used on a given system.

Support programs. The ultimate operational system consists of supervisory programs and application programs. However, a third set of programs are needed to install the system, including diagnostics, testing aids, data generator programs, terminal simulators, etc. These are referred to as *support programs*.

Suppressed carrier transmission. That method of communication in which the carrier frequency is suppressed either partially or to the maximum degree possible. One or both of the sidebands may be transmitted. (1).

Switch hook. A switch on a telephone set, associated with the structure supporting the receiver or handset. It is operated by the removal or replacement of the receiver or handset on the support. (*See also* **Off hook** *and* **On hook.**) (1).

Switching center. A location which terminates multiple circuits and is capable of interconnecting circuits or transferring traffic between circuits; may be automatic, semiautomatic, or torn-tape. (The latter is a location where operators tear off the incoming printed and punched paper tape and transfer it manually to the proper outgoing circuit.) (1).

Switching message. (*See* **Message switching.**)

Switchover. When a failure occurs in the equipment a switch may occur to an alternative component. This may be, for example, an alternative file unit, an alternative communication line or an alternative computer. The switchover process may be automatic under program control or it may be manual.

Synchronous. Having a constant time interval between successive bits, characters, or vents. The term implies that all equipment in the system is in step.

Synchronous system. A system in which the sending and receiving instruments are operating continuously at substantially the same frequency and are maintained, by means of correction, if necessary, in a desired phase relationship. (Contrast with **Start-stop system.**) (2).

Synchronous transmission. A transmission process such that between any two significant instants there is always an integral number of unit intervals. (Contrast with **Asynchronous** or **Start-stop transmission.**) (1).

Tandem office. An office that is used to interconnect the local end offices over tandem trunks in a densely settled exchange area where it is uneconomical for a telephone company to provide direct interconnection between all end offices. The tandem office completes all calls between the end offices but is not directly connected to subscribers. (1).

Tandem office, tandem central office. A central office used primarily as a switching point for traffic between other central offices. (2).

Tariff. The published rate for a specific unit of equipment, facility, or type of service provided by a communications common carrier. Also the vehicle by which the regulating agencies approve or disapprove such facilities or services. Thus the tariff becomes a contract between customer and common carrier.

TD. Transmitter-distributor, q.v.

Teleprocessing. A form of information handling in which a data-processing system utilizes communication facilities. (Originally, but no longer, an IBM trademark.) (1).

Teletype. Trademark of Teletype Corporation, usually referring to a series of different types of teleprinter equipment such as tape punches, reperforators, page printers, etc., utilized for communications systems.

Teletypewriter exchange service (TWX). An AT&T public switched teletypewriter service in which suitably arranged teletypewriter stations are provided with lines to a central office for access to other such stations throughout the U.S.A. and Canada. Both Baudot- and ASCII-coded machines are used. Business machines may also be used, with certain restrictions. (1).

Telex service. A dial-up telegraph service enabling its subscribers to communicate directly and temporarily among themselves by means of start-stop apparatus and of circuits of the public telegraph network. The service operates world wide. Baudot equipment is used. Computers can be connected to the Telex network.

Terminal. Any device capable of sending and/or receiving information over a communication channel. The means by which data are entered into a computer system and by which the decisions of the system are communicated to the environment it affects. A wide variety of terminal devices have been built, including teleprinters, special keyboards, light displays, cathode tubes, thermocouples, pressure gauges and other instrumentation, radar units, telephones, etc.

TEX. (*See* **Telex service.**)

Tie line. A private-line communications channel of the type provided by communications common carriers for linking two or more points together.

Time-derived channel. Any of the channels obtained from multiplexing a channel by time division.

Time-division multiplex. A system in which a channel is established in connecting intermittently, generally at regular intervals and by means of an automatic distribution, its terminal equipment to a common channel. At times when these connections are not established, the section of the common channel between the distributors can be utilized in order to establish other similar channels, in turn.

Toll center. Basic toll switching entity; a central office where channels and toll message circuits terminate. While this is usually one particular central office in a city, larger cities may have several central offices where toll message circuits terminate. A class 4 office. (Also called "toll office" and "toll point.") (1).

Toll circuit (American). *See* **Trunk circuit** (British).

Toll switching trunk (American). *See* **Trunk junction** (British).

Tone dialing. (*See* **Pushbutton dialing.**)

Touch-call. Proprietary term of GT&E. (*See* **Pushbutton dialing.**)

Touch-tone. AT&T term for pushbutton dialing, q.v.

Transceiver. A terminal that can transmit and receive traffic.

Translator. A device that converts information from one system of representation into equivalent information in another system of representation. In telephone equipment, it is the device that converts dialed digits into call-routing information. (1).

Transmitter-distributor (TD). The device in a teletypewriter terminal which makes and breaks the line in timed sequence. Modern usage of the term refers to a paper tape transmitter.

Transreceiver. A terminal that can transmit and receive traffic. (1).

Trunk circuit (British), **toll circuit** (American). A circuit connecting two exchanges in different localities. *Note*: In Great Britain, a trunk circuit is approximately 15 miles long or more. A circuit connecting two exchanges less than 15 miles apart is called a *junction circuit.*

Trunk exchange (British), **toll office** (American). An exchange with the function of controlling the switching of trunk (British) [toll (American)] traffic.

Trunk group. Those trunks between two points both of which are switching centers and/or individual message distribution points, and which employ the same multiplex terminal equipment.

Trunk junction (British), **toll switching trunk** (American). A line connecting a trunk exchange to a local exchange and permitting a trunk operator to call a subscriber to establish a trunk call.

Unattended operations. The automatic features of a station's operation permit the transmission and reception of messages on an unattended basis. (1).

Vertical parity (redundancy) check. (*See* **Parity check, vertical.**)

VOGAD (Voice-Operated Gain-Adjusting Device). A device somewhat similar to a compandor and used on some radio systems; a voice-operated device which removes fluctuation from input speech and sends it out at a constant level. No restoring device is needed at the receiving end. (1).

Voice-frequency, telephone-frequency. Any frequency within that part of the audio-frequency range essential for the transmission of speech of commerical quality, i.e., 300–3400 c/s. (2).

Voice-frequency carrier telegraphy. That form of carrier telegraphy in which the carrier currents have frequencies such that the modulated currents may be transmitted over a voice-frequency telephone channel. (1).

Voice-frequency multichannel telegraphy. Telegraphy using two or more carrier currents the frequencies of which are within the voice-frequency range. Voice-frequency telegraph systems permit the transmission of up to 24 channels over a single circuit by use of frequency-division multiplexing.

Voice-grade channel. (*See* **Channel, voice-grade.**)

Voice-operated device. A device used on a telephone circuit to permit the presence of telephone currents to effect a desired control. Such a device is used in most echo suppressors. (1).

VRC. Vertical redundancey check. (*See also* **Parity check.**)

Watchdog timer. This is a timer which is set by the program. It interrupts the program after a given period of time, e.g., one second. This will prevent the system from going into an endless loop due to a program error, or becoming idle because of an equipment fault. The Watchdog timer may sound a horn or cause a computer interrupt if such a fault is detected.

WATS (Wide Area Telephone Service). A service provided by telephone companies in the United States which permits a customer by use of an access line to make calls to telephones in a specific zone in a dial basis for a flat monthly charge. Monthly charges are based on the size of the area in which the calls are placed, not on the number or length of calls. Under the WATS arrangement, the U.S. is divided into six zones to be called on a full-time or measured-time basis. (1).

Word. 1. In telegraphy, six operations or characters (five characters plus one space). ("Group" is also used in place of "word.") 2. In computing, a sequence of bits or characters treated as a unit and capable of being stored in one computer location. (1).

WPM (Words per minute). A common measure of speed in telegraph systems.

INDEX

461